EVOLUTIONS OF CAPITALISM

Historical Perspectives: 1200–2000

Edited by
Catherine Casson and Philipp Robinson Rössner

BRISTOL
UNIVERSITY
PRESS

First published in Great Britain in 2022 by

Bristol University Press
University of Bristol
1-9 Old Park Hill
Bristol
BS2 8BB
UK
t: +44 (0)117 954 5940
e: bup-info@bristol.ac.uk

Details of international sales and distribution partners are available at bristoluniversitypress.co.uk

British Library Cataloguing in Publication Data
A catalogue record for this book is available from the British Library

ISBN 978-1-5292-1480-2 hardcover
ISBN 978-1-5292-1481-9 ePub
ISBN 978-1-5292-1482-6 ePdf

Cover design: Namkwan Cho
Front cover image: Shutterstock_106366754
Bristol University Press uses environmentally responsible print partners.
Printed in Great Britain by CPI Group (UK) Ltd, Croydon, CR0 4YY

Contents

List of Figures and Tables   iv

Notes on Contributors   v

Acknowledgements   vii

1   Introduction   1
      Catherine Casson and Philipp Robinson Rössner

2   The Market as an Institution: Theory and History   29
      Mark Casson

3   Regulating Capitalism   53
      Philipp Robinson Rössner

4   Capitalism and State Ownership Models   73
      Sverre A. Christensen

5   Comparative and Connected Global Capitalism(s)   100
      Edmond Smith

6   Capitalism, Imperialism and the Emergence of an   127
      Industrialized Global Economy
      Colin M. Lewis

7   Religion and Capitalism   156
      David J. Jeremy

8   Capitalism and the Environment   187
      Geoffrey Jones

9   Capitalism and Income Inequality   212
      Catherine Casson

10   Conclusion   237
      Catherine Casson and Philipp Robinson Rössner

Index   251

List of Figures and Tables

Figures

2.1   Social network linking different groups of customers to shops   41
9.1   Ratio of net national wealth to net national income, 1850–2015   214
9.2   UK Real GDP per capita and average real earnings, 1801–2010 222
9.3   US Real GDP per capita and money wage of unskilled labour,   222
       1800–2010

Tables

1.1   Five functions relevant to capitalism and their dates of emergence   19
2.1   List of eight groups of consumers classified by the shops with   42
       which they are in contact, showing the shops at which they
       will make a purchase
4.1   State ownership in companies on the Oslo Stock Exchange   83
       (OSE), 8 February 2021
6.1   The Great Divergence: continental share of global GDP (%)   132
7.1   Relative sizes of main Nonconformist sects, 1750–1850,   165
       in England and Wales
7.2   Major Nonconformist groups among cotton masters   166
       compared with Nonconformists' shares of the population,
       in Lancashire
7.3   Nonconformist inventors of new technology active in   167
       England and Wales, 1700–1850, in the *Oxford Dictionary of
       National Biography*
7.4   John Gladstone's slave holdings in the British West Indies   177

Notes on Contributors

Catherine Casson is Senior Lecturer in Enterprise at Alliance Manchester Business School, University of Manchester. Her publications include articles in *Urban History*, *Business History Review*, *Business History* and the *Economic History Review* and the co-authored book *Compassionate Capitalism: Business and Community in Medieval England* (Bristol University Press, 2020).

Mark Casson is Professor of Economics at the University of Reading and Director of the Centre for Institutions and Economic History. He has published in *Economic History Review*, *Explorations in Economic History* and *Business History Review*. He is the co-author (with Catherine Casson) of *The Entrepreneur in History* (Palgrave Macmillan, 2013).

Sverre A. Christensen is Associate Professor at the Norwegian Business School. He has co-authored several company histories and anthologies with emphasis on (foreign) ownership and corporate governance. He has also published extensively on Norwegian state ownership, including in *Scandinavian Economic History Review*.

David J. Jeremy is Emeritus Professor of Business History, Manchester Metropolitan University. His publications include *Capitalists and Christians: Business Leaders and the Churches in Britain, 1900–1960* (Oxford University Press, 1990) and the prize-winning *Transatlantic Industrial Revolution: The Diffusion of Textile Technologies between Britain and America, 1790–1830s* (MIT Press and Basil Blackwell, 1981).

Geoffrey Jones is the Isidor Straus Professor of Business History at Harvard Business School. His publications include *Multinationals and Global Capitalism: From the Nineteenth to Twenty First Century* (Oxford University Press, 2005) and *Profits and Sustainability: A Global History of Green Entrepreneurship* (Oxford University Press, 2017).

Colin M. Lewis is Professor Emeritus of Latin American Economic History at the London School of Economics and Political Science. He has held visiting professorships and/or taught at institutions including the University of São Paulo in Brazil and the Economics Faculty of the University of Buenos Aires, Argentina.

Philipp Robinson Rössner is Professor of Early Modern History, Department of History, University of Manchester. He received PhDs from the University of Edinburgh and the University of Leipzig. His publications include *Economic Growth and the Origins of Modern Political Economy: Economic Reasons of State, 1500–2000* (Routledge, 2016).

Edmond Smith is Presidential Fellow in Economic Cultures, Department of History, University of Manchester. He has published in *Economic History Review* and the *Journal of Imperial and Commonwealth History* and is co-investigator on the AHRC-funded project 'Legacies of the British Slave Trade'.

Acknowledgements

We are grateful for funding from the Alliance Manchester Business School Research Support fund, which allowed us to hold a workshop as preparation for this volume. We would also like to thank the anonymous referees for their feedback.

Introduction

Catherine Casson and Philipp Robinson Rössner

Definition of capitalism

Capitalism is a topic with many thematic strands and both geographical and chronological dimensions. As a result, its definition and interpretation have generated a significant amount of discussion. Regarding thematic strands, some scholars have focused on the political dimension, for example, and others the financial (including Hall and Soskice, 2001; Murphy, 2009; Neal and Williamson, 2014; Piketty, 2014; Kocka, 2016; Banaji, 2020; Lipartito and Jacobson, 2020). Assessments of capitalism's impact are also diverse. While aiding economic growth for some sectors and individuals, significant questions remain regarding the extent to which capitalism has had a positive or negative impact on society as a whole (Piketty, 2014; Beckert, 2015; Lipartito and Jacobson, 2020; Yazdani and Menon, 2020).

It is generally accepted that to understand capitalism fully we should situate it in a wider historical context (Cain and Hopkins, 1986). Marx's analysis of capitalism went back to the Middle Ages, although his primary focus was on the 19th century. Sombart (1927) proposed that a capitalist spirit originated in medieval rulers, administrators, noble estate owners and military leaders, and was disseminated from them to the wider population. Braudel and Britnell saw the Middle Ages as an important step in the transition from a market economy to a later capitalist one. Examining 1000–1500, Britnell (1993) used the concept of commercialization to describe economic transformation that led to urbanization, entrepreneurship and the provision of a strong institutional framework. Braudel (1981, 1982, 1985) described how, during the 15th–18th centuries, an informal 'everyday' economy developed into a market one and subsequently a capitalist one. In Braudel's analysis finance, in the form of access to credit, created a more sophisticated economy and aided a transition to capitalism by allowing merchants to participate in international markets, where higher profits could be made (Braudel, 1982: 81, 91, 100).

Weber identified the Reformation as a key transition point. He associated capitalism with the 'accumulation of wealth for its own sake, rather than for the material rewards it can serve to bring' (Weber, 2001: xi, 18). Protestantism, Weber argued, encouraged individuals to engage with 'worldly affairs' rather than try to transcend them (Weber, 2001: xii). Strong performance in their work allowed a Protestant to engage with worldly affairs and confidently demonstrate that they had been chosen by God for salvation. This 'clarity of vision' and 'command' of confidence became attributes of successful entrepreneurship (Weber, 2001: 30–1). Strong performance accumulated wealth. Protestantism discouraged excessive consumption and charitable giving to the poor. Wealth was thus either preserved for future generations (children or grandchildren), reinvested in the existing business or invested in other businesses (Weber, 2001: 30, 32).

The period *c.* 1600–1750 is a key turning point for many historians, who have associated it with the rise of the fiscal state, characteristics of which included the raising of taxation to fund warfare, the creation of national debt, the development of financial markets and overseas expansion (Sombart, 1913; De Vries and van der Woude, 1997, O'Brien, 2011; Parthasarathi, 2011; Neal and Williamson, 2014; Yun Casalilla et al, 2012; Vries, 2015; Ashworth, 2017).

The Industrial Revolution of 1760–1860 attracted the attention of Marx and continues to be recognized as a milestone in the development of capitalism (for example Taylor, 2006; Allen, 2009; Hudson, 2014). The combination of improved transport infrastructure (canals and coal) and mechanization extended the range of markets that firms could reach and allowed them to expand production capacity in conjunction. There remains debate, however, over the extent to which changes in this period should be attributed to entrepreneurial initiative or to the availability of cheap energy and labour productivity (Mokyr, 1990; Allen, 2009).

This book takes a novel approach to the history of capitalism. It provides a series of case studies with the aim of further broadening the historical and thematic perspective. The chronological range of the book is 1200–2000, which encompasses all the potential start dates for capitalism proposed in the existing literature. The geographical focus is on Western capitalism, including non-Western countries subject to Western political and cultural influences. Rather than seeking to identify a single starting point or location, the chapters in this volume instead show the evolution of capitalism to be connected to the emergence of five distinct economic functions: entrepreneurship, finance, management, workers and political leaders. Some functions emerged as more dominant in particular locations and periods, and other functions in different locations and periods. Thus, capitalism can be seen as a series of evolutions rather than a single one.

While acknowledging the complexities inherent to framing capitalism conceptually, it is important to position the volume by adopting a definition. For the present purpose, we define capitalism as an economic system with the following characteristics. The ability for firms to enter and exit is a requirement. Entry is necessary to enable entrepreneurs to implement new ideas or improvements on existing ones. Exit is required to remove unsuccessful ideas or products and to allow investment to be redirected to more successful firms, to help them flourish. The ability to pool finance from multiple individuals, with legal protection to limit their risks, is a requirement. This enables more ambitious projects, beyond the financial reach of a single investor, to be launched. In a capitalist system a firm should have access to an international market in which to sell goods and services, and the capacity to increase production accordingly. As the market grows, and transactions become more impersonal, a capitalist system should have a political and legal framework that provides procedures to follow when transactions are made and a means of redress if problems occur. There should be a feedback mechanism whereby the population can input into that political process, and the process should not give prominence to the interests of some groups over others.

Five functions relevant to capitalism

Theoretical work on capitalism has reflected the circumstances in which it was written. Malthus (1798) and Ricardo (1817) wrote when agriculture was the most significant economic sector in England and France. Malthus witnessed how a rising population resulted in a stagnation of agricultural wages and an increase in land rents. He saw a resulting concentration of wealth in the hands of landlords and a corresponding decrease in the share available to the rest of the population. The resulting dissatisfaction among many in the population contributed to the French Revolution of 1789. Malthus proposed that to avoid a potential revolution in Britain overpopulation needed to be prevented. Ricardo, in contrast, proposed a solution of steadily increasing taxation on landlords.

Marx, writing in 1867, transferred analysis to an industrial economy. Its distinctive feature was that in industry there was potentially no limit to growth, unlike agriculture where the amount of land was finite. Marx believed that capital would become increasingly concentrated in the hands of industrialists. Like Malthus, Marx proposed a revolutionary culmination in which either the rate of return of capital would start to diminish, causing conflict among industrialists, or the workers would unite to revolt against them. In 1942 Schumpeter engaged directly with Marx's analysis in the first part of his book *Capitalism, Socialism and Democracy*. His main contribution was to include the role of the entrepreneur in the narrative of capitalism.

Schumpeter was writing after seeing the impact on government policy of the economist John Maynard Keynes's 1936 book *The General Theory of Employment, Interest and Money* and at a time when economists and politicians were reflecting on the social and economic transformations wrought by the Second World War. As such, the second part of his book is a reflection on the future of capitalism. Schumpeter proposed that capitalism would end as a result of a move towards socialism, which would occur peacefully through the democratic process.

Everyone in the economy has a function. This chapter examines five functions that are relevant to the topic of capitalism: entrepreneurship, finance, management, workers and political leaders. Three of these functions, entrepreneurship, workers and political leaders, were considered by Marx and Schumpeter. The addition of finance and management extends the analysis to topics that received less attention in their work but have been raised in subsequent scholarship.

The first function, entrepreneurship, can be associated with two different views, that of Kirzner and that of Schumpeter. Kirzner emphasized the entrepreneur as a coordinator, who used price information to identify an opportunity to buy an item from one person at a low price and sell it to another at a high price. The difference in prices provided the entrepreneur with their profit (Kirzner, 1973). In contrast, Schumpeter's entrepreneur was an innovator who restructured the economy by moving resources from mature sectors to novel sectors (Casson and Casson, 2013a). In order for innovations to occur, someone needs to spot the opportunity to introduce them. Entrepreneurs perform this role by identifying and solving problems with existing goods and services. While Kirzner's entrepreneurs were the 'mechanism, or agent, through which the market system operates', Schumpeter's were 'the very creators of the system itself' (Casson, 2003: 230).

Finance is required to found a firm, particularly to bridge the gap between creation and first sales. Some business opportunities can be pursued with finance provided by an individual. More ambitious ones require multiple sources of finance, for example from several people. Marx did not examine in detail how finance was obtained to fund production (Schumpeter, 1992: 15–16). Addressing that gap, Schumpeter noted that the most common way to obtain finance to start a business was by borrowing money (Schumpeter, 1992: 16). He said that the prospective business owner might also acquire capital by saving from their salary, but that would usually still need to be supplemented by borrowing (Schumpeter, 1992: 16).

Management, the third function, was first examined in detail by Knight (1921). Before Knight it was generally assumed that owners would not want to delegate any control of their firm, and would want to take sole responsibility for all decisions. Knight suggested that a primary characteristic of an entrepreneur was the ability to exercise good judgement, including the ability to select appropriate managers to whom to delegate (Knight, 1921). However, a joint-stock company has many owners. Berle and Means (1932) examined how management operated in such circumstances. They found that managers in joint-stock companies became increasingly independent of owners and exhibited two tendencies: absorbing profits in the form of managerial perks and spending profits on hiring more staff, in order to enhance their authority. Not all aspects of the division of management and ownership were negative, however. Chandler's (1977) work on US industry examined why managers were required during firm growth and the positive contribution they could make to growth, while Porter identified the contribution of managers to company strategy (Porter, 1980).

Workers had little autonomy in Marx's theory of capitalism. Their position was static: they were unable to advance their status or to progress to entrepreneurship. In Marx's interpretation, the employer appropriated all the gains from the workers' labour. He defined labour hours as comprising both those hours used for production and also the hours that went into the 'production' of the stock of labour – the number of hours it takes to 'rear, feed, clothe and house' the worker (Schumpeter, 1992: 16). When workers sell their labour to employers the wages they receive, Marx said, should reflect the value of both elements of the labour hours. However, Marx believed that once employers received the services of the workers, they would make them work more hours than the labour hours; that is, make them work more hours than they were paid for. The 'surplus value' obtained this way was kept by employers and represented their exploitation of the workers (Marx, 1961: 244–321; Schumpeter, 1992: 27). Schumpeter's view was more optimistic. He proposed that, by saving, a worker might be able to move to the position of business founder – though he admitted this could be hard and would usually require additional capital (Schumpeter, 1992: 16).

Political leadership is relevant to capitalism in two ways: first in the identity of the leaders and secondly their actions when in office. Both Schumpeter and Marx and Engels were interested in the identity of political leaders. Marx and Engels felt that the background of many political leaders meant that they represented the interests of 'owners' rather than 'workers'. They suggested, however, that there were ways for workers to improve their representation. Industrialization had one benefit, as the concentration of workers 'in greater masses' in the industrial cities increased their perceived and actual strength (Marx and Engels, 1868). This facilitated the creation of trade unions. Industrialization also improved communication. New railways connected groups of workers from different locations, aiding the further expansion of the worker movement.

Schumpeter had a different view about the relationship between those who were political leaders and the rest of the population. He perceived a close connection between capitalism and democracy, but advocated that greater power for decision making be transferred from voters to elected representatives, who should be selected in a competitive process according to their capacity to make informed decisions (Schumpeter, 1992: 250, 269).

The actions of political leaders when in office attracted attention from other social scientists. For Marx, the mercantilist state had acted as capitalism's handmaiden in the early modern period, facilitating processes of alienation, dispossession and enclosure of the commons. However, North (1990) proposed that political leaders helped to create formal rules that governed the movement of goods and enforcement of contrasts, along with institutions, such as courts, where those rules were enforced. The rules and institutions reduced the risks faced by traders, but potentially also reflected some self-interest on the part of political leaders, for example if they derived income from the operation of the institutions.

Key dates for entrepreneurship

The period 1200 to 1350 was one of commercial boom. The Cistercian monastic order dominated large-scale entrepreneurship in England and France as it had access to land that contained natural resources and held development potential, and had the technological knowledge to manage water supplies (Bell et al, 2007). The function of towns as defensive military sites began to be overtaken by a commercial function as they became manufacturing and trading centres. There was significant horizontal specialization, which increased productivity and generated a surplus, which could be traded to provide variety. This provided opportunities for small-scale enterprises. There were, however, restrictions on business entry and growth. The ability to employ workers and sell goods was frequently restricted to individuals who had been granted residency in the town, undertaken seven years of training and paid an entry fee to a guild (Hunt and Murray, 1999: 34–5; Casson, 2020). Guilds emphasized standardization of practices among members. This maintained product standards, benefiting consumers, but limited growth. Guild members were prevented from extending their product range by diversifying the raw materials used or expanding the range of items manufactured. Some guilds also prohibited the use of labour-saving technology, such as the employment of water power. Rural locations without guilds and with readily available power and fuel increasingly became more attractive than towns to prospective entrepreneurs (Britnell, 2009: 174–5).

In contrast to the preceding boom, the period 1350–1500 can be seen as one of stasis for entrepreneurship. Access to credit, it is proposed, became harder in both 1350–70 and 1450–1500 (Goddard, 2016; Nightingale, 2018). The main entrepreneurial group to emerge in this period was the yeoman farmer, the opportunities for whom derived from labour shortages in the aftermath of the plague of 1348–9. Historians estimate that across Europe one third to a half of the population perished (Horrox, 1994). With increasing wage costs, and peasant tenants reluctant to perform their labour service, some lords decided to stop the direct management of their estates and instead lease them in order to move from arable to less labour-intensive pasture, and to venture into wool production, adopting what has been termed a capitalist mentality (Allen, 1992; Dyer, 2012).

The Church was no longer the only dominant player in large-scale enterprise. In Germany the Fugger family began to lease mineral mines from local rulers in the 1450s, making permanent loans of copper and silver to the rulers in return. They vertically integrated the mining process, operating extraction, processing and distribution of copper, silver and gold, with the silver and gold being used for, among other things, the creation of currency (Ehrenberg, 1928; Häberlein, 2012).

From 1536 onwards two features facilitated business entry. First, the decline of the guild system in England made it easier for outsiders to set up businesses and to introduce process and product innovations (Toulmin Smith et al, 1870; Rosser, 2015: 64–5). Secondly, the dissolution of English monasteries in 1536–40 removed the Church's dominance in certain sectors and gave private individuals the opportunity to acquire land and buildings that had previously been owned by the Church. This contributed to an early shift towards the centralization of production in textiles. The traditional form of textile manufacturing was the decentralized putting-out system, in which a merchant invested money (capital) in raw materials that they then 'put out' to home-workers. The workers were paid piece rates, which reflected the amount they made, while the merchant's profits were obtained by selling the finished items (Lee, 2018: 65–6). The advantage of the system was that the merchants did not incur overheads, as production occurred in the workers' homes. If the market contracted they had few outgoing costs, while in an expanding market they had the flexibility to increase production without the need to acquire larger premises or new machinery. The disadvantage of this was that it was hard to monitor quality, and the process of travelling around the home workers to distribute and collect items was time-consuming. Yet with cheaper property available it was easier for a merchant to acquire affordable premises and to centralize production, allowing workers to be directly supervised, reducing the opportunities for fraud, allowing quality to be monitored and removing the time spent travelling (Lee, 2018: 67). The entrepreneur John Winchcombe II used the Reformation as an opportunity to create a textile manufactory in a former monastic building, employing approximately 1,000 workers and 50 looms (Davids, 1982; Peacock, 2003; Jackson, 2008; Casson and Casson, 2013a: 84–5; Lee, 2018).

The year 1600 was a significant date in the development of entrepreneurship associated with new forms of business organization and new markets. Technological improvements in ship-building permitted larger and faster ships that utilized wind power and cargo space more efficiently. Improvements in navigation identified new sea routes and new locations. While expanding opportunities for international trade, these developments also increased up-front costs. The chartered company was a new form of organization whose purpose was to allow merchants to undertake ventures overseas that were too expensive to be funded by a single individual. Initiated by the Dutch and English, they were structured as joint-stock companies that enabled merchants to pool capital. The charter was provided by national government, and provided the company with a trading monopoly for a specified location and duration (Carlos and Nicholas, 1988, 1996; Jones and Ville, 1996). The English East India Company, founded in 1600, was granted a monopoly of trade with India for the English market and traded primarily in cotton, silk and tea. The Dutch East India Company, founded in 1602, received a similar monopoly from the Dutch state to conduct the spice trade with Asia.

The trade in enslaved people was undertaken from the 15th century onwards by the Portuguese and from the mid-16th century by the Dutch and English using chartered companies (Klein and Vinson, 2007). The Dutch and English East India companies engaged in the slave trade. In 1672 the Royal African Company was granted a monopoly on the trading of enslaved people from Africa by the Crown (Carlos and Brown Kruse, 1996). Ships from Europe transported manufactured goods, including cloth, guns and iron, to the west coast of Africa. They exchanged them for enslaved people, who were then transported across the Atlantic to plantations in the West Indies and North America (Inikori, 2002). They were forced to work on sugar cane, cotton, coffee and tobacco plantations. The produce from those plantations was then transported to Europe to be sold, and the profits were retained by the plantation owners and companies.

The 1640s saw development of the contractor state, a situation that offered new opportunities for entrepreneurship but primarily to those with the right connections (Knight and Wilcox, 2010). The Crown subcontracted public offices to private entrepreneurs and authorized monopolies for the private sector to undertake economic projects including mineral exploitation and infrastructure (Yamamoto, 2018: 53). The main motivation was the maximization of royal revenues, which were stretched by warfare and the cost of maintaining the court (Braddick, 2004). The contractor state was employed as an alternative to unpopular tax rises and as a form of royal patronage to reward individuals for royal service. Critics argued that there was corruption in the awarding of contracts, with opportunities allocated on basis of political lobbying rather than on skill or merit (Tawney, 1958; Prestwich, 1966; Yamamoto, 2011). However, the Crown had a counter-narrative that justified the awarding of contracts according to their demonstration of 'innovation and improvement' and their benefits to the public, including employment opportunities (Yamamoto, 2018: 53, 540–1). The most positive impact seems to have been in infrastructure, where there is evidence that monopolies allowed private enterprise to undertake projects that the Crown lacked the skills or finance to directly coordinate, including improvements to the navigation of the River Stour in 1661 (Yamamoto, 2018: 132–72).

The agricultural revolution of *c.* 1700–60 increased the volume of land under cultivation, introduced higher yielding crops and utilized new technology to cultivate and harvest them (Parker, 1975; Overton, 1996). The enclosure of open fields intensified, and the practice was extended to common land. The invention of the mechanical seed drill allowed labour to be redirected to the manufacturing sector and improved the quality of the crop, by allowing more accurate placing of seed (Sayre, 2010).

Transport changes between 1760 and 1860 enabled entrepreneurs to expand their market and thereby their volume of production. Canals significantly reduced transport time, and thereby cost, and opened up new markets, which encouraged expansion in production. The Bridgewater Canal, opened in 1761, was England's first canal. An entrepreneurial initiative initiated by the Duke of Bridgewater, it transported coal from his estate's coalfields on the outskirts of Manchester into the city centre. The canal network expanded through further entrepreneurial initiative. The Duke of Bridgewater and pottery manufacturer Josiah Wedgwood supported the construction of the Trent and Mersey Canal, which was completed in 1777 and connected the Midlands to both the port of Hull on the east coast of England and that of Liverpool on the west. Wedgwood's Etruria factory, opened in 1769, was situated alongside the canal, which brought clay from Cornwall and sent finished pottery to international markets via Liverpool (Casson and Dodgson, 2019).

Transport was further improved by the railways. The Stockton and Darlington Railway opened in 1825 in the north-east of England as a mineral railway connecting coalfields near Bishop Auckland with the estuary of the River Tees at Stockton. The individual elements of the railway, including 'an early steam locomotive, iron rails, a rope-worked incline and a timetabled passenger service (though the main traffic was meant to be freight)' were not unique but their combination was (Casson and Casson, 2013b: xxxix). In 1830 the Liverpool and Manchester Railway opened, 'the world's first inter-urban high-speed trunk railway line that was dedicated equally to passengers and freight' (Casson and Casson, 2013b: xxxix).

Joint-stock companies were founded to raise the large amount of capital required to construct a railway and to finance the purchase of the land. They were limited liability, meaning that shareholders were only responsible for losses to the limit of the price they had paid for their shares. Railway companies also needed rights for compulsory purchase of land. Without compulsory purchase, a single landowner could disrupt the entire construction by refusing to sell unless an excessive price was received, or all landowners might demand huge prices at the outset (Casson, 2009: 288). Authorization by an Act of Parliament was required to establish a joint-stock company with powers of compulsory purchase (Casson, 2009: 288–9, UK Parliament, 2020a).

The period 1870–1914 has been termed the second Industrial Revolution (Scranton, 1983, 1991, 1997; Mokyr, 1990, 1999). Focus shifted from Britain to the US, and innovations extended into the fields of 'energy, materials and chemicals' (Mokyr, 1999: 219). Thomas Edison characterized this extension of activity, contributing innovations to sectors including communication and entertainment. With the support of venture capital funding, he created the world's first research and development facility in 1886 at Menlo Park, US (Millard, 1990). A large team of staff provided a competitive edge in the speed and scope of development, allowing innovations to be quickly constructed, tested and altered, and working prototypes to be demonstrated to prospective investors (Rutgers, 2020).

Key dates for finance

Coinage was the first significant financial instrument, but it was inconvenient to move between locations (Nightingale, 1990; Bolton, 2012; Rössner, 2012; Nightingale, 2018: 7; Battilossi et al, 2020). Credit allowed money to be advanced to an individual to be repaid at a future date. Small amounts of short-term credit were available at a local level, underpinned by 'relationships of trust based on personal knowledge', for example shared membership of a guild (Muldrew, 1998; Nightingale, 2018: 10). However, methods of debt recovery were limited, the amounts were insufficient for national or international trade, and the reliance on personal information was obstructive (Nightingale, 2018: 27).

The bill of exchange was a credit arrangement that originated with Italian merchants in about 1300 (Blomquist, 1971; Hunt and Murray, 1999; Denzel, 2008). It facilitated the transfer of funds between countries for trading purposes, without requiring large amounts of coin to be moved. Its significance in the evolution of capitalism was noted by Braudel (1982) and Fredona and Reinert (2020). The bill of exchange had two elements: first, it enabled a loan of funds in one location; and secondly, it allowed the transfer or remittance of the funds from that location to another location in a different country, with a different currency (Munro, 2013). The focus on two different currencies being exchanged was practical in international trade and avoided problems with Canon Law by concealing the potential profit and interest implicit in the transaction (Day, 1978; Spufford, 2002; Denzel, 2008). Four parties were involved when the bill was used as a transfer or credit instrument: 'two principals and two agents, in two cities, using two different currencies' (Munro, 2013). The following example demonstrates the process. Piero de Don (the deliverer) is in Bruges where he lends money in the local currency of gros tournois to Giacomo Gabrieli (the taker) (Bell et al, 2017: 138; Munro, 2013). He does this by buying from Gabrieli a bill of exchange that will be presented to a third party, Gabrieli's agent in Venice, Chacharia Gabrieli, who is referred to as the payer. That bill orders Chacharia Gabrieli to 'pay a sum in ducats, equivalent to the original delivery of gros tournois at the current exchange rate' to a fourth party, the payee. The payee is Piero de Don's representative in Venice, Bortolomio Michele. The exchange rate is adjusted to allow the deliverer to make a profit in a manner that circumvents usury restrictions (Munro, 2013; Bell et al, 2017: 138).

Bills of exchange were endorsed by being signed on the back. The endorsement made a claim to a specific account. It was also possible for a bill of exchange to be used by the holder (the deliverer) to settle their own debts if the person it was offered to thought that the payment described was going to be honoured and was interested in having money transferred to the opposite location, for example from Venice back to Bruges.

The creation of the bank account was connected to the bill of exchange. International trade was conducted through the bills that were then presented to the taker's bank to be paid. A key difference between the medieval merchant banks and their later counterparts was that medieval banks were not banks of issue, as they did not issue their own notes. The Medici bank, founded in 1397, focused on provided services of exchange and transfer of credit for its clients, rather than on accepting deposits and providing loans (De Roover, 1946, 1963; Goldthwaite, 1987).

The Italian innovations did not, however, enable the large-scale pooling of capital and were still closely connected to trade between merchants. It was not until the late 17th century that finance evolved into a distinct function. In May 1689 King William III and parliament declared war on France. William needed to raise money to finance the construction of a navy. Substantial funds had already been raised through taxation, but the costs of the campaign continued to rise. In 1694 the Bank of England was founded by an Act of Parliament and a royal charter to raise further money for the war. The bank's capital was raised by subscription, with the king and queen among the 1,268 subscribers. This was then lent to the government to fund naval construction. Support for the Bank of England was encouraged by the Commission of Public Acts of 1690, which monitored revenue raised by the Crown and allocated it for specific purposes. Investors in 1694 could thus be confident that their loans to the bank would be repaid by taxation (UK Parliament, 2020b).

The Bank of England issued its own notes, which represented the money or gold that the bank would provide if the bearer of the note produced it and requested it – known as payment on demand. Theoretically, many people could go to a bank and demand gold or coins to the value of the note. Any issuer of a note consequently needed a working stock of gold to cover that eventuality. The king had a lot of gold and could raise additional cash by taxation if required. People therefore had confidence that notes issued by the Bank of England could be redeemed because it was supported by the Crown. In practice, however, most banknotes circulated many times as payment for goods and services and were only redeemed when they wore out and needed to be replaced with a new one.

Financial speculation by the public became more common after the establishment of the Bank of England. The bank improved investor confidence in projects that were supported by royal charter, and made investors less interested in examining in detail the potential risks. Many projects were based in England and in locations that were well known to investors, allowing information provided by companies to be cross-checked with relative ease. However, the risks were greater in overseas investment opportunities, where the only source of information was a company prospectus and where no independent accounts were available to verify its contents. Significant points in speculative investment were with the Darien Scheme of 1695 and the foundation of the South Sea Company in 1711. The Darien Scheme was a Scottish initiative led by one of the advocates of the Bank of England, William Paterson. Intended to found an entrepôt with access to both the Atlantic and Pacific oceans in present-day Panama, it was supported by Scottish investors eager to develop an export market and to prospective settlers escaping famine and the aftermath of the 1692 Glen Coe massacre. They did not appreciate the risk involved. Paterson had never visited Panama himself, and in reality the harbour site had strong tides, making it unsafe for mooring; it was also close to Spanish-controlled silver mines. The settlement was abandoned in 1700 after the deaths of many settlers and an attack by Spanish troops (University of Glasgow, 2005; Watt, 2007; Armitage, 2010). Its political legacy was more significant, as Scotland's consent to the Act of Union with England in 1707 was motivated by the provision of financial assistance for Darien losses and by the securer opportunities for overseas investment via England's established territories.

Despite this high-profile failure, the English Crown continued to promote overseas schemes because the more ambitious the project, the greater the number of investors and the more popular the investment opportunity, the more money the king could charge for the monopoly charter. The South Sea Company was founded in London in 1711. It had two strands of activity: the trade of enslaved Africans to Spanish colonies in the Americas and the management of government debt. It was hoped that the company would pave the way for Britain to extend her economic and political influence in North and South America. In return for its monopoly, the South Sea Company helped with the management of national debt, offering stock in return for government debt instruments (Paul, 2010: 53). This allowed the government to repay interest more efficiently, as it only had to make interest payments on the debt to one organization rather than to many individual bond holders. It also appeased government creditors who were concerned that repayments might not be made, as they had the option to convert debt to shares, to receive dividends derived from both the interest payment and the trading activities, and to cash in by selling their shares (Paul, 2010, 2020). The combination of royal and government support and the perceived potential of the trading links with scheme made the stock very desirable and people rushed to invest. Ultimately the stock ended up being overvalued and, while some exited in time, many did not (Carlos and Neal, 2006; Laurence, 2006).

Banking provision extended significantly in 1825 with the repeal of the Bubble Act and the passing of the Banking Co-Partnership Act in 1826, the final key dates for finance. Prior to the Acts, partners in private local banks had to operate with unlimited liability, and the number of partners was limited to six, making it hard to raise significant capital (Barnes and Newton, 2016). Local banks were able to issue notes, but their ability to lend was largely restricted by what was received from customer deposits. If many customers withdrew money simultaneously those deposits would decrease. Banks therefore preferred to make short-term loans rather than long-term ones (Wilson, 1995). This restricted the ability of entrepreneurs and industrialists to access long-term finance. The Acts enabled the establishment of joint-stock banks as profit-making ventures and removed the limitation on the number of partners. With greater capital the banks were able to make long-term loans and thus improve their offering to businesses.

Key dates for management

Literature on the prudent management of agrarian estates commenced in 1500 in England, Sweden and Germany. It drew on the New Testament depiction of God as the supreme steward of salvation and heavenly treasure, described using the Greek word for steward (*oikonomos* or householder) (Agamben, 2011; Leshem, 2016; Singh, 2018). It became particularly popular as a source of advice during economic depression, such as in Germany in 1660–1720 (Tribe, 1978; Burkhardt and Priddat, 2000).

The Industrial Revolution generated an interest in factory management. The management of workers to ensure productivity was an issue that engaged some factory owners and factory supervisors. Two distinct approaches emerged. Robert Owen, whose ideas Marx engaged with positively in his preparatory work for *Capital*, advocated a reduction of hours in the working day, the provision of infant education and access to affordable food for workers (Leopold, 2014). He applied these principles during 1800–24 at New Lanark Mills, Scotland (Claeys, 2004). Scientific management was a concept developed by Frederick Wilson Taylor during the 1880s and 1890s and published in 1911. It was aimed at improving productivity and professionalizing management in US manufacturing, particularly the mechanical engineering sector. Factories, such as the steelworks where Taylor was chief engineer, usually paid workers on a piece rate system, essentially payment by result. Some factories sought to increase productivity by lowering the amount they paid per item, forcing workers to produce more in order to reach their previous level of pay. Taylor motivated workers and increased efficiency by setting differential rates – a high rate for quick and accurate completion and a low rate for slow or imperfect work, for example. Taylor's manager was expected to plan and supervise work, select appropriate employees and match them to tasks, and engage with the worker to ensure that the task was untaken in the required manner (Witzel, 2012: 86).

Separation of ownership from management, which begun in 1600 with the creation of joint-stock companies, intensified with the establishment of railway companies from 1825 onwards. Railways were a complex environment because they were in continuous operation and their staff were dispersed, rather than concentrated at headquarters or trading posts. Chandler proposed that the managers of US railroads in the 1840s and 1850s became 'the first group of modern business administrators in the United States' (Chandler, 1977: 87). The need for constant coordination and control on the railways drove the new administrative framework. This was highlighted in 1841 when a fatal accident on the Western Railway was attributed to a lack of coordination in scheduling between the three separate managerial teams who each had a responsibility for a section of the line (Chandler, 1977: 94). A report into the accident required that the company move from informal personal management to a new structure featuring a central headquarters for coordination, a line manager structure for reporting and clear allocated responsibilities for each staff member – particularly in relation to the authorizing of timetabling.

From the 1880s onwards the management structure in the railroads began to be applied to the new mass production and mass distribution enterprises (Chandler, 1977: 285). They grew through a three pronged investment in manufacturing, marketing and management (Chandler, 1977: 288).

Managers aided the growth by aligning structure with strategy and developing appropriate control and coordination procedures.

Key dates for workers

The position of workers in the countryside was a key aspect of Marx's interpretation of the evolution of capitalism. Marx was interested in the operation of the feudal system and its implications, in particular for peasants with unfree tenure. Examining England, he proposed that 'serfdom had practically disappeared' by the end of the 14th century (Marx, 1961: 717). Newly freed peasants became farmers or wage labourers. However, two events negatively impacted on their status. First, from 1475 onwards peasant farmers were 'hurled on the labour market' owing to the decision of landowners to switch from arable to less labour-intensive pasture (Marx, 1961: 718–19). Secondly, the dissolution of the monasteries in 1536–40 that saw 'the estates of the church were to a large extent given away to rapacious royal favourites, or sold at a nominal price to speculating sub farmers and citizens, who drove out, *en masse*, the hereditary sub-tenants and threw their holdings into one' (Marx, 1961: 721). Marx argued that by the 18th century the resulting large farms had become 'capital' or 'merchant' farms and the agricultural population had become 'proletarians for manufacturing industry' (Marx, 1961: 725).

Marx paid less attention to the situation in towns of the Middle Ages. He indirectly suggested that to be a 'free-seller of labour-power' the worker must have 'escaped from the regime of guilds, their rules for apprentices and journey-men, and the impediments of their labour regulations' (Marx, 1961: 715). As discussed earlier, the guild system did impose limitations on competition. However, in an urban economy characterized by self-employment they also offered opportunities for members, including access to trade networks and infrastructure, training and quality control, and welfare provision during sickness and devotion after death (Rosser, 1994; Epstein and Prak, 2008; Grafte and Gelderblom, 2010; Casson, 2020).

The first key date for peasants and wage workers was the Black Death of 1348–9, which had significant implications for both groups. Before the Black Death, historians have suggested, population levels were fairly high, and therefore demand for labour could be easily met. This gave peasants and wage workers little bargaining power over their conditions or over the levels of wages. However, the plague killed a significant proportion of the population, and as a result the labour of survivors became more valuable. Wage labourers started to demand higher wages and both free and unfree peasants asked lords for incentives for them to remain on their holdings, or took the opportunity of the disruption to relocate to places with more favourable living and working conditions. The Statute of Labourers of 1351 attempted to prevent requests by workers for higher wages and to limit movement in search of better opportunities in England, and similar legislation was enacted in Italy and France (Routt, 2008). However, historians generally consider that 1350 was an important step in increasing 'the choices available to serfs and villein tenants in England' (Bailey, 2014: 337).

The 1760s can be considered the second key date for workers. The ability of entrepreneurs to grow their markets through improvement in transport from 1761 (the opening of the Bridgewater Canal) onwards encouraged the establishment of factories and changes in the organization of labour. Rather than have a single worker undertake all aspects of a multi-stage process, employers sought to improve productivity. This involved reducing a complex task to a series of simple ones. Adam Smith (1791 [1776]) used the example of a pin factory to illustrate how this could be achieved in a multi-stage process. He proposed that by dividing the manufacturing of a pin into 18 steps, with each worker specializing in one step, or at the most three, a factory with ten employees could significantly increase its volume of production compared with one worker attempting to make the whole pin themselves. Josiah Wedgwood's Etruria pottery factory, opened in 1769 in Staffordshire, England, was organized on the principle of vertical division of labour.

Breaking tasks into separate stages also facilitated mechanization. This had implications for the skills required from the workforce and the way in which workers needed to be deployed. Mechanization occurred rapidly in textiles. The spinning jenny, invented in 1764, allowed one worker to operate around eight spools, whereas previously eight workers would have been needed to operate eight individual spinning wheels to achieve the same effect. It was followed swiftly in about 1765 by Arkwright's water frame, which was powered by water and spun 96 strands of yarn simultaneously, and in 1779 by Crompton's spinning mule, which extended capacity further (Age of Revolution, 2021). Mechanization enabled greater use of semi-skilled or unskilled labour. In 1769 Arkwright founded his first factory in Cromford, Derbyshire, with new machines powered first by waterwheels and later from stationary steam engines. Operating continuously, they were more efficient than human workers.

Workers were only required to keep the machines fed with cotton, repair breaks in the yarn, replace bobbins and check no dirt got into the mechanism (Science and Industry Museum, 2020). Such tasks were easy but benefited from dexterity, for example the ability to crawl under machinery. Children had worked before the Industrial Revolution, in order to earn additional income for the family, but the use of child labour intensified during the Industrial Revolution (Humphries, 2011; Griffin, 2014). Working conditions were dangerous, with greater potential for injuries that could limit a child's future ability to earn a living. There was little potential to progress to more skilled roles. However, in 1833–80 a series of Acts were passed to address child labour, a third key date for workers. The Factory Act of 1833 prevented the employment of children under 9 years old and restricted the number of hours that children could work to no more than 9 hours a day for 9–13-year-olds and no more than 12 hours a day for 13–18-year-olds. Children were not to work at night and were to receive two hours' schooling each day (The National Archives, 2020a). In 1842 the Mines Act stated that 10 years old was the minimum age to commence mining work. This minimum age was extended to all trades with the Factory Act of 1879, while the Education Act of 1880 made schooling compulsory until the age of 10.

For adult workers, unskilled roles also offered little opportunity for progression and workers were vulnerable to redundancy as mechanization intensified. One solution was for workers to seek change by uniting formally. Trade unions were 'groups of workers who have joined together to negotiate with their employers as a group rather than as a series of individuals' (Working Class Movement Library, 2020). This process intensified in the 1830s, our next key date, as smaller unions amalgamated and new organizations with national objectives were founded (Thompson, 1963: 503; The National Archives, 2020b). Some unions took a defensive stance aimed at preventing change. Others accepted that some change was inevitable and took a more proactive stance, helping workers adapt to change through education and reskilling, for example.

In Rochdale in 1844, the final key date, a group of 28 weavers founded a consumer cooperative to address the challenges in accessing safe and affordable food in new industrial towns (Alman, 2010). Textile factories clustered in areas such as the Manchester hills, where they could easily access water power for their machinery. Workers relocated to the vicinity of the factories, but the intensive construction of housing in the new industrial centres made no provision for gardens where workers could cultivate their own food. Instead they were reliant on expensive, and often poor-quality, food purchased in shops run by factory owners. The Rochdale cooperative was structured as a 'mutual self-help organization … based on members' share contributions and retained profits' (Van Opstal, 2010). Each member invested £1 to establish a shop selling 'butter, flour, sugar, oatmeal and candles' (Van Opstal, 2010; Working Class Movement Library, 2020). By 1850 the Rochdale branch had 500 members, and cooperatives were founded in other locations and for additional provisions, such as burial (Van Opstal, 2010).

Key dates for political leaders

The separation of royal patronage from business began in the US and France, and this represents the first key date for political leaders. The first engagements of the US revolutionary war took place in 1775, while the French Revolution occurred in 1789. In his comparison of the Glorious Revolution of 1688 in England, the American Revolution and the French Revolution, Piketty suggests that the French Revolution was the most ambitious politically as it 'abolished all legal privileges and sought to create a political and social order based entirely on equality of rights and opportunities' (Piketty, 2014: 30). In contrast, the overthrowing of James II and the arrival of William of Orange in 1688, he proposes, established 'modern parliamentarism' but retained 'royal dynasty, primogeniture on landed estates and political privileges for the hereditary nobility'. Meanwhile, the American Revolution 'established the republican principle' but 'allowed slavery to continue for nearly a century and legal racial discrimination for nearly two centuries' (Piketty, 2014: 30).

In the post-Revolutionary US there remained areas where the political leaders and private enterprise sometimes needed to work collaboratively. While the UK government authorized rights that helped entrepreneurs raise the necessary capital for railway construction, in the US government was itself a source of funds (Dobbin, 1994). From the 1850s onwards, the second key date, sections of public land, usually in 20 mile or 50 mile blocks, were awarded to companies by the federal government. Companies raised money to build the railway by selling parcels of the land, often to immigrants from Europe (Library of Congress, 2021a, 2021b). Money for the track and locomotives was sought from private investors via the New York stock market (Chandler, 1977: 90–1).

Summary of chronological change

This chapter has identified the five functions relevant to capitalism. For each function, key dates have been identified, which are summarized in Table 1.1. This chapter has suggested that the transition to capitalism, as associated with the ability for firms to enter and exit the market, to pool finance from multiple individuals and to operate in a political and legal framework with input from the population, was connected to the emergence of each distinctive function.

Functions that were initially combined gradually separated into the five categories across the 13th century to the 20th century. In the period 1200–1350 the activities of a merchant would generally combine the functions of entrepreneurship, finance and management. In 1300 Italian banking introduced reforms that facilitated financial transactions between merchants.

Table 1.1: Five functions relevant to capitalism and their dates of emergence

Function	Key dates of emergence
Entrepreneurship	1200–1350 Commercial boom but with some limitations on business entry 1350–1500 Stasis but some opportunities for business entry in agriculture 1536 Firm entry becomes easier 1600 New forms of business organization and new markets. First chartered company 1640s Contractor state 1700–60 Agricultural revolution 1760–1860 Industrial Revolution, characterized by improvements in transport infrastructure and creation of joint-stock companies with compulsory purchase rights 1870–1914 Second Industrial Revolution, focused on the US and characterized by intensive investment in research and development
Finance	1300 Bill of exchange aids international trade 1694 Establishment of the Bank of England 1695 Darien Scheme 1711 South Sea Company 1825 and 1826 Joint-stock banks established as profit-making ventures
Management	Late 1500s Agrarian and household management 1800 Robert Owen's approach to managing factory workers 1825 Joint-stock companies result in separation of ownership and management 1840 Management practices introduced on US railways 1880s Management practices spread to innovative sectors 1880s and 1890s Taylor's approach to managing workers in a factory environment
Workers	1348–49 Black Death 1500s Enclosures 1760s Increased mechanization and deskilling of workers and rise of factories 1830s Trade unions emerge 1833–80 Efforts to regulate the use of child labour 1844 Cooperative movement founded
Political leadership	1775 First engagement in American Revolutionary wars 1789 French Revolution 1850s Land grants to railways in US

However, it was not until the foundation of the Bank of England in 1694 that finance became a distinct function. In the mid-19th century finance began to be separated from management, and management became more specialized. Partnerships became joint-stock companies and increasingly unwieldy. As a result, managers began to be hired to run the organization on behalf of the board, with owners delegating to managers. The divorce of ownership and control was to become a significant feature of capitalism in the US in the 20th century (Berle and Means, 1932; McKenna, 2006).

In industry, the function of worker and manager also arguably separated from the mid-18th century. In the Middle Ages most manufacturers had essentially been self-employed, but by the mid-18th century they were increasingly likely to be an employee in a factory. Marx described early modern manufactories, their processes of division of labour and the gradual emergence of the modern manager as an important transitory state of society as it moved from feudalism to capitalism proper. The division between worker and entrepreneur was more complex. In agriculture, some workers were able to become entrepreneurial yeoman farmers in the period 1350–1450.

The relationship between political leaders and the economy manifested itself in the fiscal-military state in early modern Europe. Through princes and kings and their incessant demand for military and materiel, and also infrastructure and strategic industrial policy applied since the Middle Ages, the relationship between economy and the state became increasingly symbiotic, often giving rise to virtuous cycles and synergies of development. Many scholars even see the role of the state as crucial in laying the foundations of economic development and industrialization (O'Brien, 2011; Parthasarathi, 2011; Vries, 2015). In England the development of chartered companies in 1600 and the rise of the contractor state in the 1640s created a close connection between politics and entrepreneurship. This was a relationship of patronage. These ties arguably loosened during the period 1750–1860, with private entrepreneurship initiating projects to a greater extent than previously. However, in the US in the 1850s there was a closer partnership between political leaders, entrepreneurs and private investors.

References

Agamben, G. (2011) *The Kingdom and the Glory: For a Theological Genealogy of Economy and Government*, Stanford, CA: Stanford University Press.

Age of Revolution (2020) 'Crompton's spinning wheel', *Age of Revolution*, [online] 20 December. Available from: https://ageofrevolution.org/200-obj ect/cromptons-spinning-mule/ [Accessed 20 December 2020].

Allen, R.C. (1992) *Enclosure and the Yeoman: The Agricultural Development of the South Midlands 1450–1850*, Oxford: Clarendon Press.

Allen, R.C. (2009) *The British Industrial Revolution in Global Perspective*, Cambridge: Cambridge University Press.

Altman, M. (2010) 'Cooperatives, history and theories of', in H.K. Anheier and S. Toepler (eds) *International Encyclopedia of Civil Society*, New York: Springer. Available from: https://doi-org.manchester.idm.oclc.org/10.1007/978-0-387-93996-4_102 [Accessed 20 December 2020].

Armitage, D. (2010) 'Paterson, William (1658–1719)', *Oxford Dictionary of National Biography*.

Ashworth, W.J. (2017) *The Industrial Revolution: The State, Knowledge and Global Trade*, London: Bloomsbury.

Bailey, Mark (2014) *The Decline of Serfdom in Late Medieval England: From Bondage to Freedom*, Woodbridge: Boydell and Brewer.

Banaji, J. (2020) *A Brief History of Commercial Capitalism*, Chicago: Haymarket Books.

Barnes, V. and Newton, L. (2016) 'The introduction of the joint-stock company in English banking and monetary policy', *University of Reading Centre for International Business History Discussion Paper*, [online]. Available from: https://assets.henley.ac.uk/v3/fileUploads/research/IBH-2016-01_Barnes_and_Newton-mtime20170410170908_2020-10-14-084158.pdf?mtime=20201014094158&focal=none [Accessed 20 December 2020].

Battilossi, S., Cassis, Y. and Yago, K. (2020) *Handbook of the History of Money and Currency*, Singapore: Springer.

Beckert, S. (2015) *Empire of Cotton: A New History of Global Capitalism*, London: Penguin Books.

Bell, A.R., Brooks, C. and Dryburgh, P. (2007) *The English Wool Market, c. 1230–1327*, Cambridge: Cambridge University Press.

Bell, A., Brooks, C. and Moore, T. (2017) 'The non-use of money in the middle a ges', in N. Mayhew (ed) *Peter Spufford's Money and Its Use in Medieval Europe – Twenty-Five Years On*, London: Royal Numismatic Society, pp 137–51.

Berle, A. and Means, G. (1932) *The Modern Corporation and Private Property*, New York: Macmillan.

Blomquist, T.M. (1971) 'Commercial association in thirteenth-century Lucca', *Business History Review*, 45(2): 157–78.

Bolton, J.L. (2012) *Money in the Medieval English Economy 973–1489*, Manchester: Manchester University Press.

Braddick, M.J. (2004) 'Cranfield, Lionel, first earl of Middlesex (1575–1645)', *Oxford Dictionary of National Biography*.

Braudel, F. (1981) *Civilization and Capitalism Fifteenth to Eighteenth Century: Volume 1 The Structures of Everyday Life*, London: Collins.

Braudel, F. (1982) *Civilization and Capitalism Fifteenth to Eighteenth Century: Volume 2 The Wheels of Commerce*, London: Collins.

Braudel, F. (1985) *Civilization and Capitalism Fifteenth to Eighteenth Century: Volume 3 The Perspective of the World*, London: Collins.

Britnell, R.H. (1993) *The Commercialisation of English Society 1000–1500*, Cambridge: Cambridge University Press.

Britnell, R. (2009) *Markets, Trade and Economic Development in England and Europe, 1050–1550*, Aldershot: Ashgate.

Burkhardt, J. and Priddat, B. (eds) (2000) *Geschichte der Ökonomie*, Frankfurt: Deutscher Klassiker Verlag.

Cain, P.J. and Hopkins, A.G. (1986) 'Gentlemanly capitalism and British expansion Overseas I: the old colonial system, 1688–1850', *Economic History Review*, 39(4): 501–25.

Carlos, A.M. and Nicholas, S. (1988) ' "Giants of an earlier capitalism": the chartered trading companies as modern multinationals', *Business History Review*, 62(3): 398–419.

Carlos, A.M. and Nicholas, S. (1996) 'Theory and history: seventeenth-century joint-stock chartered trading companies', *Journal of Economic History*, 56(4): 916–24.

Carlos, A.M. and Brown Kruse, J. (1996) 'The decline of the Royal African Company: fringe firms and the role of the charter', *Economic History Review*, 49(2): 291–313.

Carlos, A.M. and Neal, L. (2006) 'The micro-foundations of the early London capital market: bank of England shareholders during and after the South Sea Bubble, 1720–25', *Economic History Review*, 59(3): 498–538.

Casson, C. (2020) 'Guilds', in T. da Silva Lopes, H. Tworek and C. Lubinski (eds) *The Routledge Companion to the Makers of Global Business*, Abingdon: Routledge, pp 159–70.

Casson, C. and Dodgson, M. (2019) 'Designing for innovation: cooperation and competition in English cotton, silk and pottery firms c. 1750–1860', *Business History Review*, 93(2): 247–73.

Casson, M. (2003) *The Entrepreneur: An Economic Theory* (2nd edn), Cheltenham and Northampton, MA: Edward Elgar.

Casson, M. (2009) *The World's First Railway System: Enterprise, Competition, and Regulation on the Railway Network in Victorian Britain*, Oxford: Oxford University Press.

Casson, M. and Casson, C. (2013a) *The Entrepreneur in History: From Medieval Merchant to Modern Business Leader*, Basingstoke: Palgrave Macmillan.

Casson, M. and Casson, C. (eds) (2013b) *History of Entrepreneurship: Innovation and Risk Taking, 1200–2000*, 2 vols, Cheltenham: Edward Elgar.

Chandler, A.D. Jr. (1977) *The Visible Hand*, Cambridge, MA: Harvard University Press.

Claeys, G. (2004) 'Owen, Robert (1771–1858)', *Oxford Dictionary of National Biography*.

Davids, R.L. (1982) 'Winchcombe, alias Smallwood, John (1488/89–1557), of Newbury, Berks.', *History of Parliament*, [online]. Available from: http://www.historyofparliamentonline.org/volume/1509-1558/member/winchcombe-john-148889–1557 [Accessed 20 December 2020].

Day, J. (1978) 'The great bullion famine of the fifteenth century', *Past and Present*, 79(1): 3–54.

De Roover, R. (1946) 'The Medici bank organization and management', *The Journal of Economic History*, 6(1): 24–52.

De Roover, R. (1963) *The Rise and Decline of the Medici Bank, 1397–1494*, Cambridge, MA: Harvard University Press.

De Vries, J. and Woude, A.M. van der. (1997) *The First Modern Economy: Success, Failure, and Perseverance of the Dutch Economy, 1500–1815*, Cambridge: Cambridge University Press.

Denzel, M.A. (2008) *Handbook of World Exchange Rates, 1590–1914*, Farnham: Ashgate.

Dobbin, F. (1994) *Forging Industrial Policy: The United States, Britain, and France in the Railway Age*, Cambridge: Cambridge University Press.

Dyer, C. (2012) *A Country Merchant, 1495–1520: Trading and Farming at the End of the Middle Ages*, Oxford: Oxford University Press.

Ehrenberg, R. (1928) *Capital and Finance in the Age of the Renaissance: A Study of the Fuggers and their Connections* (trans H.M. Lucas), London: Cape.

Epstein, S.R. and Prak, M.R. (2008). *Guilds, Innovation, and the European Economy, 1400–1800*, Cambridge: Cambridge University Press.

Fredona, R. and Reinert, S. (2020) 'Italy and the origins of capitalism', *Business History Review*, 94(1): 5–38.

Goddard, R. (2016) *Credit and Trade in Later Medieval England, 1353–1532*, London: Palgrave Macmillan.

Goldthwaite, R.A. (1987) 'The Medici bank and the world of Florentine capitalism', *Past & Present*, 114: 3–31.

Grafe, R. and Gelderblom, O. (2010) 'The rise and fall of merchant guilds: re-thinking the comparative study of commercial institutions in premodern Europe', *The Journal of Interdisciplinary History*, 40(4): 477–511.

Griffin, E. (2014) *Liberty's Dawn: A People's History of the Industrial Revolution*, New Haven, CT: Yale University Press.

Häberlein, M. (2012) *The Fuggers of Augsburg: Pursuing Wealth and Honor in Renaissance Germany*, Charlottesville: University of Virginia Press.

Hall, P. and Soskice, D. (eds) (2001) *Varieties of Capitalism: The Institutional Foundations of Comparative Advantage*, Oxford: Oxford University Press.

Horrox, R. (ed) (1994) *The Black Death*, Manchester and New York: Manchester University Press.

Hudson, P. (2014) *The Industrial Revolution*, London: Hodder Arnold.

Humphries, J. (2011) *Childhood and Child Labour in the British Industrial Revolution*, Cambridge: Cambridge University Press.

Hunt, E.S. and Murray, J.M. (1999) *A History of Business in Medieval Europe, 1200–1550*, Cambridge: Cambridge University Press.

Inikori, J.E. (2002) *Africans and the Industrial Revolution in England: A Study in International Trade and Development*, Cambridge: Cambridge University Press.

Jackson, C. (2008) 'Boom-time freaks or heroic industrial pioneers? Clothing entrepreneurs in sixteenth- and early seventeenth-century Berkshire', *Textile History*, 39: 145–71.

Jones, S.R.H. and S.P. Ville (1996) 'Theory and evidence: understanding chartered trading companies', *Journal of Economic History*, 56(4): 925–6.

Keynes, J.M. (1936) *The General Theory of Employment Interest and Money*, London: Macmillan.

Kirzner, I.M. (1973) *Competition and Entrepreneurship*, Chicago: University of Chicago Press.

Klein, H.S. and Vinson, B. (2007) *African Slavery in Latin America and the Caribbean* (2nd edn), New York: Oxford University Press.

Knight, F.H. (1921) *Risk, Uncertainty and Profit*, Boston, MA: Houghton Mifflin.

Knight, R. and Wilcox, M. (2010) *Sustaining the Fleet: War, the British Navy and the Contractor State*, Woodbridge: Boydell and Brewer.

Kocka, J. (2016) *Capitalism A Short History*, Princeton, NJ: Princeton University Press.

Laurence, A. (2006) 'Women investors, "that nasty south sea affair" and the rage to speculate in early eighteenth-century England', *Accounting, Business and Financial History*, 16(2): 245–64.

Lee, J.S. (2018) *The Medieval Clothier*, Woodbridge: Boydell Press.

Leopold, D. (2014) 'Karl Marx and British socialism', in W.J. Mande (ed) *The Oxford Handbook of British Philosophy in the Nineteenth Century*, Oxford: Oxford University Press [online].

Leshem, D. (2016) *The Origins of Neoliberalism: Modeling the Economy from Jesus*, New York: Columbia University Press.

Library of Congress (2021a) 'The beginnings of American railroads and mapping', *Library of Congress*, [online]. Available from: https://www.loc.gov/collections/railroad-maps-1828-to-1900/articles-and-essays/history-of-railroads-and-maps/the-beginnings-of-american-railroads-and-mapping/ [Accessed 11 January 2021].

Library of Congress (2021b) 'Land grants', *Library of Congress*, [online]. Available from: https://www.loc.gov/collections/railroad-maps-1828-to-1900/articles-and-essays/history-of-railroads-and-maps/land-grants/ [Accessed 11 January 2021].

Lipartito, K. and Jacobson, L. (2020) *Capitalism's Hidden Worlds*, Philadelphia: University of Pennsylvania Press.

Malthus, T. (1798) *An Essay on the Principle of Population*, London: J. Johnson, *Internet Archive*, [online]. Available from: https://archive.org/details/essayonprincipl00malt [Accessed 17 January 2021].

Marx, K. (1961 [1867]) *Capital Volume 1* (trans S. Moore, S. and E. Aveling and ed F. Engels), Moscow: Foreign Languages Publishing House.

Marx, K. and Engels, F. (1868) 'Manifesto of the Communist Party', Marxists.Org, [online]. Available from: https://www.marxists.org/arch ive/marx/works/1848/communist-manifesto/ch01.htm#007 [Accessed 6 January 2020].

McKenna, C. (2006) *The World's Newest Profession: Management Consulting in the Twentieth Century*, Cambridge: Cambridge University Press.

Millard, A.J. (1990) *Edison and the Business of Innovation*, Baltimore, MD, and London: Johns Hopkins University Press.

Mokyr, J. (1990) *The Lever of Riches: Technological Creativity and Economic Progress*, Oxford and New York: Oxford University Press.

Mokyr, J. (1999) 'The second industrial revolution, 1870–1914', in V. Castronovo (ed) *Storia dell' Economia Mondiale*, Rome: Laterza Publishing, pp 219–45.

Muldrew, C. (1998) *The Economy of Obligation: The Culture of Credit and Social Relations in Early Modern England*, Basingstoke: Macmillan.

Munro, J. (2013) 'The bill of exchange', *Department of Economics, University of Toronto*, [online]. Available from: https://www.economics.utoronto.ca/ munro5/BILLEXCH.htm#:~:text=The%20Medieval%20Bill%20of%20E xchange&text=A%20Simple%20Definition%3A%20The%20bill,merch ant%20in%20that%20distant%20city [Accessed 6 January 2021].

Murphy, A. (2009) *The Origins of English Financial Markets Investment and Speculation before the South Sea Bubble*, Cambridge: Cambridge University Press.

Neal, L. and Williamson, J.G. (eds) (2014) *The Cambridge History of Capitalism, Volume 1, The Rise of Capitalism: From Ancient Origins to 1848*, Cambridge and New York: Cambridge University Press.

Nightingale, P. (1990) 'Monetary contraction and mercantile credit in later medieval England', *Economic History Review*, 43(4): 560–75.

Nightingale, P. (2018) *Enterprise, Money and Credit in England before the Black Death, 1285–1349*, London: Palgrave Macmillan.

North, D.C. (1990) *Institutions, Institutional Change and Economic Performance*, Cambridge: Cambridge University Press.

O'Brien, P. (2011) 'The nature and historical evolution of an exceptional fiscal state and its possible significance for the precocious commercialization and industrialization of the British economy from Cromwell to Nelson', *Economic History Review*, 64(2): 408–46.

Overton M. (1996) *Agricultural Revolution in England: The Transformation of the Agrarian Economy 1500–1850*, Cambridge: Cambridge University Press.

Parker, R.A.C. (1975) *Coke of Norfolk: A Financial and Agricultural Study, 1707–1842*, Oxford: Clarendon.

Parthasarathi, P. (2011) *Why Europe Grew Rich and Asia Did Not: Global Economic Divergence, 1600–1850*, Cambridge: Cambridge University Press.

Paul, H. (2010) *The South Sea Bubble: An Economic History of its Origins and Consequences*, London: Taylor and Francis Group.

Paul, H. (2020) '300 years since the South Sea Bubble: the real story behind the iconic financial crash', *The Conversation*, [online] 20 August. Available from: https://theconversation.com/300-years-since-the-south-sea-bubble-the-real-story-behind-the-iconic-financial-crash-143861 [Accessed 6 January 2021].

Peacock, D. (2003) *The Winchcombe Family and the Woollen Industry in Sixteenth-Century Newbury* (Unpublished PhD thesis, University of Reading).

Piketty, T. (2014) *Capital in the Twenty-First Century* (trans A. Goldhammer), Cambridge, MA, and London: The Belknap Press of Harvard University.

Porter, M.E. (1980) *Competitive Strategy*, New York: Free Press.

Prestwich, M. (1966) *Cranfield: Politics and Profits Under the Early Stuarts. The Career of Lionel Cranfield, Earl of Middlesex*, Oxford: Clarendon Press.

Ricardo, D. (1817) *The Principles of Political Economy and Taxation*, London: John Murray, *Internet Archive*, [online]. Available from: https://archive.org/details/in.ernet.dli.2015.12715 [Accessed 17 January 2021].

Rosser, G. (1994) 'Going to the fraternity feast: commensality and social relations in late medieval England', *Journal of British Studies*, 33(4): 430–46.

Rosser, G. (2015) *The Art of Solidarity in the Middle Ages: Guilds in England 1250–1550*, Oxford: Oxford University Press.

Rössner, P.R. (2012) *Deflation – Devaluation – Rebellion: Geld im Zeitalter der Reformation*, Stuttgart: Franz Steiner.

Routt, D. (2008) 'The economic impact of the Black Death', *EH.Net Encyclopedia*, [online] 20 July. Available from: http://eh.net/encyclopedia/the-economic-impact-of-the-black-death/ [Accessed 12 December 2020].

Rutgers University (2020) 'Edison and innovation series-the invention factory', *Thomas A. Edison Papers*, [online]. Available from: http://edison.rutgers.edu/inventionfactory.htm [Accessed 17 December 2020].

Sayre, L.B. (2010) 'The pre-history of soil science: Jethro Tull, the invention of the seed drill, and the foundations of modern agriculture', *Physics and Chemistry of the Earth. Parts A/B/C*, 35(15): 851–9.

Schumpeter, J.A. (1992 [1942]) *Capitalism, Socialism and Democracy*, London: Routledge.

Science and Industry Museum (2020) 'Richard Arkwright', *Science and Industry Museum*, [online]. Available from: https://www.scienceandindustrymuseum.org.uk/objects-and-stories/richard-arkwright#arkwright-on-trial [Accessed 28 December 2020].

Scranton, P. (1983) *Proprietary Capitalism: The Textile Manufacture at Philadelphia, 1800–1885*, New York: Cambridge University Press.

Scranton, P. (1991) '"Diversity in diversity": flexible production and American industrialization, 1880–1930', *Business History Review*, 65(1): 27–90.

Scranton, P. (1997) *Endless Novelty: Specialty Production and American Industrialization, 1865–1925*, Princeton, NJ, and Chichester: Princeton University Press.

Singh, D. (2018) *Divine Currency: The Theological Power of Money in the West*, Stanford, CA: Stanford University Press

Smith, A. (1791 [1776]) *An Inquiry into the Nature and Causes of the Wealth of Nations* (4th edn), N.S.

Sombart, W. (1913) *Krieg und Kapitalismus*, Munich and Leipzig: Duncker and Humblot.

Sombart, W. (1927) *Der Moderne Kapitalismus, Volumes 1 and 2* (4th edn), Munich and Leipzig: Duncker and Humblot.

Spufford, P. (2002) *Power and Profit: The Merchant in Medieval Europe*, London: Thames and Hudson.

Tawney, R.H. (1958) *Business and Politics under James I: Lionel Cranfield as Merchant and Minister*, Cambridge: Cambridge University Press.

Taylor, J. (2006) *Creating Capitalism: Joint-Stock Enterprise in British Politics and Culture, 1800–1870*, Woodbridge: Royal Historical Society and Boydell Press.

The National Archives (2020a) 'The 1833 factory act', *The National Archives*, [online]. Available from: https://www.nationalarchives.gov.uk/education/resources/1833-factory-act/ [Accessed 20 December 2020].

The National Archives (2020b) 'Trade unions', *The National Archives*, [online]. Available from: http://www.nationalarchives.gov.uk/pathways/citizenship/struggle_democracy/trade_unionism.htm#:~:text=The%201871%20Trade%20Union%20Act,to%20organise%20picketing%20and%20strikes [Accessed 20 December 2020].

Thompson, E.P. (1963) *The Making of the English Working Class*, New York: Pantheon Books.

Toulmin Smith, L., Toulmin Smith, J. and Brentano, L. (1870) *English Gilds: The Original Ordinances of More than One Hundred Early English Gilds*, London: Early English Text Society.

Tribe, K. (1978) *Land, Labour and Economic Discourse*, London: Routledge Kegan & Paul.

UK Parliament (2020a) 'Fire and steam', UK Parliament, [online]. Available from: https://www.parliament.uk/about/living-heritage/transforming society/transportcomms/roadsrail/overview/fireandsteam/ [Accessed 27 December 2020].

UK Parliament (2020b) 'The financial revolution', UK Parliament, [online]. Available from: https://www.parliament.uk/about/living-heritage/evolut ionofparliament/parliamentaryauthority/revolution/overview/financialrev olution/ [Accessed 27 December 2020].

University of Glasgow (2005) 'The Darien scheme', *University of Glasgow*, [online]. Available from: https://www.gla.ac.uk/myglasgow/library/files/special/exhibns/month/may2005.html [Accessed 27 December 2020].

Van Opstal, W. (2010) 'Rochdale Society of Equitable Pioneers', in H.K. Anheier and S. Toepler (eds) *International Encyclopedia of Civil Society*, New York: Springer. Available from: https://doi-org.manchester.idm.oclc.org/10.1007/978-0-387-93996-4_820 [Accessed 20 December 2020].

Vries, P. (2015) *State, Economy and the Great Divergence: Great Britain and China, 1680s–1850s*, London: Bloomsbury.

Watt, D. (2007) *The Price of Scotland: Darien, Union and the Wealth of Nations*, Edinburgh: Luath Press.

Weber, M. (2001) *The Protestant Ethic and the Spirit of Capitalism* (trans T. Parsons), London and New York: Routledge.

Wilson, J.F. (1995) *British Business History 1720–1994*, Manchester and New York: Manchester University Press.

Witzel, M. (2012) *A History of Management Thought*, London and New York: Routledge.

Working Class Movement Library (2020) 'The Co-operative movement', *Working Class Movement Library*, [online]. Available from: https://www.wcml.org.uk/our-collections/working-lives/the-cooperative-movement/ [Accessed 27 December 2020].

Yamamoto, K. (2011) 'Piety, profit and public service in the financial revolution', *English Historical Review*, 126: 806–83.

Yamamoto, K. (2018) *Taming Capitalism Before its Triumph: Public Service, Distrust, and 'Projecting' in Early Modern Europe*, Oxford: Oxford University Press.

Yazdani, K. and Menon, D.M. (2020) *Capitalisms. Towards a Global History*, Oxford: Oxford University Press.

Yun Casalilla, B., O'Brien, P.K. and Comín Comín, F. (2012) *The Rise of Fiscal States: A Global History, 1500–1914*, Cambridge: Cambridge University Press.

The Market as an Institution: Theory and History

Mark Casson

Introduction

Evolution of the market

Markets occupy a central role in economic theory. It is assumed that we understand them – but do we really? This chapter suggests that we do not. We know a lot, but not so much as we should. Markets remain a subject of controversy in popular debates over economic policy and historical debates over commercialization and capitalism. That is why we need to learn more.

Markets facilitate trade. Trade, it is often assumed, developed from small beginnings in chance encounters; for example, two people meet on a country path and one swaps their coat for the other's piece of jewellery. But there is little evidence for this 'chance encounter' theory. The key question is 'Can you really trust a stranger?' Why does the stronger person not just rob the weaker one? So why would the weaker person go out alone? Trade, it would seem, needs a secure environment. Security needs to be provided by someone who can observe a situation and has the power to detain and punish a wrongdoer. Hopefully, the threat of being captured and punished will deter the wrongdoer. Trade therefore requires a strong individual who can provide that security, such as a tribal leader.

Archaeological evidence from the Stone Age suggests that neighbouring tribes would meet at ceremonial centres to marry off their children, worship their gods and trade some goods as well. Provided the tribal leaders were at peace with one another, the ceremony would provide a safe environment where trade could take place. By the Bronze Age, long-distance trade was common in many parts of the world, supported by a network of small cities. Trade, it seems, typically flourished at big events (later known as fairs), which fulfilled important social and religious purposes (Cunliffe, 2008; Howell, 2010; Barjamovic et al, 2019).

Trade can take the form of simple reciprocity, barter or a monetary transaction. The problem with reciprocity is that the gifts may not be exactly what the recipients wanted. Some preliminary negotiation would therefore be helpful, and this may lead to barter, namely the exchange of gifts of equivalent value. Negotiation also implies communication; which requires some sort of common language; this could involve sign language or written text.

Trade may also rely on credit, which in turn implies some notion of obligation that is understood by both the parties (Muldrew, 1998). Credit relies on memory, which is aided by record keeping, which also depends on writing.

Trade and credit do not imply the existence of a market, however. It is trade on a large scale, focused on some specific location, that indicates the presence of a market. A market provides a choice of trading partner, which requires the presence of several people rather than a single pair.

According to Adam Smith (1976 [1776]), there is a natural human propensity to truck and barter. Trade facilitates the division of labour. People are more productive when they specialize in doing a single thing, such as being a butcher or a baker. But life would be very monotonous if people only ever consumed their own product. A market allows each person to trade their surplus product for the surpluses of other people and therefore consume a variety of products. Trade is therefore rational from a collective point of view. Smith is unsure, however, whether people trade because it is rational or because they like to trade for its own sake.

Modern trade takes place without the need for ceremony, but people must still find a convenient place at which to meet. The market provides a safe and convenient environment for trade. Many towns and cities where trade takes place are also ceremonial centres, even today; but nowadays trade occurs almost daily, while ceremonial is intermittent; furthermore, the urban spaces used for trade (including the market square and shopping centre) are no longer those that are used for ceremony (such as the town hall, sports stadium and local church).

The expansion of markets has driven the growth of towns. Buyers and sellers can both benefit from trade. This benefit generates surplus value that can be appropriated, and thereby encourages the development of markets for private profit. These profits can in turn be taxed, so that the state has an interest in markets too. Furthermore, the state is in a good position to regulate them since it makes and enforces laws. Some writers have portrayed markets and the state as rivals and even enemies (Walgorski, 1990). They presume that the state would like to plan the economy.

But this argument appears to be overstated: many states have historically promoted markets.

Definition of a market

'Market' is a term that is used by different people in different ways. Modern economists often describe markets as institutions that promote exchange by reducing transaction costs. Unfortunately, however, they cannot always agree on what precisely they mean by 'institution' or by 'transaction costs'. For example, are they referring to a formal rule-driven institution or an informal institution based on social ties, or both? Do transaction costs include not only the costs of negotiating and enforcing contracts, but also the costs of searching for a trading partner? This terminology is too vague for the purposes of this chapter.

A market may be defined as a forum that facilitates transactions between property holders. A forum is a site, either real (marketplace, shopping centre, organized exchange) or virtual (website, internet). Property holders possess alienable claims on the use of proprietary resources. Transactions are exchanges of property or claims on resources. Facilitation includes contact-making between buyer and seller; product inspection; standardized weights and measures; protocols for price comparison and negotiation; provision of reputable money to act as unit of account, medium of exchange and store of value; regulation; and impartial monitoring and enforcement of agreements (Priestly, 1987; Casson, 2011; Casson and Lee, 2011).

Plan of the chapter

The definition here points to seven key issues in the analysis of markets. These concern the meaning and significance of (1) the ownership of private property; (2) the alienability of property; (3) the nature of the incentive to trade; (4) the meaning and role of money (5) the significance of substitutability and its importance for the comparison of price and quality; (6) the role of trust in ensuring contractual compliance; (7) the role of intermediation in facilitating trade. These issues are addressed in the second section, entitled 'Key Concepts in the Analysis of Markets'.

Section 3, 'Economic Theories of Markets', critically reviews economic theories of markets. Neoclassical economic theory emphasizes the equilibrium of the market rather than the process by which that equilibrium is reached. This chapter takes a broader view. It examines the most common types of process used and focuses on the shopping process. It presents a social network approach to shopping behaviour that produces plausible results regarding price dispersion within urban towns. This approach generates an outcome that is conditional on the structure of the social network; it passes a 'reality check' that orthodox theories fail.

Section 4, 'Location of Towns', discusses the determinants of the location of towns. This builds on existing theories of urban and regional economics and applies them in a broad historical context. It also discusses the topography of streets and markets within towns.

The final thematic section, 'Policy Intervention: Regulation of the Market', shows that the concept of free markets is ambiguous; it may refer to freedom of entry (sometimes called contestability) or freedom from regulation, or both. While freedom of entry enhances long-run competition and boosts market performance, freedom from regulation normally has a negative effect; it allows fraudulent sellers to escape punishment. Regulation has been a feature of successful markets for over 800 years. Conclusions and policy implications are summarized in the final section.

Key concepts in the analysis of markets

Private property

The origins of private property are lost in the mists of time. When early man made an artefact he may have thought 'this is mine', and if his fellow tribespeople agreed they may have buried his artefacts with him when he died. Alternatively his children may have inherited them instead.

In early societies the most important economic resource was land. For a religious tribesperson, the land was made not by humans, but by God. So who could rightfully claim it? In practice land seems to have been claimed by tribes through their leader. The leader would normally be a warrior who defended the land against the claims of neighbouring tribes and other potential invaders.

The leader de facto owned the land because, as the most powerful person, they could regulate its use. An elected leader would normally hold the land on behalf of the people, but a dynastic leader, or one who fought for their title, might hold it in their own right. An ordinary person would own land if they were given it by the leader. Managing leadership succession, and constraining the arbitrary exercise of power, was a major political challenge for societies then, just as it is today.

Alienability

In Norman England (post-1066) the chief warriors and administrators, such as earls and sheriffs, held large tracts of land from the king. They paid rent in kind, in the form of knight's service, namely an obligation to equip a specified number of fully armed knights who would lead their local troops into battle. Knight's service could, however, be commuted for a monetary fine, which was in effect a money rent on the land held by the knight (Hudson, 2012).

The knights held land from earls in the same way that earls held it from the king. Their property was *alienable*. Earls would normally consult the king over the sale of their property, but in practice knights had more discretion. They often exchanged land with other knights in order to concentrate their property portfolios in convenient parts of the country. This became much easier after the law of property was reformed by Henry II in the 1170s.

Knights could split up their properties into manors, selling out to manorial lords, who in turn could sell to local farmers. This process was known as sub-infeudation. Knight's service gradually became archaic, and by 1300 most people held land in return for a perpetual money rent. Sub-infeudation was terminated about this time, and thereafter people held their land directly from the king. The rights of the English king persist today in the right of the state to compulsorily purchase land.

Under normal law an owner had exclusive control over the use of their resources. This power was highly valued; the king would reward his faithful servants with grants of land, which in practice meant that they acquired the rents paid by the occupiers. The creation of numerous small parcels of property held by individual occupiers, such as farmers and tradesmen, decentralized decision making over the use of resources. It empowered small proprietors, and encouraged them to take advantage of business opportunities that came their way.

Private property could also be held by institutions such as abbeys, churches, hospitals, towns and guilds (Gilchrist, 1969). Secular institutions normally required a charter for this purpose.

Incentives to trade

Trade is a voluntary process in which two agents agree to exchange certain rights on specified terms. As explained earlier, Adam Smith believed that two factors combined to motivate trade: specialization in work and a desire for variety in consumption. He understood specialization as the continuous repetition of a simple task. Modern economists emphasize that education rather than simple repetition is the key to productivity: workers should be versatile rather than focusing on just a single task. This enriches their job and makes them better citizens, and if they lose their job it enables them to switch to other work.

Ricardo (1817) was concerned with international trade rather than local trade, although his analysis applies to both. He emphasized differential access to productive resources as the basis for trade. He enunciated the principle of specialization according to comparative advantage. A country that is relatively well endowed with minerals should specialize in manufacturing and a country relatively well endowed with land should specialize in food production. Even if one country is better endowed with everything, it should still focus on its relative strengths; for if it produced everything then the other country would produce nothing, and that would be a waste of resources. Ohlin (1933), following his mentor Heckscher, later expressed comparative advantage in terms of factor proportions, arguing that capital-intensive industries should be concentrated in countries with a high capital/labour ratio and labour-intensive industries in countries with a low capital/labour ratio. Trade therefore involves the exchange of goods with different factor intensities.

Comparative advantage can also be applied to people. Most people have a natural aptitude for specific kinds of work and are therefore suited for different trades. Artisan production, for example, requires people with craft skills and shopkeeping requires social skills. If one person has outstanding craft skills and excellent social skills, and another has modest social skills and weak craft skills, then the former should become an artisan and the latter a shopkeeper, even though the former would make a better shopkeeper than the latter.

Nineteenth-century utilitarians such as Jevons (1871) and Edgeworth (1881) believed that differences in personal preferences were key to trade. Suppose that in a subsistence economy one person prefers bread to meat and another meat to bread. The meat-eater owns arable land that is only suitable for bread production and the bread-eater owns pasture that is only suitable for meat production. Clearly they should swap meat for bread. A straight swap has the potential to make both parties better off. Edgeworth developed a famous box diagram to make this point; he also developed a contract curve, which shows that, under his assumed conditions, an efficient market equilibrium was not necessarily unique.

Overall, therefore, there are three main motives for trade: gains from specialization, a preference for variety and differences in preferences. Gains from specialization come in four main forms: simple repetition, learning from experience, exploiting personal aptitudes and exploiting privileged access to resources. One factor does not preclude another; they all work together to promote trade.

Money

In economic theory, money is defined not by what it is but by what it does. So far as markets are concerned, money *functions as a medium of exchange*. Money supersedes barter: it separates the sale of one product from the purchase of another, and so avoids the need for a double coincidence of wants.

Money needs to be *widely acceptable* so that whoever a person meets will accept it as payment; *durable* because it may not be spent right away; *portable* so that it is easy to carry; and *difficult to counterfeit* so that the recipient is confident of the quality. Coins made out of precious metal are ideal for this purpose. In a modern economy, banknotes and credit limits are ultimately claims on precious metals deposited in central banks.

Comparison

A market facilitates *comparison*, which addresses two main questions. (1) Are the terms of sale the best available; could the buyer get a lower price or the seller a higher price? (2) Do the characteristics of the product provide the best possible match with the customer's needs?

To address these questions a buyer needs to contact multiple sellers and vice versa; a market provides a suitable forum. Bargaining is simplified because buyers can play off the sellers against each other and sellers can play off the buyers. Buyers are usually in a stronger position, however, because they bring money to the market, while the sellers bring stock that must be removed and stored if unsold. On the other hand, sellers attend the market regularly; they are more experienced than buyers and may be able to collude (by fixing prices, for example).

Co-location of transactions

A market town acts as a one-stop shop for a customer who requires a range of different products. Markets for similar products are co-located in a market square or in one of the neighbouring streets. This promotes competition through comparison shopping. A typical market town is also a service centre, providing facilities for education, healthcare, sport and religious activities.

Trust

How does the buyer know that the quantity and quality of the product is correct or, indeed, that it has not been stolen? How does the seller know that the money offered is not counterfeit? How are contractual disputes between buyer and seller to be resolved?

Trust may be defined as a confident expectation that another party will respect the rules. These rules involve universal ethical norms such as honesty; social norms such as respect for other members of the community; and specific rules governing trade. Such rules have always been a prominent feature of markets. Trust needs to warranted, for otherwise a trusting person can be exploited by others (Casson, 2010). Compliance with the rules may be encouraged by internal peer-group pressure such as through a trade association or merchant guild, or by external regulation such as trading standards enforced by law.

Medieval markets invoked all these mechanisms (Davis, 2012). Religious belief encouraged honesty; the shipwreck of the wealthy wool merchant

Laurence of Ludlow was widely regarded as demonstrating divine retribution on a dishonest trader (Summerson, 2005). Social status was conferred by the respectability of a merchant's trade, which would be protected by the local trade guild. The king supervised the assizes of bread and ale, which verified the quantities and qualities of food and drink, using standard weights and measures and official inspections. 'Pie-powder' courts, meeting on market days, dispensed instant justice, so that merchants travelling through the town on a circuit of markets could have their disputes settled on the spot without having to change their itinerary.

The main weakness of the medieval system lay in the power of some of the guilds (Rosser, 2015). They could act as cartels, maintaining high prices. Merchant guilds could oppress craft guilds by buying artisan products at low prices and reselling them with a substantial mark-up (Swanson, 1989). The burgesses of the town, together with the bailiffs they elected and the officers they appointed, formed a governing elite that also possessed considerable power. Both the guilds and the burgesses were often opposed to immigrant artisans, because they feared the emergence of low-cost local competition in their trades.

These urban elites could not stifle competition *between* towns, however. The more enlightened elites promoted the reputation of their towns, emphasizing competitive prices and fair trading, and stole trade away from other towns where the emphasis was simply on exploiting a local monopoly. For example, England's leading towns such as London, Bristol, York and Norwich had a very high density of churches near their centre, sending a clear signal to visitors of the religiosity and reputation of the merchants of the town.

Intermediation

Markets benefit from having specialists permanently present during opening hours, displaying products, taking orders, organizing delivery and so on. These specialists can monitor price movements and take speculative positions, either purchasing and storing or making forward contracts. They can also identify unsatisfied customer demand and match it to under-utilized producer assets. In general, they can profit from *intermediating* between the customers and producers; the intermediator who is the first to recognize an opportunity can pre-empt it, buying cheap and selling dear.

These intermediators act as information hubs who coordinate the market system (Casson, 2001). There are two main types: the retailer and the wholesaler. Typically the retailer operates a shop and the wholesaler a warehouse. Sometimes retailers integrate back into wholesaling to 'cut out the middleman' and source their supplies directly. Conversely, wholesalers may integrate forward into retailing.

Wholesalers generally operate on a larger scale than retailers. Warehouses afford substantial economies of scale, because the costs of construction and heat loss are both proportional to the surface area of the warehouse or the square of its basic dimension, while its capacity is proportional to the cube. Wholesalers generally manage transport and logistics; their skills include inventory management and scheduling deliveries. Because wholesalers deal with many customers, and usually many suppliers too, they are in a good position to monitor trends in the market. They can therefore take speculative positions by stocking up on products they believe will be in short supply. While retailers have a more direct knowledge of the customer, their information is more localized and does not encompass wider trends in production and supply.

Interventions by well-informed intermediators can increase the efficiency of a local market. Successful intermediators can become extremely wealthy; on the other hand, unsuccessful intermediators can destabilize a market by aggravating problems, especially if they go bankrupt with debts to their suppliers.

Markets and innovation

It is often assumed that innovation is driven by scientific breakthroughs or the imagination and creativity of entrepreneurs; but science and creativity benefit from being informed by market information. Market information may identify a gap in the market – a need for a product that does not yet exist (Godley and Casson, 2015). The entrepreneur must provide the imagination required to design this product and science may be needed to produce it and make it work.

The market provides the indication that demand exists; it may also indicate the likely quantity demanded and the price that potential consumers will be willing to pay. The market also provides a channel through which the product can be distributed and sold. Markets are therefore a stimulus to innovation.

Markets also contain a built-in dynamic. Not only does demand for products tend to grow over time, as news about them spreads and their production costs fall, but new products may also emerge to fill gaps in the existing product range. Products that are radically new may even create new markets altogether. For example, Henry Ford's mass-produced Model T not only added to the range of existing motor cars, but created a whole new market for the family car. Existing markets therefore create new markets by informing and stimulating innovation.

There is creative destruction too (Schumpeter, 1934). Old products become obsolete as new products appear. The motor car replaced the horse and carriage, local radio replaced the local newspaper and so on. Markets therefore have a dynamic that many standard economic models lack. These models assume that the range of products is fixed; but markets are self-renewing, old products disappear, new products appear and radical novelty creates new markets altogether.

Economic theory of markets

Analysis of market behaviour

Markets have played a central role in economic theory from the very beginning of the subject. Economic theory provides a simple classification of market structures. The benchmark is perfect competition, which prevails under idealized conditions of perfect rationality and costless perfect information. The main alternatives are monopoly and oligopoly (Baumol et al, 1982).

Monopoly involves a single seller who charges above the competitive price and appropriates a 'super-normal' profit. The higher price discourages buyers and leads them to purchase less. Customers pay a higher price for the amount they continue to buy and miss out altogether on the additional amount they would have bought at the lower price.

Oligopoly, as its name suggests, involves just a few producers. Oligopoly may involve homogeneous products such as a specific grade of wheat traded on a commodity exchange, or differentiated products such as a brand of luxury chocolate.

Monopoly can be exploited in several ways. The monopolist could insist that customers purchase an all-in bundle for a high all-in price. If the bundle was priced at the maximum price that customers would pay then each customer would continue to consume the same amount as under competition, and would pay about the average price as before. Monopoly profit would approximately double as a result.

Monopolies are often associated with large and powerful companies. Utilities are often described as natural monopolies because they exploit significant economies of scale. Their infrastructure has the capacity to serve a very large number of customers, and so the marginal cost of serving an additional customer is very low. The average costs is much higher because that includes the recurrent fixed costs of the infrastructure averaged over all the customers. Utilities are often nationalized or heavily regulated by the state.

A powerful consumer brand may also possess monopoly power. Consumers regard each branded product as distinctive and superior to any unbranded product. An exclusive brand may act as a signal of the owner's wealth. Successful brands command premium prices. Indeed, if consumers regard price as a signal of quality, a product may sell in greater quantity at a higher price than at a lower price.

Typology of market processes

Economic theory is often criticized as being inherently static. This is because economists typically focus on equilibrium states. In Alfred Marshall's (1890) theory of supply and demand, based on his scissors diagram, a uniform equilibrium price prevails throughout a market; this price balances demand and supply, and determines the output of the product (Loasby, 1978; Casson, 1999).

The assumption of a uniform equilibrium price warrants examination (Birner and Garrouste, 2004; Brousseau and Glachant, 2014). There are two possible reasons why such a price could prevail. The first is that there is costless arbitrage and the second is that the product is auctioned, and that no trade takes place until everyone is satisfied with the outcome (for example, they believe that they have got the best possible price). But in practice arbitrage is costly, and auctions of the kind assumed are almost never held. The assumption of a uniform equilibrium price dramatically simplifies the economic theory of markets, but it is difficult to justify on any other grounds.

In practice, four main forms of market process are observed. None of them guarantees a uniform equilibrium price.

Open auction. Supply is fixed by the time the auction begins. Different buyers value individual items differently, and the highest bidder wins. Auctions operate at both the wholesale level (including livestock and fish) and the retail level (including antiques and second-hand cars). Bids may be open calls during the auction or closed bids submitted beforehand, and sellers may set reserve prices. Most auctions are ascending price but a few are descending price (McAfee and McMillan, 1987).

Competitive procurement. Customized products such as buildings and public works are often procured through competitive bidding. The process is a mirror image of a sealed-bid auction: other things being equal, the winner quotes the lowest price rather than the highest one. Bidders may be invited to tender or there may be open competition; the process is usually governed by strict rules to mitigate corruption.

Arbitrage. The object of arbitrage is to buy cheap and sell dear, and to pocket the difference as a quick profit (Kirzner, 1973). Speculation is similar, except that the buyer waits for the product to appreciate in value before reselling. Arbitragers and speculators normally believe they have superior knowledge. They are confident that the product is underpriced and that there is another buyer who is unaware the product is for sale, and would be willing to pay more than the others.

Arbitrage is costly. The costs vary with the type of product involved. Buying and selling standardized financial products such as government debt is relatively cheap; arbitrage is therefore common and the spread between buying and selling prices is correspondingly small. The costs are higher in wholesale commodity markets. These markets trade physical products rather than legal claims to income. The quality of the product needs to be checked by inspection, and the product itself may need to be transported and/or stored before it is resold.

Shopping is the paradigm of the market. Window shopping is conducted by customers who compare the product varieties available and the prices at which they are sold. Shopping is often modelled as a process of consumer search, in which customers buy as soon as the quoted price falls below the maximum price that they are willing to pay. Customers searching for specific types of product may head for specific streets where speciality shops agglomerate. Online markets expedite search, but they also introduce biases. Advertisers can pay to have their products listed first. Price comparison websites simplify search, but because they charge for listing products, average prices may be higher than elsewhere.

Retailing and local market competition

Small shops are often promoted as examples of atomistic competition. There are hundreds of thousands of them in many countries, but they do not all compete against each other. Many small shops acquire a loyal clientele. People are served by the same person, or group of people, every time they visit. The shop, like the pub or coffee bar, becomes a social hub. Moreover, shops in a small town can differentiate themselves. They can segment the market, with one coffee bar, for example, catering for young people and another for families and older people. There is, therefore, a degree of local monopoly in the retail sector.

There are also economies of scale. The rent, rates and utility charges paid by shopkeepers are largely independent of the number of customers who visit their shops. For most of the week the shop is not full, and so there is excess capacity. The marginal cost of serving an additional customer is relatively low. If the shopkeeper's mark-up on merchandise reflected only marginal costs then they would not survive. The retail price must equal average costs for the shop to break even. This explains why retail mark-ups are usually high.

Where two shops compete directly, competition between the owners could bid down price to marginal cost, causing both shops to close. However, if one owner has deeper pockets than others (access to greater financial reserves, for example) then they may survive while other does not.

The main alternative to competition is cooperation. For example, the shopkeepers may agree on a price-matching strategy. In practice this means that competition becomes focused on non-price factors such as the location of the shop within the town or the quality of customer service.

In an ordinary retail market price variation is mainly constrained by price-conscious consumers, seeking to save money on essential items, who have little loyalty to specific suppliers and have time to shop around. Such shoppers are targeted, for example, by budget price retailers, who advertise lower prices than their competitors. These retailers specialize in stocking large quantities of a limited range of products. Mid-range retailers remain viable, however, because they are patronized by wealthier people who prefer to choose from a wider range and can afford to pay higher prices (Davis, 2010; Charalambos, 2015).

Neighbouring market towns also compete with each other. Rivalry between towns is potentially more serious than within towns. Towns compete through investment in cultural facilities and transport infrastructure. Their reputation for cultural ambience, product quality, friendly service and availability of credit is an important asset. Large towns provide a wide range of services that allow the town to function as a 'one-stop shop'; the larger volume of transactions may also facilitate lower prices. However, large towns are spread more thinly over space, and so on average are more costly to visit than smaller ones.

A social network approach to retail markets

A common weakness of the economic models reviewed here is that they fail to address the social embeddedness of markets; this section presents one way in which this problem can be overcome (Cantor et al, 1992; Casson and della Giusta, 2007; Preda, 2009).

Consider a large town that is a regional market centre. Shops in the town supply customers who live in its suburbs and neighbouring villages. Some customers are more aware of their options than others. Consider a specific product sold by three shops identified as A, B and C. Some customers are aware of just one shop, some are aware of two and some of all three. A few may be aware of none at all (see Figure 2.1). The customers may be classified in terms of their information networks into the eight categories

Figure 2.1: Social network linking different groups of customers to shops

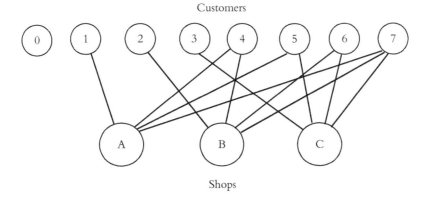

Table 2.1: List of eight groups of consumers classified by the shops with which they are in contact, showing the shops at which they will make a purchase

Consumer category identifier	Set of identified shops	Lowest attainable price available at:		
		Shop A (lowest price)	Shop B (mid-price)	Shop C (highest price)
0	None			
1	A	Yes		
2	B		Yes	
3	C			Yes
4	A, B	Yes		
5	A, C	Yes		
6	B, C		Yes	
7	A, B, C	Yes		
Total		4	2	1

numbered 0 to 7 shown in the figure. They are also listed in the left-hand column of Table 2.1. Customers in each category are aware of a specific set of shops, as indicated by the lines in the figure and summarized in the second column of the table.

Suppose to begin with that the shopkeepers are relatively passive; they simply post their prices in the shop, or provide quotations on request. Since they all sell the same product, customer decisions are based mainly on price. Those who know only one shop have to buy there. Those who know two or three shops compare their prices before they buy.

Figure 2.1 shows that each shop is in touch with four of the eight categories of buyer. If a shop quotes the lowest price then, under pure price comparison, they will win the custom of all their four groups. The shop with the second-lowest price will capture two of the three remaining groups and only the final group will patronize the high-price shop, because that is the only shop that they know about. Provided that the dispersion of prices is not too great, the low-price shop will make the most profit and the high-price shop the least.

This simple model is useful because it predicts the volume of sales of each shop according to the price it charges and the sizes of the groups for which it caters. With additional information on costs it is possible to calculate profits. Having calculated profits it is possible to predict whether there is an opportunity for further entry (the marginal firm makes a profit, for example) or whether one of the shops is likely to close (the marginal firm makes a loss).

Suppose now that the shopkeepers are more proactive. Their obvious strategy is to advertise. They could just put up posters around the town, but it may be more profitable to target their advertising (Gelper et al, 2020). With price-conscious customers, there is little point in the high-price shop advertising to people already in contact with the other shops. So long as these customers compare before they buy, they will continue to buy elsewhere. The only target for the high-price shop has to be those who are unaware of any shop at all. This may be a limited market and the potential customers extremely difficult to reach. By contrast, the low-price shop has the potential to capture the entire market; but they have about half the market already. They also need to target, therefore, but on a much larger scale. They could make a big impact, for example, by advertising prices on posters placed near to the other shops, where most of their target people will go.

The shopkeepers can also make use of mediators or multipliers. Commercial mediation is supplied by TV and radio, magazines and social media. Non-profit intermediation is provided by membership organizations; cookery classes can disseminate information about grocery shops, for example. Satisfied customers can also be encouraged to promote a shop to their friends.

In practice, many products are sold on design and quality, as well as price. This qualifies the analysis but does not change its essentials; customers will still be concerned about overall value for money. The high-price shop can now trade on personal service, since there will be few customers in the shop at any given time. It may also stock an exclusive range of products that differs from the standard ranges of the lower-price shops. The low-price shop will tend to do the opposite, focusing on 'everyday value for all the family'. Unlike the high-price shop, it will cater for bulk-purchasing, self-service and easy parking.

Locations of towns

Roles of towns: historical evidence

The location of market towns has been extensively studied by urban economists and historical geographers. Six main factors influence the location of these towns (Beresford, 1967; Aston and Bond, 1976).

Defence and administration. Many Anglo-Saxon towns were established as burghs where troops could be garrisoned. They often occupied high ground overlooking bends in rivers, such as Bristol, Wallingford and Malmesbury. Rivers often defined borders between ancient tribal territories. Invading troops were vulnerable when crossing a bridge or fording a river, and so it was convenient to keep crossing points under surveillance. Many defended places also served as administrative centres for tax collection and law enforcement.

Culture and leisure. Early religious settlements, from hermits' caves to grand abbeys, were often built in isolated positions where there was a good supply of fresh water. Many became centres of pilgrimage, such as Durham, Bury St Edmunds and St Davids. Adjacent shrines could form a circuit or 'pilgrimage trail'. As leisure society became more secular, mountain scenery, spas, coastlines and beaches became the preferred attractions, with associated towns including Bath, Brighton and Windermere.

Transport hubs. In the 14th century there was significant investment in infrastructure. Skills developed in the construction of abbeys and churches were redeployed to bridge-building and road improvement. This in turn created more bridging points where goods could be trans-shipped from river to road. Key locations were the first bridge upstream and the 'head of navigation' beyond which ships could not pass, including Gloucester (first bridging point on the River Severn) and Nottingham (head of navigation on the River Trent). Some bridging points, such as London, became heads of navigation by making their bridges impassable to sea-going craft. Trans-shipment encouraged the processing of bulky imports (such as timber) into smaller items (wooden utensils) that were distributed by road. Trans-shipment points also developed into points of sale: the producer sold to the wholesaler, who sold to the retailer, who sold to the public.

Agricultural specialization. As transport improved, agricultural regions were able to specialize more intensively in those products where their altitude, climate or soil gave them a comparative advantage. Upland areas were increasingly devoted to sheep farming, fertile plains to growing crops and riverside pasture to fattening cattle. Local markets developed on the borders of these areas, where the products of different types of farming could be exchanged. Some developed into large towns that were visited regularly by wholesalers from the cities, examples being Shrewsbury, Lancaster and York.

Industrial centres. These emerged in the textile industry in about 1300, when clusters of local villages began to specialize in different stages of textile production (carding, spinning, weaving, bleaching, dyeing). Textile production was centred initially in Suffolk, then in Wiltshire and finally in Lancashire and Yorkshire. In the early years of the Industrial Revolution, about 1760, small-scale factories harnessed water power, and a rapid switch to steam power in about 1800 saw large factory complexes developing close to major coalfields. The development of inter-urban steam railways and international steam shipping in about 1830 encouraged further growth of industries, stimulated by the emergence of mass markets. Manchester, Birmingham and Sheffield, for example, became major manufacturing centres, trading internationally through their neighbouring ports of Liverpool, Gloucester and Hull respectively.

Knowledge centres. These include prominent university towns and places that service agglomerations (or ecosystems) of high technology and/or creative businesses. They may be fashionable districts or suburbs within large sprawling towns or rural districts that support a high quality of life. These centres cater specifically for the needs of an educated elite and not for the mixed population typically found in more traditional towns (Cooke et al,

2007). Major agglomerations of high technology start-ups in England today include Cambridge, London, the Thames Valley and Manchester.

The urban marketplace: topography

Some large medieval towns had Roman origins. The Roman forum occupied a central position in a town and acted as a periodic marketplace. It typically comprised a basilica facing onto a square surrounded by colonnades. Roman towns in England functioned as administrative centres and some as legionary fortresses. Some names (including Noviomagus and Venta Belgarum, which became Chichester and Winchester) suggest important markets, which probably sold local agricultural produce and imported luxury products. However, when these towns revived, they were not usually reconstructed directly on the original Roman plan, but were refounded as river ports, such as Chester, Exeter and Worcester (Macmullen, 1970; de Ligt, 1993; Frayn, 1993; Ellis, 2018).

When the Normans took control in 1066, they built castles in many towns and developed large spacious urban markets, which were usually square or rectangular. The sites of the smaller Anglo-Saxon markets were sometimes repurposed, for handling cattle, sheep and horses, for example (Haslam, 1964; Aston and Bond, 1976). The Norman rebuildings were very disruptive, but as the economy grew in the 13th century these spacious markets became major assets (Norwich is an example).

Marketplaces were often marked by a tall cross with steps on which people could sit and from where announcements could be made. Large urban markets were usually equipped with buildings variously used for administration, law courts, storage of goods and hospitality. The market square was often overlooked by a church; and from the 15th century onwards the chimes of the church clock would often signal the opening and closing of the market (Martin, 1968; Lloyd, 1984; Slater, 1988; Courtney, 1998; Sheeran, 1998; Kirkpatrick, 2005).

Markets were often specialized. Some relied on rows of temporary stalls, with each row handling a particular speciality. Specialization extended into neighbouring streets, which were often known by the occupation of their residents. Common names that survive include Buttermarket, Neetmarket (for cattle), Lacemarket, Leathermarket, Butchers' Shambles, Horsefair, Cloth Hall and Sheep Street. Cattle markets and shambles were often located on high ground, from which waste could be conveniently drained away. To minimize pollution, smiths (ironworkers) and leatherworkers were often banished from the town centre. In pilgrimage centres the market for visitors and pilgrims was sometimes located near to the attractions and away from the market for local provisions (as in Bury St Edmunds).

Arrangements of a similar kind have persisted into the 21st century. The old medieval town remains the core of many big cities. Even if the buildings have changed, the streets and the plots that face onto them have not. Sometimes adjacent plots have been merged or subdivided, but otherwise the medieval street plan remains.

Policy intervention: regulation of the market

Objectives

The objectives of policy intervention in a market include (1) providing security for transactors by monitoring product quality, enforcing the payment of debts and so on; (2) promoting competition between suppliers and controlling the abuse of monopoly power; and (3) encouraging innovation by reducing the barriers to entry faced by new producers offering novel products.

Medieval market regulation is generally regarded as being good at (1) and weak at (2) and (3). It was not until the 17th century that there were systematic state-led initiatives to promote innovation (Yamamoto, 2018; Neal, 2014) and not until the end of the 20th century that attempts were made to promote new firm entry and break up monopolies; England did not formally regulate monopoly until 1948.

The focus here is on policy intervention implemented through rules and regulations. An effective system of rules needs to be (1) *easily understood*, being transparent, quick to learn and easy to follow; (2) *inclusive*, applying to everyone; (3) *respected*, being derived from widely accepted principles; (4) *incentive-compatible*, discouraging self-interested 'gaming' strategies, for example; (5) *easy to enforce*, with it being easy to detect offenders; and (6) *just*, with punishments sufficient to deter repetition of offences, but not unduly punitive.

Origins of regulation

The earliest recorded market regulations in England were designed to prevent suppliers of basic necessities such as food and drink setting their prices unnecessarily high (Young, 1961; Casson, 2012; Davis, 2012). A 'forestaller' intercepted sellers bringing goods to market and offered to buy their stock, thereby saving them the time and money of attending the market themselves. The higher the proportion of sellers that the forestaller could intercept on a given day, the greater their monopoly power. A 'regrator' was an arbitrager; they bought and resold at a profit. Their operations were short term and local; they did not add significant value through storage (such as purchasing hay in autumn for use in winter), nor did they transport their produce long distances to alleviate shortages elsewhere. An 'engrosser' bought up as much produce as they could in order to resell at a monopoly price. Some of the product bought by an engrosser might well remain unsold and go to waste, because more revenue could be appropriated by selling a small amount at high price rather than a large amount at a low price.

All three practices involved some form of arbitrage. Regulation was directed at specific forms of arbitrage that were believed to be harmful. They were not directed against merchants who traded over long distances or bought supplies in advance for wealthy customers, but at opportunistic local hawkers and petty traders.

Regulation of wholesale trade: role of civic customs

Wholesale trade was particularly important in large towns, and especially those that had a seaport. Such towns were typically run by a civic elite composed of burgesses, namely freeholders who held burgage plots near the centre of the town, and most of whom belonged to a local merchant or artisan guild. In royal boroughs the burgesses elected a mayor and bailiffs who managed the town's affairs and collected local taxes and tolls by agreement with the king. Boroughs compiled books of custom, while guilds made regulations governing their members' behaviour, and these provide a wealth of information on the conduct of local wholesale trade. Excerpts from some of the records are presented here.

Rights of free-holders. Freeholders, such as retail fishmongers, were able to purchase wholesale from a fishing vessel returning to port, provided that they were present at the quayside.

> [Grimsby, 1259] All freeholders of this county shall buy herring, fish and such like victual without hindrance, as long as they themselves or their servants are present at the unloading of the boat carrying the victuals. (Bateson, 1906: 169)

Obligations of wholesale buyers. A buyer at the quayside was obliged to give 'lot' to other citizens provided they applied promptly. A lot appears to have been an amount sufficient for a person to carry on their trade until the next ship arrived. A regulation from Cork, Ireland, dating from 1139 suggests that transactions at the quayside were often effected over dinner and that the outcome was, to some extent, public knowledge among citizens of the town (Bateson, 1906: 173). Agreements could be made in advance to give lot, but if the partner was not a freeman then they had to pay all the customs charges due (Bateson, 1906: 171). A freeman could demand lot from another. The regulation quoted here suggests that merchants operated in close association with one another and were bound to provide for their fellow merchants in the same trade.

[London, 1272] If anyone from the liberty of the city buys cordwain [leather] from any merchants wholesale, and a cordwainer of the liberty by chance appears, he may have, in his own name, or in the name of others, his share of the purchase without any hindrance, provided that he finds sufficient security for payment to the seller. (Bateson, 1906: 172)

Subsistence rights. In certain circumstances allowances might be required purely for subsistence consumption. These were paid to 'neighbours', who appear to have been fellow members of a guild. There was no element of profit on these allowances (Bateson, 1906: 172).

Rights of precedence for office-holders. The principle of first come first served or joining a queue was slow to become established. From early times the nobility demanded precedence, and later so did important civic office-holders such as the mayor (Bateson, 1906: 166, 171).

Supervision of merchants from other countries residing in a town. Foreign merchants were welcome to reside in a town because of their valuable trading links with other countries. They were normally supervised by local merchants; each foreign merchant would have a host, who would ensure that they did not steal trade secrets – but would do their best to steal the foreigner's secrets instead (Bateson, 1906: 181).

Quality control

Quality assurance was recognized as a key issue from an early date. A group of reputable peers were convened to resolve a dispute. This avoided recourse to courts, which could prove expensive and damaging to the reputation of the trade.

[Berwick-on-Tweed. 1249]. If it happens that a buyer of anything discovers any of his purchases to be good above and worse below, the seller of the thing ought to amend it by the view and decision of honest men appointed for the purpose. (Bateson, 1906: 182)

A similar provision is reported in Exeter in 1282 regarding the sale of beasts. Similar arrangements applied in Grimsby for fish (Bateson, 1906: 182).

Conclusions

This survey of market development in England has shown that the modern market system dates back to about 1200 and possibly earlier. Schumpeter (1939) dated capitalism from the growth of Italian banking in the 14th century, and Braudel (1981, 1982, 1984) followed a similar approach.

Modern capitalism did not develop from the emergence of equity markets of the 17th century or the factory system of the 18th century, but from the 'commercial revolution' of the 13th century.

Despite the crucial role of markets as a building block of the capitalist system, the economic analysis of markets has remained relatively superficial. The social embeddedness of markets has not always been fully appreciated. Access to markets plays an important role in stimulating innovation. In the short run innovators are often rewarded by monopoly profits, based on their possession of intellectual property rights such as patents and trademarks, but their power tends to wane as new innovations render older innovations obsolete. The main exception concerns infrastructure, where private ownership of utilities can result in entrenched monopoly power. There is a strong case, therefore, for public ownership of certain types of infrastructure. Public ownership still requires markets, however, in order to regulate access to the infrastructure and ensure that it is utilized efficiently.

This survey has revealed the superficiality of the concept of free markets. This concept owes more to political philosophy than to real world economics (Walgorski, 1990). As noted at the outset, and highlighted here, markets have always been regulated. The proliferation of markets in the early 14th century led to a standardization of regulations. When financial markets developed in the 17th century, they quickly became regulated, because of the dangers of trading in paper and the promises revealed by the South Sea Bubble and speculations in numerous fraudulent schemes. Regulation has been a feature of successful markets for over 800 years.

References

Aston, M. and Bond, J. (1976) *The Landscape of Towns*, London: J.M. Dent.

Barjamovic, G., Cheney, T., Cosar, K. and Hortacsu, A. (2019) 'Trade, merchants, and the lost cities of the Bronze Age', *Quarterly Journal of Economics*, 134(3): 1455–503.

Bateson, M. (ed) (1906) *Borough Customs: Volume 2*, London: Selden Society.

Baumol, W. J., Panzar, J. and Willig, R.D. (1982) *Contestable Markets and the Theory of Industry Structure*, New York: Harcourt Brace Jovanovich.

Beresford, M. (1967) *New Towns of the Middle Ages: Town Plantation in England, Wales and Gascony*, London: Lutterworth Press.

Birner, J. and Garrouste, P. (eds) (2004) *Markets, Information and Communication: Austrian Perspectives on the Internet Economy*, London: Routledge.

Braudel, F. (1981) *Civilization and Capitalism Fifteenth to Eighteenth Century: Volume 1 The Structures of Everyday Life*, London: Collins.

Braudel, F. (1982) *Civilization and Capitalism Fifteenth to Eighteenth Century: Volume 2 The Wheels of Commerce*, London: Collins.

Braudel, F. (1984) *Civilization and Capitalism Fifteenth to Eighteenth Century: Volume 3 The Perspective of the World*, London: Collins.

Brousseau, E. and Glachant, J.-M. (2014) 'Conclusion: tatonnement in the manufacturing of markets', in E. Brousseau and J.-M. Glachant (eds) *The Manufacturing of Markets: Legal, Political and Economic Dynamics*, Cambridge: Cambridge University Press, pp 441–69.

Cantor, R., Henry, S. and Rayner, S. (1992) *Making Markets: An Interdisciplinary Perspective on Economic Exchange*, Westport, CT: Greenwood Press.

Casson, C. (2012) 'Reputation and responsibility in medieval English towns: civic concerns with the regulation of trade', *Urban History*, 39(3): 387–408.

Casson, M.C. (1999) 'Marshall on marketing', in R.E. Backhouse and J. Creedy (eds) *From Classical Economics to the Theory of the Firm: Essays in Honour of D.P. O'Brien*, Cheltenham: Edward Elgar, pp 194–222.

Casson, M. (2001) *The Entrepreneur: An Economic Theory* (2nd edn), Cheltenham: Edward Elgar.

Casson, M. (2010) *Entrepreneurship: Theory, Networks, History*, Cheltenham: Edward Elgar.

Casson, M. (ed) (2011) *Markets and Market Institutions: Their Origin and Evolution*, Cheltenham: Edward Elgar.

Casson, M. and della Giusta, M. (2007) 'Entrepreneurship and social capital: analysing the impact of social networks on entrepreneurial activity from a rational action perspective', *International Small Business Journal*, 25(3): 220–44.

Casson, M. and Lee, J.S. (2011) 'The origin and development of markets: a business history perspective', *Business History Review*, 85(1): 9–37.

Charalambos, C. (2015) 'The countervailing power hypothesis in the dominant firm – competitive model', *Economics Letters*, 126: 110–13.

Cooke, P., de Laurentis, C., Todtling, F. and Trippl, M. (2007) *Regional Knowledge Economies*, Cheltenham: Edward Elgar.

Courtney, P. (1998) *The Archaeology of Leicester's Market-Place*, Leicester: Leicester City Museums.

Cunliffe, B. (2008) *Europe between the Oceans, 9000BC–AD1000*, New Haven, CT: Yale University Press.

Davis, J. (2012) *Medieval Market Morality*, Cambridge: Cambridge University Press.

Davis, P. (2010) Spatial competition in retail markets: movie theaters, *RAND Journal of Economics*, 37(4): 964–82.

De Ligt, L. (1993) *Fairs in Markets in the Roman Empire*, Leiden: Brill.

Edgeworth, F.Y. (1881) *Mathematical Psychics*, London: C. Kegan Paul.

Ellis, S. (2018) *The Roman Retail Revolution*, Oxford: Oxford University Press.

Frayn. J. (1993) *Markets and Fairs in Roman Italy: Heir Importance from the Second Century BC to the Third Century*, Oxford: Oxford University Press.

Gelper, S., van der Lam, R. and van Bruggen, G. (2020) 'Competition for attention in online social networks: implications for seeding strategies', *Management Science*, 67(2): 1026–47.

Gilchrist, J.T. (1969) *The Church and Economic Activity in the Middle Ages*, London: Macmillan.

Godley, A.C. and Casson, M. (2015) ' "Doctor, doctor…" Entrepreneurial diagnosis and market-making', *Journal of Institutional Economics*, 11(3): 601–21.

Haslam, J. (ed) (1964) *Anglo-Saxon Towns in Southern England*, Chichester: Phillimore.

Howell, M.C. (2010) *Commerce before Capitalism in Europe, 1300–1600*, Cambridge: Cambridge University Press.

Hudson, J. (ed) (2012) *The Oxford History of the Laws of England: Volume 2, 871–1216*, Oxford: Oxford University Press.

Jevons, W.S. (1871) *Theory of Political Economy*, London: Macmillan.

Kirkpatrick, G. (2005) *Nine Centuries of Tavistock Markets*, Tavistock: Tavistock Market Charter Group.

Kirzner, I.M. (1973) *Competition as a Dynamic Process*, Chicago: University of Chicago Press.

Lloyd, D.W. (1984) *The Making of English Towns: A Vista of 2000 Years*, London: Victor Gollancz.

Loasby, B.J. (1978) 'Whatever happened to Marshall's Theory of Value?', *Scottish Journal of Political Economy*, 25(1): 1–12.

MacMullen, R. (1970) 'Market-days in the Roman Empire', *Phoenix*, 24(4): 333–41.

Marshall, A. (1890) *Principles of Economics*, London: Macmillan.

Martin, G.H. (1968) 'The town as palimpsest', in H.J. Dyos (ed) *The Study of Urban History*, London: Edward Arnold, pp 155–70.

McAfee, R.P. and McMillan, J. (1987) 'Auctions and bidding', *Journal of Economic Literature*, 25(2): 699–738.

Muldrew, C. (1998) *The Economy of Obligation: The Culture of Credit and Social Relations in Early Modern Capitalism*, Basingstoke: Palgrave Macmillan.

Neal, L. (2014) 'The microstructure of the first emerging markets in Europe in the eighteenth century', in E. Brousseau and J.-M. Glachant (eds) *The Manufacturing of Markets: Legal, Political and Economic Dynamics*, Cambridge: Cambridge University Press, pp 295–314.

Ohlin, B. (1933) *Interregional and International Trade*, Cambridge, MA: Harvard University Press.

Preda, A. (2009) *Information, Knowledge and Economic Life: An Introduction to the Sociology of Markets*, Oxford: Oxford University Press.

Priestly, U. (1987) *The Great Market: A Survey of Nine Hundred Years of Norwich Provision Market*, Norwich: Centre of East Anglian Studies, University of East Anglia.

Ricardo, D. (1817) *On the Principles of Political Economy and Taxation*, London: John Murray.

Rosser, G. (2015) *The Art of Solidarity in the Middle Ages: Guilds in England, 1250–1550*, Oxford: Oxford University Press.

Schumpeter, J.A. (1934) *The Theory of Economic Development* (trans R. Opie), Cambridge, MA: Harvard University Press.

Sheeran, G. (1998) *Medieval Yorkshire Towns: People, Buildings and Spaces*, Edinburgh: Edinburgh University Press.

Slater, T. (1988) 'English medieval town planning', in D. Deneke and G. Shaw (eds) *Urban Historical Geography: Recent Progress in Britain and Germany*, Cambridge: Cambridge University Press, pp 93–108.

Smith, A. (1976 [1776]) *The Nature and Causes of the Wealth of Nations*, Oxford: Oxford University Press.

Summerson, H. (2005) '"Most renowned of merchants": the life and occupations of Laurence of Ludlow (d.1294)', *Midland History*, 30(1): 20–36.

Swanson, H. (1989) *Medieval Artisans*, Oxford: Blackwell.

Walgorski, C.P. (1990) *The Political Theory of Conservative Economists*, Lawrence: University of Kansas Press.

Yamamoto, K. (2018) *Taming Capitalism Before Its Triumph: Public Service, Distrust, and 'Projecting' in Early Modern England*, Oxford: Oxford University Press.

Young, C.R. (1961) *The English Borough and Royal Administration, 1130–1307*, Durham, NC: Duke University Press.

3

Regulating Capitalism

Philipp Robinson Rössner

The scholastic heritage and beyond

Since the last millennium modern capitalism in the West has evolved around two seemingly diametrically opposed notions – one being the assumption of the market as a manifestation of providential or God-given natural order, the other being about order as a result of deliberate, possibly even planned, human action and sometimes proactive interventions of the state. The earlier notion found its way into neoliberalism and other models of free-marketeerism from the Physiocrats (Kaplan and Reinert, 2019) to Friedman. The other has informed coordinated capitalism from post-1600 cameralism to post-1945 ordoliberalism. This tension has shaped evolutions of political economy of markets and regulation in the West.

In this chapter the tension is resolved by demonstrating that it was only fairly recently (post-1900) that political economy has come to misunderstand what initially was a result of a symbiotic and logical relationship – order and freedom – as opposites. Certainly the Second World War (1939–45) and post-war ideological manifestos such as Hayek's *Road to Serfdom* or Friedman's *Capitalism and Freedom* have wrought considerable damage in the collective economic mind by positing that human economy was, above all, about choice; and that human agency could only be guaranteed by a lean state (Friedman, and his other popular works co-authored with his wife); that capitalism was above all a question of freedom (not true) and that government needs, in the political and economic process, to be principally understood as a potential enemy, not friend, of the people (or individual).[1] Human choices should unfold freely according to individual rational preferences in the marketplace.[2] The metaphor of market has influenced neoliberal historians to the present day, and it is not uncommon to portray the rise of a European 'culture of growth' (Mokyr, 2017) as a trajectory based on 'markets for ideas', just to name a fairly recent influential contribution. But as was understood by the medieval schoolmen, reformers such as Luther or the cameralists and mercantilists (Schumpeter, 1954; Elmslie, 2015; Rössner, 2015; Rössner, 2020), we cannot conceive freedom in the market without the notion of order: only unregulated or weakly regulated markets (with an absence of order) allow rent-seekers, monopolists, cartels, profiteers and other wolves to devour the unbeknown sheep in the marketplace. Accordingly post-war economic conceptions of ordoliberalism (mainly Röpke, Rüstow and Eucken, see Kolev, 2017) incorporated strong models of state-enforced law and order as foundations for economic and individual freedom. In the post-war continental European models of coordinated capitalism practised in Germany and France, equilibrium and equitable market outcomes required dense regulation, monitoring and enforcement of such regulation. Not all participants in the market can be assumed to be altruistic or perfectly willing to comply with the commands of equitability in the market. There is thus a negative sense of perfect competition in which invariably the big and powerful players in the market win the game: the result is arbitrage, speculative profits, exploitation, rent seeking, price fixing, profiteering and a number of other offences modelled very precisely by Luther in his 1524 bestseller *On Commerce and Usury* (Rössner, 2015).

It is not the aim here to be either presentist or eclectic. There were many traditions in economic thinking, and each time and age developed their own systems and traditions. Mainstream systems included (all variants of) liberalism, of mercantilism, of cameralism (Seppel and Tribe, 2017; Nokkala and Miller, 2019), of scholasticism (for example Langholm, 1992; Langholm, 1998) or *Hausväter*/management of large estates literature (Tribe 1978). Sometimes there were even regional variations and modifications. It is, accordingly, difficult to determine – and perhaps not important in the grand scheme of things – whether there were certain core sets of ideas or codes commonly shared across actors in time and space that may or may not have constituted bodies of theory we may recognize and label accordingly as *Alteuropäische Ökonomik* (Burkhardt and Priddat, 2000) or an 'Other Canon' (Reinert, 2019) that became gradually displaced by post-Smithian Anglo-Saxon liberalism. But one can, in order to distil the basic idea, focus on certain representative or key thinkers known to have influenced their respective traditions in a broader sense by means of wider reception – authors including, for scholasticism and the post-scholastic traditions Thomas Aquinas and Martin Luther, or Johann Heinrich Justi for cameralism. Put simply, modern capitalism has for the last millennium built on key instruments and ideas developed long before modern capitalism came to exist, and market regulation represents a core pillar of laissez-faire capitalism and economic development in the West.

Key tools of modern capitalism emerged in Italy during the so-called Commercial Revolution (Lopez, 1976; Spufford, 2002). These include giro and deposit banking, interest, double-bookkeeping, marine and other commercial insurance, and last but not least the bill of exchange and cashless payment system (Denzel, 2010). The latter arose in close cooperation, even symbiotic relationship with the Church, especially the Papal See: the invention of Purgatory and indulgences (as a means of buying oneself out of it) was the key religious innovation that made the pursuit of business less mentally painful for merchants – who always stood with one foot in hell even during their lifetime, because of usury, for greed, for avarice, for profit, for chrematistics. It also facilitated the rise of cashless payments as manifested by the *instrumentum ex causa cambii* and later bill of exchange, which since the later Middle Ages had grown to European-wide dimensions, regularly used as a means of financing long-distance trade and settling debts at the large international fairs of Champagne and Flanders (LeGoff, 1990; Denzel, 2010). The Italian cities also developed manufacturing and production, and new research has suggested the origins of a new political economy of the entrepreneurial state – outlines of a system of manufacturing going back to Botero and his book on *Ragion di Stato* (1588/9), influencing later political economy such as cameralism and mercantilism in the flourishing capitalistic urban commonwealth of Medici Florence (Fredona and Reinert, 2020). Modern capitalism as we know it is thus old and partly anachronistic; building on rules and resting on institutions developed long before during the Middle Ages and Renaissance.

The scholastic heritage in the political economy of markets shines through every single letter and page of modern regulation and political economy in the capitalist nations of the West. Scholastic theory assumed markets to be competitive and free. It was not uncommon for schoolmen in the 13th or 14th centuries to argue that, in the words of a leading scholar:

> Properly conducted, economic exchange is not only approved of by natural law; it is praiseworthy because exchange at a just price is profitable to both parties, whether residing in different regions or in the same region. The just price will naturally be higher where the good in question is scarce than where it is plentiful. Different goods abound in different regions. Long distances and dangers on the roads make barter difficult. Money was invented to meet this problem. Merchants carry goods from places of plenty to places of scarcity, buying and selling at prices favourable to the people of each region and yet making a profit on price differences. Similarly, in any given locality, where the relative just price is an expression of value equivalence between any two goods, exchange at just prices will be profitable to both parties

in terms of personal utilities, because each will place a lower value on that of which he has more and desires to sell, than on that of which he has less and desires to buy. (Langholm, 2003: 114f)

Kings and municipal authorities – who in the Middle Ages often represented common functions and powers of state – neither desired nor had the means at their disposal of controlling market outcomes such as price formation. Only in times of crisis and scarcity was temporal authority expected to regulate prices and quantities for foodstuffs that were considered vital, mostly grain but usually also meat. What government and temporal authority did control and watch was good market behaviour and people sticking to the rules when doing market transactions, usually within an urban environment (Kaye, 2004: 25; Vries, 2019). In the countryside, where markets were more informal, involved less written documentation and where market enforcement was often devolved to the respective village community, laissez-faire may have been even more prevalent by default rather than intent; at least the state had a much weaker grip in the villages. Since village economy has only left traces of writing indirectly through manorial records, or accounts where the state acted as tax collector, we know very little about rural markets and exchanges. Monetization and marketization can be glimpsed indirectly, mainly through numismatic evidence (on coin finds) or written complaints on territorial diets, such as those made habitually by the Saxon towns in the late 15th and early 16th centuries regarding rural brewers infringing with what were principally considered an urban monopoly (Goerlitz, 1928). The frequency and recurrence of such complaints provide a sound indicator of the degree and permanence of capitalism and competitive laissez-faire that had taken hold in the Saxon lands at that time.

For urban markets, government and temporal authority tended to regulate the times and spatiality of market access. Usually natives were allowed into the market a few hours earlier than foreigners, regraters, resellers, hucksters and other brokers. According to Sombart (1921–7), an increasing frequency of pedlars and other middlemen (brokers) indicates that capitalism was gaining momentum from the later Middle Ages, and between the 15th and 19th centuries urban authorities habitually picked on such brokers as a very specific focus of market regulation. Temporal authority also regulated the spatial design of markets, the height and number of market stalls, the different corners and places in town where different markets could take place. Fish, flesh and fowl markets were usually to be kept separate from vegetable markets, for example. Temporal authorities regulated and supervised the weights and measures to be used at markets, including the currencies that were permitted. Regulation generally followed the aim of keeping the *bonum commune* (common weal) intact.

Many medieval market ordinances specifically encouraged competition by waiving certain restrictions, especially the numbers of butchers and other vital suppliers on the market, where competition among suppliers – by means of keeping the market price down – was seen as foundational for a healthy urban *bonum commune* (Isenmann, 2014; Patel and Moore, 2020).

Market regulation and market design thus framed need to be seen as part of a potentially much bigger portfolio of states governing the economy (see Rössner, 2022 for more detail). The portfolio as well as possibility and efficiency of enforcement changed considerably between the Renaissance and the Industrial Revolution. Early modern mercantilist-cameralist fiscal military states, especially France and England, but also Saxony and Prussia in the Holy Roman Empire, and Scandinavian composite multi-ethnic monarchies such as Denmark–Norway or Sweden have often been described as interventionist,[3] based on an unfortunate simultaneous misunderstanding by historians of both the concept of absolutism (purely discursive in the early modern period, with low chances of enforcement) as well as mercantilism/cameralism (see Rössner, 2020, 2022). But the basic parameters of political economy governing the economy had been set since the Middle Ages. On government, Aquinas, the leading philosopher of the Middle Ages wrote (*De Regno*):

> Therefore, since the beatitude of heaven is the end of that virtuous life which we live at present, it pertains to the king's office to promote the good life of the multitude in such a way as to make it suitable for the attainment of heavenly happiness.

From Sweden to Italy, early modern Natural Law and cameralist political economy emphasized public happiness (*Felicita* in Italian; *Glückseligkeit* in German) as a superordinate social goal; happiness thus framed included good government, safe roads, freedom of business, competitive markets, good 'rules of the game', infant industry protectionism, entrepreneurial states, industrial policy and a good Sunday sermon in church (Rössner, 2020). It was a concept of managed or coordinated capitalism, where the interests of the ruler were principally aligned with the interest of the governed individual (Brückner, 1977; Nokkala, 2019). Regarding market regulation, mercantilists/cameralists and later contributors to political economy by and large stuck to medieval templates of market regulation, which were often replicated for centuries verbatim. Neither medieval nor early modern authorities would principally want or try to control prices at markets permanently or for all goods; interventionism was practised only in times of crisis and scarcity, to avoid price inflation, hunger and misery from the people (being the duty of any good Christian administrator or ruler). Generally, the Middle Ages knew free bargaining and competitive price formation, which is what in most cases the 'natural' or 'just price' so often evoked in the literature seems to have amounted to (Wood, 2002: 132–8). The Salamanca theologian Domingo de Soto (1494–1560), a contemporary of Martin Luther, made the point that the very posing of the question 'what is a just price' did not lead anywhere in particular, because 'if someone asks you how much he can sell for, and you answer "What justice dictates", you tell him nothing that he did not already know' (Rössner, 2015: 134). In *Von Kauffshandlung vnd Wucher*/On commerce and usury (1524), Martin Luther essentially adopted the late scholastic laissez-faire stance, if grudgingly, since he began thus:

[10] […] the best and safest way would be for the temporal authorities to appoint over this matter wise and honest men who appraise the cost of all sorts of wares and fix accordingly the target price at which the merchant would get his due share and have an honest living, just as at certain places they fix the price of wine, fish, bread and the like. (Rössner, 2015: 177)

But in the next sentence he made an important modification, by taking a departure from what principally reads like a pledge for price control. Alluding to the omnipresent unholy habit of binge-drinking that had gripped (or rather drained) the German lands at his time, Luther claimed that:

as we Germans are so busy drinking and dancing that we cannot bear any such regulation. Since, then, we cannot hope for such an institution or edict, the next best thing will be to hold our wares at the price which they fetch in the common market, or which is customary in the neighbourhood. In this matter we can accept the proverb: 'Do like others and you are no fool.' Any profit made in this way, I consider honest and well earned, since there is risk of loss in wares and outlay, and the profits cannot be all too great. (Rössner, 2015: 177)

In this way Luther – whose treatise remained an economic bestseller during his time (Reinert and Reinert, 2018) – belongs to the school of pragmatic market liberals who view laissez-faire as an outcome of government or state regulation in service of a bigger common good.

This, in varying shapes and with nuances, has marked modern notions of coordinated capitalism and social market economy in the West, realizing the imperfections of capitalism while simultaneously acknowledging markets' potential to generate positive welfare outcomes when designed carefully and managed well (Rössner, 2015). The scholastic heritage continued into later centuries (see also Stanziani, 2012). James Steuart, an 18th-century Scottish economist and Jacobite who spent years of exile in France,

Frankfurt-am-Main and the south-west German university of Tübingen, where he became acquainted with cameralist political economy, argued that 'The prices of subsistence are made to fluctuate, in markets by the same principle which regulates the prices of all commodities, viz. the proportion between the demand and the supply', and that 'Private Interest is the great spring of all actions in political life' (Steuart, 1769: 289–90). 'We must emphasise', wrote Johann Heinrich Gottlob von Justi (contemporary of Steuart's and 18th-century Germany's star economist) in his 1760 treatise on the principles of political economy, 'that freedom is more conducive to the flourishing of the common weal than any government support' (Justi, 1760–1). Early modern cameralism thus principally based its assumptions of price formation on free and competitive markets and sketched merchants and entrepreneurs – as long as they increased the nation's wealth – in principally positive and very similar terms to the scholastic, even relaxing upper ceilings on interest (usury) and profit rates and fully exploring the possibility of modelling market economy in abstract conceptual and formalistic terms (Elmslie, 2015; Rössner, 2020).

The sheer increase in number and spread of monetary/currency and market regulations since the Middle Ages is sound evidence of capitalism gaining momentum outside its medieval hothouses of Upper Italy, and will be dealt with separately. For the moment it will simply be explained how different transitions towards capitalism changed and modified the regulatory requirements needed to establish it. Evidence from the German Peasant War (1524–25) and the late medieval processes of specialization and commercialization provides a case in point.

Transitions towards capitalism: case study of late medieval Germany and the Reformation, 1470s–1530s

A common misconception in the modern historian's and economist's literature has Martin Luther – whom we have encountered above as part-rooted in scholasticism – as a medieval ignoramus helplessly shouting against modern capitalism.

The problematic nature of this assumption has been briefly explained here, and elsewhere (Rössner, 2015). Briefly speaking, it rests on a doubly misplaced focus: first what modern economic thinking is and how pre-modern theories fit into its genealogy (most scholars deny the scholastic and post-scholastic heritage of cameralism and mercantilism its place here; and secondly the assumption that Martin Luther was ignorant in matters economic. However, he trained both as a lawyer/administrator and an academic theologian (he gained his divinity doctorate in 1512), and these were the main accredited 'economics' degrees of his time – and therefore the only way to acquire academic economic knowledge. The first university chairs to be specifically endowed in economics were those in *Kameralwissenschaften* (cameral sciences) at the Prussian universities of Halle/Saale and Frankfurt/Oder in 1727. Luther was thus far from being an ignoramus; on the contrary, he was firmly situated within mainstream economic knowledge and doctrine as taught in his days. His major political and economic writings include the *Address to the Christian Nobility of the German Nation* (1520) and the (consolidated) sermon *On Commerce and Usury* (1524) (Rössner, 2015). In these key writings Luther laid out the major challenges of his age, presenting his models for managing political and economic change.

The Marxist tradition as well as mainstream Western interpretations before 1991 often associate Luther's Reformation (1517) within an imputed rise of capitalism, following Tawney and Weber. Both schools emphasized a new wave or 'rise' of capitalism as a crucial undercurrent of religious and political change of the time. The central European mining booms of the 1470s–90s, the rise of interoceanic trade, big family firms and overseas trading houses such as Fugger, Welser and Höchstetter as the last medieval super-companies on German soil in the Upper German imperial cities, and trading *metropoleis* such as Nuremberg and Augsburg – where Luther's Reformation fell on particularly fertile grounds – were interpreted as evidence of a boom of capitalism that would explain away these religious critiques and political developments.

While non-Marxist materialist models of the Reformation of 1517 have seen a revival in the economist's literature (for example Becker et al, 2016), modern historians have largely avoided this topic. This is a pity because both the economic data as well as the political-economic literature of the day allow us to study the architecture of capitalism rising and then declining. Mainstream interpretations of Luther – in East and West, before and beyond 1991 (the collapse of the USSR being the hegemonic force in the discourse) – have rested upon a double misunderstanding of where Luther came from, in theory and practice – assuming that Luther shouted against a rise in capitalism when capitalism and economic development actually were temporarily, during 1500 to 1525, undergoing a period of decline and contraction. Mainstream histories of the Reformation have also suffered from a downplaying of the role played by markets and capitalism in engineering, in a sense, the landslide religious, cultural, political and social changes triggered by Martin Luther's Reformation.

A common (mis-)dating has the 'Price Revolution' – providing key metrical data on which the 'rise of capitalism' hypothesis rests – beginning in the 1470s. The downswing of central European prices between the 1590s and 1520s, however, before secular inflation gained its final momentum in the 1530s and 1540s, has often been overlooked but is crucial here. The 1520s were a key period that decided whether Luther's Reformation would 'make' or 'break'. But the 1510s and 1520s were a time of price deflation, not inflation, and monetary as well as economic contraction. Major political economy texts were written in the 1520s addressing the situation, including Luther's *Address to the Christian Nobility* and his major economic work *On Commerce and Usury* (1524; Rössner, 2015). During the crisis and depression of the central European market economies, prices for consumables had fallen, especially grain prices, to new lows, after the penultimate mining boom in the Erz Mountains and the Tyrol had led to price inflation across the Germanies during the mid-1470s to early 1490s. This deflation caused a human generation's worth (*c.* 25 years) of contracting sales revenues for middling rank farmers, urban artisans and the upper echelons of village society. These people had deep connections with the market and deployed or experienced increasingly capitalist techniques in order to make a living. Along with this came a complementary factor. As prices for agricultural goods were falling, depressing market-orientated peasant farmers' revenue, profits and mark-ups on Indian spices from the big firms involved in interoceanic trade were soaring. Capitalist business profits among Upper German high financiers (Stromer von Reichenbach, 1970; Harreld, 2007) and the last medieval super-companies, including Fugger, Welser, Höchstetter, Imhof and Rem, often skyrocketed at the same time and in the wake of Vasco da Gama and the exponential growth of Portuguese trading posts alongside the Atlantic, Indian Ocean and into the Chinese Sea (Safley, 2020). The Reformation fell on particularly fertile grounds and open ears among urban and rural middle-rank people who felt left behind and 'carried' the Reformation in its different idiosyncratic variations across the Germanies and beyond. Combining quantitative data on grain markets, including previously unpublished price data from Leipzig covering the 1470s–1560s, with other economic data and texts, pamphlets and writings of contemporary economic analysis, the early Reformation (1500–20s) can thus be reassembled as a period of capitalism in crisis, and a select analysis of Luther's and other contemporaries' writings traces out the main currents of economic analysis and the humanists'/reformers' stance on capitalism and market economy, in particular hoarding, saving and investment. Luther grew up and spent the majority of his adult life as a theologian, economist and religious reformer in what at the time was among Europe's most dynamically growing commercial, industrial and urbanized areas (Mansfeld–Thuringian–Erz Mountain silver mining region). And the specific opposition to hoarding and unproductive forms of saving money that comes across in the Reformation's political economy can be explained by referencing this period of secular contraction and capitalism in decline.

The combination of the last central European medieval mining booms, expanding population levels and growing cities, an expansion of the interoceanic trades, commercial capitalism and the increasingly close connection between Upper German banking houses with Portuguese crown capitalism and the creating of the Portuguese Indian Ocean trading empire during the 1470s to 1520s created new fields of state intervention and new demands of regulation. This was not only regarding indulgences and pilgrimages – which became big business during the later 15th century, giving rise to Luther's indulgence critique and subsequent Reformation – but also extended from market and currency regulation to church service, religious management and other fields. The remainder of this chapter discusses two aspects of economic policy in particular that arose from the Renaissance and Reformation transitions to and from capitalism: monetary regulation and industrial policy.

Monetary regulation

Monetary ordinances, *Ordonnances* as they were called in medieval French (Kaye, 2004: 20), or *Münzordnungen* in the German-speaking realms (Rössner, 2012), belong to the oldest instruments of economic policy. Known since antiquity, they grew in number from the high Middle Ages as central governments emerged – and in the German case imperial prerogatives such as currency and market regulation as well as mining. Regalia had been devolved from the emperor to individual territories in the mid-13th century. At times when states were weak and temporal authorities' grasp on markets and economic lives were light touch, high taxation regimes and interventionism as in the later fiscal-military paradigm of the post-1600 state were off the table. Indirect measures such as setting the monetary parameters – how many units of currency were to be struck from one unit (usually a mark at around 250 grams) of silver or gold – were the only means of influencing, if indirectly, the amount of money in circulation and thus economic lives, monetization and market-based exchange (Rössner, 2012, 2015, 2020). If handled wisely by the state, money could be used to influence the economy in a positive way, stabilizing the well-being of the common weal by putting market trade and exchange on a sound footing, stabilizing exchange rates and avoiding social imbalances such as profiteering, coin exchange rate speculation and other monetary manipulations that were considered usurious. Martin Luther and his contemporaries in the later 16th century still referred to such dealings as 'asymmetrical bargain' or *ungleiche hendel* (literally unequal exchange). If handled badly, coin debasement could lead to important weaknesses in property rights and contract enforcement, driving up transaction costs and leading to a decline in 'good government'. Revaluations (increases in the amount of precious metal in coins) were infrequent and often occasioned popular resistance, especially among urban economic actors who were liable to pay rents or interest payments in a fixed amount of currency units (Kaye,

2004: 24). Debasement, on the other hand, seems to have been almost the norm; between the later 14th and the 19th centuries, for instance, the south German penny currencies lost about 90 per cent of their intrinsic value measured in official grams of silver (Rössner, 2014). Popular unrest, such as in Paris in 1358 (Kaye 2004: 21), or numerous German peasant uprisings since the 1460s frequently picked up on debasement. Currency debasement was perhaps *the* common uniting feature underpinning popular unrest in the Germanies on the eve and in the wake of the Great German Peasant War and the so-called Revolution of 1525 (Blickle, 2004).

In 1500 the rulers of Saxony issued a new monetary ordinance, the Leipzig Currency Reform of 1500, which signified long-term changes of considerable social and economic importance. This therefore serves as an excellent example of a larger point. The Saxon-Thuringian lands belonged to the commercially and economically most developed areas in the contemporary Holy Roman Empire. Silver mining was centred in the Saxon Erzgebirge. Silver and copper smelting took place in large-scale capital intensive production processes in the Thuringian Forest and the Mansfeld mining area. Money payment for wages were ubiquitous. Saxony-Thuringia was heavily urbanized and industrialized; it also lay at the crossroads of important long-distance roads, and important long-distance trade fairs were held at Leipzig and Naumburg. Although it closely resembled earlier medieval ordinances in terms of wording and composition, the Leipzig Monetary Ordinance was more modern than any that preceded it. In a way it laid the foundations of a new monetary paradigm of state capacity and economic policy, although contemporary economic actors certainly would not have been fully aware of that. The Saxon *thaler* represented the first instance of a permanent substitution of silver for gold in the top-level currency in central Europe, marked by leading denominations known as the florin from its Italian roots, Guldengroschen in the German lands or cruzado in Portugal. One thaler or *Groschen so ein gulden gilt* (groat equalling 1 florin in value), as it was known, was equal to 1 Rhenish or gold florin. It became the leading currency in central Europe; gold subsequently being replaced by silver in real minting in most central European states in the early modern period.

When the Saxon duke and elector thus issued the Leipzig Monetary Ordinance (Leipziger Münzordnung) of 1500 they established a new currency paradigm which was based on stability, credibility of the state in safeguarding property rights, and a substitution of silver for gold for the highest denomination coins. In their commitment to currency stability and safeguarding of commerce and trade, the Leipzig Monetary Ordinance took a new approach that was also indicative of a new vision of money, statehood and commercial society. The ordinance established a six-tiered monetary system for the Saxon lands, comprising the silver florin (*Groschen so ein gulden gilt*, later on nicknamed thaler after Joachimsthal (today Jàchymov in Czechia) at 21 zinsgroschen (the biblical 'tithe groat' according to Martin Luther's translation) and 252 pfennige (pennies, d.). This system also knew further subdivisions that were infrequently used, including the Schreckenberger groschen at 3 *Zinsgroschen* or one seventh florin, the half schwertgroschen (half Zins groats), as well as the heller (halfpenny) at 1/504th to the florin or thaler.

Like previous ordinances, the legislation contained the requirement that all new silver minted in Saxony had to go through the mint at Freiberg or any other of the Saxon mints before it entered circulation. All existing debts were to be paid in the new currency, and the common distinction of payments made 'in gold' (namely gold florins, which usually included an *agio* or premium) and 'in gelt' (silver currency, usually at a discount) was to be waived. Instead the new silver florin was to be fully convertible to any other circulating gold coin corresponding to the Rhenish florin standard. The Leipzig ordinance also included regulations as to how the currencies of the regional adjacent states were to be used, including the counties of Schwarzburg, Henneberg, Stolberg and Hohnstein, but also the free imperial cities of Mühlhausen and Nordhausen, as well as Erfurt, a big trading city that belonged to the Archbishopric of Mainz but was not formally under suzerainty to the Saxon dukes and electors.

The Leipzig currency ordinance had some aspects in common with other currency regulation of the high Middle Ages. However, it also had key differences. It was the type of normative regulation that had become common since the high Middle Ages, specifying – often year by year – among other things the amount and fineness of precious metal that each current coin had to contain, what types and nominals of coin were to be used on Saxon markets, spot exchange rates of Saxon compared with other coins and which moneys were generally forbidden. Pre-modern concepts of money were hybrid inasmuch as legislation differentiated between 'foreign' and 'domestic' only regarding their intrinsic content: did coins contain enough silver or gold to match the domestic standard? Foreign coins were frequently admitted as legal tender (in the same way as Montenegro uses the euro as the country's national currency albeit being member of neither the eurozone nor the EU). In some cases, authorities would forbid foreign coin entirely, commanding that all payments had to be made in domestic coin, and merchants using foreign currency had to bring their coins to the princely mint to be reminted into domestic money before it could be used on the market. Often, though, these regulations only pertained to the specified and privileged urban markets and yearly or quarterly trade fairs, with day-to-day business being considerably less heavily regulated. Monetary regulation was relevant for certain types of formal contracts relating for instance to rent payment, credit sales or property transactions as well as the payment of taxes, tithes and customs to the feudal lords, states and their officials. In day-to-day payment actors could – and would – deviate from official standard, renegotiating exchange rates for different coins that were not in accordance with official legislation. However, the Leipzig ordinance included hefty fines even including corporeal punishment (the severing of one hand) upon transgressions of 'official' legislation in certain cases; albeit we know from numerous contemporary documents relating to private transactions, contracts and property sales that official rates were habitually, consciously and continuously evaded (Rössner, 2012).

In some key aspects the Leipzig Monetary Ordinance of 1500 was quite extraordinary, and worth reconsidering in the light of recent histories of state formation and capitalism because it showcased a new understanding of currency as a tool of economic intervention by one of the strongest fiscal states of its age (Schirmer, 2000). As a major player in the Reformation, with Elector Frederick 'the Wise' being protector of Luther in the crucial early phase of the Reformation, and leading global supplier of silver (and thus European monetary material) Saxony was in the midst of ongoing economic transitions to capitalism, a rise in globalization and interoceanic trade. The ramifications of whether or not the Saxon currency was to be kept stable cut across contemporary society, urban and rural alike. Above all it was people receiving fixed income streams (including tithe, rent, annual interest payment, mortgages or *Rentenkauf*, meaning annuities) who would be immediately disadvantaged by currency debasement. This included creditors and people who had lent money in a specified currency, but also paupers and the poor. This somewhat contradicts Spufford's dictum that those who paid a rent, an interest or a debt would generally have *profited* from coin debasement, as devaluation would have implied a reduction in real rent or debt (as measured in grams of silver/gold). But, as research on coin debasement and rural economy has shown (Rössner, 2012), whenever new currency contained less silver than the old but recipients of the respective payment insisted on accepting coins minted to the new standard at discounted rates, problems ensued. This *agio* on payments made in debased coin, or discounting of small change was called *Aufwexl*, or upward exchange in contemporary German economic language, and represented the most common cause for unrest documented in the numerous peasant rebellions of the time. On the other hand, in an urban capitalist rentier environment, whoever received a fixed income would immediately be put at a disadvantage as well. Even the feudal lords and the state, when collecting taxes, would be losing income if new (debased) coins were not generally accepted to the new standard.

Money was thus an important instrument of state economic policy. The Saxon standard remained higher than in adjacent territories for a long period. Saxon rulers tried to use it as a tool of hegemony over adjacent smaller states by exporting their monetary regulation. Saxon denominations usually circulated at a premium across the German-speaking lands. Saxon rulers also tended to debase their currency less frequently than other German states, and the Saxon lands were notably spared of the bigger skirmishes and battles of the Peasant War, 1524–25 (apart from some southern Thuringian stretches bordering the Hesse frontier region). Overall, they provided a safer and more stable system in which institutions safeguarded property rights and put economic lives on somewhat sounder footings than other rulers who were – if we measure institutional quality by the frequency and rates of debasement over time (Henriques and Palma, 2019) – more predatory, at least in monetary terms. Monetary policy also acted as a tool of hegemonic policy (at least for Saxon rulers) within central Germany, as new balances and imbalances arose between the emperor and the emerging territorial fiscal states. The monetary edicts and ordinances from the period abound with notions of monetary use, imbalances, debasement and profits from 'unjust' exchange rates of higher to smaller denomination coins. Merchants who travelled long distances with coinage in order to realize arbitrage gains were ubiquitous also on complaints heard and proceedings at the level of imperial diets in the 1540s to 1570s (Volckart, 2017).

Industrial policy

To Marxists and to Marx himself (Marx and Engels, 1968) the early modern European state acted as a sinister handmaiden of capitalism, facilitating capital accumulation, exploitation and inequality in the West. Modern neo-institutionalists tend to agree with Marxists on the basic outcome – proactive state institutions that positively influence capital formation and economic development, but with different conclusions regarding what states can and ought to do for economic development, through the nature and quality of institutions and regulatory frameworks applied to market exchange, trade and other economic activity (for example North and Thomas, 1976; Acemoglu and Robinson, 2012). As some have suggested regarding global comparisons of state capacity and economic development, strong night-watchman states – states providing credibly enforceable inclusive institutions and good government without trying to actively influence or alter the economic outcome and market process – may also in theory influence economic development positively (Wong, 1997; Rosenthal and Wong, 2012; and, for much counter-evidence, Vries, 2015). Some of the new literature would accept the above premises on industrial policy but tends to downplay states' enforcement capabilities before the 19th century (Johnson and Koyama, 2017).

This section suggests that there were plenty of examples of successful state-led policy in the early modern period. Industrial policy was known and practised by European states from the Middle Ages. From a deep-historical point of view, industrial policy (Oqubay et al, 2020) and 'entrepreneurial' and 'developmental states' (Kattel and Mazzucato 2018; Mazzucato, 2018, 2021) represent an old way of doing things (Reinert, 2005; Reinert, 2019; Reinert and Fredona, 2020). Since the Middle Ages Italian city states or English kings actively promoted domestic manufacturing and value-added activities by prohibiting the export of raw wool (which had provided the main input to the flourishing cloth industry in Flanders) and other measures. After the Restoration the increasingly powerful English (and after 1707 the British fiscal-military state) furthered its grip and became increasingly more proactive in targeting specific industries with bounties and premiums, abolishing customs duties on (most) exports and vital raw material imports, keeping high duties on Indian cotton manufactures (Brisco, 1907; Parthasarathi, 2011); in a parliamentary speech in 1727 Prime Minister Robert Walpole – after a series of customs reforms supporting domestic industry since 1721 – emphasized the role of manufacturing and industry in making the nation rich. Manufacturing was understood, since the writings of Jesuit pastor Giovanni Botero and his books on the reason of state and on cities (1588/9), to be a most convenient way of increasing the nation's wealth. A common trope in political economy that we find in English, German, Swedish and other languages during the 17th and 18th centuries was about manufacturing being the nations' gold mine – referring to the unhappy example of Spain that had, after being the world's richest nation with her American silver and gold, sunk into economic dependency and underdevelopment by exchanging silver for manufactures and other higher-order imports. Nations did not need gold or silver mines to get rich; in fact, writers such as Austrian state servant, economist and bestselling writer Philipp Wilhelm von Hörnigk (Austria Supreme, 1684) (Rössner, 2018) suggested that having too much of it may actually make countries weak by preventing them from focusing policy on promoting real value-added activities.

The manufacturing paradigm was based on an understanding that industry is usually more dynamic in generating employment, income and knowledge transfer through adding value. The basic rationale is that industry/manufacturing means transforming materials into a higher order stage, and such higher order goods are usually more income elastic than foodstuffs and other goods (Reinert, 2019). Since the days of Botero this was understood by political economists and consultant administrators (Schumpeter, 1954), and as a real-life political economy it had been practised in Italy since the days of the Medici (Reinert and Fredona, 2020). It is nowadays understood that economic growth is not sufficient to generate economic development: it is the nature and qualitative difference between different types and branches of economic activity that predicts whether economic development will happen or be sustained in terms of lasting income and job growth (Kattel and Mazzucato, 2018; Mazzucato, 2021). One key indicator (among others) is value added, and in the Middle Ages and early modern era, value added was most dynamic – or most likely to be generated through manufacturing.

This is one reason why in the early modern period nearly all European fiscal-military states – from Scotland to Prussia – focused economic policy on aspects of industrial policy, supporting the erection of large industrial enterprises where labour processes were divided into their most simple components and concentrated under one roof, run by professional managers and businessmen. Called manufactories, they represent an important transitory stage in the process of modern capitalism, but virtually vanished into oblivion when after 1800 the modern industrial factory took centre stage in the industrializing nations. Marx had discussed the manufactories in *Kapital* as important features empowering transitions to modern capitalism; and so had Sombart (1921–27). Adam Smith's *Wealth of Nations* (1776) famously commenced with such a manufactory, but the principle had represented common fare in German political economy since the 1750s and 1760s: Germany's leading Enlightenment economist Johann Heinrich Justi (1717–71) used the example of a mint rather than a pin factory. Modern economic historians have tended to dismiss the manufactories and their role in the germination of modern capitalism (for example Heckscher, 1954): they were often unprofitable, some of them did not live long; most were in some form privileged by some sort of state monopoly and after all they gave way to the factory and mechanization. That, however, is a dangerously short-sighted assessment. Manufactories were privileged and supported by princes and kings precisely to break up the grip of urban guilds on trade restrictions: they were meant to contribute to a freeing of the market. They embodied aspects that became key features for modern capitalism, including scientific management, rationalization, division of labour and the drive to shift economic activity into more dynamic value-added activities. Their importance – but also industry in a wider sense, including decentralized household-based manufacturing (*Verlag* or putting out) – cannot be underestimated.

Since the Renaissance political economy thus advocated the role of the state in 'getting the nation into the right business' (Reinert, 2019: chapter 2). Industrial policy was seen as one key tool (among others) to achieve these goals and to empower capitalism. Industrial policy was often directed at specific enterprises and businesses, usually run by private entrepreneurs and under capitalist auspices. It was coupled with wider tariff policies of protecting and nurturing industry, including elements of what became later, during the 20th century, known as infant industry protection and import substitution industrialization. In this way Renaissance and early modern states in practice far exceeded the remit traditionally allowed for them by modern historians as passive regulators that only provide frameworks of good government but otherwise keep their hands off the economy (Wong, 1997). This was certainly not the model of governmentality practised by European states or laid down in the contemporary works of political economy – which from the late Middle Ages were both more proactive and interventionist.

Modern capitalism has until recent times itself been based upon practices and theories developed in the Middle Ages. This includes scholastic doctrines (and sometimes sophistries) about 'just' prices (which were competitive, and often involved laissez-faire/free markets), monetary management, and regulation of monetary and currency matters, or industrial policy – all of which applied in the 20th century as they had in the 13th and 14th (albeit in different forms and to a different extent), or were resuscitated as industrial policy in the 21st century.

Notes

[1] A counterpoint to this is in Besley and Persson (2011).

[2] This philosophy has also generated a host of other interesting epistemic assumptions, including the proposition that there are 'markets' for everything, including sexual preferences, love, emotions and so on. From an anthropological viewpoint the approach is profoundly sinister and psychologically disturbing (and conveys a lot about its authors' emotional household). But it has influenced thinking in the post-war Western world to the present day.

[3] In the 17th century the Swedish state comprised, apart from Sweden, Finland, wide parts of the Eastern Baltic and Germany, through Swedish Pomerania, located in the Holy Roman Empire.

References

Acemoglu, D. and Robinson, J.A. (2012) *Why Nations Fail: The Origins of Power, Prosperity, and Poverty*, New York: Random House.

Becker, S. O., Pfaff, S. and Rubin, J. (2016) 'Causes and consequences of the Protestant Reformation', *Explorations in Economic History*, 62(C): 1–25.

Besley, T. and Persson, T. (2011) *Pillars of Prosperity: The Political Economics of Development Clusters*, Princeton, NJ: Princeton University Press.

Blickle, P. (2004) *Die Revolution von 1525* (4th edn), Berlin: Oldenbourg Wissenschaftsverlag.

Brisco, N.A. (1907) *The Economic Policy of Robert Walpole*, New York: Macmillan.

Brückner, J. (1977) *Staatswissenschaften, Kameralismus und Naturrecht: Ein Beitrag zur Geschichte der politischen. Wissenschaft im Deutschland des späten 17. und frühen 18. Jahrhunderts*, Munich: Beck.

Burkhardt, J. and Priddat, B.P. (eds) (2000) *Geschichte der Ökonomie*, Frankfurt-am-Main: Deutscher Klassiker Verlag.

Denzel, M.A. (2010) *Handbook of World Exchange Rates: 1590–1914*, Farnham: Ashgate.

Elmslie, B. (2015) 'Early English mercantilists and the support of liberal institutions', *History of Political Economy*, 47(3): 419–48.

Goerlitz, W. (ed) (1928) *Staat und Stände Unter Den Herzögen Albrecht und Georg, 1485–1539*, Leipzig: Teubner.

Harreld, D. (2007) *High Germans in the Low Countries: German Merchants and Commerce in Golden Age Antwerp*, Leiden and Boston, MA: Brill.

Heckscher, E.F. (1954) *An Economic History of Sweden*, Cambridge, MA: Harvard University Press.

Henriques, A. and Palma, N. (2019) 'Comparative European institutions and the little divergence, 1385–1800', CEPR Discussion Paper No. DP14124.

Isenmann, E. (2014) *Die Deutsche Stadt im Mittelalter* (2nd edn), Cologne: Böhlau.

Johnson, N.D. and Koyama, M. (2017) 'States and economic growth: capacity and constraints', *Explorations in Economic History*, 64: 1–20.

Justi, von J.H.G. (1760–1) *Die Grundfeste zu der Macht und Glückseeligkeit der Staaten; oder Ausführliche vorstellung der gesamten Policey-Wissenschaft*, Königsberg and Leipzig: Hartungs Erben.

Kaplan, S. and Reinert, S. (2019) *The Economic Turn: Recasting Political Economy in Enlightenment Europe*, London and New York: Anthem.

Kattel, R. and Mazzucato, M. (2018) 'Mission-oriented innovation policy and dynamic capabilities in the public sector', *Industrial and Corporate Change*, 27(5): 787–801.

Kaye, J. (2004) *Economy and Nature in the Fourteenth Century: Money, Market Exchange, and the Emergence of Scientific Thought*, Cambridge: Cambridge University Press.

Kolev, S. (2017) *Neoliberale Staatsverständnisse im Vergleich* (2nd edn), Berlin and Boston, MA: De Gruyter Oldenbourg.

Langholm, O.I. (1992) *Economics in the Medieval Schools: Wealth, Exchange, Value, Money and Usury According to the Paris Theological Tradition 1200–1350*, Leiden: Brill.

Langholm, O.I. (1998) *The Legacy of Scholasticism in Economic Thought. Antecedents of Choice and Power*, Cambridge: Cambridge University Press.

Langholm, O.I. (2003) *The Merchant in the Confessional: Trade and Price in the Pre-Reformation Penitential Handbooks*, Leiden and Boston, MA: Brill.

LeGoff, J. (1990) *The Birth of Purgatory*, London: Scolar Press.

Lopes, R.S. (1976) *The Commercial Revolution of the Middle Ages, 950–1350*, Cambridge: Cambridge University Press.

Marx, K. and Engels, F. (1968) *Werke, Vol 23, 'Das Kapital', Vol. I*, Berlin: Dietz.

Mazzucato, M. (2018) *The Entrepreneurial State: Debunking Public vs. Private Sector Myths*, London: Penguin.

Mazzucato, M. (2021) *Mission Economy: A Moonshot Guide to Changing Capitalism*, London: Allen Lane.

Mokyr, J. (2017) *A Culture of Growth: The Origins of the Modern Economy: The Graz Schumpeter Lectures*, Princeton, NJ: Princeton University Press.

Nokkala, E. (2019) *From Natural Law to Political Economy: J.H.G. von Justi on State, Commerce and International Order*, Zurich: LIT.

Nokkala, E. and Miller, N. (eds) (2019) *Cameralism and the Enlightenment: Happiness, Governance and Reform in Transnational Perspective*, London and New York: Routledge.

North, D.C. and Thomas, R.P. (1976) *The Rise of the Western World: A New Economic History*, Cambridge: Cambridge University Press.

Oqubay, A., Cramer, C., Chang, H.-J. and Kozul-Wright, R. (eds) *The Oxford Handbook of Industrial Policy*, Oxford: Oxford University Press.

Parthasarathi, P. (2011) *Why Europe Grew Rich and Asia Did Not: Global Economic Divergence, 1600–1850*, Cambridge: Cambridge University Press.

Patel, R. and Moore, J.W. (2020) *A History of the World in Seven Cheap Things: A Guide to Capitalism, Nature, and the Future of the Planet*, Oakland: University of California Press.

Reinert, E. and Reinert, F.A. (2018) '33 Economic bestsellers published before 1750', *The European Journal of the History of Economic Thought*, 25(6): 1206–63.

Reinert, E.S. (2019) *The Visionary Realism of German Economics: From the Thirty Years' War to the Cold War*, London and New York: Anthem.

Reinert, S.A. (2005) 'The Italian tradition of political economy: theories and policies of development in the semi-periphery of the Enlightenment', in J.K. Sundaram and E.S. Reinert (eds) *The Origins of Development Economics: How Schools of Economic Thought Have Addressed Development*, London: Zed Books, pp 24–47.

Reinert, S.A. and Fredona, R. (2020) 'Political economy and the Medici', *Business History Review* 94(1): 125–77.

Rosenthal, J.-L. and Wong, R.B. (2012) *Before and Beyond Divergence: The Politics of Economic Change in China and Europe*, Boston, MA: Harvard University Press.

Rössner, P.R. (2012) *Deflation – Devaluation – Rebellion: Geld im Zeitalter der Reformation*, Stuttgart: Franz Steiner.

Rössner, P.R. (2014) 'Monetary instability, lack of integration and the curse of a commodity money standard: The German Lands, c.1400–1900 A.D.', *Credit and Capital Markets*, 47(2): 297–340.

Rössner, P.R. (2015) *Martin Luther on Commerce and Usury (1524)*, London and New York: Anthem.

Rössner, P.R. (ed) (2018) *Austria Supreme, If It So Wishes (1684): A Strategy for European Economic Supremacy*, London and New York: Anthem.

Rössner, P.R. (2020) *Freedom and Capitalism in Early Modern Europe: Mercantilism and the Modern Economic Mind*, Cham: Palgrave Macmillan.

Rössner, P.R. (2022) *Managing the Wealth of Nations*, Bristol: Bristol University Press.

Safley, T.M. (2020) *Family Firms and Merchant Capitalism in Early Modern Europe: The Business, Bankruptcy and Resilience of the Höchstetters of Augsburg*, Abingdon and New York: Routledge.

Schirmer, U. (2000) *Kursächsische Staatsfinanzen (1456–1656) Strukturen – Verfassung – Funktionseliten*, Stuttgart: Franz Steiner.

Schumpeter, J.A. (1954) *History of Economic Analysis*, New York: Oxford University Press.

Seppel, M. and Tribe, K. (2017) *Cameralism in Practice: State Administration and Economy in Early Modern Europe*, Woodbridge: Boydell and Brewer.

Smith, A. (1776) *An Inquiry into the Nature and Causes of the Wealth of Nations*, London: Strahan & Cadell.

Sombart, W. (1921–7) *Der Moderne Kapitalismus: Volumes 1 and 2*, Munich and Leipzig: Duncker and Humblot.

Spufford, P. (2002) *Power and Profit: The Merchant in Medieval Europe*, London: Thames and Hudson.

Stanziani, A. (2012) *Rules of Exchange: French Capitalism in Comparative Perspective, Eighteenth to Early Twentieth Centuries*, Cambridge: Cambridge University Press.

Steuart, Sir J. (1769) *Considerations on the Interest of the County of Lanark*, Glasgow: Duncan.

Stromer von Reichenbach, W. (1970) *Oberdeutsche Hochfinanz 1350–1450*, Wiesbaden: Franz Steiner.

Tribe, K. (1978) *Land, Labour, and Economic Discourse*, London: Routledge and K. Paul.

Volckart, O. (2017) *Eine Währung für das Reich: die Akten der Münztage zu Speyer 1549 und 1557*, Stuttgart: Franz Steiner, 2017

Vries, J. de (2019) *The Price of Bread. Regulating the Market in the Dutch Republic*, Cambridge: Cambridge University Press.

Vries, P. (2015) *State, Economy and the Great Divergence: Great Britain and China, 1680s–1850s*, London: Bloomsbury.

Wong, R.B. (1997) *China Transformed: Historical Change and the Limits of European Experience*, Ithaca, NY: Cornell University Press.

Wood, D. (2002) *Medieval Economic Thought*, Cambridge: Cambridge University Press.

4

Capitalism and State Ownership Models

Sverre A. Christensen

Introduction

Private ownership of the means of production is essential in Marx's definition of capitalism. Norway is an outlier in the Western world with its extensive state ownership, particularly in listed companies. The state is a direct owner of about 25 per cent of the values listed on the Oslo Stock Exchange, and controls companies that account for almost half of the market value. The ownership is mainly in large companies, and can thus be seen as a solution to the challenges regarding ownership and control in large companies (Berle and Means, 1932)

Different countries chose different paths to accommodate these challenges. In the US, and later in Great Britain, ownership in large companies was diffused. This diluted the owners' control and paved the way for managerial capitalism. On the European continent, ownership was more concentrated, with individuals, families and/or business groups staying in control over the large and capital-intensive companies, often by using cross-holdings, pyramid ownership and/or dual-class shares. Hence they controlled companies, without providing the corresponding capital.

The Norwegian state ownership does not fit easily into either of the two models. On the one hand, it is a kind of concentrated ownership. On the other hand, the state ownership shares features with the Anglo-Saxon model, for instance with a challenging agency problem. Norway has also settled for a market-conforming state ownership model, respecting minority shareholders and ensuring that shareholder value is at the top of the agenda (Christensen, 2018; Ministry of Trade, 2020b). State ownership in Norway has often been seen as a sign of weakness, compensating for the lack of private capital and entrepreneurs. The inescapable comparison with Sweden has reinforced this notion.

Sweden was an archetype of the continental model, with a few families and groups controlling the lion's share of the values on Stockholm's Stock Exchange by way of pyramid ownership, vote differentiation and Hausbanken, with close relation to the family and which the company had a primary relationship to. Several of the companies were successful multinationals. Many Norwegians envied the strong owners in Sweden, not least the Wallenberg family, 'the leading exponent of the Swedish corporate control model' (Henrekson and Jakobsson, 2012: 216). Then again, the Wallenbergs also had a strong position in Norway and were considered a threat by many (Tanderø, 1974). Moreover, being a neighbouring country of comparable size, Sweden often served as an explicit and implicit comparison with Norwegian development. This chapter will explore this more explicitly, contributing to the historical explanation and understanding of Norwegian state ownership by analysing it against the background of corporate governance literature in general and the Swedish case in particular.

As will be evident already, the Norwegian and Swedish ownership models are very different. We are therefore not comparing apples; at best we are comparing apples and oranges. The aim is thus not to compare explanatory variables in a stringent manner, but rather to generate reflections that can contribute to our understanding.

Comparative analysis thrives on similarities and differences. If everything is equal or everything is different, then a comparison has little to offer. For outsiders, Norway and Sweden have much in common, both being small Northern European countries, with a relatively high gross domestic product (GDP) per capita, similar welfare systems and ranking high on the majority of indexes for well-being and development. More specifically, regarding legal ramifications of ownership and corporate governance, there are many similarities. Both countries protect minority shareholders and prioritize shareholders' right over those of managers/companies (Eklund, 2009; Lekvall, 2014; Thomsen, 2016a). Still, this chapter will show that the differences are perceptible.

It is challenging and interesting to compare entities that interact with each other (Sejersted, 2003b). Norway entered into a union with Sweden after the Napoleonic wars in 1814. Both countries experienced decent growth between 1820 and 1870, based on the export of natural resources, and shipping was also important for Norway. Both countries modernized their society and infrastructure, and mercantilist privileges were dismantled, allowing for entrepreneurship and innovation (Fellman et al, 2008). After 1870, with the second Industrial Revolution and organized capitalism, the economic development of the two countries diverged. Swedish industry thrived, and several companies were founded in the new knowledge and capital-intensive industries. Norway struggled with this transition, and it is pertinent that the Wallenbergs were instrumental in founding the Norsk Hydro, which became the Norwegian industrial champion. Norway was inferior to Sweden in business and economic growth for decades, and did not catch up with Swedish GDP until the latter part of the 20th century. This was largely because of the discovery of petroleum, but also because Norwegian business in general, and state ownership in particular, adjusted better to the new era of Anglo-Saxon capitalism.

Apart from providing a better understanding of state ownership in Norway, this chapter will also contribute to the corporate governance literature. First, it will show that active ownership was applauded in the post-war years in both Norway and Sweden, but that it became less important after the Anglo-Saxon corporate governance model made its mark in Scandinavia from the 1980s. Secondly, the chapter accentuates the importance of national ownership and control in understanding the development of ownership models. Finally, it discusses Mark Roe's argument that the strength of social democracy explains concentrated ownership (Roe, 2003). Despite it being a social democratic stronghold, nobody has viewed Norwegian state ownership from this perspective. The chapter argues that the dichotomy between weak or strong social democracy is too simplistic, and that a perspective including nationalism would strengthen Roe's argument.

After the brief literature review that follows, two sections look at the historical background of Sweden's and Norway's ownership models. Similarities and differences between the two models are highlighted, before concluding remarks are made in the final section.

Literature review

The Swedish ownership model has been thoroughly analysed in view of the corporate governance literature (Högfeldt, 2005; Henrekson and Jakobsson, 2012). There are many analyses of state ownership in Norway, but none of them uses corporate governance literature to shed light on Norwegian development (Grønlie, 1989; Christensen, 2003, 2018; Lie, 2016).

La Porta et al launched an influential theory that emphasized legal origin, claiming that common law countries had better protection of minority shareholders, which allowed for diffused ownership; whereas civil law countries did not protect minority shareholders well enough for diffused ownership to transpire (La Porta et al, 1997). The underlying assumption is that diffused ownership is preferable. Morck talks disdainfully of family and business groups that control companies, and portrays them as 'oligarchic family dynasties that jealously safeguard their power, sometimes at great cost to their host economies' (Morck and Steier, 2007: 2). This does not sit well with the economic success that Sweden, Germany and Japan enjoyed in the post-war era. It also seems strange from the Norwegian perspective, where the lack of strong owners, such as the Wallenbergs, has been a persistent complaint for years (Sejersted, 1993). La Porta et al's contribution has received much criticism for confusing cause and effect, and for being normative (Roe, 2003; Morck and Steier, 2007; Musacchio and Turner, 2013). Moreover, it is less relevant for Scandinavia, which has a high concentration of ownership and high protection of minority shareholders (Lekvall, 2014; Thomsen, 2016b).

Roe's contribution is more relevant for Norway and Sweden, as he finds that concentrated ownership correlates with the strength of unions and social democracy. 'Social democracies press managers to stabilise employment, to forego some profit-maximising risks with the firm, and to use up capital in place rather than to downsize when markets no longer are aligned with the firm's production capabilities' (Roe, 2000: 1). Thus, concentrated ownership is required to make sure managers prioritize shareholder value (Roe, 2003). Roe 'finds strong evidence that weak labour correlates with strong diffusion' of shareholding (Gourevitch, 2002: 1830). Still, Roe's explanation may require refinement (Gourevitch, 2002).

Roe starts his book by claiming that 'before a nation can produce, it must achieve social peace' (Roe, 2003: 1). This is an important insight and points to the need for legitimacy for companies to operate. Another relevant term, used by Sven-Olof Collin, is 'political efficiency', and this is also relevant for large companies (Fear, 1997; Collin, 1998). Roe relates this to concessions to the labour movement, taking place on the traditional political axis of left–right. As important, however, is national ownership and control over the companies. A desire for this was not limited to the left, but was shared by many conservatives. 'Our students may know much about economic liberalism and economic socialism', says David Levi-Faur, 'but they usually know very little, if anything, about economic nationalism' (Levi-Faur, 1997: 155). This seems to be the case for many scholars as well.

Owing to the dominance of Anglo-Saxon thinking and globalization, the political economy of both Friedrich List and Alexander Hamilton is easily overlooked. This is essential, however, to understand the development of an ownership model for large companies during the 20th century. Despite this, politicians' desire for national ownership is disregarded by many scholars, or even mocked. Randal Morck portrays it as suspicious nationalism, 'a symptom of elite entrenchment', and a way to protect top executives' careers (Morck et al, 2005: 45, 48). He claims that Swedish social democrats wanted 'a stable large corporate sector controlled by Swedes, who were thought more susceptible than foreign owners to political pressure' (Morck and Steier, 2007: 23). Morck let his normative views blur his historic understanding.

The emergence of the Swedish ownership model should be understood as a variant of industrial nationalism (Kilander, 1991; Fridlund, 1997; Sejersted, 2011). Sjögren emphasizes that there 'was a strong component of nationalism behind the striving for market expansion and economic growth' (Sjögren, 2008: 34). In comparing Norway and Sweden, Sejersted (2011: 11) quotes Robinson (1962), who said that the 'very nature of economics is rooted in nationalism'. In Scandinavia and other places, large companies were bound together with political authorities in a common destiny. In investing large sums of capital, erecting company towns, building infrastructure and moving people, politicians and shareholders had a common interest in succeeding. Moreover, companies needed energy, research and development, capital and access to foreign markets, which entailed cooperation with the government (McCraw, 1997). Finally, in many countries, politicians would only prioritize companies that were under national ownership and control.

The securing of national ownership in for instance Switzerland, Sweden and the Netherlands has been coined as selective protectionism (David and Mach, 2003; Lüpold and Schnyder, 2006). The concept draws inspiration from Katzenstein (1985), who argues that small European states, largely because of the small size of their domestic market and the early extroversion of their economies, developed some specific traits to cope with their international environment: international liberalization, domestic compensation and flexible adjustment to fluctuations in international markets through corporatist institutions. This selective protectionism often took the form of shielding companies from corporate control. This is the main motivation for state ownership in Norway; it is thus a variant of selective protectionism (Christensen, 2003).

Sweden: historical background for ownership model

Sweden underwent exceptional growth and industrial development from the 1870s, when it entered the phase of organized capitalism and the second Industrial Revolution (Barkin, 1975; Sejersted, 2001; Sejersted, 2003a). Germany served as a role model (Sjögren, 2008), and the government pursued a policy in line with Friedrich List's infant industry argument – protecting the national industry in the early stages of development – with high tariff barriers (Angell, 2002; Högfeldt, 2005). Sweden had a technologically oriented academia and a tradition for combining science, technology and industry (Sejersted, 2011). The period 1870–1914 was formative for industrial development: '35 of the 50 largest Swedish firms in terms of sales in 2000 were established before 1914' (Henrekson and

Jakobsson, 2005: 7). Many of these were called 'genius companies', including Atlas Copco (1873), L.M. Ericsson (1876), Alfa-Laval (1883), ASEA (1883), AGA (1904) and SKF (1907).

The interwar years were formative for the ownership model. Sweden experienced an economic boom after the First World War, with intense speculation in stocks. Companies issued new shares to finance expansion, and banks gave loans with securities in the shares (Glete, 1978). The deflation crisis from the early 1920s made loans heavier to bear, and banks became owners in many of the crisis-ridden companies. The Wallenberg Bank, Stockholms Enskilda Bank and Den Svenska Handelsbanken bought insolvent companies, which were then able to survive the financial crisis that knocked out their owners and the entrepreneurs who had set them up (Högfeldt, 2005). Swedish business therefore emerged from the crisis both consolidated and strengthened. An example is the telecom company Ericsson, which was in disarray after the infamous match king Ivar Kreuger sold his share in the company to its American competitor, ITT, in 1931. The Wallenbergs negotiated a deal with the Americans, so Ericsson came under Swedish control (Glete, 1978; Christensen, 2006). Industrivärden/ Handelsbanken and the Wallenberg sphere had joint control, using an extreme voting differentiation of 1:1,000 between A- and B-shares (Högfeldt, 2005).

The banks were prohibited from holding shares in the companies, but after the Kreuger Crash a law allowed the banks to set up closed end investment funds (CEIFs), which were owned by the banks' shareholders (Högfeldt, 2005). This was a solution that avoided putting depositors at risk, but at the same time gave the banks a key role as so-called Hausbanken for the companies (Högfeldt, 2005; Stafsudd, 2009). The Swedish ownership model consisted of a family or business group at the top, a CEIF in between and listed firms with dual-class shares at the bottom (Högfeldt, 2005). Many countries had dual-class shares: one study showed that 24 per cent of European firms had dual shares in 2005, while in Sweden the corresponding figure was 62 per cent (Bennedsen and Meisner, 2006; Eklund, 2009).

'The 15 families' became an expression for Sweden's dominating business families. There were actually three family and business groups, namely Handelsbanken, Skandinaviska Banken and the Wallenbergs with Stockholms Enskilda Bank, which came to control the lion's share of the companies noted on the Stockholm stock exchange. They controlled companies that accounted for two thirds of employment, sales and total assets of the 270 largest corporations in Sweden (Folster and Peltzman, 1997). The Wallenberg sphere was the most dominant: in 1998, it 'controlled – directly and indirectly – about 42 per cent of total market capitalisation of the Stockholm Stock

Exchange, but held only 1 per cent of capital' (Schnyder, 2012b: 1440).

An important dimension of the ownership model is that it laid the ground for close cooperation between business and different parts of the government, like public utilities, to develop business and secure innovation. This was common in western countries in the post-war period, where governments 'bestow[ed] favours on large firms, especially national champions' (Fear, 1997). Many of the 'Wallenberg-companies', such as Ericsson, Asea and Saab, engaged in tight cooperation with Swedish authorities based on public technology procurement (Carlsson, 1997; Fridlund, 1999, 2000a, 2000b; Christensen, 2021a). These technologies and innovations were the foundations for these companies' foreign direct investments abroad, not least in Norway, to which we will turn now.

Norway: historical background for state ownership

Norway falling behind after 1870

Norway was better suited to the liberal era prior to 1870 than to organized capitalism under the second Industrial Revolution. Owing to its shipping and export industries, it was leaning towards Britain and was more influenced by Adam Smith's liberal ideas than Sweden was (Heckscher, 1953; Grove, 2002; Munthe, 2005). It was also more geared towards transactions than manufacturing, which partly explained why a technical university was not established until 1910 (Hanisch and Lange, 1985; Sejersted, 2011; Berg, 2020). Sejersted (1993: 171) emphasizes that Norway lacked a 'strong major industrial and financial bourgeoisie', like the Wallenbergs and strong investment banks. Furthermore, he claims that Norwegian elites lacked legitimacy to play the role of national strategists and attributed this to an egalitarian norm structure.

Sandvik (2010: 390) is in line with Sejersted, claiming that it was an 'almost instinctive fear of economic concentrations of power' in Norway. This partly explains why most large companies in Norway in around 1900 were established by foreigners (Christensen, 2021a). Shortly after the dissolution of the union in 1905, Marcus Wallenberg (1864–1943) stated that Sweden ought to reconquer Norway by peaceful means, particularly by foreign direct investment (Affärsvärlden, 1905). The Wallenbergs became among the largest owners in Norwegian industry during the 20th century, for instance in the mining company Orkla in 1905, with the family becoming a large and influential shareholder (Bergh et al, 2004). Marcus Wallenberg cooperated with the Norwegian entrepreneur Sam Eyde in setting up Elkem in 1904 (Electro-Chemical) and Norsk Hydro in 1905 (Andersen, 2005). The family also invested in other projects related to hydro power, partly motivated by exporting electronic technical equipment from ASEA. The foreign capital that was attracted to Norwegian natural resources 'motivated a number of concession laws regulating the ownership of natural resources' (Lie, 2016: 910). Sweden also introduced a law in 1916 that restricted foreign ownership in companies owning natural resources (Henrekson and Jakobsson, 2005). These laws were important to maintain national control; this provided legitimacy that was important in the process of industrial expansion (Sejersted, 1993).

As the interwar crisis led to a consolidation of Swedish ownership and industry, the opposite happened in Norway; banks, companies and families struggled (Sogner and Christensen, 2001; Sogner, 2002; Knutsen, 2007, 2020), and many companies were sold abroad (Hodne, 1981). The Wallenbergs fastened their grip on the electro-technical industry in Norway, as ASEA and Ericsson took over struggling Norwegian companies (Christensen, 2014). In the mid-1930s, there was a class compromise in Norway, encompassing both politics and industrial relations. It was not necessary, however, to forge a compromise on ownership, as there were few large companies that encountered the problem of ownership and control. Economic growth in Norway from the mid-1930s has actually been attributed to a Schumpeterian 'growth through crisis' in small companies (Sejersted, 1982), where a 'swarm of new, small enterprises took over as driving forces' (Lange, 2015).

The Norwegian mindset during most of the 20th century involved the exploitation of natural resources for exports. Thus, many saw a future for large-scale industry based on hydro power. Several projects were considered in the interwar period; but the resistance to big business was significant, and many wanted to allocate electrical power to small businesses and civilians before large businesses (Wicken, 1992; Thue, 2006). This opposition was stimulated by the fact that some companies that had been set up in relation to newly erected power stations went bankrupt, leaving local communities without an economic basis. The Second World War was an important stimulus for large-scale industries, as Nazi Germany made big investments in power stations and also in factories that manufactured light metals for the Luftwaffe (Frøland and Kobberrød, 2009; Andersen and Storeide, 2016), the largest being an aluminium plant in Årdal. Norsk Hydro was also involved in the plans, both of which led to state ownership after the war.

State ownership after the Second World War

The state became owner or part-owner of many companies after the war, particularly in the fields of fisheries, electronics and mining, and of large companies based on hydro-electric power (Grønlie, 1992). One of these was Norsk Hydro, which stood out in three major ways. First, the government became owner after a dramatic war settlement, an integral part of which was well-founded allegations of collaboration between Hydro and the German armament industry (Christensen, 1999; Andersen and Storeide, 2016). The government attained 47 per cent of the shares in Hydro and the former French owners kept around 35 per cent. Second, unlike the case with many of the other state-owned companies, the government could have sold their Hydro shares for a decent price on the market. The Labour government did not want to do this, as they wanted to secure national ownership of the company. There was a campaign to let private investors increase their ownership in Hydro at the expense of the state, but the government declined, arguing that in order for their preferred national control to come about it was essential that the largest owner of Hydro was Norwegian (Christensen, 2003).

Third, Hydro retained its private identity and method of operation as a public listed company. The state respected the management's overarching goal of generating a profit for their shareholders and the government respected the interests of the minority shareholders. This came to be known as the Hydro model (Christensen, 1997, 2003, 2018; Grønlie, 2006). It fostered managerial capitalism, where the manager had close contact with key representatives from the government (Christensen, 1997). This dealt with capital requirements, the lease of hydro power, research, sensitive products such as heavy water and magnesium, and, later on, oil. Even though the state was passive as an owner, it secured national ownership; this provided the company with a legitimacy that paved the way for industrial expansion (Christensen, 1997). Hydro was prioritized by the Labour government in terms of water power and scarce necessities, and stimulated investment by way of favourable depreciation rules. Thus, Hydro's production of fertilizer multiplied during the first decades after the war. In the 1960s it started to produce aluminium, and it then became involved in the oil and gas industry. Hydro became the largest company in Norway, and until 2000 it was the largest company listed on the Oslo Stock Exchange, accounting for as much as 30 per cent of the total market capitalization (NTB, 1994).

The Hydro model was very different from companies where the government owned all the shares. These were established to fulfil objectives such as employment, regional policies and the exploitation of natural resources. Profitability was not a goal in and of itself, but a means to an end: this meant that other interests superseded the profit objective. Lie (2016: 61) has described how trade unions and local politicians in Årdal visited decision makers in Oslo to prevent 'cost cuts, downsizings or shutdowns' and thus contributed to 'weakening the decision centres that were working for efficient and rational operations'.

After oil was discovered in the North Sea in 1969, Statoil (now Equinor) was established, with the ambition to develop an integrated company that could match the multinational oil companies in terms of industrial and technological insight. Moreover, Statoil was to be used as a tool of industrial policy, aiding the development of a Norwegian supplier industry. The exploitation of natural resources, in the form of water power, had induced the need for national ownership and control in the post-war years. This dimension was only reinforced with the discovery of oil. Statoil was granted beneficial political and economic terms for its first ten years of existence.

The nationalistic petroleum policy was stimulated by political circumstances. The European Community referendum, the oil crisis and the economic crisis in the 1970s created 'an ideal climate for ambitious industry politicians' (Grønlie, 1995: 118). The phenomenon was far from uniquely Norwegian; several European governments practised an ambitious industrial policy with a strong element of state ownership (Foreman-Peck and Federico, 1999; Bohlin, 2014). There was strengthened optimism from the Labour party regarding state ownership and ambitious industrial policies. This was combined with a point made earlier: that some companies and parts of the state apparatus were vulnerable to pressure from stakeholders. This included pressure from employees or from powerful industrial players who were more interested in further refining natural resources than assessing financial risk. The result was that many companies faced big financial losses in the 1970s (Byrkjeland and Langeland, 2000; Lie et al, 2014; Christensen, 2018).

Liberalization and embracing of the Hydro model

By the end of the 1970s, partly owing to problems with 100 per cent state-owned companies, the Labour party moved in a liberal economic direction in which 'the primary focus was that business and industry should be profitable' (Fossen, 2013: 26). The Conservatives' prime minister from 1981 had always been sceptic of Statoil's dominant role, claiming it was 'a combination of business, administration, political agency and propaganda machine' (Willoch, 2002: 432–3; Aven, 2014: 1). The Conservatives stripped Statoil of its privileges, and awarded Norsk Hydro operatorship in the North Sea, thus turning it into a fully integrated oil company. Moreover, the conservatives also let Hydro take over the 100 per cent state-owned aluminium company, Årdal, in 1986. In doing this, the conservatives embraced the Hydro model. Furthermore, Statoil and other state companies experienced industrial scandals and overruns in the 1980s. The Conservative leader saw the Hydro model, with its private owners and market monitoring, as a suitable vaccine 'against the disease that, based on experience, afflicts pure state companies' (Willoch, 1986). Another Conservative noted that 'the Hydro model [was] in fact an excellent way for the state to contribute long-term capital', not least because 'the company's performance is constantly measured in the share market through the fact that it is listed on the stock exchange' (*Bergens Tidende*, 1995).

Hence, the Hydro model was accepted by most political parties, and this formed the basis for increasing state ownership in listed companies in Norway in the 1990s (see Table 4.1). The former defence contractor Kongsberg was partly privatized and listed, with the government keeping a 50 per cent share. After the bank crises in Norway in the early 1990s, the government held a stake in several banks and kept a 33 per cent stake in DnB to secure Norwegian ownership in one large bank. In the year 2000, Statoil and the old telecoms operator Telenor were partly privatized and listed. A key argument for the listing of Statoil was to attain market monitoring of the company (Ministry of Petroleum and Energy, 2000). In 2004, Norsk Hydro demerged its fertilizer business, now called Yara. In 2007, Statoil took over Norsk Hydro's oil and gas business; thus Norsk Hydro is at present an aluminium company. At the turn of the century, the Progressive party also supported state ownership, arguing that it made no sense to sell and put money in the Petroleum fund (Christensen, 2018).

Table 4.1: State ownership in companies on the Oslo Stock Exchange (OSE), 8 February 2021

Millions of Norwegian kroner	Market value	State's share	Market value state's share	Share of state ownership
Listed companies				
1. Equinor	510,805	67%	342,239	55%
2. Telenor	201,172	54%	108,633	17%
3. DnB	265,887	34%	90,402	14%
4. Norsk Hydro	83,649	34%	28,441	5%
5. Yara International	111,516	36%	40,146	6%
6. Kongsberg Gruppen ASA	30,598	50%	15,299	2%
Sum	1,203,627		625,160	99%

Note:

Market value on Oslo Stock Exchange (OSE) 2 957 729

State owns 21 per cent of the values at OSE directly

State controls companies which account for 41 per cent of the values at OSE.

Source: Oslobørs (2021a, 2021b)

The state ownership model became a true compromise, with those who were sceptical to a strong state emphasizing that Telenor and Statoil were privatized. Others saw this as a way to ensure that the state had an important role and retains control (Christensen, 2018). Herein lay the background for broad political support.

The next section compares different features of the state ownership in Norway according to the Hydro model, and the Swedish model of family/business group associated with a bank, using a CEIF, which owns A-shares with voting rights in listed firms.

Comparing ownership models of Norway and Sweden

It has been suggested that historical accidents play a role in the forming of corporate governance systems (Morck and Steier, 2007). This applies to both Norway and Sweden. The Swedish model was a result of an economic crisis in the 1920s and 1930s, and the Norwegian model was a result of Norsk Hydro's collaboration with the Germans during the Second World War. Still, it was no coincidence that the Swedish and Norwegian national champions came under national control; this was a favoured solution. Hence, this is an example of how influential groups in societies can exploit crises and historical fluctuations, and cement situations that appear beneficial.

Collaboration between business and Social Democrats

Both models were sanctioned by the Social Democrats and laid the foundation for close cooperation between the companies and the government for the next decades. The Social Democrats did not seek to abandon private ownership, but aimed to make sure that the companies delivered the goods in terms of growth and employment. Moreover, a key political goal for the Social Democrats in both countries was to gain more influence and control over the economy. There was therefore close cooperation between business and government in both countries (Barkin, 1968).[1] This cooperation was induced by the experience of the Second World War and of the Cold War. This kind of cohesion has been more typical in small countries, and it is also reflected in the Nordic Welfare model (David and Mach, 2003). Notwithstanding this, the cooperation reflected a social contract that also existed in many large countries, including the US (Reich, 2007). Still, the Wallenbergs' position was unique: Olsson has claimed that they 'acted at a middle level – a "meso level" – between the private enterprise at the micro level and the national macro level' (Olsson, 1986: 263; Sejersted, 2011: 242). Norway had nothing like this. Moreover, the Swedish ownership model included most of the large companies in Sweden, and was thus important for the relationship with the unions. This was not the case in Norway, even after the Hydro model became the norm for state ownership.

National ownership and control

Cooperation between the government and business was aimed at industrial expansion and innovation. In Sweden, many of the Wallenberg companies benefited from public procurement of technology (Carlsson, 1997; Fridlund, 1999; Christensen, 2021a). Thus, the Swedish policy was aimed at stimulating user–producer relations, which would foster innovation and competitive industries Lundvall, 1985; Dahmén, 1988; Taalbi, 2017). It was partly inspired by the Schumpeterian economist Erik Dahmén's (1988) work on development blocks. Marcus Wallenberg (1899–1982) hired the young Dahmén to work at Stockholms Enskilda Bank in 1951. They became friends and met weekly to discuss industrial development and innovation, sometimes accompanied by the Social Democrat minister of finance, Gunnar Sträng (Olsson, 2013). The companies that were involved in this, cooperating with the government, had to be under national ownership and control. If the loyalty and future of the companies was unclear, it was meaningless for the government to engage in fostering innovation and technological development with a long-term perspective.

In Norway, the relationship between state and industry was more about facilitating industrial expansion based on natural resources than on fostering innovation and technological development. A common economic reasoning in Norway was to secure the resource rent, either from waterfalls or from petroleum resources (Claes, 2003; Ministry of Trade, 2014). Natural resources were also important in Swedish business, and large parts of Norwegian business were technology and knowledge intensive, such as the oil business and Kongsberg. Still, there was a difference: national ownership and control in Sweden was more about stimulating and protecting innovation and technology, while in Norway it was more about legitimizing industrial expansion based on natural resources and comparative advantages.

International agreements related to the World Trade Organization and the European Union (EU) has limited the scope for such cooperation today, but they were important for the historical origin of the ownership models. Today, the government argues that national ownership will secure potential 'positive spill-over effects of maintaining head office' in Norway (Ministry of Trade, 2020a). The wish for national ownership has always been explicit regarding Norwegian state ownership, but is more implicit in the Swedish ownership model. Still, a public inquiry from 1986 stated that dual-class shares could be useful to ascertain that 'Swedish firms remain controlled by Swedish interests' (SOU, 1986: 23; Högfeldt, 2005: 565). During the 1980s, 30–40 per cent of the companies listed on the Stockholm Stock Exchange used dual-class shares (Henrekson and Jakobsson, 2012). The importance of national ownership and control was also evident when ASEA merged with Brown Boveri to form ABB. The only comment from the Swedish cabinet was that it demanded that the Swedes (the Wallenbergs) maintained 50 per cent ownership and voting rights in the new company (Christensen and Rinde, 2009).

It may seem to be a paradox that state ownership in Norway attained cross-party support from the 1990s and that calls for national ownership became more explicit in Sweden from the 1980s, given that liberalization and globalization were strengthened at the time. There is, however, a logic to this. With European integration and the abolishment of currency controls, it was more difficult to protect ownership in domestic companies. A core idea behind the EU was the facilitation of mergers and acquisitions to create European champions that could compete with US and Japanese companies (Christensen, 2006). As Norway joined the European Economic Area (EEA), state ownership was the only accepted means to protect national ownership.[2] The Wallenbergs and the Social Democrats lobbied the EU to maintain the system with dual-class shares in order to protect national ownership (Högfeldt, 2005).

Active ownership

The most explicit argument for the Swedish ownership model in general, and for dual-class shares in particular, is that it secures stable and knowledgeable management in the companies, thus allowing active ownership. First, it reduces the agency problem, in as much as large owners have incentives to monitor management effectively (SOU, 1986, 1988). Institutional owners can aim to minimize agency costs by using incentives, and perform active financial ownership, such as stipulating requirements for profitability, returns, capital structure and transparency. Concentrated ownership allows for a more direct active ownership, sometimes called industrial ownership: owners may have opinions about markets, technology, vertical integration and so on (Reve, 2013), thus providing the company with valuable knowledge (Grünfeld, 2010). The traditional agency problem is shirking, as it does not address poor and bad management; industrial owners can deal with both shirking and bad management (Gourevitch, 2002; Roe, 2003). Active ownership does not imply weak managers: 'strong presidents have always been a part of the Wallenberg philosophy of management' says Glete (1993: 42), 'but their power has been derived from the dominating owner, not from their position in the managerial hierarchy'. This is why they were often recruited from other companies.

The Wallenbergs handled three electro-technical companies, ASEA (ABB), Ericsson and Electrolux, as an entity, and moved managers and business around them (Glete, 1993; Collin, 1998; Christensen and Rinde, 2009). A classic argument for business groups is that they allow deficiencies in the market for labour or for managers to be handled (Collin, 1998). This is also an argument for conglomerates, as they create an internal market for leaders. Norsk Hydro was a conglomerate before it was split up after 2004. Managers there were often shifted through different divisions, which had different features and challenges, in order to provide them with broader experience and to test them (Lie, 2005). Moreover, the company provided an important pool of managers, not least for other Norwegian companies that needed managers with international experience.

The role of the Hausbanken in Sweden, and later the CEIFs, can also be seen as part of active ownership, in as much as companies used the financial and industrial expertise of the banks and CEIFs for their own purpose (Lindgren, 1994). The banks and CEIFs were staffed by former managers and board members who contributed their expertise; they became an intelligence centre for the companies (Lindgren, 1994). The industrial structure was a key issue, not least as increasing globalization demanded economies of scale. There were attempts in Norway to create a holding model for state-owned companies in the early 1970s, which would play a similar role as the banks and CEIF in Sweden, but this did not materialize, partly because Norsk Hydro protested fiercely – as it insisted on its private identity and did not want to be grouped with 100 per cent-owned companies (Tveite, 1995; Christensen, 2003).

Monitoring and free-riding

The state-owned companies lack strong owners and an active ownership. Moreover, their structure leads to managerial capitalism and high agency costs (Jakobsen et al, 2001; Reve et al, 2001; Christensen, 2003; Bøhren, 2011). Bøhren (2006: 1) has said that 'good ownership is characterized by direct, long-term and involved owners'. This is something the state never can aspire to as an owner. Thus, the lack of owners who play such a role has been accentuated as a problem in Norway for many years. 'Norwegian industry has not had a Wallenberg' complained a commentator in 1989, 'Swedes are professionals. Strategies are drawn up, and followed', unlike short-sighted Norwegians (Aftenposten, 1989). Still, the market monitoring of the state-owned companies has been the key argument for part-privatizing companies. In a sense, the Norwegian state relies on minority shareholders' willingness to monitor the state-owned companies. In a sense the state free-rides the minority shareholders. This is the opposite of the concentrated ownership in Sweden: where the minority investors rely on, in a sense, a free-ride, the controlling owners' are willing and able to monitor the companies.

The present standing of the ownership model

In the wake of the economic crises of around 1990, the Swedish (ownership) model came under increased criticism. Several announced the 'failure' or 'death' of the Swedish model, including the ownership model (Schnyder, 2012a). First, liberalization and deregulation, such as a new tax regime, have challenged the model. This has led to an increase in institutional and foreign ownership (Högfeldt, 2005). Second, the Wallenbergs have been accused of distancing themselves from the social democrats and the union (Schnyder and Jackson, 2013). Furthermore, the model has been attacked by business leaders and scholars inspired by the Anglo-Saxon corporate governance school. Some claim that companies with dual-class shares make poorer investments (Eklund and Wiberg, 2006) and that there is a discount on the companies' market value (Högfeldt, 2005). Others insist that the model has pacified the financial markets, protected incumbents and hampered entrepreneurship (Magnus and Jakobsson, 2001; Högfeldt, 2005).

This critique intensified after ABB and Ericsson experienced a spectacular drop in their market value around the turn of the century (Carlsson and Nachemson-Ekwall, 2003; Christensen and Rinde, 2009). A result was that institutional owners demanded reform of the dual-class share system, claiming that the companies' problems did not hurt the Wallenbergs enough to motivate necessary change (Engzell-Larsson, 2017). The critics were met halfway: the voting differentiation was reduced from 1:1,000 to 1:10 in Ericsson and abolished altogether in many other companies. The chief executive officer (CEO) of ABB, Percy Barnevik, was lauded as a European Jack Welch, as someone who had introduced shareholder value to Sweden. He took over as CEO of Investor, Wallenberg's CEIF, to balance traditional 'Family's Values With Shareholder Values' (*WSJ*, 1998). He had to resign from Investor in disgrace after a pension scandal in 2003. The troubles at ABB and Ericsson led to much soul-searching about the value of the Swedish ownership model. All these troubles endangered the legitimacy and political efficiency of the Swedish ownership model.

There have been scandals related to the state ownership in Norway as well, but none of the same magnitude. Traditionally, representatives from business have been critical of state ownership. A new trend appeared in the 1990s, namely that leading players in business and industry came forward to praise and support the state ownership of listed companies. A former chairman of Hydro's board, said in 1997 that a long-term and major owner such as the state gave Hydro considerable stability. The Statoil chief financial officer spoke warmly of the Hydro model in 2002 and argued that since the state had a long-term industrial perspective it could be a guarantee against 'Enron conditions' (*Aftenposten*, 2002). Others accentuated that state ownership curbs short-termism and quarterly capitalism (Roland, 2020). The former CEO of Statoil, Harald Norvik, stated in 2014 that the 'state ownership in Norway is remarkably successful' and that the state has exercised exemplary ownership (*Aftenposten*, 2014).

The Norwegian economy has had unprecedented growth since 1993, so there is less fertile ground for criticism. The petroleum resources were vital, but Norwegian business and productivity were strong regardless of this (Fagerberg, 2009). An example is the former public telephone operator, Telenor, which has developed successfully and is on a par with Ericsson in market value (Christensen, 2021b). Many commentators perceived that Norway did not have any choice if it wanted to maintain national ownership and control over key companies. Furthermore, state ownership seemed less controversial in view of the increase in institutional ownership. The latter contributed to an increased interest in corporate governance in the Western world and Norway (Lie et al, 2014; Cheffins, 2015). Corporate governance principles were designed for institutional owners, performing active financial ownership but passive industrial ownership. These principles have become normative for the state's exercise of ownership and are stipulated in the state's '10 principles for good ownership' (Ministry of Industry and Trade, 2002; Ministry of Trade, 2014). It has also helped that the Ministry of Trade and Industry has invested in its Ownership department since the early 2000s and has professionalized ownership (Bråthen, 2018). State ownership therefore appears to be less controversial under Anglo-Saxon hegemony.

Conclusions

Roe has interpreted concentrated ownership as a means to balance stakeholder claims emanating from countries with strong social democratic norms (Roe, 2003). He has received some support with regard to Sweden (Henrekson and Jakobsson, 2008). Still, Roe's argument that concentrated ownership was necessary to reduce agency costs is anachronistic when applied to the post-war environment when there has been close cooperation between the Social Democrats and business. It is also important to bear in mind that stakeholders and representatives from the labour movement preferred strong owners with the discretion to take decisions. A government report stated that 'the presence of a strong owner can therefore facilitate the union work' (SOU, 1986; Reiter, 2003: 108). Moreover, it is misleading to present the companies striving for efficiency from an agency perspective where the ultimate goal was to reward shareholders. The overall goal was to secure that these exporting companies remained competitive in an international market (Högfeldt, 2005).

Finally, Roe's dichotomy is a blunt instrument: not all Social Democrats were anti-capitalists, and not all shareholders and businesspeople were pro-capitalist. In Norway and Sweden, Social Democrats initiated and orchestrated several market- and shareholder-friendly reforms from the 1980s. Moreover, many business people in Norway and Sweden have opposed an Anglo-Saxon shareholder value norm (Gourevitch, 2002; Schnyder, 2008; Christensen, 2003). This could be because they are protecting their interests and privileges, as Morck and others will have us believe (Morck and Steier, 2007); but it might also be that owners and capitalists are concerned with national interests as well. When the Norwegian stock market experienced a wave of hostile takeovers in the 1980s, for example, the Social Democrats and unions could not care less; it was mainly Conservatives who protested fiercely against predatory capitalism (Christensen, 2003; Christensen and Rinde, 2009).

Roe's theory does not seem relevant for state ownership as it is predicated on the shareholder's quest for value. This might be why his theory has not been applied to Norway. Still, it is useful to explain the development of state ownership in Norway. In the 100 per cent state-owned companies, the top managers were vulnerable to stakeholder claims. It was difficult to push through restructuring and rationalization, as stakeholders could mobilize against it and contact political authorities. The companies also pursued unrealistic and costly industrial ambitions. The success of the Hydro model in the post-war period, on the other hand, can be ascribed to its ability to prioritize cost efficiency and to fend off stakeholder claims. The same goes for the principles of state ownership today: the government laid down that it will not interfere with companies' operations and that it will respect that shareholder value is the dominating guiding principle. Hence, any stakeholder claim is met by this principle. Consequently, Roe's emphasis on the ability to withstand stakeholder claims is pertinent when attempting to understand the considerable state ownership in Norway today.

This chapter also corroborates the importance of nationalism, namely the wish for national ownership and control over the largest companies, in explaining the emergence of the ownership model. More research is needed to explain and understand why national ownership and control have been desired in most countries, and how this has affected the emergence of different ownership models and corporate governance systems. Roe's argument regarding companies' ability to withstand stakeholder claims has something to it. Still, the agency theory seems anachronistic in attempting to explain the origins of the ownership model, and his emphasis on the strength on social democracy is too divisive. The element of industrial nationalism needs to be included. The Scandinavian ownership model suggests that this would refine and strengthen Roe's political argument.

Finally, it is striking that the corporate governance literature does not recognize the desire for active ownership. This was a prominent argument for the Swedish ownership model and an argument against the Norwegian model. There are probably several reasons why national ownership and active ownership is not valued in the literature. One reason might be that it leads to the concentration of power, which in many countries inevitably leads to misuse of that power. Hence, maybe the high level of trust and transparency in Sweden allows for such concentration of power without the danger of corruption.

Still, after the Anglo-Saxon corporate governance system and values came to dominate in Europe, fuelled by an increase in institutional ownership, it has led to more criticism of and scepticism towards the Swedish ownership model. Norwegian state ownership, on the other hand, has proved more acceptable, as it resembles institutional ownership.

Notes

[1] In Norway it has been called top-level partnership; in Sweden it was called the Harpsund democracy, referring to the estate of the prime minister where he often met representatives from industry and other organizations. 'The four men usually considered to be the key figures in this junta of understanding are the Prime Minister, the Presidents of LO (labour union) and SAF and a Wallenberg' (Barkin, 1968; Bull, 1982).

[2] The EEA Agreement was made between Norway – along with Iceland and Liechtenstein – and the EU to provide these countries with access to the 'internal market'. It stipulates that they must adopt most EU legislation concerning the single market.

References

Affärsvärlden (1905) 'Emissionsbanker', 21 December.

Aftenposten (1989) 'Norge savner industrihistorie', 6 January.

Aftenposten (2002) 'Staten forsikring mot norsk Enron', 19 August.

Aftenposten (2014) 'Det statlige eierskapet i Norge er oppsiktsvekkende vellykket', 7 November.

Andersen, K.G. (2005) *Flaggskip i Fremmed Eie: Hydro 1905–1945*, Oslo: Pax forlag.

Andersen, K.G. and Storeide, A.H. (2016) 'A quest for diversification? Norsk Hydro, IG Farben, and the German Light Metal Programme', in H.I.M. Frøland and J. Scherner (eds) *Industrial Collaboration in Nazi-Occupied Europe*, London: Palgrave, pp 299–329.

Angell, S.I. (2002) *Den Svenske Modellen og det Norske Systemet: Tilhøvet Mellom Modernisering og Identitetsdanning i Sverige og Noreg ved Overgangen til det 20. hundreåret*, Oslo: Samlaget.

Aven, H.B. (2014) *Høgres Syn på Statleg Eigarskap i Norsk Oljeverksemd 1970– 1984*, Oslo: Universitetet i Oslo.

Barkin, K.D. (1975) 'Organized capitalism', *The Journal of Modern History*, 47(1): 125–9.

Barkin, S. (1968) ' "Fleisher, Frederic:" the new Sweden: the challenge of a disciplined democracy' (Book Review). *Journal of Economic Issues*, 2: 246.

Bennedsen, M. and Meisner, K. (2006) 'The principle of proportionality: separating the impact of dual class shares, pyramids and cross-ownership on firm value across legal regimes in Western Europe', *Center for Industrial Economics Discussion Papers*, University of Copenhagen.

Berg, R. (2020) 'Norway's foreign politics during the union with Sweden, 1814–1905: a reconsideration', *Diplomacy & Statecraft*, 31(1): 1–21.

Bergens Tidende (1995) 'Frykter maktkonsentrasjonen', 1 June.

Bergh, T., Espeli, H. and Sogner, K. (2004) *Brytningstider Storselskapet Orkla 1654–2004*, Oslo: Orion.

Berle, A. and Means, G. (1932) *The Modern Corporation and Private Property*, New York: Harcourt, Brace and World.

Bohlin, J. (2014) 'Swedish industrial policy: from general policies to crisis management, 1950–1980', in C.N.A. Grabas and A. Nützenadel (eds) *Industrial Policy in Europe after 1945: Wealth, Power and Economic Development in the Cold War*, Basingstoke: Palgrave Macmillan, pp 113–33.

Bøhren, Ø. (2006) 'Eierskap og lønnsomhet', *Praktisk Økonomi and Finans*, 22(3): 91–103.

Bøhren, Ø. (2011) '*Eierne, styret og ledelsen: Corporate governance i Norge*', Bergen: Fagbokforl.

Bråthen, T. (2018) 'Legal challenges of state ownership', in A. Sasson (ed) *At the Forefront, Looking Ahead: Research-Based Answers to Contemporary Uncertainties of Management*, Oslo: Universitetsforlaget, pp 119–33.

Bull, E. (1982) *Norgeshistorien etter 1945*, Oslo: Cappelen.

Byrkjeland, M. and Langeland, O. (2000) *Statlig Eierskap i Norge 1945–2000*, Oslo: Fafo-notat.

Carlsson, B. (1997) 'On and off the beaten path: the evolution of four technological systems in Sweden', *International Journal of Industrial Organization*, 15: 775–99.

Carlsson, B. and Nachemson-Ekwall, S. (2003) *Dangerous Management – The History of the Crash of ABB.*, Stockholm: Ekerlids Förlag.

Cheffins, B.R. (2015) 'Corporate governance since the managerial capitalism era', *Business History Review*, 89: 717–44.

Christensen, S.A. (1997) *Statens Forhold til Norsk Hydro 1945–1952* (Unpublished MA thesis, University of Oslo).

Christensen, S.A. (1999) *Hydromodellens Opprinnelse: Oppgjøret om Norsk Hydro etter Andre Verdenskrig*, Sandvika: Handelshøyskolen BI.

Christensen, S.A. (2003) 'Statlig eierskap og nasjonal kontroll', in S.A. Christensen, H. Esepli, E. Larsen and K. Sogner (eds) *Kapitalistisk Demokrati?: Norsk Næringsliv Gjennom 100 År*, Oslo: Gyldendal Akademisk, pp 67–148.

Christensen, S.A. (2006) *Switching Relations: The Rise and Fall of the Norwegian Telecom Industry* (PhD thesis, Norwegian School of Management).

Christensen, S.A. (2014) 'Globaliseringens fortellinger – ABB Norges konsernansvar for olje- og gassvirksomhet', in E.E.A. Ekberg (ed) *Næringsliv Og Historie*, Oslo: Pax, pp 61–92.

Christensen, S.A. (2018) 'The capitalist state or the state as private owner', in A. Sasson (ed) *At the Forefront, Looking Ahead*, Oslo: Universitetsforlaget, pp 134–58.

Christensen, S.A. (2021a) 'Dubrowka – a free-standing company from a Norwegian family-network capitalism', *Scandinavian Economic History Review*, 69(1): 63–82.

Christensen, S.A. (2021b) 'A narrative approach to corporate relations: the historical background for the success of Telenor', *Enterprise & Society*.

Christensen, S.A. and Rinde, H. (2009) *Nasjonale Utlendinger: ABB i Norge 1880–2010*, Oslo: Gyldendal akademisk.

Claes, D.H. (2003) 'Globalization and state oil companies: the case of Statoil', *The Journal of Energy and Development*, 29: 43–64.

Collin, S.O. (1998)'Why are these islands of conscious power found in the ocean of ownership? Institutional and governance hypotheses explaining the existence of business groups in Sweden', *Journal of Management Studies*, 35: 719–46.

Dahmén, E. (1988) '"Development blocks" in industrial economics', *Scandinavian Economic History Review*, 36: 3–14.

David, T. and Mach, A. (2003) 'The specificity of corporate governance in small states: institutionalization and questioning of ownership restrictions in Switzerland and Sweden', in M. Federowicz and R.V. Aguilera (eds) *Corporate Governance in a Changing Economic and Political Environment: Trajectories of Institutional Change*, London: Palgrave Macmillan, pp 220–46.

Eklund, J. and Wiberg, D. (2006) 'A-mot B-laget: En match för den svenska ägarmodellen', *Ekonomisk Debatt, Årg*, 34: 17–26.

Eklund, J.E. (2009) 'Corporate governance and investments in Scandinavia-ownership concentration and dual-class equity structure', in P.-O.M. Bjuggen and C. Dennis (eds) *The Modern Firm, Corporate Governance and Investment*, Cheltenham: Edward Elgar, pp 139–67.

Engzell-Larsson, L. (2017) 'Kräv mer av de röststarka ägarna', *Dagens Industri*, 6 June.

Fagerberg, J., Mowery, D. and Verspagen, B. (eds) (2009) *Innovation, Path Dependency, and Policy: The Norwegian Case*, Oxford: Oxford University Press.

Fear, J.R. (1997) 'Constructing big business: the cultural concept of the firm', in A.A. Chandler, F. Amatori and T. Hikino (eds) *Big Business and the Wealth of Nations*, Cambridge: Cambridge University Press, pp 546–74.

Fellman, S., Iversen, M., Sjögren, H. and Thue, L. (2008) *Creating Nordic Capitalism: The Business History of a Competitive Periphery*, Basingstoke: Palgrave Macmillan.

Folster, S. and Peltzman, S. (1997) 'The social costs of regulation and lack of competition in Sweden: a summary', in R.B.T. Freeman, R. Topel and B. Swedeborg (eds) *The Welfare State in Transition: Reforming the Swedish Model*, Chicago: University of Chicago Press, pp 315–52.

Foreman-Peck, J. and Federico, G. (1999) *European Industrial Policy: The Twentieth-Century Experience*, Oxford: Oxford University Press.

Fossen, E. (2013) *Statens Industripolitikk På 1980 – Tallet: Mot en Mer Markedsliberal Industripolitikk i Norge*, Oslo: Master.

Fridlund, M. (1997) 'Nationsbyggandets verktyg: Teknisk förändring i nationalismens teori och praktik', in B. Lindberg (ed) *Nationalism: En Kursredovisning Från Avdelningen För Idéhistoria Vid Stockholms Universitet, Idéhistoriska Uppsatser*, Stockholm: Stockholm University Press.

Fridlund, M. (1999) *Den Gemensamma Utvecklingen* (Unpublished PhD thesis, KTH: Institutionen för Produktionssystem).

Fridlund, M. (2000a) 'Procuring products and power: developing international competitiveness in Swedish electrotechnology and electric power', in C. Edquist, L. Hommen and L. Tsipouri (eds) *Public Technology Procurement and Innovation*, New York: Springer, pp 99–120.

Fridlund, M. (2000b) 'Switching relations and trajectories: the development procurement of the Axe Swedish switching technology', in C. Edquist, L. Hommen and L. Tsipouri (eds) *Public Technology Procurement and Innovation*, New York: Springer, pp 143–65.

Frøland, H.O. and Kobberrød, J.T. (2009) 'The Norwegian contribution to Göring's megalomania. Norway's aluminium industry during World War II', *Cahiers d'Histoire de l'Aluminium*, 42–3: 130–47.

Glete, J. (1978) 'The Kreuger group and the crisis on the Swedish stock market', *Scandinavian Journal of History*, 3: 251–72.

Glete, J. (1993) 'Swedish managerial capitalism: did it ever become ascendant?', *Business History*, 35(2): 99–110.

Gourevitch, P.A. (2002) 'The politics of corporate governance regulation', *Yale Law Journal*, 112: 1829.

Grønlie, T. (1989) *Statsdrift: Staten som Industrieier i Norge 1945–1963*, Oslo: Tano.

Grønlie, T. (1992) 'Establishment of state-owned industrial enterprises: Norway in a West European context', *Scandinavian Journal of History*, 17: 209–25.

Grønlie, T. (1995) 'Styrenes styring-et mangfold av styreroller', in T. Grønlie and Ø.N. Grøndahl (eds) *Fristillingens Grenser: Statsaksjeselskapet– Styringsproblemer og Reformprosesser Gjennom*.

Grønlie, T. (2006) 'Hydro-modellen', *Nytt Norsk Tidsskrift*, 23: 159–64.

Grove, K. (2002) 'Mellom "non-intervention" og "samfundsvillie". Statleg og kommunal regulering av økonomisk verksemd i Norge på 1800 – talet', *Notat Stein Rokkan senter for Flerfaglige Samfunnsstudier*, Bergen: Stein Rokkan Senter for Flerfaglige Samfunnsstudier.

Grünfeld, L.A. (2010) *Kompetent Kapital og Smart Arbeidskraft*, Oslo: Menon.

Hanisch, T.J. and Lange, E. (1985) *Vitenskap for Industrien: NTH-En Høyskole i Utvikling Gjennom 75 År*, Oslo: Universitetsforlaget.

Heckscher, E.F. (1953) 'A survey of economic thought in Sweden, 1875–1950', *Scandinavian Economic History Review*, 1(1): 105–25.

Henrekson, M. and Jakobsson, U. (2005) 'The Swedish model of corporate ownership and control in transition', in H. Huizinga and L. Jonung (eds) *The Internationalisation of Asset Ownership in Europe*, Cambridge: Cambridge University Press, pp 207–46.

Henrekson, M. and Jakobsson, U. (2008) 'Globaliseringen och den svenska ägarmodellen', *Underlagsrapport nr 19 till Globaliseringsrådet*, Stockholm: Globaliseringsrådet.

Henrekson, M. and Jakobsson, U. (2012) 'The Swedish corporate control model: convergence, persistence or decline?', *Corporate Governance: An International Review*, 20: 212–27.

Hodne, F. (1981) *Norges Økonomiske Historie 1815–1970*, Oslo: Cappelen.

Högfeldt, P. (2005) *A History of Corporate Governance around the World: Family Business Groups to Professional Managers*, Chicago: University of Chicago Press.

Jakobsen, E., Goldeng, E. and Reve, T. (2001) 'Eierskap–spiller det noen rolle', in V. Norman, T. Reve and K. Roland (eds) *Rikdommens Problem*, Oslo: Universitetsforlaget, pp 120–46.

Katzenstein, P.J. (1985) *Small States in World Markets: Industrial Policy in Europe*, Ithaca, NY: Cornell University Press.

Kilander, S. (1991) *Den Nya Staten Och Den Gamla: En Studie i Ideologisk Förändring*, Uppsala: Acta Universitatis Upsaliensis.

Knutsen, S. (2007) *Staten og Kapitalen i Det 20. Århundre: Regulering, Kriser og Endring i det Norske Finanssystemet 1900–2005* (Unpublished PhD thesis, University of Oslo).

Knutsen, S. (2020) 'Profitten setter tonen, og investeringene danser deretter', *Historisk tidsskrift*, 98: 230–48.

La Porta, R., Lopez-de-Silanes, F., Shleifer, A. and Vishny, R.W. (1997) 'Legal determinants of external finance', *The Journal of Finance*, 52(3): 1131–50.

Lange, E. (2015) 'Verdenskrise og økonomisk omstilling', University of Oslo [online]. Available from: https://www.norgeshistorie.no/ [Accessed 21 January 2021].

Lekvall, P. (2014) *The Nordic Corporate Governance Model*, Stockholm: SNS, Center for Business and Policy Studies.

Levi-Faur, D. (1997) 'Friedrich List and the political economy of the nation-state', *Review of International Political Economy*, 4(1): 154–78.

Lie, E. (2005) *Oljerikdommer og Internasjonal Ekspansjon: Hydro 1977–2005*, Oslo: Pax Forlag.

Lie, E. (2016) 'Context and contingency: explaining state ownership in Norway', *Enterprise and Society*, 17(4): 904–30.

Lie, E., Myklebust, E. and Norvik, H. (2014) *Staten Som Kapitalist: Rikdom og Eierskap for det 21. Århundre*, Oslo: Pax.

Lindgren, H. (1994) *Aktivt Ägande: Investor under Växlande Konjunkturer*, Stockholm: Institutet för Ekonomisk-Historisk Forskning vid Handelshögsk.

Lundvall, B-A. (1985) 'Product innovation and user-producer interaction', *Industrial Development Research Series No. 31*, Aalborg: Aalborg University Press.

Lüpold, M. and Schnyder, G. (2006) 'Protecting insiders against foreigners? Corporate governance in three small states: Switzerland, Sweden, and the Netherlands, 1900–1960', Helsinki: International Economic History Conference.

Magnus, H. and Jakobsson, U. (2001) 'Where Schumpeter was nearly right – the Swedish model and capitalism, socialism and democracy, *Journal of Evolutionary Economics*, 11(3): 331–58.

McCraw, T.K. (1997) 'Government, big business and the wealth of nations', in A.A. Chandler, F. Amatori and T. Hikino (eds) *Big Business and the Wealth of Nations*, Cambridge: Cambridge University Press, pp 522–45.

Ministry of Petroleum and Energy (2000) 'Ownership of Statoil and future management of the SDFI', in Energy NMOPA (ed) Regjeringen.no., Oslo: Ministry of Petroleum and Energy.

Ministry of Trade, Industry and Fisheries (2014) 'Diverse and value-creating ownership', in Ministry of Trade, IAF (ed) Regjeringen.no., Oslo: Ministry of Petroleum and Energy.

Ministry of Trade, Industry and Fisheries (2020a) 'Why the state is an owner', *Ministry of Trade, Industry and Fisheries* [online]. Available from: https://www.regjeringen.no/en/topics/business-and-industry/state-ownership/hvorfor-staten-eier/id2607021/ [Accessed 22 January 2021].

Ministry of Trade, Industry and Fisheries (2020b) 'The state's ten principles for good corporate governance', in Norwegian Ministry of Trade, IAF (ed) Regjeringen.no., Oslo: Ministry of Petroleum and Energy.

Ministry of Industry and Trade (2002) 'Et mindre og bedre statlig eierskap', in Trade, MOIA (ed) Regjeringen.no., Oslo: Ministry of Industry and Trade.

Morck, R. and Steier, L. (2007) 'The global history of corporate governance: an introduction', in R. Morck (ed) *A History of Corporate Governance Around the World: Family Business Groups to Professional Managers*, Chicago: University of Chicago Press, pp 1–64.

Morck, R., Tian, G. and Yeung, B. (2005) 'Who owns whom? Economic nationalism and family controlled pyramidal groups in Canada', in L. Eden and W. Dobsob (eds) *Governance, Multinationals and Growth*, Cheltenham: Edward Elgar.

Munthe, P. (2005) 'Adam Smiths norske ankerfeste', *Tilbakeblikk På Norsk Pengehistorie*, conference proceeding, pp 103–10.

Musacchio, A. and Turner, J.D. (2013) 'Does the law and finance hypothesis pass the test of history?', *Business History*, 55(4): 524–42.

NTB (Norsk Telegrambyrå, Norwegian News Agency) (1994) 'Indeksfondene til topps med Hydro', 29 July.

Olsson, U. (1986) *Bank, Familj och Företagande: Stockholms Enskilda Bank 1946–1971*, Stockholm: Skandinaviska Enskilda Banken.

Olsson, U. (2013) 'En värdefull berättelse Wallenbergarnas historieprojekt', *Göteborg Papers in Economic History*, Gothenburg University.

Oslobørs (2021a) *Aksjer* [online]. Available from: https://www.oslobors.no/markedsaktivitet [Accessed 8 February 2021]

Oslobørs (2021b) *Hovedindeksen* [online]. Available from: https://www.oslobors.no/markedsaktivitet [Accessed 8 February 2021].

Reich, R. (2007) *Supercapitalism. The Transformation of Business, Democracy and Everyday Life*, New York: Alfred A. Knopf.

Reiter, J. (2003) 'Changing the microfoundations of corporatism: the impact of financial globalisation on Swedish corporate ownership', *New Political Economy*, 8(1): 103–25.

Reve, T. (2013) 'Eierskapsmangfold og verdiskapning', *Statens Eierberetning for 2013*, Oslo: Nærings- og fiskeridepartementet.

Reve, T., Roland, K. and Norman, V. (2001) *Rikdommens Problem: Oljeformue, Eierskap og Fremtidens Pensjoner*, Oslo: Universitetsforlaget.

Robinson, J. (1962) *Economic Philosophy*, Piscataway, NJ: Transaction Publishers.

Roe, M.J. (2000) 'Political preconditions to separating ownership from corporate control', *Stanford Law Review*, 53(3): 539–606.

Roe, M.J. (2003) *Political Determinants of Corporate Governance: Political Context, Corporate Impact*, Oxford: Oxford University Press.

Roland, K. (2020) 'Delprivatiseringen av Statoil var god sosialdemokratisk politikk', *Aftenposten*, 30 April.

Sandvik, P.T. (2010) 'Såpekrigen 1930–31 – lilleborgsaken, venstrestaten og norsk økonomisk nasjonalisme', *Historisk tidsskrift*, 89: 389–424.

Schnyder, G. (2008) 'Does social democracy matter? Corporate governance reforms in Switzerland and Sweden (1980–2005)', Cambridge: Cambridge Centre for Business Research, University of Cambridge. Available from: https://papers.ssrn.com/sol3/papers.cfm?abstract_id=1233194 [Accessed 14 December 2021].

Schnyder, G. (2012a) 'Like a phoenix from the ashes? Reassessing the transformation of the Swedish political economy since the 1970s', *Journal of European Public Policy*, 19(8): 1126–45.

Schnyder, G. (2012b) 'Varieties of insider corporate governance: the determinants of business preferences and corporate governance reform in the Netherlands, Sweden and Switzerland', *Journal of European Public Policy*, 19(9): 1434–51.

Schnyder, G. and Jackson, G. (2013) 'Germany and Sweden in the crisis', in V.A. Schmidt and M. Thatcher (eds) *Resilient Liberalism in Europe's Political Economy*, Cambridge: Cambridge University Press, pp 313–45.

Sejersted, F. (2003a) 'Nationalism in the epoch of organised capitalism – Norway and Sweden choosing different path', in A. Teichova and H. Matis (eds) *Nation, State and the Economy in History*, Cambridge: Cambridge University Press, pp 96–112.

Sejersted, F. (1982) *Vekst Gjennom Krise: Studier i Norsk Teknologihistorie*, Oslo: Universitetsforlaget.

Sejersted, F. (1993) *Demokratisk Kapitalisme*, Oslo: Universitetsforlaget.

Sejersted, F. (2001) 'Capitalism and democracy: a comparison between Norway and Sweden', in S.M. Haldor Byrkjeflot and C. Myrvang (eds) *The Democratic Challenge to Capitalism*, Bergen: Fagbokforlaget, pp 87–119.

Sejersted, F. (2003b) *Sannhet Med Modifikasjoner*, Oslo: Pax.

Sejersted, F. (2011) *The Age of Social Democracy: Norway and Sweden in the Twentieth Century*, Princeton, NJ: Princeton University Press.

Sjögren, H. (2008) 'Welfare capitalism. The Swedish economy 1850–2005', in S. Fellman, M. Iversen, H. Sjögren and L. Thue (eds) *Creating Nordic Capitalism: The Business History of a Competitive Periphery*, Basingstoke: Palgrave Macmillan, pp 24–74.

Sogner, K. (2002) 'Det norske næringsborgerskapet under den andre industrielle revolusjon', *Historisk tidsskrift*, 81: 231–51.

Sogner, K. and Christensen, S.A. (2001) *Plankeadel: Kiær- og Solberg-familien under den 2. industrielle revolusjon,* Oslo: Andresen & Butenschøn for Handelshøyskolen BI.

SOU (1986) 'Aktiers röstvärde. Betänkande av röstvärdeskommittén', Justitie Departementet, Stockholm: Liber.

SOU (1988) 'Ägande och inflytande i svenskt näringsliv Ownership influence in Swedish industry]. Ekonomisk Debatt', Industry, SMO, Stockholm: Swedish Government.

Stafsudd, A. (2009) 'Corporate networks as informal governance mechanisms: a small worlds approach to Sweden', *Corporate Governance: An International Review*, 17(1): 62–76.

Taalbi, J. (2017) 'Development blocks in innovation networks: the Swedish manufacturing industry 1970–2007', *Journal of Evolutionary Economics*, 27: 461–501.

Tanderø, N.P. (1974) *Den Svenske Utfordring: Multinasjonale Selskapers Innflytelse i Norsk Næringsliv: Hvorledes Kan Oljepenger Endre Forholdet?*, Oslo: Bedriftsøkonomens Forlag.

Thomsen, S. (2016a) 'The Nordic corporate governance model', *Management and Organization Review*, 12(1): 189–204.

Thomsen, S. (2016b) 'Nordic corporate governance revisited', *Nordic Journal of Business*, 65(1): 4–12.

Thue, L. (2006) *Statens Kraft 1890–1947: Kraftutbygging og Samfunnsutvikling*, Oslo: Universitetsforlaget.

Tveite, T. (1995) 'Forvaltningsselskap for statsindustri?', in T. Grønlie and G. Øyvind Nordbrønd (eds) *Fristillingens Grenser – Statsaksjeselskapet, Styringsproblemer og Reformprosesser Gjennom 50 År.*, Bergen: Fagbokforlaget.

Wicken, O. (1992) 'Teknologi som politisk skillelinje – Et teknologihistorisk perspektiv på norsk politikk ca 1850–1990. Framtidsretet teknologipolitikk', Oslo: NTNF programmet.

Willoch, K. (1986) 'KV til Statoil: en snarvei til subsidier', *Aftenposten*, 27 November.

Willoch, K. (2002) *Myter og virkelighet: Om Begivenheter Frem til Våre Dager Med Utgangspunkt i Perioden 1965–1981*, Oslo: Cappelen.

WSJ (*Wall Street Journal*) (1998) 'Investor AB chairman tries balancing family's values with shareholder values', 18 May.

5

Comparative and Connected Global Capitalism(s)

Edmond Smith

Introduction

Bitu, also known as Bighu or Begho, was a market town that lay in the Banda region of West Africa just south of the River Volta in what is present-day Ghana. It was identified as something akin to Eldorado within the Arab world – something immensely wealthy and just beyond reach – a perception adopted by European actors as they became familiar with the region. In the 17th-century history of the Songhai Empire, the Ta'rīkh al-Fattāsh, the historiographer Ibn al-Mukhtar recorded that during the rise of the Malian empire 'the gold mines' of the western Niger 'have no parallel in all the Takrūr, except in the land of the Bergo' at Bitu. Even though merchants (known as Wangara) from Timbuktu and other cities within the Malian and Songhai empires had regularly participated in the trading caravans southward, al-Mukhtar could only identify the trading centre at Bitu as a source of gold and had no knowledge of the actual Akan mining centres further south (Wise, 2011: 74–5; Nobili and Shahid Mathee, 2015: 37–73). The Moroccan physician and author Wazir al-Ghassani similarly wrote about 'a place called Bitu where there are mines of gold and of gold dust'. He understood that the town was where 'those who have the salt of Taghaza origin and those who have the gold of Bitu origin meet each other' but remained unable to describe the origins of the gold, only that it was a source 'without equal in the universe' and that 'everyone finds great profit in going there to trade, and thus fortunes are made of which God alone knows the size'. Indeed, from al-Ghassani's perspective, Timbuktu itself owed its wealth to the Bitu caravans, and he argued that 'it is because of this blessed town that caravans converge at Timbuktu from all points of the horizon, from east, west, south, and north' (Wilks, 1982a: 343).

For these commentators, Bitu was a site of international trade that served to connect the merchants of the western Niger – from cities with their own advanced economies – with a precious commodity that underpinned economic activity across northern Africa and beyond. This was not an occasional trade or one that was riven with regular failures and uncertainties, but one that functioned year in, year out through careful institutional arrangements that made Bitu a successful cross-cultural and international market town. Wilks identified that 'Bitu was a frontier town', and extensive archaeological excavation at the site (and other markets in the Banda region) have revealed strict practices of urban planning that separated visiting merchants from the rest of the community despite shared economic interests (Wilks, 1982a: 343). The central market of the town was dominated by a community of traders and retailers, the east quarter by local Akan landowners, the west quarter by 'Kramo' *qabilas*, that is, the wards of the Wangara, who lived near the town's mosque; and to the north lived artisans – especially blacksmiths. Near the town, in what might be called "greater" Bitu, there is evidence of further manufacturing sites, including furnaces at Dapaa where iron slag has been unearthed in considerable quantities and a pottery-producing community at Bandakile (Stahl, 2009: 107–47; Posnansky, 2015). As the source, from the perspective of visiting merchants at least, of the gold that stimulated the trans-Saharan trading networks, towns such as Bitu provided an opportunity for Akan traders to access important international markets. They also provided security against potential threats by strictly limiting participation in different types of economic activity and contributed to the control of commercial activity within the wider economy remaining in Akan hands. As Daaku has highlighted:

> […] by the end of the 16th century the Akan economic production had become highly specialised, both regionally and locally. The salt and dry fish of the coastal dwellers were exchanged for food stuff and other forest produce and the gold mining areas of Awowin and Wassa depended on their food-producing neighbours for their sustenance. At the same time, Akan traders scoured the inland markets of the Wenchi-Bono-Takyiman area and beyond for manufactured [goods]. (Daaku, 1972: 237)

Thus, from an Akan perspective, these divisions of economic activity among the quarters of Bitu reflected common practices across the wider Akan economy, with specialization of manufacturing practice fuelling the dense commercial webs that criss-crossed the region. Yet this was no small, insignificant or disconnected economic region – the Akan goldfields produced a commodity that shaped markets across the world. Why then do towns such as Bitu or the economic practices of the Akan appear so infrequently in histories of capitalism? How should such a town at Bitu be interpreted within our histories of capitalism? How might it compare with the market towns in England considered elsewhere in this volume? What, if anything, might an analysis of sites such as Bitu tell us about economic cultures in other sites of global exchange such as Macao, Xinjiang or Livorno and their relationship to 'capitalism' (Millward, 2007; Barreto and Zhiliang, 2012; Trivellato, 2012)?

The challenges in examining non-Western 'capitalisms' in contexts like these are numerous, in part from a paucity of sources about some of the economic practices that took place, but also owing to a lack of analysis that offers a clear link between these activities and 19th- or 20th-century capitalism as defined by European and American powers. Bitu, for instance, essentially ceased to function as a market town and was depopulated in the 17th century, in part owing to climate change and war reshaping the commercial landscape of the Niger delta region and partly through the impact of the transatlantic slave trade on the regional economy. Does this diminish the practices of 'capitalism' that emerged in Bitu in the 15th century? If we conceive capitalism as a series of practices or a set of values and beliefs, rather than a narrative ending inevitably in 'Western Capitalism's' (probably brief) ascendancy in the 19th to 21st centuries, how might it change the way we approach the economic histories of different parts of the world?

As Yazdani and Menon (2020: 1) highlight in their introduction to the recent *Capitalisms: Towards a Global History*, 'it is imperative that we ask what historical roles different world regions played in the making of capitalism(s)' and that in doing so we might 'help shed new light on contemporary aspects of industrial and financial capitalism, particularly the reasons underlying socio-economic development and underdevelopment'. As they note, holistic explanations for capitalism remain rare, and the challenge of successfully entangling the processes of capitalist development in ways that effectively recognize the intra-European, extra-European, short-term, continuous and contingent factors is, to say the least, a difficult proposition. Understanding the emergence of modern capitalism therefore requires recognition and effective integration of global conjunctures and dimensions that include 'African slave labour; Asian-African consumer demands; Asian dynamism; and competitiveness in global markets' (Yazdani and Menon, 2020: 3). That is not to say, of course, that historians of capitalism are unaware of these trajectories, and historians such as Bayly (2004) and Williams (1944) have highlighted the importance of factors such as the East India Company, empire, colonialism, slavery and sugar in Britain's economic development. Rather, the challenge in using capitalism as a useful framework for understanding global and local economic developments in diverse contexts is in identifying not just whether activities were capitalist, but whether they represent an alternative mode or process of capitalism, whether they form part of a connected capitalist system that could be brought together within the same analytical framework or whether they are processes that are disconnected and distinct from what we might describe as capitalist. Importantly, though, these processes of exchange in global contexts provide an important means to examine our preconceptions of Western capitalism and challenge us to question the ways in which it evolved through processes of interaction and exchange on scales ranging from the global to the local.

In this chapter, these questions will be interrogated through three case studies that approach this topic through comparative and connected perspectives, and on different scales of analysis. In the first, we will examine the evolution of Chinese 'capitalism' from the Song to the Qing dynasties, drawing attention both to how particular economic processes took place in this context and how a long-term history of Chinese capitalism might be brought together with similarly long-term histories of Western capitalism – such as those presented elsewhere in this book. Secondly, this chapter will turn to the Armenian commercial diaspora that conducted trade across much of the early modern world, and use this to question the role of national and transnational institutions within capitalist trajectories, and, again, to consider some of the ways in which global commercial exchange might have encouraged the European adoption and adaptation of non-European economic practices during the evolution of capitalism. Finally, the third case study returns to West African economies, but rather than examining practices of the Akan at Bitu it instead considers trade with the Portuguese on the Atlantic coast and the requirement of European traders to meet local market demands and expectations. Across these case studies, there is one prevalent question – how might different perspectives change the way we define and understand what 'capitalism' means?

Capitalism(s) before divergence

If we are thinking about comparative capitalisms in global contexts other than Europe, perhaps the most obvious place to start is China. In histories of divergence, the comparison with China is often presented as the most significant (and, indeed, China's resurgence in the 21st century might suggest that historians need to reassess their long-term chronologies of capitalism), with Pomeranz's *The Great Divergence* (2001) representing an important effort to change how we approach questions related to industrial and capitalist development. In intellectual histories of capitalism, too, the position of China vis-à-vis the development of capitalist ideas in Europe is similarly being re-evaluated. For instance, while it is perhaps not surprising that many early modern writers expressed their awe of China's perceived wealth and power, increasingly historians are also noting that practices in

China appear to have influenced efforts by thinkers to challenge 17th- and 18th-century economic practices in Europe. As Yazdani and Menon have argued, in political and intellectual discourse in Europe, authors as diverse as Turgot, Adam Smith, Leibniz and Voltaire have all been identified as drawing, to one extent or another, on contemporary knowledge about China. De Halde, for instance, lauded Chinese institutions, technologies and economic ideas, while Quesnay 'advocated the alleged Chinese lack of government interference and regulation of the economy' that he saw as contributing to high agricultural productivity, a well-functioning revenue system and meritocratic administration – notably in contrast to the hereditary succession found across Europe (Yazdani and Menon, 2020: 6–7). However, despite these links, if we are seeking to identify the place of China within long-term trajectories of capitalism, this later period is perhaps not the only place where we should look to draw these comparisons and, possibly, connections. In the history of science, for example, a longer-term focus has proven fruitful in questioning the trajectories of the birth and growth of modern science, and similar approaches would be suitable for the study of capitalism (Bala and Prasenjit, 2016). If, as this book effectively shows for the evolution of Western capitalism, we need to understand trajectories of development from as early as the 12th-century market towns of England, perhaps our understanding of global capitalism would likewise benefit from a similarly long-term perspective of China's relationship with capitalism.

Such a refocusing would draw attention to Song China (960–1279), which often sits uncomfortably within histories of capitalism, representing as it does a seemingly anomalous entity within broader trajectories of economic development. During this period, China led the world in science, technology, commerce, urbanization and economic development – the cause of which might be identified as comparable with those that we would expect in capitalist systems elsewhere (Deng and Zheng, 2015). As Deng has argued, 'the double whammy of agricultural vulnerability caused by climatic change and military weakness' contributed to radical socio-economic changes in China that created a situation whereby the Song state was 'chiefly responsible for internalising the exogenous shocks and turning them positively towards unprecedented monetisation, marketisation, and openness' (Deng, 2020: 227–30). Central to Song China's economic growth were mining and metallurgical industries (that according to Hartwell (1962) produced more iron than any other economy in the world until 1750), predominantly undertaken by state-owned businesses. However, despite government involvement in licensing and taxing most aspects of the Song economy – practices that would surely be familiar in any modern capitalist system – this did not make entrepreneurial activity and innovation impossible. As Kent Deng suggests, the 'hand of the state was visible and busy in the Song economy' (2020: 242) – but should this diminish our identification of Song China as an example of 'one-off capitalism' or encourage us to reassess our preconceptions of what we mean by capitalist development in the first place? During the Song period, for instance, the development of quartz-based based ceramics to produce genuine porcelain was achieved for the first time, an innovation that was still relevant in Wedgwood's factories half a millennium later (Berg, 2002). Similar connections might be drawn between the development of calico printing in India and the later British adoption and adaption of these technologies (Riello, 2010). Innovation in international maritime trade was likewise undertaken and expanded as larger and more efficient ships were designed and new trade routes were developed to destinations as far flung as the Arabian Peninsula and East Africa – creating new webs of exchange that would similarly outlast the Song dynasty (Deng, 1997; Soon, 2001).

It is perhaps in these international trading networks that we find a means for conceptualizing the development of capitalist practices that might serve to offer some useful connection between Song China's economic development and the emergence of connected, even global, capitalisms across South East Asia and the Indian Ocean World in the early modern period (Chaudhuri, 1985; Ptak and Rothermund, 1991; Ptak, 1999). As Gang Deng has suggested, 'private trade in China was more active than government-sponsored trade in that Chinese merchants were motivated by profit; they traded to regions bypassed by the government; and they were discouraged neither by heavy taxes nor by bans on foreign trade' (1997: 261). In the Chinese historian Zhao Rukuo's *Zhu Fan Zhi* (1225 [1911]), a geographical description of the world and catalogue of trade goods, we are presented some insight into how the Chinese conceptualized their involvement in international trade during the Song period. Across the text, we learn of Chinese trading relationships with nearby Sumatra, Java and the Malay Peninsula and in distant markets in Gujarat, Oman and Zanzibar, where they traded goods including mineral and agricultural, raw and manufactured commodities. In describing trade with the Ta'shï (Arabs), who are described as 'pre-eminent among all foreigners for their distinguished bearings', Rukuo explains how the distance was too great for direct voyages, so instead Arab commodities were 'for the most part brought to San-fo-ts'i [Palembang], where they are sold to merchants who forward them to China'. In Egypt itself, which Rukuo understood to be 'an important centre of trade for foreign peoples', he described how 'markets are noisy and bustling, and are filled with great store of gold and silver damasks, brocades, and suck like wares' and also noted that 'the artisans have the true artistic spirit'. Rukuo continued to describe how 'the Ta'shï have come repeatedly to our court to present tribute' and noted the existence of a Arab community in China that had been home to the Arab merchant Shï-na-weï, who had 'established himself in the southern suburb of Ts'üan-chóu [Quanzhou]' and built a 'charnel house' as 'a last resting place for the abandoned bodies of foreign traders' (Rukuo, 1911: 114–24). These descriptions, coupled with the experience of living alongside foreign traders in China itself, contributed to descriptions of the world available in China, such as those by near contemporary Zhou Qufei, who wrote the *Lingwai Daida* in 1178. Qufei wrote that 'of all the wealthy foreign lands which have a great store of precious and varied goods, none surpass the realm of the Arabs. Next to them comes Java; the third is Palembang; many others come in the next rank' – and highlighted the great number of ships that reached China, especially through the entrepôt at Palembang (extract in Rukuo et al, 1911: 23–4). These extensive routes were not only characterized by long-distance, luxury trades, but also for staple trade across East and South East Asia.

The density of international trading networks across South East Asia and the Indian Ocean World increased dramatically as Chinese as well as other Asian actors contributed to the flourishing of international maritime trade over consequent centuries, despite changing ideas in China about how international trade should be conducted and controlled (Pin-tsun, 1989; Ray, 1993). As we might expect, agricultural goods were traded only with nearby markets, while long-distance trade supported the manufacture of goods including ceramics, silk, cotton, iron, silver, gold, beads and copper – with ceramics and silk each reaching over 50 different international destinations (Deng, 1997: 272–3). By the 16th century, and the arrival of the Europeans in Asian waters in large numbers for the first time, there were already sophisticated commercial systems in place that rested on practices – on the part of rulers across the region as well as individual actors – that served to provide institutional frameworks for traders in this diverse cross-cultural space. From the perspective of the Ming state, as we learn from the *Ming Shi-lu,* the arrival of Dutch and Portuguese traders disturbed the institutional status quo that had provided commercial stability in the region, and many reports noted that these new entrants were too willing to use force and violence to enter markets, rather than adapt and function within existing frameworks (Wade, 2005: entries for *Fo-lang-ji*). Yet despite these challenges, even during the Ming and Qing periods (1368–1911) when maritime trade from China was restricted owing to the adoption of strictly mercantilist policies, Gang Deng has noted that 'legal trade with Japan and Manila in the seventeenth and eighteenth centuries is well documented' – reaching a peak between China and Japan in 1688 when 9,128 Chinese merchants aboard 193 Chinese ships visited Nagasaki (Deng, 1997: 261–2). Similarly, after the establishment of Manila by the Spanish in 1572, Chinese merchants regularly visited the port city, trading in high value goods, and this trade provided 91.5 per cent of customs revenue of Manila, which became 'one of the largest centres for privately owned Chinese maritime businesses' (Deng, 1997: 266). If illegal trade, conducted in contravention of the Chinese state's attempted monopoly, is considered, thousands more Chinese ships can be seen as active and essential participants in Asia's maritime commerce. The scale of these practices included the entrepreneurial development of necessary infrastructure such as ports and the implementation of cross-cultural practices that supported smuggling operations; these 'included Japanese, Malaccans, Siamese, Portuguese, Africans, as well as Chinese' participants (Deng, 1997: 269). Chinese participation in trade across South East Asia was widespread, often as private entrepreneurs and businesses operated in environments beyond the reach of the Chinese state (Kispal-van Deijk, 2013). Working effectively in this environment demanded not only Chinese commercial practices that made it possible to conduct trade effectively but also the integration of these into wider, adaptable and responsive trading networks that developed long before the arrival of European actors in the region.

China's engagement in the emergence of what we might see as capitalist practices in these international contexts can also be traced back to China, where efforts to engage with new global patterns of exchange contributed to innovative and entrepreneurial activity and the restructuring of manufacturing industries. As Deng has noted, 'both the private sector and the government specialised. The latter dealt mainly in livestock and had less interest in consumer good, especially luxuries' (1997: 273). Porcelain production in China, especially, has received significant attention as a manufacturing sector where we might recognize many of the practices seen as capitalist – whether in its financing, organization, specialization or responsiveness to international markets (Wen-Chin, 1988). As Gerritsen has recently shown in her extensive study of the Jiangdezhen (home to the imperial kilns of the Ming and Qing dynasties), the success of the site as a productive centre depended on 'sophisticated labour management policies, waged labour, and production for global markets, pointing to a capitalist environment' (2020: 307). At this site, which depended on the sophisticated division of labour to ensure high quality and efficient production, we can see numerous 'features compatible with Neal and Williamson's definition of capitalism' (Gerritsen, 2020: 307). At Jiangdezhen, 'private property rights were in operation, as the wares in produced in *minyao* were sold by merchants and generated profits for investors; enforceable contracts governed both production quotas and those labouring in the kilns; and goods were produced here in response to demand from local, regional, and ultimately global market' (Gerritsen, 2020: 314), as well as extensive waged labour and sophisticated training practices (Moll-Murata, 2013). During its heyday in the 17th and 18th centuries, responding to the demands of international markets, Chinese porcelain exports 'could easily have reached the level of one million pieces a year' (Deng, 1997: 276). Through China, then, from the Song dynasty of the 10th century through to the evolution of new productive processes to cater to global markets during the 18th-century Qing dynasty, we can trace many of the processes that we might define as capitalism taking shape in different forms, at different times and in places different from those that we might expect. With this in mind, if we are considering the evolution of capitalism over the long term, what trajectories and chronologies might histories of Chinese trade and manufacturing encourage us to reconsider (Frank, 1998)?

Capitalism(s) and the institutions of global trade

Capitalism depends on commerce, whether domestically, to allow for specialization within communities or states, or internationally. In histories of European capitalism, the role of global trade, often seen to have been generated and sustained by European maritime expansion, is a common feature. The role of European empires, and corporations, in changing the structure and operation of global trade has received considerable attention, and the institutions of global trade that had become dominant by the 20th century emerged from this environment and through the dominance of European imperial, military and economic systems (Harris, 2020; Sharman and Phillips, 2020). Yet, of course, the arrival of Europeans into new markets in the early modern period was not the first time that trade had been brought to these regions, and European practices of trade were only slowly imposed in these spaces (Bavel, 2016; Spek et al, 2019). For instance, English merchants, during their first encounters with non-European economies, were often surprised by the sophistication and scale of the commercial activities they encountered. For example, on reaching sub-Saharan Africa for the first time in 1553, English factors employed by 'certain merchant adventurers of the City of London' (Eden, 1555: 343) were unprepared and surprised when they learned that the King of Benin was not just willing to trade through barter for the goods they carried, but instead suggested a multi-year credit agreement. The African traders observing the transaction may have been less impressed, as the lack of functioning organization on the part of the English expedition soon led to mutiny among their crew and the abandonment of the merchants on the African coast (Eden, 1555: 343–60). In South Asia, early English experiences of trade were similarly beset by limited expectations. The merchants Thomas Aldworth and William Edwards, for instance, sought to highlight the scale of commercial society in Gujarat to their superiors in London, noting that 'great and small are merchants' and that Ahmadabad was 'the great city of the Gujarat's, and is well near as big as the City of London'–features that the East India Company had not yet come to realize in their efforts to sell what they would soon learn was unwanted English broadcloth in the region (BL, IOR/E/3/1, ff. 198–9; BL, IOR/E/3/2, ff.

157–8). In each case, the tone of reports suggests surprise by these English entrants, representing the most sophisticated commercial organizations of their home country, at finding such well-developed economic systems – and that they had to fit themselves into them. Should historians of capitalism share in their surprise? If not, how should the recognition that sophisticated economic practices have never been limited to Europe change the way we conceptualize capitalism to account for global economic cultures and try to understand them together?

Practices for conducting trade were adopted or adapted from existing practices – even if individual participants brought with them the institutional baggage of their home (Curtin, 1984). As Ibn Khaldun had noted in the 14th century the basic premise of markets was a means of equitable and profitable exchange: he remarked that 'commerce means the attempt to make a profit by increasing capital, through buying goods at a low price and selling them at a high price' – a practice at the heart of global trade throughout the intervening centuries (Haddad, 1977; Khaldun, 1989: 309). This would suggest that if one of the functions of capitalism is the integration of international markets, the adaption of economic practices in response to changing circumstances to facilitate exchange would attest that access to and adaption to international markets were a common feature in non-European capitalisms too. The principle-agent problem, for instance, has often been explored in reference to practices of trade and exchange that are not typically Western precisely because of the effectiveness of diasporic or other non-national traders to operate successfully in cross-cultural and cross-institutional spaces (Greif, 1989; Trivellato, 2012). In this environment, how do we align national with transnational examinations of trade and capitalism? Can capitalism only take place within nation-states – or are David Washbrook (1990) and Eric Tagliacozzo (2020) correct that the lack of Western conceptions of territorial control are a key reason why South East Asia, for instance, fits uncomfortably within histories of capitalism? Do the institutions that support capitalism only exist if European participants understood them – or is the expectation that we should view European efforts to impose their own legal ideas as the origin of commercially viable institutions (Smith, 2018)?

As the next case study will demonstrate, the institutional arrangements by which economic actors facilitated impersonal and personal transactions were not necessarily maintained by states, and commercial communities functioning across different legal and political boundaries helped create the institutional frameworks vital for global exchange. As Sebouh David Aslanian has convincingly argued, Armenian merchants from New Julfa operated as 'transimperial cosmopolitans' who were able to effectively do business across the Mughal, Ottoman, Safavid, Muscovite, Qing, Portuguese, Spanish, British and Dutch economies in the early modern period (Aslanian,

2011: 66). It was the very contested, or more generously cosmopolitan, qualities of these spaces that made it possible for this network to operate effectively as businesses. Indeed, it was the 'informal and semiformal institutions' that underpinned this community that enabled its great success (Mauro, 1990: 273; Aslanian, 2011: 166–201). In international trading environments, where trans-imperial and cross-cultural activity was the norm, the Armenian diaspora was well suited to adapting to new conditions as they arose, and making the activities of other empires – whether Asian or European – work for them (McCable, 2010).

Spread outwards from New Julfa, a city within Safavid Persia not far from the empire's major commercial ports on the Persian Gulf, the Armenian mercantile network helped facilitate this diasporic community's business across the world. Founded in 1605, following their expulsion from Old Julfa by the Safavid ruler Shah 'Abbas, New Julfa presented a centralizing force within this commercial network, acting as a nodal centre that could provide capital, support relationships and act as a home base – even if neither New Julfa nor the Safavid state offered military support or facilitated monopolistic interests in the way that might be considered common practice among European traders and companies active in the same regions (Aslanian, 2011: 44–65). Elsewhere within Safavid Persia, Armenian merchants settled in port towns – including Basra, Bandar Kung and Bandar 'Abbas – which acted as key points within a network that had its nodal centre in New Julfa. Through these towns, a circulatory commercial network drew together capital, people and information. The expanding network rested on a practice whereby young merchants were sent abroad, settling in new towns, alongside or independently of other Armenians, where they were expected to act as agents (Sarkissian, 1987). Their success depended on their rapid integration into new environments – adapting to local conditions. As Shireen Moosvi (1998) has indicated, this adaptability was part of the reason Armenian merchants and small firms remained competitive against European corporate entrants. One consequence, and a key strength of Armenian merchants, was a willingness and ability to integrate their trading activities with investment in, and direct relationships with, the producers of key goods – whether textile manufacturers in Gujarat and Sindh or buyers of silk in Marseilles, Lyon and Tours (Aslanian, 2011: 48, 75). Similarly, in South Asia, Armenian merchants utilized financial practices adapted from both Asian and European trading partners, facilitating credit agreements between members of the diaspora and trans-imperial partners (Hussain, 1990). From the perspective of histories of capitalism, this suggests a radically innovative and entrepreneurial approach to business that depended more on the free functioning of markets than European actors more familiar with mercantilist involvement in trade on the part of their respective states.

As Armenian merchants from New Julfa spread eastward from their Persian home, their linguistic abilities – often speaking Persian as well as Armenian – as well as flexible business practices when acting as cross-cultural brokers provided them with favourable trading and living conditions. For example, the Mughal emperor Akbar invited Armenian merchants to locate to Agra around the middle of the 16th century, and they quickly obtained prominent positions within the empire's court (Hosten, 1916). In the kingdom of Golconda, Armenian merchants were among the most prominent 'portfolio capitalists', with links to the highest echelons of power (Aslanian, 2011: 50–1). In these spaces, where trade was contested between local Hindu and Muslim traders as well as numerous foreign merchants, the Armenian community proved particularly successful in bridging gaps between different groups – providing a framework for commercial interaction that could overcome less adaptive participants (Hussain, 2011). Further east still, in Spanish Manila, Armenian merchants were able to maintain similarly prominent roles despite weak Spanish protections for property rights – either as ship owners, ship captains or partners for Dutch and English interlopers who the local authorities sought to exclude from the city's trade (working, incidentally, alongside the Chinese merchants in Manilla discussed earlier) (Aslanian, 2011: 59–60, 62–4). Indeed, the strength of the Armenian network in the region even encouraged European merchants to fly the Armenian flag to obtain access to the region's markets. The Englishman Charles Lockyer, a former merchant in the region, even went so far as to counsel future traders that 'Manila under Armenian colours is a profitable voyage' (1711: 15). Through their Indian Ocean network, Armenian merchants traded in markets as diverse as those in Mughal India, the Coromandel Coast, Syriam in Burma, Dutch Batavia, Melaka, Canton, the Spanish Philippines and even as far as Acapulco in the Americas (Yang, 2009; Aslanian, 2011: 44–65).

To the west, Armenians had begun to settle in port cities on the Mediterranean coast in the early 16th century – most prominently at Aleppo – and would come to hold a prominent position in markets ranging from Izmir and Constantinople in the Ottoman Empire to Venice, Cadiz and Amsterdam further west. In Aleppo especially, where they operated as brokers for the Persian silk trade, dealing especially with European merchants increasingly drawn to the port, Armenian merchants were able to obtain great wealth. Described by a visiting Portuguese merchant in the 1590s as living in palaces 'fit to harbour princes', this community's wealth soon 'triggered a cultural flourishing of the city's Armenian community as a whole … new churches were constructed and illuminated manuscripts were commissioned' (Teixeira, 1902: 113). Yet as opportunities arose elsewhere, whether owing to reduced customs in Izmir or tax-free trade in Livorno, Armenian merchants remained adaptable and quickly shifted operations into more lucrative spaces (Masters, 1998: 84, Aslanian, 2011: 69). Where they faced less welcoming circumstances – such as protectionist efforts in France – flexible economic behaviour helped maintain their presence in markets (Herzig, 1991: 137). In towns where they settled, the process of building churches, warehouses, places of business and their homes enabled the retention of a distinct social and cultural identity within the Armenian commercial network (Aslanian, 2011: 47–50, 52, 55, 67, 70–1, 85). Indeed, this was an essential for traders in the region as the monsoon-driven trading calendar meant it was very difficult for them to return to New Julfa or other settlements in Safavid Persia within a year of their departure (Aslanian, 2011: 48). By shaping economic spaces in this way, Armenian merchants were not only creating the cultural conditions necessary for a more comfortable and familiar life but also fashioning an environment where they could internalize commercial disputes and respond communally to shared challenges.

Across their extensive business undertakings, the Armenian merchant community became 'an important bridge in the early modern period for economic and cultural encounters between the two great zones of the world economy, the Mediterranean and the Indian Oceans, as well as the Eurasian landmass' (Aslanian, 2011: 66). Aslanian suggests that the success of the Armenian merchant community rested especially on how its institutions and networks helped maintain trustworthiness across its disparate members even as they entered and settled in new markets across the world. To do so, they depended on 'a code of conduct' that was applied across the diaspora, a set of rules 'not codified in writing' but that 'was most likely customary in nature' (Aslanian, 2011: 174). Instead of relying on local courts, for instance, in towns with larger Armenian populations the community joined together through an 'Assembly of Merchants' that could oversee disputes between members of the community (Aslanian, 2011: 175–92). Hussain has shown how Armenian merchants in Mughal India were 'able to blend with the local merchant' groups through a willingness to actively participate in the wider community – even going so far as to invite local merchants to join the *joomiat* that oversaw disputes between Armenian merchants (Hussain, 2011: 400). This was reinforced through coalitions and partnerships between individual merchants who depended on common behavioural practices that could be applied in different circumstances across the globe.

Through their networks, Armenian merchants were not just able to, and highly competent at, accessing international markets, but their strong communal institutions, separate from those of the empires that they crossed, made them ideal partners for many merchants. Indeed, Baghdiantz McCabe has demonstrated how 'it was European companies that longed to carry their [the Armenians'] goods' in recognition of their influence in global trading routes (2010: 125). In Madras, for instance, the English East India Company was heavily reliant on Armenian merchants as social and economic brokers, business partners, financiers and informants (Braudel, 1992: 490). For the English merchants in the region, the Armenian commercial community had long been a source of some consternation, and were believed to hold such a dominant role in Indian cloth and indigo trades that they obtained goods 30 per cent cheaper than the East India Company's agents found possible (Chaudhuri, 1978: 335; Moosvi, 1998: 268–9). Indeed, the relationship between Armenian merchants and the East India Company helps demonstrate their enduring role – and the importance of their institutional adaptability to cross between different economic cultures. In 1688, the 'English East India Company and the Armenian Nation' signed an agreement that was intended to encourage Armenians to 'alter and invert the ancient course of their trade to and from Europe' (Ferrier, 1970: 438–42). That is to say, rather than transporting goods overland to the Mediterranean through their long-standing networks in Safavid Persia and the Ottoman Empire, it was hoped Armenian merchants would start shipping large quantities of silk in English ships. To try and woo their new partners, the East India Company and English state offered incredibly generous terms – including the treatment of Armenian merchants 'as if they were Englishmen born' and low customs fees (Aslanian, 2011: 48–9). Such was the importance of this seemingly boundaryless network of merchants that the English corporation was willing to throw out decades of policy and monopolistic fervour in an attempt to win them over.

For Armenian merchants then, enduring success in the globalizing early modern economy depended on a set of common cultural standards that meant 'rather than elbow their way in', they 'comported themselves to local arrangements wherever they went'. In doing so, they were able to enter 'into relations with locals that were more intimate, sticky, and prolonged than the Europeans could countenance' (Ho, 2006: xxi). Despite crossing imperial boundaries, Armenian merchants could depend on common institutions to sustain the long-distance trading relationships that made them so valuable, while developing relationships with fellow merchants, local producers and the political elites of regions within which they did business.

If we return to Ibn Khaldun's analysis, the Arab author suggested that the revenues of rulers 'can be improved only through the equitable treatment of people with property and regard for them, so that their hopes rise, and they have the incentive to start making their capital bear fruit and grow' (1989: 234). This was the arrangement in Asia that Armenian merchants were able to operate in so successfully – their internal institutional framework that their diasporic network provided helped them stay connected and effective across borders, while their adaptive approach to different economic cultures and political structures made them effective partners. Returning again to the question of how we understand the evolution of capitalism – especially in reference to the development of international markets and the institutions of global trade – how does the Armenian experience fit into our analysis?

Whose capitalism?

One of the most interesting aspects of the Armenian merchants' success described here is how these traders adapted effectively to different and changing conditions. In taking part in global trade, merchants such as these, and of course European traders too, were required to innovate and evolve in recognition of the markets they sought to enter. Traders entering London, for instance, were expected to act in ways that recognized local laws and customs: if they did not do so they would be unlikely to succeed (unless of course the state stepped in and overruled existing agreements in their favour). In markets in Africa, Asia, Europe or America the same dynamic held true – traders were required to find ways to do business together, either by adopting the existing local conditions, but adapting them with their new partners to find new ways of doing business, or by enforcing the business practices they were bringing with them, often through violence. Such dynamics mean that the evolution of capitalist modes of exchange can hardly be seen as being a European phenomenon: they developed through processes of adaptation and the exchange of ideas about how business could be conducted. Even within Europe, the sharing and exchange of ideas about how to organize business was common practice – for example the adoption of corporate structures for organization or the use of double entry bookkeeping. Globally, European merchants needed to adapt to be successful, but it remains unclear how and where practices of trade developed – and how the experience of adapting to local conditions in different places might have affected the economic practices of Europeans elsewhere. Did the experience of trading globally feed back into the networks that sustained them? Did the English merchants in Benin mentioned earlier learn from their mistake? Did the East India Company change how it did business in light of new information, and in what ways did its own business model change in light of recognizing the effectiveness of Armenian traders? If capitalism evolved during a period of intense global exchange, how much of what we understand as Western capitalism might have been influenced by these experiences?

In the following case study, the question of European adaptation towards local conditions is examined through the Akan–Portuguese commercial relations that defined trade on what became known as the Costa da Mina or Gold Coast. As in the market town of Bitu discussed at the start of this chapter, the same mentality of restricting access to the hinterland and conducting trade in carefully selected market locations was exhibited by local rulers along the Atlantic coast. By 1600, around twenty or so European forts had been established on the coast and provided further opportunities for access to international markets for local gold traders. Some Akan polities such as Komenda or Cara (Accra) used their access to these markets to grow into powerful regional centres (Daaku, 1970: 78–95). This was facilitated in part by Portuguese practices across their empire whereby they 'inserted themselves as a militarized commercial elite' alongside communities 'with an established commercial and political life but with every intention of encouraging the existing commercial order to continue' (Pearson, 1976; Subrahmanyam, 1993; Newitt, 2008: 105). In this context, by overseeing the practices by which Akan gold reached international markets, different Akan polities across this region could maintain significant control of the movement of people through their territories while simultaneously encouraging commercial engagement.

Environmental conditions, whether dense forest and steep hills that made inland travel arduous, difficult navigation of the region's rivers or the prevalence of heat and disease, contributed to the maintenance of a strong border between the Akan hinterland and visiting traders. Cultural and linguistic boundaries likewise made it more difficult for outsiders to penetrate deeply into the main regions of Akan gold production. In this context, it should be of little surprise that Akan traders, rulers and other local actors were able to impose strict frameworks about how, where and when trade would be conducted – even if European diasporic groups along the coast have received more attention from historians (Mark and Horta, 2004; Silva, 2012). In the north this meant dedicated trading entrepôts were established, such as that at Bitu discussed at the start of this chapter (Effah-Gyamfi, 1987; Stahl, 1999), while to the south European actors were restricted mainly to small coastal trading posts (Blake, 1970). Coastal and riverine trade, as well as overland traffic, were kept in the hands of Akan traders, who navigated the 800-mile stretch between the Portuguese factories on the southern coast and the northern entrepôts and helped connect the regional economy to global commercial webs. By enforcing strict boundaries between local and global commercial activity, Akan efforts to ensure that the sources of gold production remained in their hands were remarkably successful (Sanders, 1979). For instance, even by the 17th century Portuguese ships still struggled to enter the river systems, depending on help from 'pilots from the land', and even much of the coastal trade remained in the hands of 'local people who are called *alaus*, big fishermen' with 'their canoes or *almadias* in which they navigate along the coast' (BNP, COD 7698, n. 10, f. 1). From the perspective of

Portuguese imperial administrators, this context defined their practices of empire on the Costa da Mina, and seeking viable means of establishing a secure supply of gold was a key objective across this period.

The viability of the Portuguese position depended on them being perceived as valuable trading partners, especially if they were to offer an attractive alternative to the trans-Saharan trade routes dominated by markets further north (Silva, 2002: 146). Engaging in trade only with their immediate neighbours was not enough to justify the expense and risk of establishing a Portuguese presence on the coast, and attracting merchants from nearby 'kingdoms' – a term used by the Portuguese to represent polities ranging from individual towns to much larger territories – was vital. The main Portuguese trading fortress, São Jorge da Mina, lay between the wider territories of the Eguafo and Fetu polities, which each stretched from the coast to settlements further inland, and beyond these there were numerous other African kingdoms that attracted Portuguese interest (Ballong-Wen-Mewuda, 1993: 76, 95–106). With this in mind, the newly built fortress was intended primarily as a trading post rather than as a base for military and territorial expansion, and the built environment the Portuguese created reflected these aims. The site was defensible from attacks by sea or by land, but more importantly it provided a physical structure that established a Portuguese market as a permanent destination for African merchants. As well as its walls, towers and military paraphernalia, São Jorge da Mina was constructed with warehouse facilities, a chapel, accommodation for permanent administrative staff and solders, and space for a market to be held (DeCorse, 2001).

In 1503, after two decades of reasonably successful trade, Diogo Lopes de Sequeira, the captain of São Jorge da Mina, wrote to King Manuel I to explain that 'there [was] work to do in the factory' if it was going to prove an effective commercial site for engaging with traders from across the region. In particular, Sequeira warned that 'it seems to be a big waste in such an important trade not to have a house where these cloths cannot be damaged every day the way it is nowadays'. The situation was so bad, he argued, that visiting African merchants were currently forced to trade in the 'small house' where 'it is not even possible to show them all the cloths' available, and those that were displayed could only be placed on the floor (ATT, CC, 1-4-42). Another Portuguese resident, Fernão Lopez, reported 'how small this house is and how in there we cannot fold or shake the *lambeis*' (coloured cotton cloths) that were a principal commodity in the trade for gold. In order to cater to the demands of African merchants, Sequeira encouraged Manuel to invest in improving the site's commercial infrastructure, arguing that 'it would be possible to perfectly do this work in a short time' if they received support from the Crown, a charge that would be repaid after only one or two years (ATT, CC, 1-4-42). For

Sequeira, the success of São Jorge da Mina depended on the viability of the fortress as a marketplace, and the Portuguese administration would need to recognize and meet the needs and expectations of the people they were seeking to trade with.

To encourage visiting merchants, and keep trade routes to São Jorge da Mina open, it became widespread practice for the Portuguese to engage diplomatically with Akan rulers across the region. The captains of São Jorge da Mina between 1517 and 1524, Fernão Lopes Correia, Duarte Pacheco Pereira and Afonso de Albuquerque, maintained these relations carefully through visits and gift-giving (ATT, CC 2.70–113). In this way, Portuguese communication, if not necessarily friendship or support, with the rulers of Bixau, Piã, Futo, Sabú, Sáa, Apuato, Assas, Acave, Cabo das Redes, Komani, Labidão and Abermus, as well as 'local black merchants' around Axim could be secured (ATT, CC 2.101). Among the most common gifts were *lambeis* and *algeravias* (burnouses), but also red caps, *caldeirões* (a type of cauldron), *bacias de mijar* (shallow bronze bowls for washing gold), wine, goats and pigs. These relationships developed over time. For example, in 1518 a goat was given 'to two black merchants for opening up the way to Assas' in advance of the King of Assas visiting in São Jorge da Mina, where he was given 'a painted cloth of Gonçalo Vaz and an *algeravias*' (ATT, CC 2.77.31; ATT, CC 2.77.134). The following year, the representative and two of the sons of the King of Assas returned to the fortress where they received further gifts, before the king's brother was given two goats during another visit (ATT, CC 2.86.80; ATT, CC 2.86.115). By 1520, the Portuguese were able to send João Vieira as an ambassador to Assas, carrying not only gifts but also new wares available at São Jorge da Mina (ATT, CC 2.89.80). The programme was, it seems, relatively successful. For instance, by 1519 the King of Futo had become a trusted intermediary and helped 'facilitate a peace with the King of Acomane' on behalf of the Portuguese and was given a portrait of Manuel I, ivory bowls and a number of cloths as thanks (ATT, CC 2.85.9; ATT, CC 2.85.44). Diplomatic relations were not limited to these engagements in Africa, and the *Xarife*, joined by the King of the Assas and 'those from this village', asked for 'a clerk to write to our Highness', although unfortunately this has not survived (ATT, Núcleo Antigo, n. 348). As well as improving relations in general, such exchanges could also be used to serve a specific objective, such as obtaining permission from a king to let the merchants to pass through his lands or to secure peace.

The Portuguese therefore had to provide enough goods and respond to local demands regarding their quality. Failure to do so could be devastating to their business. For example, in 1518 Fernão Lopez Correia, now captain at São Jorge da Mina, complained that declining trade at the outpost reflected reduced local interest in Portuguese products. Following orders from Manuel I, *lambeis* were sold for 20 *pesos*, but Correia said that because of the price only two had been sold, and new samples of *algeravias tenezes* (burnouses from Tunis) brought by Gonçalo Vaz had likewise failed to attract local interest. The Portuguese had either been unable or unwilling to understand local expectations and tastes effectively. Akan traders had dismissed the new goods 'because the *tenezes* are made with another pattern' not corresponding to the ones they first saw, 'and are more covered and with the inside-out as a tapestry' (ATT, CM, Maco 3, n. 179). Correia reported that locals appreciated the *tenezes* because find them 'soft and warm, which they really enjoy, because they use it as during the day as evening', but as these were not of the same quality they would not pay more than 5 *pesos* per item – far less than expected by Portuguese authorities. Similarly, 'algeravias from Fez, which are now being taken here' were considered inferior quality and attracted little interest. In the end, Correia recommended that higher quality *lambeis* should be the priority, especially if Manuel's insistence on higher prices continued (ATT, CM, Maço 3, n. 179).

Nonetheless, Correia was keen on increasing shipments to São Jorge da Mina in general, and encouraged Manuel that if 'it seems to your highness that the amount of *algeravias* might impede the *lambeis* to be sold, your highness should not be afraid'. Akan traders sought each product for different markets 'because in the expenses and use of them they are different', as 'men bring the algeravias all as a cape' while 'they cut the lambeis to use it for *bragas* [short trousers] and skirts for their wives' (ATT, CM, Maço 3, n. 179). Indeed, Correia warned that without more consistent delivery of goods the Portuguese risked losing the interest of local merchants who were already kept waiting for deliveries – either directly from Portugal or from Portuguese ships that had obtained slaves from other parts of the African coast. Unable to stay at São Jorge da Mina for long, 'many times they go without anything'. The problem was exacerbated when slaving ships from Cabo Verde or São Tomé 'bring so little goods that two merchants that go can take all of it with them and the rest of the time they stay without doing nothing until another ship' arrived. When they did eventually arrive, a fully laden ship carrying 'three thousand *manilhas* and two hundred and fifty *algeravias* and two hundred *bacyas de myjar*' only provided enough goods as could be 'taken in one day'. It was clear to Correia that if they could provide a more reliable supply and local merchants learned that they would always 'find in it all the goods that they ask in abundance', then 'with this fundament come many that never came here before'. He hoped that Manuel I would recognize the opportunity and send more of these 'goods that they very much desire' (ATT, CM, Maço 3, n. 180).

By 1529, efforts to ensure goods sought by Akan traders were in regular supply had succeeded, and the factor at São Jorge da Mina was ordered to 'always have all things in the factory to sell to the black'. Whether for people 'from the village [who] will sometimes desire and enjoy buying dresses and other things for gold' or 'for the merchants, when they come to that city', he was expected to stock 'all things of all qualities, that they will appreciate very much the abundance'. It was essential that the Portuguese 'can always satisfy what the Africans from that factory want to buy', otherwise their access to the precious Akan gold markets would quickly fade away (Faro, 1958: 100). During this period that meant supplying commodities including metal hardware, textiles, enslaved people and cowry shells, goods that represented around 50 per cent, 25 per cent, 19 per cent and 3 per cent of the value sold to Akan traders respectively (Vogt, 1973: 93–103). In West Africa, Portuguese efforts to meet the demands of the local market forced them to change the way they were doing business. The power of the Akan rested in their control of the supply of gold, and the possibility of diverting goods northward towards Arab traders at Bitu meant that they had little reason to choose the Portuguese market on the Atlantic coast unless the Portuguese offer was competitive. If we took this analysis further and examined Portuguese practices in, say, India or Japan, we would find similar patterns, and the same would be the case for Dutch or English traders in many international markets where they functioned primarily as traders. In this experience in Africa then, are we seeing in the Akan economic practices that are non-capitalist, that represent an alternative form of capitalism, or processes of exchange and adaptation that suggest a more connected, more inclusive form of capitalist exchange? Asking these questions, especially during periods and in places where imperial power-dynamics did not skew the functioning of economic activity, can offer new avenues for examining what 'capitalism' means and what function it can serve for our understanding of the world economy in the past, present and future.

Conclusion

Capitalism in one form or another can be viewed as a global phenomenon. Even if processes of production, exchange, consumption and accumulation differed greatly in response to local contexts, cultures and environments, they were hardly an uncommon occurrence in any part of the world. Yet to embrace a too broad definition of capitalism limits its effectiveness as a specific and precise historical tool, and it would be wrong to engross all history of human economic activity into a single, worryingly teleological, capitalist trajectory. Instead, and what the other chapters in this volume show, is that we can interrogate specific aspects of capitalism in different times and places as a means of better understanding of specific economic histories as well as recognizing the potential for comparative and connected histories across these. In this chapter, rather than tracing European influence into global markets, through maritime trade or empire, as a precursor to capitalist development, we have seen how shifting our perspective can offer alternative avenues for exploring what capitalism means, both in terms of how economies in Africa and Asia functioned prior to early modern engagement with Europe, but also how European or Western capitalist practices emerged through processes of exchange and adaption. Thus, rather than seeking to explain the Great Divergence debate and the occurrence of industrialization, this chapter has instead sought to engage with how we think about capitalism in its broader definitions, and how we might better understand the structure and significance of different economic cultures and models in our understanding of global economic history. In each of the case studies considered here – related to Chinese, Armenian and West African 'capitalisms' – it has shown how some different global conditions, especially in relation to commerce, might reflect a definition of capitalism that highlights effective cross-cultural and communal, rather than national or corporate, frameworks as a key feature underpinning global exchange. This is important not only as a means for understanding international capitalisms in a comparative perspective but also contributes to changing ideas about how new European entrants to these regions were able to effectively integrate (or not) into pre-existing networks. The evolution of capitalism took place in an environment of global connection and exchange, and interpreting it within this habitat can help show where we need a more inclusive definition of 'capitalism' and where we need to move towards a better understanding of competing, connected and more adaptive 'capitalisms'.

References

Aslanian, S. (2011) *From the Indian Ocean to the Mediterranean: The Global Trade Networks of Armenian Merchants from New Julfa*, Oakland: University of California Press.

ATT [Arquivo Nacional da Torre de Tombo, Lisbon], CC 1-4-42. Letter from the Captain of Elmina to the king, 22 December 1503.

ATT, CC 2.70–113. Receipts for gifts, 1517–25.

ATT, CC 2.77.31. Order for payment to two black merchants, 1518.

ATT, CC 2.77.134. Mandate for gift giving to the King of Assas, 1518.

ATT, CC 2.86.80. Mandate for the giving of gifts to a local ruler, 1519.

ATT, CC 2.86.115. Mandate for gift giving to local ruler, 1519.

ATT, CC 2.89.80. Ordering the giving of gifts to the King of Assas, 1520.

ATT, CC 2.85.9. Mandate of the Captain of Mina for the cost of gifts to the King of Futo, 1519.

ATT, CC 2.85.44. Preparation of gifts for a visit to Mina, 1519.

ATT, Núcleo Antigo, n. 348. Letter from Nuno Vaz de Castelo Branco to the king, [c. 1514].

ATT, CM, Maço 3, n. 179. Letter from Fernão Lopes Correia to the king, 8 October 1518.

ATT, CM, Maço 3, n. 180. Letter from Fernão Lopes Correia to the king, 23 June [c. 1510s].

Bala, A. and Prasenjit, D. (eds) (2016) *The Bright Dark Ages: Comparative and Connected Perspectives*, Leiden: Brill.

Ballong-Wen-Mewuda, B. (1993) *São Jorge da Mina, 1482–1637: la vie d'un comptoir portugais en Afrique occidentale*, Lisbon and Paris: Fondation Calouste Gulbenkian.

Barreto, L.F. and Zhiliang, W. (2012) *Port Cities and Intercultural Relations: 15th–18th Centuries*, Lisbon: Centro Científico e Cultural de Macau.

Bayly, C. (2004) *The Birth of the Modern World, 1780–1914: Global Connections and Comparisons*, Malden, MA: Blackwell Publishing.

Berg, M. (2002) 'From imitation to invention: creating commodities in eighteenth-century Britain', *Economic History Review*, 55(1): 1–30.

BL [British Library], IOR/E/3/1, ff. 198–9. Thomas Aldworth at Amadavar to the East India Company, 9 November 1613.

BL, IOR/E/3/2, ff. 157–8. William Edwards at Ahmedabad and Ajmeer to Sir Thomas Smith, 26 December 1614.

Blake, J.W. (1970) *European Beginnings in West Africa, 1454–1578*, London: Longman.

BNP [Biblioteca Nacional de Portugal, Lisbon], COD 7698, n. 10. Discourse about the defence of Elmina, [undated, c. 1610s].

Braudel, F. (1992) *The Perspective of the World: Vol. 3 of Civilisation and Capitalism, 15th–18th Centuries*, California: University of California Press.

Chaudhuri, K.N. (1978) *The Trading Worlds of Asia and the English East India Company, 1600–1760*, Cambridge: Cambridge University Press.

Chaudhuri, K.N. (1985) *Trade and Civilisation in the Indian Ocean: An Economic History from the Rise of Islam to 1750*, Cambridge: Cambridge University Press.

Curtin, P. (1984) *Cross-Cultural Trade in World History*, Cambridge: Cambridge University Press.

Daaku, K.Y. (1970) *Trade and Politics on the Gold Coast, 1600–1720: A Study of the African Response to European Trade*, Oxford: Oxford University Press.

Daaku. K.Y. (1972) 'Aspects of precolonial Akan economy', *The International Journal of African Historical Studies*, 5(2): 235–47.

DeCorse, C. (2001) *Archaeology of Elmina: Africans and Europeans on the Gold Coast, 1400–1900*, Washington DC: The Smithsonian Press.

Deng, G. (1997) *Chinese Maritime Activities and Socio-Economic Consequences, c. 2100 B.C.–1900 A.D.*, New York: Greenwood Publishing Group.

Deng, G. (1997) 'The foreign staple trade of China in the pre-modern era', *The International History Review*, 19(2): 253–85.

Deng, K. and Zheng, L. (2015) 'Economic restructuring and demographic growth: demystifying growth and development in Northern Song China, 960–1127', *Economic History Review*, 68(4): 1107–31.

Deng, K. (2020) 'One-off capitalism in Song China, 960–1279 CE', in K. Yazdani and D. Menon (eds) *Capitalisms: Towards and Global History*, Oxford: Oxford University Press, pp 227–30.

Eden, R. (ed) (1555) 'Description of the two voyages made out of England into Guinea in Africa', in P.M. d'Angiera and R. Eden (eds and trans) *The Decades of the New World or West India Containing the Navigations and Conquests of the Spaniards*, London: NS, pp 343–60.

Effah-Gyamfi, K. (1987) 'Archaeology and the study of Early African towns: the West African case, especially Ghana', *West African Journal of Archaeology*, 17: 229–41.

Faro, J. (1958) 'A Organização Fiscal de S. Jorge da Mina em 1529', *Boletim Cultural da Guiné Portuguesa*, 13(49): 75–108.

Ferrier, R. (1970) 'The agreement of the East India Company with the Armenian nation, 22nd June 1688', *Revue des Études Arméniennes*, 7: 438–42.

Frank, A. (1998) *ReOrient: Global Economy in the Asian Age*, Berkeley: University of California Press.

Gerritsen, A. (2020) 'The view from early modern China: capitalism and the Jingdezhen ceramics industry', in K. Yazdani and D. Menon (eds) *Capitalisms: Towards and Global History*, Oxford: Oxford University Press, pp 306–24.

Greif, A. (1989) 'Reputation and coalitions in medieval trade: evidence on the Maghribi traders', *The Journal of Economic History*, 49(4): 857–82.

Harris, R. (2020) *Going the Distance: Eurasian Trade and the Rise of the Business Corporation, 1400–1700*, Princeton, NJ: Princeton University Press.

Haddad, L. (1977) 'A fourteenth-century theory of economic growth and development', *Kyklos*, 30(2): 195–214.

Hartwell, R.M. (1962) 'A revolution in Chinese iron and coal industries during the northern Sung, 960–1123 A.D.', *Journal of Asian Studies*, 21(1): 153–62.

Herzig, E. (1991) *The Armenian Merchants from New Julfa: A Study in Premodern Trade* (Unpublished PhD thesis, University of Oxford).

Ho, E. (2006) *The Graves of Tarim: Genealogy and Mobility across the Indian Ocean*, Oakland: University of California Press.

Hosten, H. (1916) 'Mirza Zul Qarnian, a Christian grandee of three great Moghuls, with notes on Akbar's Christian wife and the Indian bourbons', *Memoirs of the Asiatic Society of Bengal*: 115–94.

Hussain, R. (1990) 'Credit techniques in Armenian commerce in Mughal India', *Proceedings of the Indian History Congress*, 51: 327–31.

Hussain, R. (2011) 'The Armenians in India: trading together but separately', *Proceedings of the Indian History Congress*, 72(1): 400–7.

Khaldun, I. and Rosenthal, F. (eds and trans) (1989) *The Muqaddimah: An Introduction to History*, Princeton, NJ: Princeton University Press.

Lockyer, C. (1711) *An Account of the Trade in India*, London: NS.

Mark, P. and Horta, J. (2004) 'Two early seventeenth-century Sephardic communities on Senegal's Petite Côte', *History in Africa*, 31: 231–56.

Masters, B. (1998) *The Origins of Western Economic Dominance in the Middle East: Mercantilism and the Islamic Economy of Aleppo, 1600–1750*, New York: New York University Press.

Mauro, F. (1990) 'Merchant communities, 1350–1750', in J. Tracy (ed) *The Rise of Merchant Empires: Long-Distance Trade in the Early Modern World, 1350–1750*, Cambridge: Cambridge University Press, pp 255–86.

McCabe, I.B. (2010) 'Small town merchants, global ventures: the maritime trade of the New Julfan Armenians in the seventeenth and eighteenth centuries', in M. Fusaro and A. Polónia (eds) *Maritime History as Global History*, Liverpool: Liverpool University Press, pp 125–57.

Millward, J. (2007) *Eurasian Crossroads: A History of Xinjiang*, New York: Hurst Publishers.

Moll-Murata, C. (2013) 'Guilds and apprenticeship in China and Europe: the Jingdezhen and European ceramics industries', in M. Prak and J.L. van Zanden (eds), *Technology, Skills and the Pre-Modern Economy in the East and the West*, Leiden: Brill, pp 225–56.

Moosvi, S. (1998) 'Armenians in the trade of the Mughal Empire during the seventeenth century', *Proceedings of the Indian History Congress*, 59: 266–78.

Newitt, M. (2008) 'Mozambique island: the rise and decline of a colonial port city', in L. Brockey (ed) *Portuguese Colonial Cities in the Early Modern World*, Farnham: Routledge, pp 105–29.

Nobili, M. and Shahid Mathee, M. (2015) 'Towards a new study of the *Tārīkh al-fattāsh*', *History in Africa*, 42: 37–73.

Pearson, M.N. (1976) *Merchants and Rulers in Gujarat: The Response to the Portuguese in the Sixteenth Century*, Oakland: University of California Press.

Pin-tsun, C. (1989) 'The evolution of Chinese thought on maritime foreign trade from the sixteenth to the eighteenth century', *International Journal of Maritime History*, 1(1): 59–65.

Pomeranz, K. (2001) *The Great Divergence: China, Europe and the Making of the Modern World Economy*, Princeton, NJ: Princeton University Press.

Posnansky, M. (2015) 'Begho: life and times', *Journal of West African History*, 1(2): 95–118.

Ptak, R. (1999) *China's Seaborne Trade with South and Southeast Asia, 1200–1750*, Aldershot: Routledge.

Ptak, R. and Rothermund, D. (eds) (1991) *Emporia, Commodities and Entrepreneurs in Asian Maritime Trade, c. 1400–1750*, Stuttgart: Franz Steiner Verlag.

Ray, H. (1993) *Trade and Diplomacy in India-China Relations: A Study of Bengal in the Fifteenth Century*, New Delhi: Radiant Publishers.

Riello, G. (2010) 'Asian knowledge and the development of calico printing in Europe in the seventeenth and eighteenth centuries', *Journal of Global History*, 5(1): 1–28.

Rukuo, Z., Hirth, F. and Rockhill, W.W. (eds and trans) (1911) *Chau Ju-Kua: His Work on the Chinese and Arab Trade in the Twelfth and Thirteenth Centuries, entitled Chu-fan-ehï*, St Petersburg: Imperial Academy of Sciences.

Sanders, J. (1979) 'The expansion of the Fante and the emergence of Asante in the eighteenth century', *Journal of African History*, 20(3): 349–64.

Sarkissian, M. (1987) 'Armenians in South-East Asia', *Crossroads: An Interdisciplinary Journal of Southeast Asian Studies*, 3(2/3): 1–33.

Sharman, J.C. and Phillips, A. (2020) *Outsourcing Empire: How Company-States Made the Modern World*, Princeton, NJ: Princeton University Press.

Silva, A. (2002) *A Manilha e o Libambo: a África e a escravidão, de 1500 a 1700*, Rio de Janeiro: Editora Nova Fronteira.

Silva, F. (2012) 'Forms of cooperation between Dutch-Flemish, Sephardim and Portuguese private merchants for the Western African trade within the formal Dutch and Iberian Atlantic empires, 1590–1674', *Portuguese Studies*, 28(2): 159–72.

Smith, E. (2018) 'Reporting and interpreting legal violence in Asia: the East India Company's printed accounts of torture, 1603–24', *Journal of Imperial and Commonwealth History*, 46(4): 603–26.

Soon, D.H.T. (2001) 'The trade in Lakawood products between South China and the Malay world from the twelfth to fifteenth centuries', *Journal of Southeast Asian Studies*, 32(2): 133–49.

Stahl, A. (1999) 'The archaeology of global encounters viewed from Banda, Ghana', *African Archaeological Review*, 16: 5–81.

Stahl, A. (2009) *Making History in Banda: Anthropological Visions of Africa's Past*, Cambridge: Cambridge University Press.

Subrahmanyam, S. (1993) *The Portuguese Empire in Asia 1500–1700: A Political and Economic History*, London: Longman.

Tagliacozzo, E. (2020) 'Capitalism's missing link: what happened to Southeast Asia?', in K. Yazdani and D. Menon (eds) *Capitalisms: Towards and Global History*, Oxford: Oxford University Press, pp 180–96.

Teixeira, P. and Sinclair, W. (eds and trans) (1902) *The Travels of Pedro Teixeira; with His 'Kings of Hormuz', and extracts from His 'Kings of Persia'*, London: Hakluyt Society.

Trivellato, F. (2012) *The Familiarity of Strangers: The Sephardic Diaspora, Livorno, and Cross-Cultural Trade in the Early Modern Period*, New Haven, CT: Yale University Press.

van Bavel, B. (2016) *The Invisible Hand? How Markets have Emerged and Declined Since AD 500*, Oxford: Oxford University Press.

Van der Spek, R.J., van Zanden. J.L. and van Leeuwen, B. (eds) (2019) *A History of Market Performance: From Ancient Babylonia to the Modern World*, London: Routledge.

Vogt, J. (1973) 'Portuguese gold trade: an account ledger from Almina, 1529–31', *Transactions of the Historical Society of Ghana*, 14(1): 93–103.

Von Kispal-van Deijk, G. (2013) 'Ubiquitous but elusive: the Chinese of Makassar in VOC times', *Journal of Asian History*, 47(1): 81–103.

Wade, G. (ed and trans) (2005) 'Ming Shi-lu [The Veritable Records of the Ming Dynasty]', [online]. Available from: http://epress.nus.edu.sg/msl/ [Accessed 17 February 2021].

Washbrook, D. (1990) 'South Asia, the world system, and world capitalism', *Journal of Asian Studies*, 49(3): 479–508.

Wen-Chin, H. (1988) 'Social and economic factors in the Chinese porcelain industry in Jingdezhen during the Late Ming and Early Qing period, ca. 1620–1683', *The Journal of the Royal Asiatic Society of Great Britain and Ireland*, 1: 135–59.

Wilks, I. (1982a) 'Wangara, Akan and Portuguese in the fifteenth and sixteenth centuries: 1, the matter of Bitu', *The Journal of African History*, 23(3): 333–49.

Wilks, I. (1982b) 'Wangara, Akan and Portuguese in the fifteenth and sixteenth centuries: 2, the struggle for trade', *The Journal of African History*, 23(4): 463–72.

Williams, Eric (1944) *Capitalism and Slavery*, Chapel Hill: University of North Carolina Press.

Wise, C. (ed and trans) (2011) *Ta'rīkh al-Fattāsh: The Timbuktu Chronicles, 1493–1599*, Trenton, NJ: Africa World Press.

Yang, X. (2009) 'Some possible Chinese records about Armenia and the Armenians in mid-Qing Dynasty', *Iran and the Caucasus*, 13: 229–38.

Yazdani, K. and Menon, D. (2020) 'Introduction', in K. Yazdani and D. Menon (eds) *Capitalisms: Towards and Global History*, Oxford: Oxford University Press, pp 1–27.

6

Capitalism, Imperialism and the Emergence of an Industrialized Global Economy

Colin M. Lewis

Introduction

If imperialism is the highest stage of capitalism, marked by the growth of monopoly and finance capital, and the mechanism by which capitalism was diffused (Lenin, 2010), it is legitimate to enquire what type of capitalism was transmitted across the world, and when. It is also relevant to speculate about forms of capitalism that may have been 'globalized' by earlier expressions of colonialism. In the age of precocious commercial capitalism – the so-called Age of (European) Discoveries and Exploration beginning in the early 14th century, what was the impact of Portuguese encounters with African and Asian societies, and what form of capitalism was carried to the Americas by Iberian adventurers around 1500? Indeed, how capitalist were the seaborne empires of the Iberian kingdoms of the period, and how did the impact of these encounters differ from such later examples as the scramble for Africa and deepening penetration of Asia by Europeans at high points of the 'old' and 'new' imperialisms of the 18th and 19th centuries, successively characterized by mercantile, industrial and financial capitalism? How did these expressions of capitalism and imperialism meld and interact?

Speculating about expressions of capitalism that emerged in Western Europe, this chapter will explore the nature of overseas expansion from the North Atlantic world. It offers a stylized assessment of interactions with other regions of the global economy from the old and new imperialisms to the post-colonial (or neo-colonial) era, considering the extent to which specific manifestations of capitalism shaped the political economy of successive state–market formations. Modern capitalism, marked by the agricultural and industrial revolutions of the late 18th century, involved the internationalization of industry, and patterns of trade and investment that were quite different from earlier mercantilist overseas adventures. Changes in the nature and form of industrialization – from early North Atlantic expressions to 20th-century models such as those observed in Latin America and Asia, along with the restructuring of global trade and investment flows, have provoked renewed debate about the usefulness of the term 'imperialism'. Challenges from the left and the right have revitalized analyses of capitalism and imperialism (and neo-colonialism). They have encouraged a reappraisal of different manifestations of capitalism and of the nature of industrial development. Reviewing the 'long' 20th century, terms such as the 'concentration and centralization of capital', 'late industrialization', 'late imperialism', 'globalization' and the 'trans-nationalization of capitalism' – the consolidation of a transnational capitalist class and transnational state – have come to the fore or gained greater prominence.

Is the traditional view of imperialism dead or, as Warren (1980) asserts, does imperialism remain the pioneer of capitalism in what used to be regarded as the periphery? Has the old hierarchy of imperialism centre and dependent periphery been displaced by a multifaceted network of transnational production and finance that refines but does not displace ideas about interconnections between capitalism and globalization, while adding nuance to arguments about imperialism and different types of capitalism (Wallerstein, 2004; Foster, 2019)? These questions frame this chapter about industrial capitalism in a global context —from first-mover industrializers to early late-comers engaged in catch-up and very late-comer industrializers seeking to accelerate the processes of structural change through state-sponsored development and state capitalism. The next section provides a stylized assessment of theory and history. This is followed by accounts of different routes to industrialism suggested by such concepts as relative economic backwardness, stage theory and modernization, drawing largely on the experience of the North Atlantic economies. Then the narrative shifts to examine emergent expressions of industrial capitalism in East Asia. While state capitalism is viewed as a recent feature of industrialization in parts of Asia, the next section on 'cosy' or 'crony' capitalism reflects on earlier examples of the role of government in processes of capitalist industrialization. The section before the Conclusion re-evaluates various debates, old and new, about the capitalism–imperialism–industrialization nexus.

Some (stylized) theory and history

Debates about capitalism, imperialism and industrialization raise several related issues. Was imperialism critical to the first and second industrial revolutions in the North Atlantic world, processes that marked the 'Great

Divergence' of the modern age – the acceleration of growth at the European end of the Eurasian land mass, occasioning the rise of the West and the decline – first relative, then absolute – of the South and much of East Asia (Wallerstein, 2004; Parthasarathi, 2011; O'Brien, 2020)? Was the late imperialism of finance capital the mechanism by which modern capitalism (aka industrialization) was transferred to 'backward' areas of the globe? Does the third Industrial Revolution (often associated with the emergence of state capitalism in parts of what used to be described as the periphery or the Third World) mark the emergence of a distinct form of development that is rebalancing the global order – the 'Rise of the Rest' and the 'Rise of the Remainder', pointing to novel expressions of capitalism, industrialism and new power relationships (Amsden, 2001)?

Classical economics argued that unfettered markets and specialization (division of labour) would contribute to a growth in trade – domestic and international – thereby raising productivity, welfare and the sum of human happiness. Colonialism and imperialism had little fit with this approach. They were anathema, impediments to the free functioning of markets and exchange. The unrestricted movement of factors of production – capital and labour, and an international monetary system based on the Gold Standard – with the pound sterling serving as a reserve currency managed by the City of London, facilitated an international division of labour in which countries specialized in the mechanized production of goods or commodities in which they enjoyed a comparative (or relative) advantage. A hegemonic British state provided public goods for the international system as a whole – peace, the protection of property (rule of international law), an open regime for international trade and investment and the guarantee of an international monetary system – an action that was responsible for the dissemination of a liberal political economy that resonated across the world (Akita, 2002: 2–3). The result was the internationalization of production and trade, and a period of rapid, if volatile, growth, leading to the emergence of the modern capitalist system, a world order that would later serve as a model for neoliberals who argued the case for trade and financial liberalization (open economies and a reduction in protectionism and statism) on the eve of the second era of globalization in the late 20th century. With the collapse of communism in East Europe and parts of Africa and Asia, this later model of globalized capitalism would be based on the Washington Consensus. The US dollar performed a role similar to that of sterling for much of the pre 1914 period, and the Bretton Woods institutions provided institutional and ideological support for the new arrangement.

A different assessment was provided by Marx, Hobson, Lenin and successors. They observed a succession of distinct stages of capitalism/ imperialism: mercantile capitalism, most associated with the old imperialism; industrial capitalism, of the Industrial Revolution; and finance capitalism (the Leninist term is 'finance capital'), which triggered the new imperialism. This shift from competitive to monopoly (finance) capitalism would later provide *dependistas* and neo-Marxists with the bases of an argument that imperialism had not affected capitalist modernization in colonial (and neo-colonial) regions – the Third World to be. Although for orthodox Marxist-Leninists, imperialism – irrespective of its form – remained the route to capitalism, most recognized the implications of the shifting nature of the beast (Warren, 1980).

Finance capital had created a world quite different from that of the late 18th century, rooted in innovation in manufacturing and agriculture driven by entrepreneurial competition among small, individual family firms and the consolidation of a free market – an economy regulated by the hidden hand rather than the state. The historical provenance of this model was late 18th-century England and, a little later, New England and the soon-to-be independent US. Conveniently, US independence marked the end of mercantile capitalism in the Anglo North Atlantic world at a time when the old imperialism survived in the Spanish and Portuguese Empires, where mercantilism and monopoly remained the norm, as in French imperial territories, notwithstanding the loss of Canada.

The early Anglo model of the first Industrial Revolution gave way to an expression of capitalist modernization that entailed a closer collaboration between industry (and agriculture) and finance, supported by government. This was not state capitalism, but was state protected, linked to the emergence of large conglomerates as the focus of industrial production shifted from such early industries as cotton textiles and the industrialized production of wage goods to heavy industry and 'lumpy' technology, when follower economies such as Belgium and some German states industrialized. This was the age of maturing industrial capitalism when modest colonial expansion was again observed, prefiguring the emergence of the new imperialism of the late 19th century.

The third stage – finance capital – coincided with the second Industrial Revolution, which was the expression of capitalism that most exercised Lenin. Industry was cartelized, firms increased in size and large-scale modern conglomerates emerged among later industrializers in such sectors as steel, petrochemicals and electrical – technology-heavy and capital-intensive activities. This was the age of monopoly capitalism and of economic imperialism – the new imperialism. Neo-Marxists, especially those who wrote from a dependency perspective, questioned the progressive attributes of imperialism and capitalism in the age of finance capital while stressing the resilience of commercial-cum-mercantilist capitalism transmitted during the old imperialism. They disputed the dynamics of imperialism as a transfer/transformative mechanism (Frank, 1967; 1998). Predating dependency, though sometimes conflated with it, structuralist analyses of the 1950s and 1960s provided another pessimistic assessment of international capitalism during the first era of globalization. As decolonization gathered pace in the mid-20th century, the experience of post-colonial Latin America was held to offer insights to 'newer' colonies in Africa and parts of Asia. Foreign finance and international trade before the 1920s fostered structural impediments to national industrialization – the centre had constrained the development of the periphery (Prebisch, 1981). Development required a resetting of relations with the international economy and state action to drive modern manufacturing. Unbalanced growth meant distorting internal and external terms of trade to induce a flow of factors into manufacturing, triggering domestic multiplier effects. Strong chains of backward and forward linkages would flow from the leading, dynamic industrial sector stimulating national economic development, overcoming pre-modern constraints and delivering national autonomy (Hirschman, 1958).

State planning and pro-manufacturing national development strategies were pronounced features of several Asian, African and Latin American economies in the immediate post-Second World War decades, especially during the decolonization in parts of Africa and Asia from the late 1940s to the 1960s. Indeed, such Russia-inspired programmes were often a reaction against colonialism and imperialism. National industrialization, involving differing mixes of market and non-market devices, was equated with development and economic and political autonomy in many former colonial territories. The achievements (or failures) of state-led programmes of import-substituting industrialization remains a subject of debate. Successes influenced later manifestations of state capitalism, with failures castigated as facilitating neo-colonialism and dependence, new forms of exploitation that inhibited industrialization-cum-development. Antagonism towards the Washington agencies and the ideological underpinnings of the consensus and agencies has led to both a questioning of market economics and market capitalism and the popularizing of state capitalism, provoking a reappraisal of the role of state and market. Asia-style state capitalist industrialization is seen as a potential route to modern development. This model melds market and state mechanisms in a framework that is quite different from Soviet-socialist industrialization or state-led import-substituting industrialization in developing economies during the middle third of the 20th century. Asian state capitalism may explain the Rise of the Rest (and the Remainder), reversing the Great Divergence and – as argued in due course – has accelerated the diffusion of the third Industrial Revolution. But what about imperialism?

Table 6.1 suggests that the demise of the old imperialism also marked the beginning of the Great Divergence in the global economy – the rise of the West and the decline of Asia as the largest and most dynamic component

Table 6.1: The Great Divergence: continental share of global GDP (%)

	1500	1600	1700
Western Europe	17.9	20.0	22.5
Eastern Europe (a)	5.9	6.1	7.2
Western Offshoots (b)	0.5	0.2	0.2
Latin America	2.9	1.5	1.7
Asia (c)	65.0	65.8	61.8
Africa	7.4	6.7	6.6
	1820	**1870**	**1913**
Western Europe	23.6	33.6	33.5
Eastern Europe (a)	9.0	11.7	13.1
Western Offshoots (b)	1.9	10.2	21.7
Latin America	2.0	2.5	4.5
Asia (c)	59.2	38.3	24.6
Africa	4.5	3.7	2.7
	1950	**1973**	**2003**
Western Europe	26.3	25.7	19.2
Eastern Europe (a)	13.1	13.8	6.1
Western Offshoots (b)	30.6	25.3	23.8
Latin America	7.6	8.7	7.7
Asia (c)	18.5	24.1	32.6
Africa	3.6	3.3	3.2
	2030		
Western Europe	13.0		
Eastern Europe (a)	4.7		
Western Offshoots (b)	19.8		
Latin America	6.3		
Asia (c)	53.2		
Africa	3.0		

Source: Based on Maddison (2001, 2008)

Notes: Eastern Europe (a): Includes Russia/USSR, which accounts for a disproportionate – the preponderant – proportion from the late 19th century until the late 20th.

Western Offshoots (b): USA, Canada, Australia and New Zealand, meaning that the proportion is largely determined by US GDP).

Asia (c): Until the late 19th century the share is largely determined by China and India – for 1500 the Indian GDP contributed slightly more than the Chinese; thereafter, until the early 19th century, the continental percentage was increasingly influenced by Chinese GDP; although in 1870 the Chinese participation dwarfed the Japanese, from the 1870s until the 1980s Japanese GDP accounted for a growing proportion, followed by other East Asian economies from the 1990s, yet from c. 2003, China's contribution has increased exponentially in the continental share, notwithstanding a significant growth in the contribution of Indian GDP to the continental figure.

of the international system. Until the beginning of the 19th century, East (and South) Asia accounted for a disproportionate share of global gross domestic product (GDP) and trade. Industrialization underpinned the acceleration of growth in England, parts of Western Europe and the broader North Atlantic world after *c.* 1800, intensifying the focus on the relationship of modern capitalism, industrialization and imperialism. Divergence began at some point during the first half of the 18th century, around the highpoint of the old imperialism. By 1800, the ratio of GDP per capita of the richest to the poorest regions of the world was around 3:1. Divergence through the 19th and 20th centuries pushed the ratio to 15:1 in 2000 until it declined somewhat around 2008, standing at 10:1 in 2016 as state capitalist industrialization in China occasioned yet another pendulum swing in influence and power back to the eastern rim of Eurasia (Court, 2020: 1–2, 7–8, 32–3).

The period of deepening global divergence approximates with the consolidation of modern industrial capitalist and the new imperialism. The Great Divergence debate has refuelled older controversies about the locus of power and influence on the Eurasian land mass and in the global economy as mainland Chinese commercial and financial penetration of Africa, Asia and Latin America has accelerated. If industrialization explains divergence, did imperialism account for industrialization in the West? The divergence debate also has implications for the Marxist-Leninist assessment of the dynamic of capitalism–industrialization–imperialism – that imperialism industrialized the international economy.

The concentration and centralization of capital, backwardness, stage theory and capitalist modernization

Returning to Lenin and the concentration and centralization of capital: capital was concentrated in conglomerates that integrated production, distribution and finance – represented by the industries of the second Industrial Revolution that featured the production of steel, new sources of energy such as electricity and oil, the early manufacture of motor vehicles and electrical appliances, synthetic chemicals and new capital goods, and was centralized in the major advanced economies of the day – what would later become denominated as the centre, where such capital-intensive new technology predominated in large-scale, multi-divisional corporate entities geared towards assembly line mass production.

While orthodox economists and institutionalists such as Williamson (O'Rourke and Williamson, 2017) and others such as O'Brien (2020) would disagree, the argument that monopoly finance capitalism depended on secure supplies of essential raw materials and guaranteed access to markets, requirements that could only be delivered by an alliance of state and business and imperialism, continues to resonate. The result was late 19th-century Great Power industrial rivalry and the scramble for empire. As suggested earlier, this manifestation of capitalism was quite different from that of the first Industrial Revolution, associated with iron and coal and steam power, and the rapid modernization of communications (the displacement of canals by railways and wooden sailing ships with iron-hulled steamships), plus mechanized production, especially of cotton textiles and other wage goods. Firms tended to be small and competitive, headed by Schumpeterian inventors who pioneered sequences of (often) small-step technical improvements that reduced costs and made for a horizontal expansion of the market. These were the heroic, would-be gentlemanly entrepreneurs and the small-scale enterprises that pioneered creative destruction – for example the mechanization of factory-based spinning and weaving, leading to the demise of cottage industries and the destitution of handloom weavers. Committed to free competition, such representatives of early industrial capitalism railed against government intervention and rejected the mercantilist constraints of chartered monopoly companies and the old imperialism of protected domestic and colonial markets, with commercial opportunities in competitor markets exploited by illicit commerce – contraband or smuggling. For advocates of laissez-faire, international trade was no longer viewed as a zero-sum game whereby exports represented a gain and imports a loss of bullion.

Where Lenin noted the emergence of monopoly finance capital, others offer differing perspectives on the consolidation of large-scale modern industrial production and big business (and big banking). Arguing that capital accumulation was the principal driver of economic growth – rather than supply-side factors, innovative technology and enterprise per se – Gerschenkron was concerned with different routes to economic development; the ideas and institutions shaping late industrialization. Challenging the contemporary appeal of Soviet-style planning, he reflected on the advantages (and disadvantages) of relative backwardness and the shifting nature of industrial production that changed market–state relations. Not coming first, backward countries had the advantage of being able to borrow and learn; benefiting from follower advantage, they did not have to reinvent the wheel. Yet in the face of first-comer advantage, there was the need to catch up fast to compete and survive. In moderately backward economies, industrial or universal banks could foster industrial capital accumulation, with government encouragement. Coercive state action was required to overcome extreme backwardness in economies that lagged even further behind, providing capital, skilled labour, entrepreneurship and technology. Banks and/or state coordination were substitutes for heroic entrepreneurs; they accelerated the process of industrialization and overcame constraints that had inhibited industrial growth. Only a partnership between banks and business, with the assistance of government, could sustain the capitalism of the second Industrial Revolution. Technologies driving innovation and scale required large agglomerations of capital and extended gestation periods to achieve profitability, yet the benefit was accelerated industrial transformation, even if growth was unbalanced. Scale, technology and the agglomeration of capital were the hallmarks of the second Industrial Revolution, as were institutional substitutes that delivered a spurt to industrial development (Gerschenkron, 1962; Amsden, 1989: 12–14; Engerman, 2010: 236–44; Fishlow, n.d.).

Once a country had industrialized, the rules of the game changed for ever and for everyone, necessitating different state–market relationships among follower economies. Early expressions of industrialism such as those observed in England and New England could not be a model for second wave industrializers such as Germany and Japan in the mid-19th century – or industrial consolidation in the US itself. Infant industry needed protection. Advocates of protection for infant industries to achieve industrial catch-up would come to have a profound influence. In the US, Alexander Hamilton was a precocious campaigner against unfettered international trade, along with his near German contemporary, Friedrich List (Reinert, 2007: 71–100). Both argued that without tariff protection fledgling industrial business could not compete against British manufacturers; such was the edge gained by the first industrial nation. While recognizing the efficiency delivered by competition, protection was essential for catch-up, a process also characterized by capital-hungry technologies and scale, and the development of managerial capitalism. In the new context, development ideology and state-directed national projects were important in shaping policy and institutions in implementing industrial strategy (Gerschenkron, 1962: 73).

Although the Gerschenkron hypothesis was much challenged, it has stood the test of time, unlike the stage-model of industrialization essayed by a near-contemporary economist-cum-economic historian, Walt Whitman Rostow (Kasza, 2018: 146; Fishlow, n.d.). Rostow was similarly concerned with what he regarded the pernicious influence of socialist planning. His first major work, subtitled *A Non-Communist Manifesto*, could have been entitled *An Anti-Communist Manifesto*. In a series of publications, drawing on his research on the first Industrial Revolution and the modernization of British economy, polity and society, Rostow constructed a linear, universalist, increasingly prescriptive recipe for industrialization, designed to defend capitalism and promote free enterprise, that acknowledged Gerschenkron's notion of substitutes (Rostow, 1960, 1978). Rostow's publications represented a significant contribution to Weberian modernization theory, mapping transitions from traditional societies to modern, democratic, market welfare capitalism in a globalizing world. His treatise established a typology of phases of industrial transformation that vaunted the importance of the market, rather than government, and sought to confront what he regarded as influential (and misguided) statist route maps to industrialization advanced in newly independent countries in Africa and Asia during the Cold War. Despite its initial scholarly impact, and promotion as a policy model for developing economies in Africa, Asia and Latin America by US officials, the stages of growth hypothesis rapidly fell out of favour. In part this was because of obvious flaws in the model as the hypothesis was pushed beyond its intellectual limits – as noted by specialist in areas upon which Rostow was trespassing, as much as his role as a Washington hawk, policy advisor and official during the height of the Cold War, when he supported nuclear intervention during the Vietnam War.

Some years later, Alfred D. Chandler provided support for the thesis of scale, technology and the agglomeration of capital during the second Industrial Revolution. In works that drew on firm/company case histories from the US, Britain and Germany, Chandler disputed the primacy of the market in delivering growth, focusing on the business organization as a critical mechanism. He analysed how organization and structure evolved to enhance operational capabilities and profits, thereby fostering growth at large – even when limiting competition. In his early work, Chandler pointed to changes in business organizations (phases in the emergence of big business from the entrepreneur-owned entities engaged in trade and production to joint-stock companies in such sectors as transport, chemicals and oil, and retailing) and emphasized managers and mergers – structural change associated with amalgamation, acquisitions and the rise of impersonal, managerial hierarchies. Subsequently he wrote about finance, technology and mass production propelled by the horizontal expansion and vertical deepening of the market that underpinned a managerial revolution. Later still the scale and scope of production shaped the dynamics of industrial capitalism in the age of the multidivisional, managerial mega-corporation – with investment flowing into organizational and technical capabilities and marketing. Managerial coordination facilitated multifaceted innovation, ensuring the productive utilization of resources at firm level and growth and modernization in the wider economic and social context as marketing broadened and deepened the market. (Chandler, 1977; 1990).

Whether focusing on imperialism, relative historical backwardness, a shifting relationship between state and market or the emergence of impersonal, managerial capitalism, these approaches all emphasize the evolving nature of capitalism and industrialism.

State capitalism, imperialism and late industrialization

As suggested, Gerschenkron's research on Russia derived from a search for development insights that might apply to the Third World, particularly former colonies seeking economic independence through rapid industrialization, many of whose policy makers were influenced by the Soviet model. The emphasis was anti-Marxist, and the focus on late industrialization derived as much from a desire to debunk the contemporary vogue for Soviet-style planning as the desire to offer to Third World policy makers alternative models intellectually rooted in capitalism (Fishlow, n.d.; Engerman, 2010: 234–5, 236). In late-comer industrializers, where coercive government action was essential to combat extreme backwardness, the state was a substitute for the market, and unbalanced growth – forcing the pace of industrial transformation – an objective as much as a consequence of an industrial spurt.

Extrapolating from Gerschenkron, several examples of late industrialization, or late development (and/or very late industrialization/development), can be identified in which in the state substituted – or part substituted – for the market. Examples include those referenced by Gerschenkron, such as Russia and Japan, while others have been identified by scholars of unbalanced growth and late industrialization writing about Asia and Latin America. Czarist Russia, after around 1890, and Soviet Russia in the interwar period represented compelling examples of state and market fusion and substitution. Although serfdom had been abolished in Russia in 1861, some one third of all former serfs remained indebted to the Crown. Government was the main promoter and operator of railways and featured in the mining sector. State banks dominated the domestic financial market. State-owned factories, while declining in relative importance, remained a feature of several branches of manufacturing – notably heavy industry. Even before 1917 the Russian state produced much for itself and consumed from itself, while fostering private production via subsidies, tariff protection (which also benefited state enterprises) and access to key inputs – financial, material and human resources. Favoured cartels and monopoly producers grew, coming to dominate the market for modern industrial goods. The arrangement hardly constituted central planning, yet there was massive government intervention. Czarist Russia, an imperial power whose laggard modernization raised the spectre that it might fall victim to imperialism, was the most closed, bureaucratized market economy in early 20th-century Europe. In the 1920s, War Communism gave way to the New Economic Policy (NEP) promoted by Lenin in 1921 as a temporary measure to revive and stabilize the economy before a transition to socialism. The NEP brought a partial revival of the private sector, particularly in agriculture and some service activities. Money, which had been abolished during the phase of

War Communism, was reintroduced, and private property and the private ownership of (mainly small) business permitted. Although notionally a mixed economy, and representing a retreat from the command economy of War Communism, the system was a form of state capitalism: the state retained control of the commanding heights of activity by controlling such sectors as transport, heavy industry, banking and foreign trade, though foreign direct investment was encouraged. Yet there were echoes of the heavily statist late Czarist political economy (Gregory, 1994: 6–12; Gatrell, 1995: 47; Cheremukhin et al, 2017).

Elements of state capitalism can be observed in the first stages of industrial modernization in Japan. With the Meiji Restoration of 1868, the motto of the regime, 'enrich the nation; strengthen the army', pointed to an ideology and project of state-led industrialization – and the development of what might be described as a military-industrial complex. Only economic power would ensure autonomy and independence. Investing in technology, industrialization and defence, the regime renegotiated unequal trade treaties. Modernization was spearheaded by state enterprises and private business – the Zaibatsu (Samuels, 1994: 84–93). Beginning as family businesses, the Zaibatsu subsequently developed as quasi industrial-financial conglomerates, integrating processing and industrial activities. With one or two firms dominating specific sectors, they came to resemble the near contemporary monopoly cartels observed in the US and Germany. They were large, multi-activity private corporations in receipt of state assistance. In theory, though to a somewhat lesser extent in practice until compelled by budgetary and financial constraints, Meiji strategy incorporated the idea that pioneer state companies would be transferred to private ownership once established on a strong footing, able to compete against foreign firms enjoying first-mover and monopoly advantage. Despite the determination of the US occupation administration to dismantle the Zaibatsu, they remained the driving force behind the post-Second World War Japanese Economic Miracle, a model of state-assisted national capitalism that did not weaken until the late 20th century (Morck and Nakamura, 2007: 14–40; Addicot, 2017: 2–3, 5–7, 14). This model would inform post-1960s Korean development strategy, in which the Chaebols played a role similar to that of Japanese Zaibatsu. Such corporations and business groups were an institutional substitute for the Schumpeterian entrepreneur (Guillén, 2001: 60, 61)

In Meiji Japan, imperialism was not the vector by which capitalism was transmitted to the country. Rather, the threat of imperialism triggered a domestic response that matured as state-sponsored late industrialization. Reacting to the forced opening of the country by a US fleet in 1853 and 1854, and the imposition of unequal trade treaties - negotiated under the guns of foreign warships after 1858 – a section of the elite subscribed to an ideology of modernization, imposing a programme of industrial catch-up to increase production, promote enterprise and stimulate growth. Feudalism was abolished. Commercial and civil codes and a system of parliamentary government, based on Imperial Germany, were imported. Many economic institutions were modelled on those of late 19th-century European capitalism. Students were dispatched overseas; basic state education was made compulsory; higher education was structured along the lines of the French and German systems, with strong emphases on training for the public administration and on the technical, the scientific and the vocational. Military modernization was modelled on the Royal Navy and Prussia. The national banking system was structured along US lines. Technology was imported, along with capital and foreign advisors (Macpherson, 1987: 29–30; Amsden, 1991: 283; Morck and Nakamura, 2007: 6, 12–13). Modern industrial capitalism in late 19th-century Japan was capitalism by invitation. Japan borrowed and learnt, importing institutions and policy models, adapting them to local conditions.

The rise of the rest: late industrial capitalism in Asia

Although taking issue with elements of the approach, Amsden has contributed most to the resurgence of the economic backwardness thesis (1989, 2001). Building on Gerschenkron, she expanded the concept of late industrialization in time and space. Her focus on the diffusion of development contributes to the analysis of state-supported industrialism and state capitalism after the 1960s. This was characterized by the opening of economies and the transition from heavily subsidized import substitution to market-disciplined (manufactured), export-led industrialization (Amsden, 1991: 284–5).

Late industrialization, or very late industrialization, in its early phases depended on borrowing and learning – importing and adapting technology and organizational methods. During this process, the state itself changed, from rent-seeking to development-promoting, a change that also required a new (possibly inclusive) political and social economy. Focusing on East Asia, with occasional references mainly to South East Asia and Latin America, Amsden emphasizes the significance of technology, particularly in mid-technology sectors – industries where production techniques were accessible, easily replicable and less costly than in the most advanced technology industries. Hence the targeting of heavy industry, the motor-mechanical and electrical industries and textiles on the part of would-be late industrializers intent on catch-up. In such sectors, cheap, available, borrowed technologies gave late-comer industrializers a competitive advantage over low-wage producers of basic goods and advanced economies that had moved on to the production of high-tech items – a shifting pattern of global industrial production/specialization that reflected the emergence of a new international division of labour.

State action was critical in mid-tech sectors. The state identified and conditioned a targeted number of national leaders, directing capital towards preferred manufacturing activities, providing subsidies and other forms of aid to ensure competitivity in world markets, while curbing domestic consumption to ensure an adequate export surplus and disciplining labour – the main source of forced savings. Borrowing from Chandler, Amsden also acknowledges the rise of salaried managers in emergent conglomerates (Amsden, 1989: 8–9; Kasza, 2018: 148–51). For Amsden, the pioneering English Industrial Revolution was based on invention; for followers such as Germany and the US on innovation; while for latecomers such as Korea knowledge-based learning underwrote national industrial capitalism (Amsden, 1989: 3–6, 14, 319–21). The emergence of a strong, autonomous state was a prerequisite for such late national capitalism, and entailed the state engaging in corporate as well as national planning, not least to augment supply and demand (Amsden, 1989: 141–2, 146).

Japanese imperialism, a growing influence in the Korean peninsula from around the time of the Meiji Restoration, led to military occupation and colonization, and culminated in annexation and the incorporation of the country into the Japanese Empire in 1910. This initiated the process of building a strong state – an enduring colonial transfer. The concept of a strong state matured after the Second World War and the Korean Conflict (1950–53) in response to decades of occupation and warfare and the Japanese example (Amsden, 2001: 100–4, 119–20). The ruling class of what would become the Republic of Korea enjoyed an ambivalent relationship with Japan, which was viewed with great antagonism and as a continuing threat, yet also as a model of state-assisted industrial capitalism. The ever-present danger posed by the Democratic People's Republic of Korea to the north, plus US aid, also influenced the momentum in favour of national industrial capitalism ordered by a developmental state. In addition to an ideological and cultural bias towards a strong state that generates and channels economic rents, another feature of the Korean disciplined capitalism model was export-led industrialization pioneered by family-owned conglomerates (Amsden, 2001). There was a reciprocal relationship between business and state, and the state set performance standards for firms in exchange for subsidies and support. A strong, disciplining, developmental state did not preclude venality. The Korean model melded corruption, productivity and efficiency (Amsden, 1989: 55, 146–7; Guillén, 2001: 76–82).

A similar legacy of Japanese imperialism is observable in post-Second World War state-directed industrial capitalism in the Republic of China, though the business–state relationship was quite different from that which emerged in Korea. In Taiwan, small- and medium-sized enterprises spear-headed industrialization; in Korea, big business (Amsden, 2001: 105–7, 119–20). At the end of the first Sino-Japanese War – a contest for influence in Korea – the island was ceded to Japan by China in 1895. With the defeat of Japan at the end of the Second World War, China reasserted its authority over the island in 1945, and in 1949 it became the seat of the Nationalist (Kuomintang) government following defeat in the Chinese civil war by communist forces on the mainland. The newly formed government (and state) inherited a plethora of corporations from the Japanese imperial administration and the Japanese military, which came to constitute a component of the initial economic model (Amsden, 2001: 235). The ethos of a strong state derived from the pre-1945 colonial administration and the militaristic, authoritarian system established by Kuomintang refugees. Other common characteristics of state-led development in the Republic of China and the Republic of Korea include a rapid transformation of industrial structures as the economies moved from early, easy import substitution industrial growth to mature manufactured export-orientated industrialization, investment in human capital – facilitating relative income equality – and a cosy relationship between government and business. There was also a considerable amount of authoritarianism in the early phases of industrial upgrading (Kuznets, 1988; Kim and Heo, 2017).

The cases of Taiwan and Korea fostered the idea of an East Asian model; that is, substantial state-supported high ratios of accumulation and investment in human capital and the promotion of technology-based manufactured exports. These were distinct state assisted, disciplined, knowledge-based variants of national industrial capitalism that sustained domestic ownership of enterprises (Kuznets, 1988: S17–S34; Amsden, 2001: 14, 191; Chang, 2003: 46–51; Kim and Heo, 2017: 18–27). Local ownership also ensured that such industry leaders generated strong internal backward and forward linkage effects stimulating investment, employment and growth. This was a model of state-national, market-orientated industrial development that would inform post-1978 reforms in mainland China, a programme of pragmatic liberalization that accelerated in the 1990s, grafting market mechanisms and incentives, and quasi-market institutions, onto a planned economy. Domestic market liberalization and openness to the international economy were the two most influential factors driving post-1990s industrialization in the People's Republic, resulting in export-led growth and state capitalism – all with distinct echoes of the Meiji ethos of enriching the nation and strengthening the army, plus in the Chinese case empowering the party (Brandt et al, 2016: 2–3, 25). The East Asian pattern of industrial capitalism would accelerate the third Industrial Revolution, symbolized by electronics, information technology, robotics, artificial intelligence and renewable energy, and an associated transformation of production techniques across sectors and services by mega-corporations geared towards integrated supply chains and just-in-time delivery. This is a world economy dominated by free-wheeling Silicon Valley technology-research campuses such as Facebook and Asian state-capitalist/business conglomerates such as Huawei.

Cosy capitalism or crony capitalism?

A cosy relationship between big business and government was critical to the dynamics of industrial capitalism from the late 19th century. It was effective when guided by a disciplining, developmental state. Yet for some this was crony capitalism – a concept that applied as much to state-owned enterprises as businesses benefiting from government favours – and was inimical to long-term growth because firm performance and survival was determined not by a competitive environment but by non-market criteria than would lead to rent-seeking – the antithesis of vibrant capitalist modernization (Krueger, 2002: 2–3). For others, crony capitalism was a second-best option, necessary in backward economies plagued by political insecurity, where capital markets were shallow and underdeveloped, and where an institutional framework required for the consolidation of market capitalism was absent. Cronyism was an institutional substitute and might prove a stepping stone to market capitalism. Rent-seeking was not necessarily a bad thing if it secured property rights – for some, thereby accelerating accumulation and investment in productive enterprises – and was reformable, admittedly a difficult process (Guillén, 2001: 60–3; Haber, 2002: xx; Haber, Razo and Maurer, 2003:20, 29–36; Schneider, 2004: 3–6; Aligica and Tarko, 2014: 157). The crucial factor was potential for state capture by would-be rent-seekers. State capture scotched any likelihood of a reform of the model by a disciplining, autonomous state. These arguments are made by Chibber, drawing on Amsden and Hirschman. He contrasts the Korean and Indian experiences of post-Independence industrialization and industrial policy. State-building, state capacity and state autonomy are critical: in the absence of any one, successful late capitalist industrial development is unlikely (Chibber, 2003: 29–44).

Epitomized by *grupos económicos*, *grupo familiar* or *familias empresarias*, cronyism was much in evidence during periods of industrial growth and industrialization in Latin America in the 19th and 20th centuries. In late 19th-century Latin America, the emergent oligarchic state may be depicted as a variant of crony capitalism, as may the populist state of the mid-/late 20th century. The state granted privileges to specific groups of national and/or foreign capitalists, sufficient to provide credible commitments against government predation. This occasioned investment in activities that generated economic growth (and/or development) and a flow of fiscal resources sufficient to finance the state and secure order, a reciprocal relationship that yielded gains for business and the state, and may even have provided economic and social public goods to a broader spectrum of the population beyond the immediate beneficiaries, thereby further reducing the risk of political instability. Most associated with structural modernization, the oligarchic state embedded capitalism and oversaw the emergence of modern manufacturing (Beatty, 2001; Rocchi, 2006; Summerhill, 2015). Key beneficiaries of cronyism were, in the 19th century, family financial–commercial–industrial businesses, on many occasions owned by networks of families linked by blood and marriage. Maintaining effective political connections, and surviving political upheavals and economic crises, many such enterprises matured during the second half of the 20th century, well placed to benefit from the privatization of state-owned firms around 2000 (Fernández Pérez and Lluch, 2015). The populist state pioneered import-substituting industrialization at a time of rapid population growth and accelerating urbanization. Examples of the oligarchic state include Porfirian Mexico (1876–1911), the Argentine during the Belle Époque (1870–1914) and the Second Empire and Old Republic in Brazil (1850–89, 1889–1930). Classic exemplars of populism range from the Vargas administrations in Brazil (1930–45, 1951–4) and early Peronism in the Argentine (1946–55, 1973–74) to such later examples of democratic and authoritarian populism as the presidencies of Carlos Menem (1989–99) in the Argentine, Alberto Fujimori (1990–2000) in Peru and the regime of Hugo Chávez in Venezuela (2002–13) (Kaufman and Stallings, 1991; Weyland, 2002).

Populism required a strong state presence in the economy but did not necessarily imply a strong state. Strategy centred on a set of economic policies intended to achieve political goals – the forging of a pro-industry alliance of domestic business (later including foreign capital), the urban middle classes (professionals, ideologues, bureaucrats and the military) and organized urban labour. Monopoly rents generated resources for the industrial sector. Policies included the manipulation of factor and input prices in favour of manufacturers – for example privileged access to credit at preferential rates of interest, the skewing of exchange rates to reduce the cost of essential imports, tariff and non-tariff protection, and subsidies funded by transfers from commodity producers/exporters. Other redistributionist policies critical to demand-driven growth were wage hikes and job creation to foster domestic consumption of locally produced manufactures and engender social peace. In addition, domestic industrialists enjoyed a cosy relationship with an expanding state sector (often resulting from the nationalization of formerly foreign-owned transport, communications, energy and commercial/financial enterprises): state-owned corporations sold cheap to local industry and bought dear, while mixed corporations (public–private entities) similarly supported domestic enterprises directly and indirectly, ensuring a national presence in strategic areas (Kaufman and Stallings, 1991: 15–21; Cardoso and Helwege, 1991: 47–50). Budget deficits, inflation, exchange depreciation and balance of payments crises were the hallmarks of populist economics. The Economic Commission or Latin America provided the intellectual and policy bases for import-substituting industrial development strategies applied from the mid-20th century onwards. Rooted in analyses of the

Argentinian economist Raúl Prebisch, and drawing on Albert Hirschman's concept of unbalanced growth, *cepalismo* or structuralism may be described as a Gerschenkronian-style ideology of national, state-managed industrial development, and was rapidly disseminated after the 1940s. *Cepalismo* addressed the needs of the industrial sector while stressing structural and institutional blockages to development, distortions rooted in the prevailing international economic order.

Re-evaluating the dynamics of imperialism-industrialism: a perspective (largely) from Latin America: the imperialism of free trade, structuralism and dependency

The relationship of commodity-driven growth, capitalism and imperialism was as much debated during the Belle Époque of modernization around 1900, as was the mercantilist nature of import-substituting industrialization during the middle third of the 20th century, along with state–market interactions during both periods. Was crony capitalism most observed during the golden age, or the age of populism; was the relationship between imperialism and capitalism more pronounced during British paramountcy in the 19th century or US hegemony in the 20th?

Although the term was not used, a distinct type of cosiness may be posited as the oligarchic state was taking form – the ethos and ideology of free trade as local elites engaged with foreign financiers and commercial agents. Contributing a revisionist account of 19th-century British imperial history that rejects economic determinism, Gallagher and Robinson (1953) sought to demolish the conventional argument about a non-imperial interregnum between the old (mercantilist) and new (finance) imperialism. They advanced the argument of laissez-faire imperialism, or free trade imperialism. As argued earlier, mercantilist imperialism was associated with European conquest, colonization and conflict in the Americas and Asia from the late 15th century. Supposedly dealt a mortal blow by independence struggles in the late 18th and early 19th centuries that witnessed the emergence of new states in much of North and South America, from then until around the 1880s British policy makers were indifferent to empire-building or actively anti-imperialist. This imperial pause came to an end around the 1880s with the onset of Great Power rivalry and a new age of Hobson/Lenin-style economic imperialism. An important contribution of the thesis of free trade imperialism was to bring Latin America into the frame (Gallagher and Robinson, 1953: 8–10). For Gallagher and Robinson, unequal British commercial and financial relations with the continent (as well as not infrequent military interventions during the revolutionary and immediate post-independence decades) contributed to the subsequent evolution of their thesis in several respects. These included the formation and diffusion of the ideology of free trade, the nature of relations between official Britain and business Britain, and the elaboration of the concept of collaborative elites – a term applied to governing groups in the informal as in the formal empire. The existence, capacity and attitude of a collaborative elite was critical to the form of imperialism: informal control if possible, formal control if necessary (Gallagher and Robinson, 1953: 5–7, 13; Cain and Hopkins, 1986: 523). Where local elites were strong and rejected the ideology of free trade, gunboat diplomacy and coercion would result in conquest and formal imperialism. If local elites were weak and insufficiently able to guarantee the order required for trade and investment to flourish, colonization and formal imperialism would similarly result. When local elites were strong, capable of guaranteeing order, and embraced economic liberalism, informal empire became the norm. This was imperialism on the cheap, and local elites retained a larger share of the material benefits of economic growth, resources that might be directed towards domestic capitalist modernization.

Writing some 30 years after Gallagher and Robinson, Cain and Hopkins (1986, 1987) offer further insights on informal empire and economic imperialism. Referring to the British experience, they refute Marxist arguments that imperialism was a product of the inner logic of industrial capitalism: Marxists overestimated the role of finance capital in the dynamics of imperial expansion because the connections between banks and industry were very limited before 1914. Yet Cain and Hopkins acknowledge the transformation of industrial capitalism in the latter part of the 19th century, a reordering that also led them to take issue with Gallagher and Robinson's denial of an imperial interregnum. They argue that Gallagher and Robinson attach insufficient weight to structural changes in the British domestic economy during the 19th century and over-emphasize the degree of continuity in British imperialism. For Cain and Hopkins, such non-industrial capitalist activities as finance and the service sector were the main propellants of overseas expansion. The role of the City of London as a centre of international finance, and the growth of sterling as the engine of world trade, generated the wealth that sustained the British political and economic system, determining the political economy of external relationships with and beyond the empire. This was service capitalism, or gentlemanly capitalism, rather than industrial capitalism or finance capitalism: services (including merchant banking, high finance, commerce, shipping and insurance – and a dynamic re-export trade) created a particular type of economic development and a strong fiscal-military state, along with a new form of rentier capitalism – capitalist yet not industrial. In South America, but also elsewhere, British trade and finance fostered nation-building and the growth of liberal institutions and ideology – free trade and sound money.

Was this economic imperialism or capitalist modernization – or were they one and the same? Alluding to mid-19th-century free trade imperialism and drawing parallels with nostrums associated with the so-called Washington Consensus of more than a century later, Amsden has little doubt about the imperialism of exported ideology and policy (Amsden, 2001: 255–6). And Cain and Hopkins themselves accept that it is reasonable to describe the reliance of parts of Latin America on commercial and financial ties with Britain, no less than the 'white dominions', as one of economic imperialism. The rhythm of the economic life of these countries was dependent on the ebb and flow of London funds, and local elites were 'ideal pre-fabricated collaborators' (Cain and Hopkins, 1986: 502; see also Cain and Hopkins, 1987: 11, 2016: 265–6).

Rejecting the idea of the imperialism of free trade, and focusing on the Argentine, Ferns alludes to the social distribution of gains among local and foreign actors. Rather than supporting the concept of informal empire, though accepting a congruence of interest between what others would describe as a collaborating elite and British commercial and financial interests, Ferns suggests that it is possible to make the case that benefits accrued as much to the Argentine as Britain, and that Britain did not obtain rents from an asymmetrical commercial and financial relationship. British beneficiaries comprised the British–Argentinian business community, shareholders of some banks, railway companies, meat-processing plant and mercantile enterprises, and consumers – especially the waged working class, whose standard of living was enhanced by cheap River Plate commodities. In the Argentine, Ferns specifies as beneficiaries landowners (including immigrants), workers (whose wages and employment prospects widened owing to investment from London and trade-related growth) and the Argentinian state – though he does not use this term (Ferns 1960: 487–91). Echoing Ferns, Platt also disputes the Gallagher and Robinson thesis that official Britain sought indirect political hegemony in Latin America to promote the commercial and financial interests of business Britain. He counter-argues that British governments only intervened when international norms had been violated or lives and property threatened – that is, when public goods such as peace and the rule of law were compromised. Platt's contributions to the study of the business history of the British in Latin America sought further to question the view that corporate practices (efforts to monopolize the processing and marketing of commodities, banking activities and the predominance of London-registered railways and utilities in various markets) was consciously malign. Such activities were not imperialistic given the paramountcy of domestic actors and the queasiness of official Britain about direct action. British influence in the region was mutually beneficial and local elites were economically and politically sovereign: modernization rather than imperialism facilitated industrial capitalism. This assessment echoes that of Ferns, though critics argue that Platt's interpretation of the sources (he worked largely with printed Foreign Office and consular material and the commercial and financial press, given lack of access to business archives) too closely followed the official mind. Even Platt would accept the pervasive influence and appeal of liberal ideology and acknowledge the weight of British commerce and finance in many countries, and the potential for informal imperialism – notwithstanding his stance that this influence was benign (Platt, 1968a, 1968b, 1977; Barton, 2014: 97–100; Cain and Hopkins, 2016: 265–6).

While some questioned the appropriateness of the term 'imperialism' with regard to Latin America during British ascendancy, others pointed to the non-progressive (or anti-transformative) impact of imperialism across the continent – from the age of Iberian mercantilism and monopoly to periods of finance capital and corporate extraction/exploitation. Around the time that Gallagher and Robinson were adding further substance to their approach, within Latin America structuralism was emerging as the dominant paradigm for the analysis of the impact of international trade and finance on continental development, soon to be followed by dependency (Abel and Lewis, 2015: 1–25). Although the two were distinct in their origins and policy recommendations, there were similarities. Structuralism-cum-dependency was a theory of development from the Third World and for the Third World. Structuralists and *dependistas* blamed laissez-faire ideology, the structure of overseas trade (an exchange of commodity exports for imported manufactures) and foreign borrowing and investment as the cause of structural underdevelopment and/or deepening dependency. While drawing on Marxist theory and language, *dependistas* rejected the Marxist-Leninist argument about different forms of capitalist imperialism driving development. Quite the contrary, imperialism had strengthened the forces of underdevelopment by deepening the dependence of peripheral satellite economies on the capitalist core and was responsible for the de-industrialization of the continent in the 19th century. There had been a continuity of exploitation from the implantation of mercantilist, monopoly extractive institutions at the time of conquest and colonization in the 16th century through to transnational industrialization by invitation in the latter part of the 20th. Latin America's engagement with the core had, at best, resulted in weak, fragmented manifestations of capitalism and fragile states, strengthening forces that inhibited development. Only an indigenous socialist revolution would sever the chains of dependence between satellite economies and the capitalist centre – and sweep away the hybrid melange of feudal, pre-capitalist and anti-developmental capitalist relationships that had come to characterize the economies and societies of the continent from Iberian colonization, through British informal empire to US hegemony. In short, *dependistas* refuted modernization theory and questioned Marxian assertions about the progressive nature of imperialism.

Nevertheless, as seen, by the time that Frank was writing, structuralism had already secured a firm base in many Latin American capitals among bureaucratic, policy-making elites and advocates of state-assisted industrial modernization. Conflating industrialization and development, as argued, structuralists observed the instability and institutions associated with export-led growth of the *c.* 1870–1930 period as inhibiting economic and social progress. In part this was because of the inappropriateness of imported economic ideologies and the weakness of states, which proved incapable of resolving bottlenecks that checked development. Nevertheless, while Prebisch-inspired programmes of import-substitution industrialization came to involve a large measure of state capitalism, there was a stark contrast with East Asia. Ill-considered regulation and macroeconomic instability triggered by demand creation – monetary expansion and easy credit – led to inflation and balance of payments crises. The most advanced sector of the economy, manufacturing, was truncated and ill-integrated into the domestic economy, with limited local linkage impact. Production was capital-intensive and skewed towards the production of consumer durables, a bias resulting from inequitable patterns of income distribution. Industry was dominated by an oligopoly of conglomerates that imported technology and components, though largely financed operations from local accumulation and siphoned profits overseas. These shortcomings flowed from state weakness and lack of 'discipline'.

Like Gerschenkron, early dependency writing suggested that there was no single route to development via capitalism, imperialism and industrialization. Frank (1998) depicts *c.* 1800 as a pivotal date in the global system, marking the rise of the West in economic and demographic terms and the decline of the East in around 1800. European states used commodities, especially silver, extracted from the American colonies to buy entry into an expanding Asian market that was already flourishing before the onset of the first global age. Confronted with the superiority of manufacturing in Asia, prefiguring what some Asian economies did in the late 20th century, North Atlantic government and business systems facilitated an early form of import substitution in the 18th century. The first Industrial Revolution was based on protection and export promotion, and the under-development of 'the rest'. Warren, it must be remembered, would have none of this. Writing during the ascendant vogue for dependency theory, from what he regarded as an authentic Marxist position, Warren railed against misrepresentations of the Leninist thesis. He attempted to demolish what he regarded as faddish (and misguided) neo-Marxian theories of imperialism and anti-imperialism, seeking to revendicate the progressive nature of imperialism (and neo-colonialism). Rival transnational corporations were the new pioneers of capitalism in the Third World. Neo-colonialism was serving as the handmaiden of capitalism, bringing industrialization and development to Latin America and Asia by overcoming internal contradictions. Modern imperialism enabled capitalism to accomplish its historic mission, through increased competition rather than increased monopoly (Warren, 1980: 1–6).

The internecine debate among Marxist-Leninists and neo-Marxists about whether capitalism and imperialism were transforming the Third World triggered further assessments of imperialism at the time of the first and second industrial revolutions among scholars writing from quite different perspectives. Did monopoly, mercantilist profits finance the first Industrial Revolution – profits from the slave trade and tropical commodities produce on slave plantations in the Caribbean and the Americas (Williams, 1944)? Did the imperialism of free trade and the new imperialism sustain this process, and were later manifestations of capitalism and the spread of industrialism dependent on monopoly rents from imperial adventures? While not seeking to downplay the impact of colonialism, informal empire or imperialism, O'Brien challenges such assumptions. He argues that, among the first industrializers, domestic capital and domestic markets, rather than American treasure, colonial rents and the fruits of imperialism funded and explained industrialization. Regarding the English Industrial Revolution, 'for the economic growth of the core, the periphery was peripheral' (O'Brien, 1982: 18). Domestic growth, structural change and demography explain the diffusion of industrial revolutions among second-wave industrializers, not extractions from overseas or higher profits from foreign investment – the export of capital deployed to counter falling rates of return at home owing to Hobsonian excess saving and under-consumption. Imperialism played but a limited role in the industrialization of Western Europe: colonialism did not pay and in the long run 'imperialism turned out to be of limited benefit' to the development of core economies (O'Brien, 1997: 86–9). European industrialization, coupled with the emergence of global markets for commodities, capital, labour and technology, led to the emergence of a liberal international order that gradually included all parts of the world, not least what by the mid-20th century was called the Third World. Although income differentials widened between industrialized and non-industrial economies, per capital incomes rose in most parts of the globe (O'Brien, 1997: 85).

Revisionist analyses of capitalist modernization and state-assisted industrial growth/development since the 19th century have often focused on imperialism – in Latin America and elsewhere – for example, the impacts on state and market resulting from incorporation within the world economy after the 1870s, along with the form of that incorporation and the distribution of the gains resulting from it. Events and processes during the second age of globalization have fostered further re-evaluations, particularly policy responses to war and successive economic and financial crises such as those of the 1930s, the 1980s and early 21st century. One constant in the literature has been a focus on industrialization – how to achieve and how to sustain it.

Conclusion

Taking industrialization as the pinnacle of capitalism, imperialism has been presented as facilitating the first Industrial Revolution in the First World and the cause of de-industrialization and underdevelopment in the Third World. In turn, industrialization has been presented as facilitating autonomy – constraining or preventing the imperialization of former backward countries. Imperialism has also been depicted both as fostering the industrialization of a globalized world economy and as largely irrelevant to the first and second industrial revolutions notwithstanding recognition that imperialism was a facet of globalization. Yet colonialism (or neo-colonialism) was not an inevitable result of the globalization of capitalism. A capable state may have been key to effecting an imperial mission, but a strong state could resist imperialistic pressure. Much depended on the nature of the state, business–state engagement and the congruence of national industrial project and development ideology – whether in driving or resisting imperial adventures.

From the time of Marx, Hobson and Lenin, the interplay of capitalism, imperialism and industrialism has been contested. There is more agreement about the changing nature of capitalism, mercantile, industrial, financial and state, and to some extent about expressions of imperialism, old, new and neo-colonialism, though not necessarily between manifestations of capitalism and imperialism. Interpretations of market and state interaction have been shaped by the evolving nature of the state itself: from the nation-state, to the imperial state and the globalized transnational state. Less contested is the diffusion of industrialism – a congruence of industrialization and globalization, whether globalized industrialization or industrialized/financial globalization, processes that have accelerated at an uneven pace since the early 19th century as the dynamic locus of the process has shifted back and forth across Eurasia or the Atlantic, or between what used to be the First World and Third World. Just as there is more than one expression of capitalism, so there is now some acceptance of more than one route to industrialization – such expressions as early, late and very late industrialization have as much explanatory power as early or late development and a recognition of distinct expressions of imperialism and capitalism. Gerschenkron is persuasive. Economic backwardness in historical perspective highlights the importance of institutions and substitutes in demarcating forms of industrialization as of imperialism, as well as bringing the state back into the equation. Growth (industrialization) in one part of the world economy disrupted the system – serving as challenge, threat or model. Responses to that challenge varied across time and space, shaped by domestic political economies and global opportunities – and by emergent ideology and national projects.

References

Abel, C. and Lewis, C.M. (eds) (2015) 'General introduction', in C. Abel and C.M. Lewis (eds) *Latin America, Economic Imperialism and the State: The Political Economy of the External Connection from Independence to the Present* (3rd edn), London: Bloomsbury Press, pp 1–25.

Addicott, D.A.C. (2017) 'The rise and fall of the Zaibatsu: Japan's industrial and Economic modernization', *Global Tides*, 11(1–5): 1–16.

Akita, S. (2002) 'Introduction: from imperial history to global history', in S. Akita (ed) *Gentlemanly Capitalism and Global History*, London: Palgrave Macmillan, pp 1–16.

Aligica, P.D. and Tarko, V. (2014) 'Crony capitalism: rent seeking, institutions and Ideology', *KYKLOS*, 67(2): 156–76.

Amsden, A.H. (1989) *Asia's Next Giant: South Korea and Late Industrialization*, New York: Oxford University Press.

Amsden, A.H. (1991) 'Diffusion of development: the late-industrialization model and Greater East Asia', *American Economic Review*, Special Number: *Papers and Proceedings of the Hundred and Third Annual Meeting of the American Economic Association*, 81(2): 282–6.

Amsden, A.H. (2001) *Rise of "The Rest": Challenges to the West from Late-Industrialising Economies*, Oxford: Oxford University Press.

Barton, G.A. (2014) *Informal Empire and the Rise of One World Culture*, Basingstoke: Palgrave/Macmillan.

Beatty, E. (2001) *Institutions and Investment: The Political Basis of Industrialization in Mexico before 1911*, Stanford, CA: Stanford University Press.

Brandt, L., Ma, D. and Rawski, T. (2016) 'Industrialization in China', *Discussion Paper No. 10096*, Institute for the Study of Labour (IZA), Bonn.

Cain, P.J. and Hopkins, A.G. (1986) 'Gentlemanly capitalism and British overseas expansion: I the old colonial system, 1688–1850', *Economic History Review*, 39(4): 501–25.

Cain, P.J. and Hopkins, A.G. (1987) 'Gentlemanly capitalism and British overseas expansion: II The new imperialism, 1850–1945', *Economic History Review*, 40(1): 1–26.

Cain, P.J. and Hopkins, A.G. (2016) *British Imperialism, 1688–2015* (3rd edn), London: Routledge.

Cardoso, E. and Helwege, A. (1991) 'Populism, profligacy and redistribution', in R. Dornbusch and S. Edwards (eds) *The Macroeconomics of Populism in Latin America*, Chicago: University of Chicago Press/National Bureau of Economic Research, pp 45–74.

Chandler, A.D. (1977) *The Visible Hand: The Managerial Revolution in American Business*, Cambridge, MA: Harvard University Press.

Chandler, A.D. (1990) *Scale and Scope: The Dynamics of Industrial Capitalism*, Cambridge, MA: Harvard University Press.

Chang, H-J. (2003) *Kicking Away the Ladder: Development Strategy in Historical Perspective*, London: Anthem Press.

Cheremukhin, A., Golosov, M., Guriev, S. and Tsyvinski, A. (2017) 'The industrialisation and economic development of Russia through the lens of a neoclassical growth model', *The Review of Economic Studies*, 84(2): 613–49.

Chibber, V. (2003) *Locked in Place: State-Building and Late Industrialisation in India*, Princeton, NJ: Princeton University Press.

Court, V. (2020) 'A reassessment of the Great Divergence debate: towards a reconciliation of apparently distinct determinants', *European Review of Economic History*, 25(1): 1–42.

Engerman, D.C. (2010) 'The price of success: economic sovietology, development and the costs of interdisciplinarity', *History of Political Economy*, 42 (Annual Supplement): 234–60.

Fernández Pérez, P. and Lluch, A. (eds) (2015) *Familias empresarias y grandes empresas familiares en América Latina y España: una vision de largo plazo*, Madrid: Fundación BBVA.

Ferns, H.S. (1960) *Britain and Argentina in the Nineteenth Century*, Oxford: Clarendon Press.

Fishlow, A. (n.d.) 'Review of Alexander Gerschenkron: a latecomer who emerged victorious', EH.net: *Significant Works in Economic History: Economic Backwardness in Historical Perspective*, [online]. Available from: https://eh.net/book_reviews/economic-backwardness-in-historical-perspective-a-book-of-essays/ [Accessed 11 June 2020].

Foster, J.B. (2019) 'Late imperialism: fifty years after Harry Magdoff's *The Age of Imperialism*', *Monthly Review*, Special Number: *Late Imperialism*, 71(30): 1–19.

Frank, A.G. (1967) *Capitalism and Underdevelopment in Latin America: Historical Case Studies of Chile and Brazil*, New York: Monthly Review Press.

Frank, A.G. (1998) *Re-ORIENT: Global Economy in the Asian Age*, Berkeley: University of California Press.

Gallagher, J. and Robinson, R. (1953) 'The imperialism of free trade', *Economic History Review*, 5(1): 1–15.

Gatrell, P. (1995) 'Economic culture, economic policy and economic growth in Russia, 1861–1914', *Cahiers du monde russe*: Special Number: *Russe, Empire Russe, Union Soviétique, États Independants*, 36(1–2): 37–57.

Gerschenkron, A. (1962) *Economic Backwardness in Historical Perspective, a Book of Essays*, Cambridge, MA: Harvard University Press, pp 5–30. First published as Gerschenkron, A. (1952) 'Economic backwardness in historical perspective', in B.F. Hoselitz (ed) *The Progress of Underdeveloped Areas*, Chicago: University of Chicago Press, pp 3–29.

Gregory, P. (1994) *Before Command: An Economic History of the Russian Economy from Emancipation to the First Five-year Plan*, Princeton, NJ: Princeton University Press.

Guillén, M.F. (2001) *The Limits of Convergence: Globalization and Organizational Change in Argentina, South Korea and Spain*, Princeton, NJ: Princeton University Press.

Haber, S. (2002) 'Introduction: the political economy of crony capitalism', in S. Haber (ed) *Crony Capitalism and Economic Growth in Latin America: Theory and Evidence*, Stanford, CA: Hoover Institution Press, pp xi–xxi.

Haber, S., Razo, A. and Maurer, N. (2003) *The Political Economy of Property Rights: Political Instability, Credible Commitments, and Economic Growth in Mexico, 1876–1929*, Cambridge: Cambridge University Press.

Hirschman, A.O. (1958) *The Strategy of Economic Development*, New Haven, CT: Yale University Press.

Kasza, G.J. (2018) 'Gerschenkron, Amsden and Japan: the state in late development', *Japanese Journal of Political Science*, 19(2): 146–72.

Kaufman, R.R. and Stallings, B. (1991) 'The political economy of Latin American populism', in R. Dornbusch and S. Edwards (eds) *The Macroeconomics of Populism in Latin America*, Chicago: University of Chicago Press/National Bureau of Economic Research, pp 15–43.

Kim, H. and Heo, U. (2017) 'Comparative analysis of economic development in South Korea and Taiwan: lessons for other developing countries', *Asian Perspectives: Special Supplement: South Korea's Rise in Comparative Perspective*, 41(1): 17–41.

Krueger, A.O. (2002) 'Why crony capitalism is bad for economic growth', in S. Haber (ed) *Crony Capitalism and Economic Growth in Latin America: Theory and Evidence*, Stanford, CA: Hoover Press, pp 1–23.

Kuznets, P.W. (1988) 'An East Asian model of economic development: Japan, Taiwan and South Korea', *Economic Development and Cultural Change: Supplement: Why Does Overcrowded, Resource-Poor East Asia Succeed: Lessons for LDCs?*, 36(53): S11–S43.

Lenin, V.I. (2010) *Imperialism, the Highest Stage of Capitalism*, London: Penguin.

Macpherson, W.J. (1987) *The Economic Development of Japan, 1868–1941*, London: Macmillan/Economic History Society.

Maddison, A. (2001) *The World Economy: A Millennial Perspective*, Paris: Organisation for Economic Co-operation and Development.

Maddison, A. (2008) 'The West and the rest in the world economy, 1000–2030: Maddisonian and Malthusian interpretation', *World Economics*, 9(4): 75–99.

Morck, R. and Nakamoura, M. (2007) 'Business groups and the big push: Meiji Japan's mass privatization and subsequent growth', *Paper No 13171*, National Bureau of Economic Research, Cambridge, MA.

O'Brien, P.K. (1982) 'European economic development: the contribution of the periphery', *Economic History Review*, 35(1): 1–18.

O'Brien, P.K. (1997) 'Intercontinental trade and the development of the Third World since the Industrial Revolution', *Journal of World History*, 8(1): 75–133.

O'Brien, P.K. (2020) *The Economies of Imperial China and Western Europe: Debating the Great Divergence*, London: Palgrave Macmillan.

O'Rourke, K.H. and Williamson, J.G. (eds) (2017) *The Spread of Modern Industry to the Periphery since 1871*, Oxford: Oxford University Press.

Parthasarathi, P. (2011) *Why Europe Grew Rich and Asia Did Not: Global Economic Divergence, 1600–1850*, Cambridge: Cambridge University Press.

Platt, D.C.M. (1968a) 'The imperialism of free trade: some reservations', *Economic History Review*, 21(2): 296–306.

Platt, D.C.M. (1968b) *Finance, Trade and Politics in British Foreign Policy, 1815–1914*, Oxford: Oxford University Press.

Platt, D.C.M. (ed) (1977) *Business Imperialism: An Inquiry Based on British Experience in Latin America, 1840–1930*, Oxford: Clarendon.

Prebisch, R. (1981) *Capitalismo Periférico: Crisis y Transformaciones*, Mexico City: Fondo de Cultura Económico.

Reinert, E.S. (2007) *How Rich Countries Got Rich … and Poor Countries Stay Poor*, London: Constable and Robinson.

Rocchi, F. (2006) *Chimneys in the Desert; Industrialization in Argentina during the Export Boom Years, 1870–1930*, Stanford, CA: Stanford University Press.

Rostow, W.W. (1960) *The Stages of Growth: A Non-Communist Manifesto*, Cambridge: Cambridge University Press.

Rostow, W.W. (1978) *The World Economy: History and Prospect*, Austin: University of Texas Press.

Samuels, R. (1994) *Rich Nation, Strong Army: National Security and the Technological Transformation of Japan*, Ithaca, NY: Cornell University Press.

Schneider, B.R. (2004) *Business Politics and the State in Twentieth Century Latin America*, Cambridge: Cambridge University Press.

Summerhill, W.R. (2015) *Inglorious Revolution: Political Institutions, Sovereign Debt and Financial Underdevelopment in Imperial Brazil*, New Haven, CT: Yale University Press.

Wallerstein, I.M. (2004) *World-System Analysis: An Introduction*, Durham, NC: Duke University Press.

Warren, B. (1980) *Imperialism: Pioneer of Capitalism*, London: NLB/Verso.

Weyland, K. (2002) *The Politics of Market Reform in Fragile Democracies: Argentina, Brazil, Peru and Venezuela*, Princeton, NJ: Princeton University Press.

Williams, E. (1944) *Capitalism and Slavery*, Chapel Hill: University of North Carolina Press.

7

Religion and Capitalism

David J. Jeremy

Introduction

Like tectonic plates grinding together, the macro-economic social encounters between capitalism and religion have often had seismic effects. Capitalism is defined here as the legal accumulation and distribution of wealth. Across time numerous kinds of capitalism have been tried in most societies and, in contrast to statism, they offer systems that have more often produced economic development. The stages for encounters between capitalism and religion have varied. Some have been regional, national or global; others have been between businesses or within a single firm.

The role of religion in relation to capitalism almost wholly escapes the scope of Beckert's history of global capitalism (Beckert, 2014). Believing in the non-material world and accountability to God gave the religious mind the possibility of distanced, critical, prophetic perspectives on manifestations of capitalism. The laws of Moses and the teaching of Jesus presented capitalist societies with the highest alternative ethical standards. Therefore it might be thought that religion would offer necessary restraints on the excesses of capitalism, whatever the variety. The purpose of this chapter is to examine this assumption.

Religion could be both an obstacle and a spur to capitalist development. Epitomized in the Catholic nunnery, the Ottoman harem, the Hindu zenana, in the daily blessing of the pious Jew (thanks for not being made a Gentile, a slave or a woman) or the Victorian married man's property rights, for centuries most European and Asian societies have been patriarchal, usually with the approval of the dominant religion. Consequently, one of the greatest disservices that religion has done to capitalism until the second half of the 20th century was to deprive capitalist enterprise of half the potential talent in the population: the abilities of women (Weber, 1948: 268–9, 295–301;

156

Holcombe, 1983: 23–6; Watts, 1995: 54–6; McLeod, 1996: 156–68; Kuran, 2018: 1349). Religion could also be an apologist for exploitive capitalism. Nowhere was this more evident than in the slave trade in the Atlantic world, an aspect of which is examined later.

The chapter begins by examining the debates surrounding the role of religion in the economic divergence between East and West. It then considers the evidence about the impact of religion–capitalism interactions on ethical behaviour and also on social control at the level of the business. The chapter then turns to critical junctures in the development of capitalism in the West where religion played a significant role.

Global and firm level interactions between religion and capitalism

The role of religion in the great divide between East and West

In China for over two millennia Confucianism was the dominant religion. Under its influence, abetted by later imported Buddhism, the Chinese 'regarded their culture as the highest civilisation' in the world (Latourette 1954: 47). With the Sung dynasty (960–1279) this was probably true, for they then invented gunpowder, the magnetic compass, paper and moveable printing types, waterpower clocks, cannon, and water-powered machines for textile production (Needham, 2020). However, their successors, the Mongol-originating Ming dynasty (1368–1644), 'in government … perfected the civil service examinations based on Confucianism, but this and the education which prepared for them tended to imprison the Chinese mind and outlook in patterns framed centuries earlier' (Latourette, 1954: 42–3). The Manchus, also from the north, overthrew the Ming regime and installed their own Qing dynasty (1644–1911), preserving the Confucian-based outlook of superiority. Consequently, they were left behind by Western advances in science and technology, the tools of capitalist enterprise, from the 17th century onwards (Landes, 1998: 335–49). Evaluating China in terms of public administration, Dreschler reached a very different conclusion. Like Francis Fukuyama, he credits its centuries-long merit-based bureaucratic system as creating a civil service, essential in running a modern state (Dreschler, 2013: 327–32). However, he glosses over the increasingly obsolete content of its examination textbooks.

In Islam, in which the religious and the secular are an integrated whole, religion at first approved and developed the knowledge of its conquered peoples. Between about 750 and 1100,

> Islamic science and technology far surpassed those of Europe … Islam was Europe's teacher. Then something went wrong. Islamic science, denounced as heresy by religious zealots, bent under theological

157

pressures for spiritual conformity … For militant Islam, the truth had already been revealed. What led *back* to the truth was useful and permissible; all the rest was error and deceit. (Landes, 1998: 54)

In Landes' judgement, 'Islam's greatest mistake, however, was the refusal of the printing press, which was seen as a potential instrument of sacrilege and heresy. Nothing did more to cut Muslims off from the mainstream of knowledge' (Landes, 1998: 401–2).

A granular view has emerged within economics of religion studies on the connections between 'Islam and economic performance' (Kuran, 2018: 1292). Attention has focused on the mechanisms effecting the late 11th-century shift. Chaney argues that it was the Abbasid caliphs (in power 750–945), served by Persian bureaucrats, who sponsored the translation into Arabic of every scientific text available and thereby stimulated Islam's Golden Age of scientific advance. However, 'Opposition to this project began early on as disaffected groups began to organise opposition to government around religious ideals' (Chaney, 2019: 442). The Abbasid caliphs tried to impose rationalist interpretations of the Koran on religious leaders and for this purpose introduced slave soldiers (for centuries thereafter a feature of Islamic rulers). Countering this, the spread of madrasas across the Islamic world brought the Sunni Revival and a deeply conservative reaction in the second half of the 11th century. Kuran takes Chaney's hypothesis one stage further by pinpointing the *waqf* or trust deed as permanently locking the madrasa founder's rules, monitored by conservative Muslim clerics, into the development of the madrasas and an anti-scientific outlook (Kuran, 2018: 1329).

A novel interpretation of the changing relativities of Islam and the West has been proposed by Jared Rubin. His focus is the manner in which rulers in the respective regions propagated their rule. Islamic doctrine was more conducive to legitimizing political rule, promoting 'greater security for merchants, a common social and religious network, a common currency, a common language, and common financial instruments' (Rubin, 2017: 202). All that gave relative competitive advantage to the Muslim world. In contrast Christianity arose in the Roman Empire with its efficient legal and political institutions, and therefore Christianity had diminished leverage over the secular authorities. When after about 1050 trade expanded in the Mediterranean world, new laws and policies were required. Western Europeans, lacking close religious restraint, allowed economic elites more easily to achieve relaxed usury laws and (with greater religious pluralism after the Protestant Reformation) readily spread the use of the printing press. In contrast, as mentioned, the clerical legitimation of Muslim rulers prohibited the printing press and retarded similar pro-economic development measures. Rubin's thesis relies on broad-brush strokes and a path-dependency argument (Rubin, 2017).

From the mid-15th century progressive advances in guns and ships pushed Europeans technologically ahead of China, Japan, India and the Ottoman empire. Missionary Christianity, especially in Spain and Portugal, offered the highest of motives in driving European expansion overseas in the late 15th and 16th centuries. Motives were not unalloyed, however. Ogier Ghiselin de Busbecq (1522–92), Flemish diplomat and Austrian ambassador to Constantinople, shrewdly observed that for the 'expeditions (to the Indies and the Antipodes) religion supplies the pretext and gold the motive' (Cipolla, 1965: 133).

A situation similar to that of China arose in Japan, but the Japanese were more ready to learn from the West. Religion in Japan, it is argued, spurred the Japanese to catch up with the West by the end of the 19th century. Very influential during the Tokugawa era (1600–1868) was the Shingaku movement preached by Ishida Baigan in the early 18th century; it spread through his writings and in lecture halls. Meditation, asceticism, devotion to one's obligations and occupation, serving 'to reinforce loyalty, filial piety and a devotion to hard work in one's calling' (Bellah, 1985: 152): these were the values that Bellah believed helped to make competitive capitalism and modernization possible after the restoration of the rule of the emperor in 1868. This ethic has been compared to the Protestant ethic and its impact on 16th–17th-century Europe (discussed later). After Baigan's death 'the *shingaku* movement grew into the most influential educational institution of the merchant class'. It was not enough. 'In spite of at least partially favourable economic conditions the merchant class of Tokugawa Japan failed to evolve a liberal, progressive and self-assertive mentality' (Hirschmeier and Yui, 1975: 55).

The role of religion in the development of corporate social responsibility

Religion could also be a source of ethical behaviour. In the 20th century the concept and practice of corporate social responsibility (CSR) can be traced via three Christian initiatives. Archbishop William Temple in his influential *Christianity and Social Order* (1942) publicized the notion of middle axioms, or maxims for conduct that mediated between fundamental Christian principles and the jungle of ethical dilemmas confronting society. Middle axioms can be traced back to Plato, but well before Temple the economic historian (later Archdeacon) the Rev William Cunningham proposed them at the Church Congress in Hull in October 1890. 'What we want is middle principles to come between great Christian Truths and our personal conduct. How am I to apply the Ten Commandments to the question whether I should pay a farthing an hour more or not?' (Church Congress, 1890: 571). This method of bridging an ethical generalization on the one side and disputable particularities on the other resurfaced in the late 1930s before Temple advanced them in 1942 (Preston, 1981: 37–44).

Another source of CSR was the Christian Frontier Council (CFC) launched in 1942 by Joseph H. Oldham, missionary statesman and ecumenical pioneer, concerned about spreading unbelief and the twin threats of Right and Left in wartime Britain. Among its members were businessmen with Christian sympathies or commitment whose ideas substantially developed CSR. Samuel Courtauld, of Unitarian stock and a wealthy rayon manufacturer, lent respectability to remarkably radical ideas published posthumously as *Ideals and Industry* (1949). He favoured worker directors (1943); thought the best directors regarded themselves as servants of the shareholder, the worker and the consumer (1944); and emphasized the need for directors and managers 'to make themselves realise and sympathise with the natural feelings, needs, and aspirations of their workers, not only because it is the only possible thing for a decent man to do once the idea has crossed his mind, but because there is no other road to industrial efficiency' (1943) (Courtauld, 1949: 37, 45, 95, 126).

The other opinion former with regard to CSR was George Goyder, managing director of Newsprint Supply Co in wartime and a member of the Church of England's Church Assembly in the 1950s. In his seminal studies 'Socialism and Private Industry: a New Approach' in *Fabian News* (November 1949) and *The Future of Private Enterprise* (1951), he advanced the view, derived from the German example of the Carl Zeiss Stiftung (foundation), Samuel Courtauld and the CFC group of which he had been a member, that the company had responsibilities to the consumer and the community as much as to shareholders and employees. In his *The Responsible Company* (1961) Goyder went further, proposing that companies should issue a regular social audit. The four original stakeholders (as they came to be called) were widened in the late 1980s to include the environment, with pressure not least from Christian voices (Goyder, 1951, 1961; Jeremy, 1990: 196–209; Clapp, 1994: 58; Goyder and Goyder, 1994; Prance, 1996: 68–79; Stott, 2006: 135–60; Jeremy, 2009: 364–9).

Religion as an instrument of capitalist social control

Capitalists have tried to use religion as an instrument of social control. Famously, E.P. Thompson claimed that Methodism's emotional experiences, as 'a ritualised form of psychic masturbation', sublimated the workers' anger against their masters (Thompson, 1963: 368). But half the 292 largest Lancashire cotton manufacturers with known adult religious affiliations were Anglicans and only 11 per cent were Methodist (Howe, 1984: 62).

Thompson's thesis has been most effectively exposed as the product of the anti-Methodist prejudices of his upbringing (Hempton and Walsh, 2001: 99–120). A much more definite example of capitalist exploitation of religion to control workers was William Lever, the soap baron. At Port Sunlight on the Mersey in the 1890s he built a soap factory employing over 3,000 people and a company village housing 3,600. To exercise control, he recruited a Wesleyan minister to double as company welfare officer and as a non-denominational clergyman, whose salary he paid. Then at his own expense he built a £25,000 church whose membership was confined to his employees. All to little avail: less than a fifth of the village residents bothered to become Christchurch Port Sunlight members (Jeremy, 1991: 58–81).

Religion-based ethics eroded by capitalist structures and motives

Capitalism was also capable of subverting religion-based ethics. One outstanding case was that of the Turner family, asbestos manufacturers of Rochdale, Lancashire. Pillars of the local United Methodist Church (UMC), once they merged with Newalls of Newcastle upon Tyne (1920), to form Turner & Newall (T&N), the Turners evidently abandoned any pretence of practising a Christian ethic. When the widower of Nellie Kershaw, first of their employees to be medically diagnosed with asbestosis (in 1922), appealed to the T&N board for compensation, his case was rejected out of hand. The Turners then commenced the policy of denying the lethal effects of exposure to asbestos, and this continued through most of the rest of the 20th century, causing repeated suffering. Robert Turner (1847–1931) the last of the three founding brothers, vice-chairman of T&N until 1927 and generous chairman of the UMC Finance Board, must be especially guilty. In 1925 the UMC Conference recorded its appreciation of the reports issuing from the great Conference on Christian Politics, Economics and Citizenship held the previous year. Robert Turner must have seen the ninth report by the Conference on Christian Politics, Economics and Citizenship (COPEC) on *Industry and Property*. That report laid down that 'the first charge on industry should be a remuneration sufficient to maintain the worker and his family in health and dignity' (COPEC, Ninth Report 1924: 194; Tweedale, 2000; Jeremy, 2013: 425–31).

Skills and money from business in support of religious organizations

With respect to funding, in the 19th century the Wesleyans were heavily dependent on large contributions from those in industry and commerce, deriving from Lancashire and Yorkshire in early Victorian England and later on London donors (Jeremy, 2018: 186–200; Jeremy, 2020: 129–51).

One family, the Ranks, were massive funders of Wesleyan Methodism and its successor (after 1932) the Methodist Church. Joseph Rank, the flour miller, left £70,000, but well before he died gave £1 million to each of his seven children and several million to Methodist causes. The biographer of J. Arthur Rank, the film magnate, reached the extraordinary conclusion that 'there probably wouldn't have been much of a Methodist Church without the Rank connection' (Wakelin, 1996: 9, 31). Dependence on a few rich people presented a moral hazard. Clergy could ask for more luxurious church premises, knowing that they would not have to pay for them and that they would not lose their job if those premises were under used or abandoned. Equally, if a congregation knew that a rich donor would underwrite a scheme, the incentive to self-help was much diminished. Joseph Rank fully understood the first of these hazards and complained accordingly (Jeremy, 1990: 349).

And men of capital were organization builders. In the Church of England in the 1920s the merchant banker Lord Kindersley spearheaded fundraising for the Church Board of Finance, and more importantly advised it about investments (Jeremy, 1990: 267–81). Sir Josiah Stamp performed an important organizational role after the Methodist Church in Britain was formed in 1932 by the merger of the Wesleyan, the Primitive Methodist and the United Methodist connexions. Facing the task of unifying the legal, property and financial components of the three connexions, he brought to bear the managerial skills he learned in the Civil Service, the merger experience gained on the board of Imperial Chemical Industries and the strategic vision he possessed as President of the London Midland and Scottish Railway Co (Jeremy, 2013: 451).

Crucial interactions in the West between religion and capitalism

Religion and the rise of capitalism

Arguably the most consequential encounter between religion and capitalism was the Protestant Reformation. Convulsing Europe in the 16th–17th centuries, because theological differences had political and economic repercussions and led to violent wars, the Reformation released a torrent of revolutionary ideas. Max Weber, the father of sociology, and later Ernst Troeltsch found congruence between Protestant and capitalist values (Weber, 1904–5; Troeltsch, 1912).

Weber hypothesized that the ascetic Protestant, particularly Calvinist, virtues capable of proving the Reformed Christian's calling and election, were also those that could power bourgeois capitalism: denial of worldly pleasure, work, time-saving, honesty, frugality, restricted consumption, acquisition for investment (Weber, 1958: 90–104).

Not surprisingly, Weber's thesis has been the subject of continuing controversy. His friend the academic economist Werner Sombart detected the spirit of capitalism much earlier in the social attitudes and economic practices of Judaism and then in the teachings of the medieval School men, primarily the 14th-century Thomas Aquinas; and he flatly denied that either Luther or Calvin approved of capitalism (Sombart, 1915, in Green, 1959).

Tawney directed attention to Calvinists, not of the 16th century but of the 17th century, in Holland, Scotland, England and New England. He believed Weber missed 'large economic movements, in particular the (geographical) Discoveries and the results which flowed from them'; intellectual movements, especially Machiavelli 'as powerful a solvent of traditional ethical restraints as Calvin'; and the complexities of Calvinism (Tawney, 1926: 320). A torrent of literature on Weber's thesis has subsequently flowed (Green, 1959).

One major criticism of Weber is that his ascetic Calvinists were ideal types. Others have tried to profile them more individually. Grassby studied the business community of 17th-century England from a vast array of manuscript sources and printed records. Businessmen, he found, aspired to values for practical as much as for theological reasons. Self-denial, as in frugality and circumspection, was essential to accumulate capital. Overindulgence in food and alcohol endangered health as well as sound judgement. A work ethic could be excessive as well as threatening the Sabbath observance. Concern for honesty and reputation was replete with practical self-interest. Conscience within the framework of obligation shaped business morality (Grassby, 1995: 286–301).

From a different perspective, Stark challenges the originality of the Protestant Reformation by outlining the numerous forerunners (Cathars, Waldenses, Hussites and Lollards) who reacted against the corruptions and ultramontanism of the Roman Church. As for capitalism, he quotes Hugh Trevor-Roper's view that industrial capitalism had its antecedents in the Italian city-states of the late medieval period (Stark, 2004: 15–119).

Most recently Rubin confirms an association between Protestants and wealth having existed since the 17th century, hypothesizing that this was brought about by the Protestant adoption of the printing press to disseminate Reformation ideas (Rubin, 2017: 119–37).

The theology of the Protestant Reformation was shaped by Martin Luther and John Calvin (MacCulloch, 2004: 106–253). Implicit in the teachings of both Luther and Calvin was the concept and practice of individualism (Tawney, 1926: 175–93). For Luther the individual exercised faith for himself/herself and studied the Bible to understand that faith (Luther, 1520). For Calvin the believer proved their election to salvation by pursuing their calling and demonstrating an ascetic lifestyle (Calvin, 1559). Individualism of course was inherent in bourgeois capitalism.

The role of Nonconformists in Britain's pioneering Industrial Revolution of the 18th–19th centuries

Protestant Nonconformists (also known as Dissenters) were those who followed the 2,029 clergy driven from the established Church of England by the Restoration religious settlement after 1660. They were excluded because they refused to submit to episcopacy. The vast majority in 1660–62 were Presbyterians, but over the next two hundred years they splintered into Presbyterians, Independents (or Congregationalists), Baptists and, outside all, the Society of Friends or Quakers. From the 1770s Methodists of various kinds joined the religious outsiders collectively named Nonconformists. Before 1660 they were known as Puritans, heirs of the Protestant Reformation.

Not dissimilar to the Weber thesis has been the view that Protestant Nonconformity played a notable role in powering Britain's first Industrial Revolution. Contemporaries and subsequent historians observed the apparent over-representation of Nonconformists among the first generation of industrialists. A Unitarian minister, Israel Worsley, published *Observations on … the Manufactures of Great Britain which Have Been for the Most Part Established and Supported by Protestant Dissenters* in 1816. In his seminal essay on the Industrial Revolution, the 20th-century economic historian T.S. Ashton echoed the theme (Ashton, 1948: 18).

However, during the Industrial Revolution period Nonconformists comprised a small albeit growing proportion of the population. As Table 7.1 shows, between 1715 and 1851 they increased from about 6 to 17 per cent of the population of England and Wales. So which of them produced the capitalists who organized the firms that drove rapid industrial change and why?

In the Midlands cotton spinning industry at the end of the 18th century the leading figures were Unitarians (Chapman 1967: 194). For Lancashire, Howe studied 351 owners and partners of the largest cotton firms in 1830–60. The 292 individuals leaving evidence of religious affiliations were almost equally split between the established Church of England and Nonconformist denominations. Among the latter the Unitarians (53), Independents (27) and Wesleyan Methodists (27) dominated (Howe, 1984: 62). Watts reworked Howe's data (see Table 7.2):

Clearly Nonconformists were heavily over-represented among the elite of Lancashire cotton masters. Remarkable in their frequency were the Unitarians, 38 times over-represented, and, most remarkable of all, the Quakers, 43 times.

Table 7.1: Relative sizes of main Nonconformist sects, 1750–1850, in England and Wales

Denomination		England & Wales 1715 to 1718	England & Wales 1851
		Members	Members
New Dissent			
	Congregationalists/Independents	59,940	655,935
	Baptists	59,320	499,604
	Particular		
	General Baptist New Connexion		
Old Dissent			
	Unitarians (formerly Presbyterians)	179,350	84,190
	Society of Friends (Quakers)	39,510	16,783
Methodists			
	Wesleyan Methodists		298,406
	Methodist New Connexion		16,962
	Primitive Methodists		105,656
	Bible Christians		
	Wesleyan Methodist Association		
Nonconformists, estimated total		338,120	2,878,543
Population total		5,442,670	16,915,820
Nonconformists as percentage of the population		6.21	17

Source: Watts, 1995: 29

There are further indicators of the prominence of Nonconformists among capitalists when Britain became the world's first industrial nation. Rubinstein's work on millionaires and half millionaires dying between 1720 and 1899 showed only 15 per cent of both classes having been Dissenters, and among Dissenters the Congregationalists, Quakers and Unitarians led the way (Rubinstein, 1981: 150–3). However, Watts compared Rubinstein's data with his own analysis of the Religious Census of 1851 and found the Unitarians and the Quakers massively over-represented among the rich, the former ten times their numbers in the English and Welsh population, the latter fifty times (Watts, 1995: 331–2). Across a much longer period of time, the biographical dictionary of British Quakers in commerce and industry, 1775–1920, included over 2,800 individuals (Milligan, 2007: viii).

Table 7.2: Major Nonconformist groups among cotton masters compared with Nonconformists' shares of the population, in Lancashire

	Nonconformists among Lancashire cotton masters (Howe's elite sample 1830–60)	Nonconformists among Lancashire population in 1851
	%	%
Wesleyans	7.7	3.8
Congregationalists	7.7	2.8
Quakers	4.3	0.1
Unitarians	15.1	0.4
Other Nonconformists	5.7	4.9
Total Nonconformists	40.5	12

Source: Watts, 1995: 333

Evidence from the *Oxford Dictionary of National Biography* (*ODNB*) on inventors, as opposed to entrepreneurs, during the Industrial Revolution suggests a larger contribution than Ashton implied (see Table 7.3). Searching the *ODNB* produced a total, and hence a universe, of 89 inventors (author's data). Of these, 8 spent their careers wholly in Scotland, which left a universe of 81. Of this number, 47 evinced no evidence of Nonconformist connections. Of the 81, 11 were Scots who moved south. If they are included, on the assumption they would have been raised in the Church of Scotland (which was Presbyterian in governance and Calvinistic in theology), then 34 'Nonconformist' inventors equates to 42 per cent, much nearer Watts's figure from Howe's data on cotton masters (Table 7.2). Even excluding the 11 Scots who moved south produces 28 per cent, well above the numbers of Nonconformists in the whole population of England and Wales (Table 7.1).

The value of some of the inventions vastly outweighed numbers of individual Nonconformists of course. The Quakers appear strong in the metal industries; otherwise there are no obvious concentrations of Nonconformist denominations in any particular industrial activity.

If Nonconformists were prominent among Britain's 18th–19th-century capitalists, the latter were likewise prominent among contemporary Nonconformists. Some 20 per cent or £43,000 of the Wesleyan Methodists' Centenary Fund of 1839–44 (which raised £229,944) came from the north-west of England, and of the 59 donors giving over £200 each, 22 were textile manufacturers or merchants (Jeremy, 2020: 143, 148).

Table 7.3: Nonconformist inventors of new technology active in England and Wales, 1700–1850, in the *Oxford Dictionary of National Biography*

Name	Birth	Denomination	Association
Newcomen, Thomas	1664	Baptist	UA
Phillips, Peregrine	1800	Baptist	U
Walker, Samuel	1715	Calvinistic Methodist	A
Crossley, Francis	1817	Congregational	UA
Salt, Titus	1803	Congregational	UA
Stephenson, Robert	1803	Congregational	U
Whitworth, Joseph	1803	Congregational	U
Ewart, Peter	1767	Presbyterian	Us
Fairbairn, Peter	1799	Presbyterian	Us
Fairbairn, William	1789	Presbyterian	Us
Keir, James	1735	Presbyterian	Us
Kennedy, John	1769	Presbyterian	Us
M'Adam, John Loudon	1756	Presbyterian	Us
Muir, William	1805	Presbyterian	Us
Murdock, William	1754	Presbyterian	Us
Mushet, David	1772	Presbyterian	Us
Telford, Thomas	1757	Presbyterian	Us
Watt, James	1736	Presbyterian	Us
Bentley, Thomas	1731	Presbyterian/Arian/Socinian	UA
Roebuck, John	1718	Presbyterian/Arian/Socinian	Us
Strutt, Jedediah	1726	Presbyterian/Arian/Socinian	A
Wedgwood, Josiah	1730	Presbyterian/Arian/Socinian	UA
Champion, John	1705	Quaker	UA
Champion, Nehemiah	1678	Quaker	UA
Champion, William	1710	Quaker	UA
Darby, Abraham	1678	Quaker	UA
Darby, Abraham	1711	Quaker	UA
Huntsman, Benjamin	1704	Quaker	UA
Reynolds, William	1758	Quaker	UA
Crompton, William	1753	Swedenborgian	A
Hackworth, Timothy	1786	Wesleyan	A
Holden, Isaac	1807	Wesleyan	UA
Mercer, John	1791	Wesleyan	U
Bickford, William	1774	Wesleyan	A

continued

Name	Industry	Invention	Patent/ invention date
Newcomen, Thomas	engineering	atmospheric steam engine	1712
Phillips, Peregrine	chemical engineering	H_2SO_4 platinum catalyst	1831
Walker, Samuel	steel mfr	crucible steel furnace	1766
Crossley, Francis	carpet mfr	application of steam power	1840?
Salt, Titus	worsted mfr	mixed fibre cloths	1839
Stephenson, Robert	railway and civil engineer	axletrees, etc	1826
Whitworth, Joseph	engineering	uniform system of screw threads	1841
Ewart, Peter	engineering	coffer dam	1822
Fairbairn, Peter	engineering	flax machinery	1834
Fairbairn, William	engineering	ship designs, etc	1842
Keir, James	polymath inventor	Keir's metal	1779
Kennedy, John	cotton mfg	double speeder	1794?
M'Adam, John Loudon	road engineer	road construction	1816
Muir, William	engineering	radial drill	1840
Murdock, William	energy	gas light	1792
Mushet, David	iron mfr	direct steel in crucibles	1800
Telford, Thomas	civil engineering	Caledonian Canal	1804–22
Watt, James	engineering	steam engine, rotary	1769
Bentley, Thomas	pottery	neo-classical designs	1767–2
Roebuck, John	iron mfr	lead chambers to make H_2SO_4	1749
Strutt, Jedediah	hosiery	Derby rib machine	1758
Wedgwood, Josiah	pottery	jasper ware	1777
Champion, John	brass	toughening	1739
Champion, Nehemiah	brass	annealing technique	1723
Champion, William	brass	large-scale furnace	1738
Darby, Abraham	iron mfr	coke blast furnace	1710
Darby, Abraham	iron mfr	coke blast pig iron	1753
Huntsman, Benjamin	steel	cast steel	1751

continued

Name	Industry	Invention	Patent/ invention date
Reynolds, William	iron mfr	manganese steel	1799
Crompton, William	cotton mfr	spinning mule	1779
Hackworth, Timothy	engineering	railway locomotive	1813
Holden, Isaac	worsted mfr	wool combing machine	1848
Mercer, John	calico printing	mercerization	1844
Bickford, William	mining	safety fuse	1831

Source: ODNB

Note: Religious linkage; U by upbringing; A by adult association; Us Scottish upbringing.

A question then arises about what can explain this close relationship between Nonconformists and industrial capitalism in 18th–19th-century Britain, considering they were such a tiny proportion of the population (Table 7.4). General and particular explanations have been advanced. Common to all Nonconformists were the disabilities imposed on them by the Restoration religious settlement after 1660. This drove over 2,000 clergy from their livings; excluded religious dissenters (effectively Presbyterians, Independents and Baptists) from holding office in the Army or Navy or on municipal bodies; and prohibited religious services contrary to the 1662 Prayer Book of the Church of England. The Restoration settlement thereby created Nonconformity. Although some relief came with the Toleration Act of 1689 (which allowed the legal existence of congregations, and their buildings, outside the Church of England), the disabilities continued into the 19th century, affecting Quakers, Catholics and also Jews (Rawlings, 1902; Manning, 1952; Henriques, 1961; Watts, 1978).

Further explanation can be sought in probing the characteristics of the Quakers, Unitarians, Independents and Wesleyan Methodists separately, because each was different. The Quakers, or Society of Friends, were the most distinctive of all.

Founded by George Fox in the 17th century, by the 1720s they had become a clearly identifiable sect, numbering about 40,000 in England, but shrinking to under 20,000 by 1851 (Watts, 1978: 509, 1995: 29). A 'plain' non-worldly lifestyle characterized by black/grey garments, reduced speech, starkly built and furnished houses, and simple marriage and burial services were the most visible Quaker features. In religion they relied on the inner light of the Holy Spirit, experienced in the silence of their worship meetings, for guidance on belief and behaviour, rather than Scripture (Davies, 1961: 114–23).

In response to persecution, they developed a series of Queries and Advices that inter alia shaped their ethics in business. Fox enjoined his Meetings to appoint two or three members to admonish any Friends who 'profess the Truth [but] follow pleasures, drunkenness, gaming, or are not faithful in their callings and dealings, nor honest, but run into debt, and so bring a scandal upon the Truth' (Religious Society of Friends, 1931: xviii–xix). Those who persisted in such behaviour would be disowned (excluded). When Friends ran into financial difficulty, commercially experienced members of the Meeting would inspect the pertinent financial records, give advice and render assistance. A bankrupt would be investigated by fellow Friends and, if judged morally guilty, would be disowned (Walvin, 1997: 73–9). Bankruptcy, above all, was abhorred because it was regarded as robbing a neighbour. The overarching principle motivating the Quakers was expressed in 'Advices and Queries' issued in the 18th century by the Yearly Meeting of Ministering Friends (the Quakers' governing body): 'Finally, dear friends, let your whole conduct and conversation be worthy of disciples of Christ' (Religious Society of Friends, 1931: 39).

To the highest of business standards, and hence a huge reputation for integrity, the 'plain' living Quakers added powerful business networks. 'The Society of Friends was structured around the travels of Quakers back and forth from the local meetings to the national annual gatherings in London, but they also wrote to each other, and used each other's homes as staging posts on their various social and commercial wanderings across the country' (Walvin, 1997: 81). Networks were cemented by the strict insistence of marriage within the Society of Friends. Hence, for example, the Peases and Backhouses, Darlington bankers and investors in the Stockton and Darlington Railway (the first goods railway in Britain, opened 1825), were related by marriage; the Gurneys, Norwich bankers, were related to the Backhouses; and the Barclays married into the Gurneys (Milligan, 2007 qv). Promoting Quaker dynasties were inheritance patterns that carefully spread wealth and assets across the sons and daughters of the next generation (Walvin, 1997: 89).

Belatedly supporting the Quaker network, faced with falling numbers and tempted into habits of plenty by rising living standards in the late 18th century, was the decision to launch Quaker boarding schools. Acworth, Bootham (1829–) in York and Sidcot (1808–) in Somerset were the most heavily attended by Quakers in industry and commerce (Milligan 2007: 552–61). Quaker schools may not have been as advanced as Walvin suggests (Stewart, 1953 quoted Watts, 1995: 343–4). Of crucial importance for Quakers and other Nonconformists, according to Watts, was a teenage apprenticeship of some kind with a co-religionist in industry or commerce (Watts, 1995: 343–4). Nevertheless, Quaker schools both inculcated the Quaker lifestyle and also allowed friendships that would lead to marriage alliances.

Most successful, and exceptional, were the coca and chocolate manufacturers Fry, Cadbury and Rowntree, whose business dynasties produced two millionaires. But therein lay a conundrum. How could the plain way of life be compatible with huge material success? Fox had warned against the snare of riches. In the 19th century numbers of the Quaker elite became worldly, marrying outside the Society of Friends, abandoning the meeting house for the parish church and indulging in a luxurious lifestyle (Corley, 1988: 164–87).

Not all succeeded in business. Most spectacular were the collapses of the banking firm of Overend, Gurney & Co in 1866 and the north-east industrial conglomerate of J. & J.W. Pease in 1902 (Kirby, 1988: 142–63; entry on Henry Edmund Gurney in Milligan, 2007). Nevertheless, in their best practice firms the Quakers lent a more acceptable face to capitalism by setting standards in quality of product, labour management and the adoption of new technology (Corley, 1988).

Very different were the Unitarians. Reason, rather than the Scriptures of the Calvinists or the inner light of the Holy Spirit of the Quakers, was the source of their theology. Anti-Trinitarian views emerged in the 17th century but did not gain wide currency in England until the 18th. Two forms appeared. Arians 'acknowledged the pre-existence of Christ … the more radical Socinians denied both the divinity and the pre-existence of Christ and rejected the doctrine of vicarious atonement' (Watts, 1978: 371). Any form of anti-Trinitarianism was excluded from the benefits of the Toleration Act, a situation not reversed until the Unitarian Toleration Act of 1813.

Among Nonconformists the Trinitarian controversy came to a head in 1719 when 151 London Dissenting ministers met at Salters' Hall to settle a dispute among Presbyterian ministers in Exeter. Over the remainder of the 18th century numbers of Presbyterians adopted Arian and then Socinian views (Watts, 1978: 374–79). Universalist (universal salvation for all) theology began to appear from the 1790s (Watts, 1995: 83–95).

What then explains the prominence of Unitarians among the capitalists of the Industrial Revolution? First, multigenerational family capitalists transiting from pre-industrial to industrial society might make radical religious journeys. So a multigenerational family such as the Wanseys of Warminster remained clothiers from the late 17th century until the early 19th century, but in that time moved from Presbyterian to Arian and ultimately Unitarian religious views.

Secondly, there were the values of the Presbyterians who either moved or were tempted to move theologically. Dominant among these was watchfulness. It was the recurrent theme in the 25-year-long spiritual diary of Joseph Ryder (1695–1768), a clothier who spent his entire life in Leeds. Watchfulness meant 'the constant, anxious, subtle, and complex examination of the self, the outside world, and the depths of religious habit for evidence of God, Satan, and salvation' (Kadane, 2013: 51). George Wansey (1713–62) precisely defined his moral code in advice bequeathed to his children: a 'Scale of Duty' in three parts (Jeremy, 1970: 2):

To my God
Constant prayer to Him …
Endeavouring to attain right knowledge of Him
Sundays should be particularly devoted to this line of duty …
Patient submission to his dispensations.
To my Neighbour
Speak well of him always …
Always do to them as we would wish them to do to us.
To Ourselves
Keep my body chaste & temperate.
Avoid all occasion of intemperance, lewdness, drunkenness, loose mirth, governing manners.
Make the best use of my time.
Improve my mind in useful Knowledge.
Keep strict watch over the passions & endeavor to bring them in subjection to reason …
Dead to sin but alive to Righteousness

The next generation was not as intensely watchful. At the Unitarians' Warrington Dissenting Academy, functioning from 1756 to 1782, 'dancing, cards, the theatre, were all held lawful in moderation' (Watts, 1995: 209). In short, Unitarians inherited a Puritan moral code but became liberal in both their theology and their attitudes to the world – affording flexibilities that might lubricate their command of businesses in industry and commerce.

Thirdly, 'it was the Presbyterians, and their Unitarian successors, who made by far the most important Dissenting contribution to weekday education' (Watts, 1995: 286–7). Quality varied enormously. However, prospering Unitarians ensured that in the best of them the curriculum incorporated the classics and commercially useful as well as appropriate moral and religious subjects.

Prior to the formation of the British and Foreign Unitarian Association in 1825 (Mellone, 1925: 31–63), Unitarian networks were local or at best regional. Much networking depended on the congregations attracted to popular ministers. Imbibing the views of his uncle the Rev Thomas

Walker, minister of Mill Hill Chapel, Leeds, the Rev George Walker of High Pavement Presbyterian Chapel, Nottingham, influenced the Midlands cotton spinners with his Unitarian theology and radical politics (Chapman, 1967: 188–99; Kadane, 2013: 156–82).

Lastly, Unitarians nurtured positive attitudes towards new technology. For example, Josiah Wedgwood created the sensational ceramics Queen's ware and jasper ware in the 1760s and 1770s; Samuel and George Courtauld, silk manufacturers at Halstead, Essex, pioneered and then dominated the manufacture of Victorian mourning crape (Coleman, 1969: 24–32).

Independent congregations were distinguished by their inherited Trinitarian Calvinism, their independence of each other and government through the (usually monthly) church meeting. Church-based networks tended to be local rather than regional or national until, respectively, the emergence of county associations to promote village preaching in the late 18th century and the formation in 1832 of the Congregational Union to fund chapel building and ministerial support.

Independents exercised strong church discipline over a number of matters. For those in business the expected norm was success. Bankruptcy incurred expulsion from the chapel community: a great humiliation (Watts, 1995: 200). This kind of chapel equipped strong personalities such as the Victorian cotton magnates John Rylands or Hugh Mason and the Bradford worsted manufacturer Sir Titus Salt with the Puritan ethic and the dynamic to succeed in commerce and industry.

Independents did not match Presbyterians in the provision of denominational schools. John Rylands and Titus Salt attended local grammar schools until their mid-teens, Hugh Mason went to a private school before leaving at the age of 10 to help his father, a cotton spinner (Reynolds, 1986; Watts, 1995: 286–9; Farnie, 2004a, b; James, 2004).

As for the Wesleyans, two features shaped their early industrialists. One was their moral code, the other their powerful networks. John Wesley, their founder, preached an influential sermon on 'The Use of Money' in 1744, published in 1760. Reflecting the empiricism of John Locke, the 17th-century philosopher, Wesley inter alia urged his followers to:

> gain all you can, by common sense, by using in your business all the understanding which God has given you. It is amazing to observe, how few do this; how men run on in the same dull track with their forefathers. You should be continually learning, from the experience of others, or from your own experience, reading, and reflection, to do everything you have to do better today than you did yesterday. (Wesley, 1788: 621; Rack, 2002: 366–70)

Though Wesley regarded riches as a snare, he and his successors abhorred business failure. Bankruptcy incurred expulsion from the Methodist society (chapel).

The other huge asset of Wesleyan Methodism was its dense connectivity, offering the opportunity for capitalist networking, mostly within Methodism:

> Each of the Methodist bodies tracing their origins back to John Wesley had roughly similar pyramidal administrative structures, reaching up from the local chapel via circuits and districts to a national governing Conference. These structures were held together by Conference rules, by the rotation of professional clergy (travelling preachers, or ministers) through the circuits, by the tapping of lay abilities in leadership, preaching, teaching in Sunday Schools, and in small cell groups for prayer and spiritual counseling … Combined, these structural elements allowed distant and effective geographical reach. (Jeremy, 2020: 149–50)

What then explains the prominence and the differences between these four Nonconformist bodies among the capitalists of the 19th century? Ashton thought it was the superior education enjoyed by the Scots, but that cannot be the whole explanation – as seen from Table 7.3.

There is much truth in Watts's verdict:

> For Evangelical Nonconformists, even for those engaged in business, the chief end of their endeavours was not worldly prosperity it was the saving of souls. They looked upon their fellow men first and foremost not as potential customers but as potential converts, not primarily as men whose desires required satisfaction in this life, but as men whose souls needed saving after death. Conversely the Quakers and the Unitarians were more successful in business than the Baptists or Congregationalist not because they adhered more rigidly to the values of the Reformation, but for the quite the opposite reason that they were readier than Calvinists and Evangelicals to escape the straitjacket of Puritan restraint. (Watts, 1995: 341–2)

Slavery

Enslavement of conquered peoples characterized nearly every empire from those of the ancient world to the British Empire. Implicated were all the world's major religions, Judaism, Christianity and Islam (Stark, 2004: 291–365; Cross and Livingstone, 2005: 1519–20).

With the discovery of the Americas in the 15th and 16th centuries, sugar, highly desired in European markets, became the dominant crop in the new world empires of Spain and Portugal, especially the latter. The insatiable demand of sugar production for labour led the Portuguese to introduce the plantation system to Brazil in the 1550s, and after 1570 to resort to the mass importation of African slave labour (Klein and Vinson, 2007: 42–7).

Between 1501 and 1866 an estimated 12,521,336 men, women and children were herded from Africa; 10,547,087 arrived in the Americas and the Caribbean while another 155,569 were taken to other parts of Africa (Klein, 2010: 214–17). Of the arrivals, 4.8 million went to Brazil, 2.3 million to the British Caribbean, 1.29 million to Spanish America and 1.12 million to the French Caribbean (Klein, 2010: 216–17).

If there were two areas where religion and capitalism colluded or collided over slavery they were the British West Indies, where there were approximately 800,000 slaves in 1833, and the antebellum American South. This section considers two questions about British West Indian slavery. How did the owners of British slaves reconcile slave owning with their Christian consciences? And how critical to the abolition of slavery was the campaign of the Christian abolitionists?

The 1833 act abolishing slavery in the British Empire included a clause compensating slave owners with a grant of £20 million. Approximately 47,000 individuals applied for compensation, claiming as owners, beneficiaries or agents. Of these 3,000 lived in Britain (Hall et al 2014: 3) and came from the upper and middling classes, mostly in England and Scotland. They included 107 clergymen, of whom the highest ranking was the Rev Henry Philpotts, Bishop of Exeter, a trustee or agent (Draper, 2010: 279–322). Several generations of the Hibbert family, Unitarians, were slave owners; 11 Hibberts received compensation totalling £103,000 (Donington 2014: 203–49). Thomas Greg (17?? –1839), son of Samuel Greg, a Scottish Presbyterian who had married into a Unitarian cousinhood and built Quarry Bank cotton mill near Manchester, had 210 slaves in Dominica and St Vincent for which he was compensated £5,082 (Rose, 2012; Legacies, 2020). Benjamin Greene, Bury St Edmunds brewer and owner of 231 slaves on three plantations on Montserrat and St Kitts for which he received £4,033 compensation, was a Congregationalist (Wilson, 2004; Legacies, 2020). One slave owner, James Whitehorne, appears to have been a Baptist (Draper and Lang, 2014: 276). Two directors of the Scottish Missionary Society, an arm of the United Secession Church, William Stothert and William Stirling, were slave owners (Draper, 2010: 29–30). One of the most egregious slave owners was John Gladstone (1724–1851), Scots-born Liverpool merchant and politician (and father of a future prime minister) (Fisher, 2009; Matthew, 2016). An evangelical Anglican, Gladstone built three churches, in Liverpool, Seaforth and Toxteth. After emancipation his 2,912 slaves in British Guiana and Jamaica gave him

£112,721 compensation, the fifth highest award to merchants. Table 7.4 details Gladstone's slave holdings, and incidentally indicates his pursuit of higher value sugar plantations in the new territory of British Guiana, particularly along the Demerara River (Draper, 2010; Hall et al 2014; Legacies, 2020).

What sorts of argument allowed these avowedly Christian people to reconcile slave holding with their consciences? The most obnoxious was peddled by Edward Long in his three volume history of Jamaica. Racial stereotyping, caricature and obscenity cradled his opinion that 'Negroes' were not human (Long, 1774, II: 270, 351–86; Morgan, 2014). Such a misguided and repulsive view may have salved the planters' consciences, but it was abandoned by the next historian of the British West Indies. Bryan Edwards, owner of 600 slaves, even reported Christian conversions among the slaves of Antigua and elsewhere, implying of course that 'Negroes' – *as they were called in contemporary documents* – were just as much human and in need of salvation as white people (Edwards, 1793, I: 450–55, emphasis mine: Sheridan, 2008; Legacies, 2020).

When George Hibbert, owner of 3,671 slaves for which he was paid £67,286 compensation, stood up in the House of Commons in 1807 to oppose the abolition of the slave trade bill, his chief aim was to get compensation for the damage done to an investment of £100 million and a slave population of 600,000 in the British West Indies. While that aim failed, in the course of his three speeches Hibbert offered a cluster of conscience-calming justifications for slavery. By the laws and customs of Africa, existing from antiquity, slavery was perfectly just. It was a refuge from famine. The Old Testament was indifferent to 'the sale of men' (Hibbert, 1807: 12), and in the New Testament Paul sent the runaway slave Onesimus back to his master [which rather ignores Colossians 3:11]. While Hibbert deplored abuses in the slave trade, the slave trade was not the problem, he declared; rather it was the abuses. Furthermore, 'Slavery has been mitigated, and must be mitigated, as civilisation is extended. It is mitigated by manners, by opinion, and by examples' (Hibbert, 1807: 101–2; Murphy and Fisher, 1986; Hancock, 2008; Legacies, 2020).

John Gladstone contended that those who were enslaved were especially capable of 'the power of laboring beneath a vertical sun' but because of their indolent characters needed enslavement. Rather than appeal to the Bible, he invoked Providence:

> it is not for me to attempt to say when a system should terminate which Almighty God, in the divine wisdom of his over-ruling providence, has seen fit to permit in certain climates since the origin and formation of society in this world; whilst in other

Table 7.4: John Gladstone's slave holdings in the British West Indies

Slaves and compensation

Claimant category	Colony	Plantation	Number of slaves
awardee (owner in fee)	British Guiana	Pin Success	429
awardee (mortgagee in possession)	British Guiana	Wales	272
awardee	British Guiana	Vreedestein	193
awardee (owner in fee)	British Guiana	Vreed-en-Hoop	415
awardee (mortgagee)	British Guiana	Met-en-Meerzorg	393
claimants in list E or chancery case	Jamaica, Hanover	Fish River Estate	237
awardee	Jamaica, St Elizabeth	Holland Estate	300
awardee	Jamaica, St Elizabeth	Holland Estate	106
awardee (owner in fee)	Jamaica, St Mary	Oxford Estate	169
awardee	Jamaica, St Thomas-in-the-East	Surrey 1	231
claimants in list E or chancery case	Jamaica, Westmoreland	Petersville	167
Total			2,912

Slaves and compensation

Plantation	Number of slaves	Compensation (to nearest £)	Average £ per slave
Pin Success	429	22,275	51.9
Wales	272	14,721	54.1
Vreedestein	193	10,278	53.3
Vreed-en-Hoop	415	22,444	54.1
Met-en-Meerzorg	393	21,011	53.5
Fish River Estate	237	4,211	17.8
Holland Estate	300	5,624	18.7
Holland Estate	106	2,075	19.6
Oxford Estate	169	3,060	18.1
Surrey 1	231	4,295	18.6
Petersville	167	2,727	16.3
Total	2,912	112,721	38.7

Source: Legacies of British Slave-ownership website

climates, where man is found in a more civilised state, and was influenced by different feelings, the same purposes have been answered by those distinctions which rank and subordination have created. (Gladstone, 1830: 19–20)

Lastly he pointed to the US, 'where no want of strong religious feeling, nor of a sense of duty exists … yet even there slavery is found to exist on a far more extended scale than with us' (Gladstone, 1830: 22).

Compensation, either for lost trade or freed slaves, hinged upon the legal concept of property and whether it was possible to have 'property in men'. That was ambiguous under both English and colonial laws and produced nearly 20 years of debate. Eventually, under the 1833 Act, slaves were regarded as property in order that they might be freed from being property (Draper, 2010: 75–92). In this sense the slave owners, the capitalists, won half the legal argument and all the economic case, but lost the moral and humanitarian one.

How critical to the abolition of slavery was the campaign of the Christian abolitionists? Did religion checkmate the vilest manifestation of capitalism? The question is debatable. Other earlier thinkers such as Montesquieu and Francis Hutcheson condemned slavery. Adam Smith in 1776 dismissed slavery as uneconomic compared with free labour (Smith, 1776: 364–6). Rousseau denounced slavery as a renunciation of 'one's quality as a man, the rights and also the duties of humanity' (Rousseau, 1762, in Hirschfeld, 1964: 176) – which of course was why slave owners deployed the subhuman argument in reference to those they enslaved.

Eric Williams (1943: 149–53) claimed that British West Indian planters, suffering from overproduction, assented to abolition of the slave trade as a means of restricting sugar output. This Marxist interpretation was subsequently demolished. Roger Anstey pointed out that in parliamentary debates only two speakers voiced this concern, while Seymour Drescher demonstrated that British West Indian slave colonies expanded, rather than contracting, before 1807 (both cited in Watts, 1995: 437–8). Klein asserted that 'While the arguments against the slave trade may have had a moral origin, they were also based on the interests of European workers and capitalists and not on any concern with the African slaves themselves' (Klein, 2010: 190). Such an argument, minimizing morality, reflects the effort of modern economics to reduce everything to self-love and calculus (Sedlacek, 2011: 251–7). It ignores the reality of good and evil, particularly the Christian conviction that slavery was such an enormous evil it deserved the sacrifice of personal economic, social and political prospects.

What indispensable ingredients did Evangelical Anglicans and Nonconformists add to the voices of philosophers, economists or the abused industrial classes of Britain? First, there was the moral case against slavery based on Christian belief in human equality. This was published in the 1760s by the Philadelphia Quaker Anthony Benezet who denied assertions of innate negro inferiority (Gerona, 2004). His anti-slavery tracts convinced Thomas Clarkson, an Anglican, to begin a long career writing about the injustice of slavery and the history of the abolition of the slave trade. Clarkson's first publication, a university prize essay, persuaded William Wilberforce in 1787 to take up the anti-slavery cause in the House of Commons (Brogan, 2011). John Wesley, influenced by Benezet, issued *Thoughts upon Slavery* (1774), thereby throwing Methodists into the struggle against the slave trade (Rack, 2002: 362).

Second, there was pressure both within and outside Parliament. A London Committee for the Abolition of the Slave Trade was formed mostly by Quakers in 1787. Josiah Wedgwood, a fellow member and a Unitarian, gave away to fashionable society hundreds of the jasper ware cameos that he had produced showing a kneeling black slave on a white ground with the motto 'Am I not a man and a brother? ' (Clarkson II, 1830: 79–80; Reilly, 2013). William Cowper, the poet, wrote a seven stanza poem 'The Negro's Complaint', again arousing sympathy for and anger at the injustice and cruelty of slavery (Baird, 2013). MPs joined the committee and by 1791 an organized pressure group in Parliament had the ear of the prime minister until 1806 and an admired leader, William Wilberforce (Wolffe, 2009; Hague, 2008). Furthermore, 'Dissenters of all shades of theological opinion responded to the abolition campaign', mobilizing support across the country (Watts, 1995: 441–2).

Third, there was legal expertise and achievement. Granville Sharp, evangelical Anglican, won the Somerset case (1772) that was popularly understood as outlawing slavery in Britain (Ditchfield, 2012).

John Newton, the converted slave ship captain and Anglican clergyman, in 1764 published an *Authentic Narrative* that provided the abolitionists with graphic accounts of the transatlantic slave trade (Hindmarsh, 2010). So too did Olaudah Equiano, a former African slave, who published his *The Interesting Narrative of the Life of Olaudah Equiano* in 1789, describing the horrors of both the slave trade and slavery in the Caribbean and the US, an account that went through numerous editions before he died in 1797 (Walvin, 2017). For conditions of slavery in the British West Indies after 1794, the abolitionists received reports by James Stephen, barrister, an Anglican, and Wilberforce's brother-in-law, who had two spells living on St Kitts (Lipscomb, 2005).

Last, for about twenty years there was a cabinet for the anti-slavery movement. A small core of evangelical Anglicans, nicknamed the Clapham Sect, in the 1790s lived or lodged in houses on Clapham Common built by Henry Thornton, a wealthy banker and opponent of slavery. The group encouraged one another, planned their next moves against slavery and worshipped in the adjacent Holy Trinity parish church (Howse, 1953; Brown, 1961; Wolffe, 2005; Tolley, 2015). Apparently George Hibbert (referred to earlier), another inhabitant of Clapham, also attended Holy Trinity (Legacies, 2020; Olusoga, 2020). When he did so, he was obliged to sit in a high boxed pew and hear the rector, John Venn (d 1813), in his three-decker pulpit, preach against slavery (Cowie, 2005).

The abolition of slavery was more difficult than abolishing the slave trade. This time the reformers collided with the legal concept of 'property in men' and the rights of property under English law. In 1823 the ageing Wilberforce passed leadership of the anti-slavery group in the House of Commons to Thomas Fowell Buxton, an Evangelical Anglican, who began a parliamentary campaign against colonial slavery. In the West Indies, news from England precipitated slave rebellions in 1823 in Demerara and in 1831 on Jamaica. The planters' savage reprisals spurred many Nonconformist missionaries, numbering 87 in the British West Indies, to ignore their home boards' instructions to stay out of politics. They suffered for their agitation but it stirred public opinion in England. Critically, William Knibb, Baptist missionary, returned to England, toured the country, giving graphic accounts of slavery and rousing the conscience of the nation. All this came in 1832 just after the passage of the Reform Act. In the December 1832 election candidates were subjected to over 5,000 petitions and 1.3 million signatures calling for the abolition of slavery. The following February Buxton introduced a motion for the abolition of slavery, which, after some amendments, was passed and became law in August 1833. Wilberforce died three days after the bill passed its Third Reading, the decisive point in enactment (Watts, 1995: 442–52; Blouet, 2004; Heuman, 2004; Wolffe, 2009).

Against immense and fierce political resistance (Taylor, 2020), in a nation tenderized by the Methodist and Evangelical revivals, small but eventually swelling numbers of legislators, lawyers, preachers, campaigners, ex-slaves, missionaries, artists, poets, writers and pamphleteers focused the nation's attention on abolishing the slave trade and later slavery itself. The result was the acts of 1807 and 1833. These were the effects of 'religion' in contrast to the nugatory results of the rarefied voices of philosophers and economists.

Conclusion

Religion and capitalism interacted at both macro- and micro-levels. Religion contributed to the great pre-modern divide between East and West. Through the Reformation, religion launched the individualism essential to bourgeois capitalism. Religious Nonconformity helped to stir the Industrial Revolution. Yet religion failed to restrain the asbestos tragedy. Religious tools have been applied, without much success, to capitalist social control.

For its part capitalism could subvert religion-based ethics and use them to justify slavery in the British West Indies. More effectively the religious imperative drove the abolition of the slave trade and slavery itself in the British Empire. In short, enough examples have been presented to demonstrate the importance of considering the role of religion in any comprehensive historical analysis of global capitalism.

References

Ashton, T.S. (1948) *The Industrial Revolution, 1760–1830*, London: Oxford University Press.

Baird, J.D. (2013) 'William Cowper', *Oxford Dictionary of National Biography*.

Beckert, S. (2014) *Empire of Cotton: A New History of Global Capitalism*, New York: Alfred A. Knopf.

Bellah, R.N. (1985) *Tokugawa Religion: The Cultural Roots of Modern Japan*, New York: The Free Press.

Blouet, O.O. (2010) 'Sir Thomas Fowell Buxton', *Oxford Dictionary of National Biography*.

Brogan, H. (2011) 'Thomas Clarkson', *Oxford Dictionary of National Biography*.

Brown, F.K. (1961) *Fathers of the Victorians: The Age of Wilberforce*, Cambridge: Cambridge University Press.

Calvin, J. (1559) *The Institutes of the Christian Religion* excerpts in K.F. Thompson (ed) (1964) *Classics of Western Thought: Middle Ages, Renaissance, and Reformation*, New York: Harcourt, Brace and World, Inc, pp 322–37.

Chaney, E. (2019) 'Religion, political power and human capital formation: evidence from Islamic history', in J.-P. Carvalho, S. Iyer and J. Rubin (eds) *Advances in the Economics of Religion*, International Economic Association Conference, vol. 158, London: Palgrave Macmillan, pp 437–48.

Chapman, S.D. (1967) *The Early Factory Masters: The Transition to the Factory System in the Midlands Textile Industry*, Newton Abbot: David and Charles.

Church Congress (1890) *The Official Report of the Church Congress Held at Hull, September and October 1890*, London: Bemrose and Sons Ltd.

Cipolla, C.M. (1965) *Guns and Sails in the Early Phase of European Expansion, 1400–1700*, London: Collins.

Clapp, B.W. (1994) *An Environmental History of Britain since the Industrial Revolution*, London: Longman.

Clarkson, T. (1830) *The History of the Rise, Progress and Accomplishment of the Abolition of the African Slave-Trade, by the British Parliament* (abridged by E. Lewis, II), Wilmington, DE: R. Porter.

Coleman, D.C. (1969) *Courtaulds: An Economic and Social History*, Oxford: Clarendon Press.

COPEC (Conference on Christian Politics, Economics and Citizenship) (1924) *Reports: Volume 9: Industry and Property*, London: Longman, Green.

Corley, T.A.B. (1988) 'How Quakers coped with business success: Quaker industrialists, 1860–1914', in D.J. Jeremy (ed) *Business and Religion in Britain*, Aldershot: Gower Publishing Co, pp 164–87.

Courtauld, S.A. (1949) *Ideals and Industry: War-Time Papers*, Cambridge: Cambridge University Press.

Cowie, L.W. (2005) 'Henry Venn', *Oxford Dictionary of National Biography*.

Cross, F.L. and Livingstone, E.A. (eds) (2005) *The Oxford Dictionary of the Christian Church* (3rd edn), Oxford: Oxford University Press.

Davies, H. (1961) *Worship and Theology in England Volume 3 From Watts and Wesley to Maurice*, Princeton, NJ: Princeton University Press.

Ditchfield, G.M. (2012) 'Granville Sharp', *Oxford Dictionary of National Biography*.

Donington, K. (2014) 'Transforming capital: slavery, family, commerce and the making of the Hibbert family', in C. Hall, N. Draper, C. McClelland, K. Donington and R. Lang (eds) *Legacies of British Slave-Ownership: Colonial Slavery and the Formation of Victorian Britain*, Cambridge: Cambridge University Press, pp 203–49.

Draper, N. (2010) *The Price of Emancipation: Slave-Ownership, Compensation and British Society at the End of Slavery*, Cambridge: Cambridge University Press.

Draper, N. and Lang, R. (2014) 'Appendix 1, Making history in a prosopography', in C. Hall, N. Draper, C. McClelland, K. Donington and R. Lang (eds) *Legacies of British Slave-Ownership: Colonial Slavery and the Formation of Victorian Britain*, Cambridge: Cambridge University Press, pp 253–80.

Dreschler, W. (2013) 'Three paradigms of governance and administration: Chinese, Western and Islamic', *Society and Economy*, 35(3): 319–42.

Edwards, B. (1793) *The History, Civil and Commercial, of the British Colonies in the West Indies*, 2 vols, London: John Stockdale.

Farnie, D.A. (2004a) 'Hugh Mason', *Oxford Dictionary of National Biography*.

Farnie, D.A. (2004b) 'John Rylands', *Oxford Dictionary of National Biography*.

Fisher, D. (2009) 'John Gladstone', in D. Fisher (ed) *The History of Parliament: The House of Commons, 1820–1832*, Cambridge: Cambridge University Press, n.p.

Gerona, C. (2004) 'Anthony Benezet', *Oxford Dictionary of National Biography*.

Gladstone, J. (1830) *A Statement of Facts, Connected with the Present State of Slavery in the British Sugar and Coffee Colonies and in the United States of America*, London: Baldwin and Cradock.

Goyder, G. (1951) *The Future of Private Enterprise: A Study in Responsibility*, Oxford: Blackwell.

Goyder, G. (1961) *The Responsible Company*, Oxford: Blackwell.

Goyder, G. and Goyder, R. (1994) *Signs of Grace*, London: Cygnet.

Grassby, R. (1995) *The Business Community of Seventeenth-Century England*, Cambridge: Cambridge University Press.

Green, R.W. (ed) (1959) *Protestantism and Capitalism: The Weber Thesis and Its Critics*, Boston, MA: D.C. Heath and Co.

Hague, W. (2008) *William Wilberforce: The Life of the Great Anti-Slave Trade Campaigner*, London: Harper Press.

Hall, C., Draper, N., McClelland, C., Donington, K. and Lang, R. (2014) *Legacies of British Slave-Ownership: Colonial Slavery and the Formation of Victorian Britain*, Cambridge: Cambridge University Press.

Hancock, D. (2008) 'George Hibbert', *Oxford Dictionary of National Biography*.

Hempton, D. and Walsh, J. (2001) 'E. P. Thompson and Methodism', in M. Noll (ed) *God and Mammon: Protestants, Money, and the Market, 1790–1860*, Oxford: Oxford University Press, pp 99–120.

Henriques, U. (1961) *Religious Toleration in England 1787 to 1833*, London: Routledge and Kegan Paul.

Heuman, G. (2004) 'William Knibb', *Oxford Dictionary of National Biography*.

Hibbert, G. (1807) *The Substance of Three Speeches in Parliament, on the Bill for the Abolition of the Slave Trade*, London: Lowe, Darling and Co.

Hindmarsh, D.B. (2010) 'John Newton', *Oxford Dictionary of National Biography*.

Hirschfeld, C. (ed) (1964) *Classics of Western Thought: The Modern Mind*, New York: Harcourt, Brace and World Inc.

Hirschmeier, J. and Yui, T. (1975) *The Development of Japanese Business, 1600–1973*, London: George Allen and Unwin Ltd.

Holcombe, L. (1983) *Wives and Property: Reform of the Married Women's Property Law in Nineteenth-Century England*, Toronto: University of Toronto Press.

Howe, A. (1984) *The Cotton Masters, 1830–1860*, Oxford: Clarendon Press.

Howse, E.M. (1953) *Saints in Politics: The 'Clapham Sect' and the Growth of Freedom*, London: George Allen and Unwin.

James, D. (2004) 'Sir Titus Salt', *Oxford Dictionary of National Biography*.

Jeremy, D.J. (1970) *Henry Wansey and His American Journal, 1794*, Philadelphia, PA: American Philosophical Society.

Jeremy, D.J. (1990) *Capitalists and Christians: Business Leaders and the Churches in Britain, 1900–1960*, Oxford: Clarendon Press.

Jeremy, D.J. (1991) 'The enlightened paternalist in action: William Hesketh Lever at Port Sunlight', *Business History*, 33(1): 58–81.

Jeremy, D.J. (2009) 'Ethics, religion, and business in twentieth-century Britain', in R. Coopey and P. Lyth (eds) *Business in Britain in the Twentieth Century*, Oxford: Oxford University Press, pp 356–84.

Jeremy, D.J. (2013) 'Nonconformist business leaders, ca 1880–1940: the uses and abuses of wealth', in R. Pope (ed) *T&T Clark Companion to Nonconformity*, London: Bloomsbury, pp 407–36.

Jeremy, D.J. (2018) 'Who were the benefactors of Wesleyan Methodism in the nineteenth century?' *Proceedings of the Wesley Historical Society*, 61(5): 186–200.

Jeremy, D.J. (2020) 'Funding faith: early Victorian Wesleyan philanthropy', in C. Binfield, G.M. Ditchfield and D.L. Wykes (eds) *Protestant Dissent and Philanthropy in Britain 1660–1914*, Woodbridge: The Boydell Press, pp 129–51.

Kadane, M. (2013) *The Watchful Clothier: The Life of an Eighteenth-Century Protestant Capitalist*, New Haven, CT: Yale University Press.

Kirby, M.W. (1988) 'The failure of a Quaker business dynasty: the Peases of Darlington, 1830–1902', in D.J. Jeremy (ed) *Business and Religion in Britain*, Aldershot: Gower Publishing Co, pp 142–63.

Klein, H.S. and Vinson, B. (2007) *African Slavery in Latin America and the Caribbean* (2nd edn), New York: Oxford University Press.

Klein, H.S. (2010) *The Atlantic Slave Trade* (2nd edn), Cambridge: Cambridge University Press.

Kuran, T. (2018) 'Islam and economic performance: historical and contemporary links', *Journal of Economic Literature*, 56(4): 1292–1359.

Landes, D.S. (1998) *The Wealth and Poverty of Nations: Why Some Are so Rich and Some so Poor*, New York: W.W. Norton and Co.

Latourette, K.S. (1954) *A History of Modern China*, Harmondsworth: Penguin.

Legacies (2020) 'Legacies of British Slave-Ownership', *University College London*, [online]. Available from: https://www.ucl.ac.uk/lbs/ [Accessed 20 September 2020].

Lipscomb, P.C. (2005) 'James Stephen', *Oxford Dictionary of National Biography*.

Long, E. (1774) *The History of Jamaica or, General Survey of the Ancient and Modern State of that Island*, 3 vols, London: T. Lowndes.

Luther, M. (1520) *Address to the Christian Nobility of the German Nation* excerpts in K.F. Thompson (ed) (1964) *Classics of Western Thought: Middle Ages, Renaissance, and Reformation*, New York: Harcourt, Brace and World Inc, pp 304–21.

MacCulloch, D. (2004) *Reformation: Europe's House Divided, 1490–1700*, London: Penguin Books Ltd.

Manning, B.L. (1952) *The Protestant Dissenting Deputies*, Cambridge: Cambridge University Press.

Matthew, H.C.G. (2016) 'Sir John Gladstone', *Oxford Dictionary of National Biography*.

McLeod, H. (1996) *Religion and Society in England, 1850–1914*, Basingstoke: Macmillan Press Ltd.

Mellone, S.H. (1925) *Liberty and Religion: The First Century of the British and Foreign Unitarian Association*, London: N.S.

Milligan, E.H. (2007) *Biographical Dictionary of British Quakers in Commerce and Industry, 1775–1920*, York: Sessions Book Trust.

Morgan, K. 'Edward Long', *Oxford Dictionary of National Biography*.

Murphy, B. and Fisher, D.R. (1986) 'George Hibbert', in R. Thorne (ed) *The History of Parliament: The House of Commons, 1790–1820*, Woodbridge: Boydell and Brewer, n.p.

Needham, N.J.T.M. (2020) 'Joseph Needham', Wikipedia. Available from: https://en.wikipedia.org/wiki/Joseph_Needham [Accessed 20 September 2020].

Olusoga, D. (2020) *Britain's Forgotten Slave Owners*, BBC Four, Thursday 27 June.

Prance, G. (1996) *The Earth under Threat: A Christian Perspective*, Glasgow: Wild Goose Publications.

Preston, R.H. (1981) *Explorations in Theology; 9*, London: SCM Press.

Rack, H. D. (2002) *Reasonable Enthusiast: John Wesley and the Rise of Methodism* (3rd edn), Peterborough: Epworth Press.

Rawlings, E.C. (1902) *The Free Churchman's Legal Handbook Including a Summary of Laws Relating to Social Questions*, London: National Council of the Evangelical Free Churches.

Reilly, R. (2013) 'Josiah Wedgwood', *Oxford Dictionary of National Biography*.

Religious Society of Friends (1931) *Church Government, Being the Third Part of Christian Discipline in the Religious Society of Friends in Great Britain*, London: Friends Book Centre.

Reynolds, J. (1986) 'Sir Titus Salt', in D.J. Jeremy and C. Shaw (eds) *Dictionary of Business Biography*, 6 vols, London: Butterworths.

Rose, M.B. (2012) 'Samuel Greg', *Oxford Dictionary of National Biography*.

Rousseau, J.J. (1762) *The Social Contract*, excerpts in C. Hirschfeld (ed) 1964 *Classics of Western Thought: The Modern World*, New York: Harcourt, Brace and World Inc, pp 173–92.

Rubin, R. (2017) *Rulers, Religion and Riches: Why the West Got Rich and the Middle East Did Not*, Cambridge: Cambridge University Press.

Rubinstein, W.D. (1981) *Men of Property: The Very Wealthy in Britain since the Industrial Revolution*, London: Croom Helm.

Sedlacek, T. (2011) *Economics of Good and Evil: The Quest for Economic Meaning from Gilgamesh to Wall Street*, New York: Oxford University Press.

Sheridan, R.B. (2008) 'Bryan Edwards', *Oxford Dictionary of National Biography*.

Smith, A. (1776) *An Inquiry into the Nature and Causes of the Wealth of Nations*, ed E. Cannan (1937), New York: Random House.

Sombart, W. (1915) *The Quintessence of Capitalism*, trans M. Epstein, New York: E.P. Dutton & Co.

Stark, R. (2004) *For the Glory of God: How Monotheism Led to Reformations, Science, Witch-Hunts and the End of Slavery*, Princeton, NJ: Princeton University Press.

Stewart, W.A.C. (1953) *Quakers and Education*, London: Epworth Press.

Stott, J. (2006) *Issues Facing Christians Today* (4th edn), Grand Rapids, MI: Zondervan.

Tawney, R.H. (1926) *Religion and the Rise of Capitalism: A Historical Study*, London: John Murray.

Taylor, M. (2020) *The Interest: How the British Establishment Resisted the Abolition of Slavery*, London: The Bodley Head.

Temple, W. (1942) *Christianity and Social Order* (new edn 1976), London: SPCK.

Thompson, E.P. (1963) *The Making of the English Working Class*, London: Victor Gollancz.

Thompson, K,F (ed) (1964) *Classics of Western Thought: Middle Ages, Renaissance, and Reformation.* New York: Harcourt, Brace and World Inc.

Tolley, C. (2015) Henry Thornton, *Oxford Dictionary of National Biography.*

Troeltsch, T. (1912) *The Social Teaching of the Christian Churches Volumes 1 and 2* (trans O. Wyon, 1931, repr 1992), Louisville, KY: Westminster/ John Knox Press.

Tweedale, G. (2000) *Magic Mineral to Killer Dust: Turner & Newall and the Asbestos Hazard,* Oxford: Oxford University Press.

Wakelin, M. (1996) *J. Arthur Rank: The Man behind the Gong,* Oxford: Lion.

Walvin, J. (1997) *The Quakers: Money and Morals*, London: John Murray.

Walvin, J. (2017) 'Olaudah Equiano', *Oxford Dictionary of National Biography.*

Watts, M.R. (1978) *The Dissenters from the Reformation to the French Revolution*, Oxford: Clarendon Press.

Watts, M.R. (1995) *The Dissenters: Volume 2: The Expansion of Evangelical Nonconformity*, Oxford: Clarendon Press.

Weber, M. (1904–5) *The Protestant Ethic and the Spirit of Capitalism* (trans T. Parsons, 1958), Kettering, OH: Angelico Press.

Weber, M. (1948) *From Max Weber: Essays in Sociology*, ed. and trans. H.H. Gerth and C. Wright Mills, London: Routledge.

Wesley, J. (1774) *Thoughts upon Slavery*, London: R. Hawes.

Wesley, J. (1788) 'The use of money', in *Sermons* (repr), London: Methodist Conference Office.

Williams, E. (1943) *Capitalism and Slavery*, Chapel Hill: University of North Carolina Press.

Wilson, R.G. (2004) 'Greene family', *Oxford Dictionary of National Biography.*

Wolffe, J. (2005) 'Clapham Sect', *Oxford Dictionary of National Biography.*

Wolffe, J. (2009) 'William Wilberforce', *Oxford Dictionary of National Biography.*

Worsley, I. (1816) *Observations on the State and Changes in the Presbyterian Societies of England during the Last Half Century: also on the Manufactures of Great Britain; for the Most Part Established and Supported by the Protestant Dissenters: Tending to Illustrate the Importance of Religious Liberty and Free Enquiry to the Welfare and Prosperity of a People; Preceded by a Sermon on the Death of the Rev Dr Joshua Toulmin*, London: Longman, Hurst and Co.

8

Capitalism and the Environment

Geoffrey Jones

Introduction

The capitalist industry that began with the Industrial Revolution resulted in enormous productivity increases, wealth creation and sustenance as Earth's population soared. Yet the business system as it emerged described the varied impacts on the natural environment as 'externalities', and took little responsibility for them. The result was growing ecological damage, which persisted despite warnings by philosophers and scientists. The results were cumulative, and were magnified from the 1980s as some non-Western countries, including China, experienced fast economic growth. Most studies of this phenomenon have focused on policy and regulation, and have looked at this issue from a system-wide perspective on the negative consequences of capitalism. This chapter offers an alternative business history perspective with a more nuanced analysis of the role of business enterprises.

   This chapter proceeds chronologically and thematically. The first section reviews the ecological damage between the Industrial Revolution and the 1970s, and the limited attempts by either government or social activists to contain it. The second section reviews the endeavours of small groups of entrepreneurs to create alternative capitalisms before the 1970s that helped rather than damaged the environment. The third section examines the period of corporate environmentalism since the 1980s. These decades saw, for the first time, large corporations that were addressing environmental challenges claiming to become more sustainable. It is less evident that major environmental improvements occurred as a result. The chapter concludes by reflecting why endeavours to create an alternative, more ecological, capitalism have proved challenging.

Capitalism and the problem of environmental externalities

The evolution of humanity over history has seen the progressive taming of the natural environment and its redeployment to facilitate human development. Settled agriculture and the domestication of animals for use as food and clothing were milestones in this process. The building of cities and the development of methods to trade over distances were further milestones. By the 18th century human intervention had radically changed the natural landscape across the habitable globe. However, even in the most economically advanced regions, the autonomy of the natural world remained strong.

This situation began to change with the Industrial Revolution. Some scientists have identified 1820 as the start of a new Anthropocene Age because modern economic growth resulted in an enormous extension of humanity's ability to control, and damage, the natural environment (Jones, 2017: 4–5). The key driver of change was the shift to the use of coal instead of firewood and charcoal and the use of metals on a scale never seen before. The bio-based economy of the past was replaced by a geo-based economy of coal, iron and steel. In 1700 an estimated two thirds of energy consumed in Britain came from animals. By 1850 steam power provided 30 per cent of Britain's power (Fouquet, 2008: 125). Fossil fuel capitalism was at the heart of an ongoing negative impact of capitalism on the Earth's environment, driving climate change and the loss of biosphere integrity (Bergquist, 2019). The Earth's climate had been broadly stable for 10,000 years before the 19th century. From the 1880s, the average global temperature rose by 1.1 °C. This caused heatwaves and floods to grow in intensity, and the development of chronic hazards including droughts and rising sea levels (McKinsey Global Institute, 2020).

Fossil fuels and the rise of modern science resulted in massive increases in productivity through the spread of factory production. Steam-driven railways and steam-driven ships also opened the possibility of exploiting natural resources in distant lands. Multinational trading and shipping companies created large farms of cattle and sheep, which were transported on an industrial scale to slaughterhouses to be killed for meat and skins. Plants and crops were moved between continents and their production vastly expanded (Jones, 2005a: 44–52). Regions typically specialized in particular crops or commodities, creating monocultural agricultures that swept away traditional ecological systems, often alongside the indigenous peoples who had inhabited the lands. Globalization became a vehicle for the diffusion of the destruction of the natural environment in the industrialized West around the world.

Latin America provides a regional example of the devastation wreaked by US and European multinational corporations. The banana plantations of the United Fruit Company and other US firms in Central America were notorious for damaging the soil: the firm would simply move to another region when the ecological damage was too great. A key problem was that the companies focused on a single type of banana, the Gros Michel, which proved vulnerable to the fungal infection known as Panama disease (Miller, 2007: 129–33).

Resources that had built up over millennia were rapidly depleted on the sub-continent. A classic example was the Peruvian guano industry. From the 1840s Europeans identified Peruvian guano as possessing high concentrations of nitrogen, making it the best accessible fertilizer. British and other merchants, who mined the product from coastal islands and promontories, and exported it worldwide, exploited it under contract to the government. Their application resulted in a huge rise in yields in the West, but by the 1870s Peru had largely run out of guano. The Peruvian state responded by managing and protecting guano birds, often by killing predatory birds, and the recovering supplies were used to enhance national agriculture. However, a boom in the fishmeal industry, used to feed the chickens and pigs that transformed Western diets after the Second World War, depleted fishing stocks, causing bird populations and guano production to decline again (Cushman, 2013).

Consumer capitalism literally consumed the lives of animals. In Venezuela, egrets were protected in 1917, but only after hunters had almost destroyed the population in order to harvest the breeding plumage, which was used to adorn women's hats. Most efforts at conservation were ineffective. From Argentina and Chile's Andean slopes, chinchilla pelts were exported to North America and Europe from the 1820s to manufacture fur clothing. By the last decade of the 19th century exports averaged nearly half a million pelts per annum; a long fur coat required as many as 150. Small litters, usually one set of twins, limited chinchilla reproduction, and populations crashed at the start of the 20th century. In 1905 Argentina exported about 200,000 pelts. By 1909 exports had fallen to 28,000. Despite an international agreement in 1910 between Argentina, Chile, Bolivia and Peru, which outlawed the trade, one species became extinct and the two remaining, endangered (Miller, 2012).

Meanwhile, Western mining multinationals were hugely destructive of the natural environment in Latin America (and elsewhere) as mountains were destroyed and landscapes scarred by new and powerful technologies. The emergence of the new petroleum industry in early 20th-century Mexico and Venezuela caused extraordinary ecological devastation in both countries (Santiago, 2006).

However, and somewhat paradoxically, it was the adverse impact of industrialization on the natural environment of Western industrialized countries rather than the periphery that stirred most opposition. As whole species of animals, such as the American buffalo, were hunted to virtual extinction over a short period, critics called for the 'conserving' of the natural environment. Conservation became institutionalized as a movement during the second half of the 19th century, typically driven by social elites. In the US, conservation sentiments led to the creation of Yellowstone National Park, the world's first national park, in 1872 (Schullery and Whittlesey, 2003). In 1892 the Sierra Club was founded in San Francisco by the wilderness explorer John Muir. It became America's most influential conservation society (Guha, 2008: 49–54; Worster, 2008). In Europe, too, scientists documented environmental problems such as the loss of habitats and species. Voluntary groups were also formed to protect wildlife and conserve nature. The protection of birds from hunting, and from the growing demand for feathers to be used in women's hats and other clothes, was an early focus of attention (Matagne, 1998: 362–3).

The ongoing damage to the natural environment largely caused by business enterprises was well understood by contemporaries, then, but there was no method of accounting for it, and it became broadly accepted as a necessary evil or inevitable consequence of economic growth. Environmental destruction, or other adverse (and indeed positive) social impacts, was regarded by accounting systems as 'externalities'. The profit-making endeavours of firms, in contrast, were the 'internal' matter of business. The resulting dilemma for the natural environment was articulated by the ecologist Garrett Hardin in an essay entitled 'The Tragedy of the Commons', published in 1968. He explained that the self-interest of rational (and well-meaning) individuals can, and did, lead to the harm of the common good. 'The rational man', Hardin wrote concerning the problem of pollution, 'finds that his share of the costs of the wastes he discharges into the commons is less than the costs of purifying his wastes before releasing them. Since this is true for everyone, we are locked into a system of "fouling our own nest"' (Hardin, 1968).

The one adverse environmental impact that did come under scrutiny was industrial pollution. By the late 19th century, the smoke caused by the burning of coal had become a huge pollution problem in big Western cities. London became known as the 'big smoke'. There was considerable environmental activism against such pollution (Clapp, 1994). In Britain, legislation was passed in the 1830s and intensified in the 1860s to control pollution, especially black smoke and coal emissions, drawing on the common law of nuisances. The law reflected the anger of the aristocracy, represented in the House of Lords, about the environmental impact of chemical factories in particular on their lands (Pontin, 2007).

Meanwhile, in the US dozens of anti-smoke associations were formed to lobby for controls on smoke pollution in big cities including Baltimore and Chicago. Women's groups were prominent in many of the associations. Business leaders and organizations often opposed regulation over pollution, but they were sometimes found among the supporters of it (Meisner Rosen, 2017). Ordinances against excessive smoke were followed by pioneering legislation on smoke inspection, which the city of Chicago passed in 1907. Under this, municipal engineers enforced smoke controls and provided advice to businesses to reduce their emissions. The system spread across America's industrial cities (Meisner Rosen, 1995; Uekötter, 2009: 20–42).

Recent research has stressed that business was not simply a black box emitting environmental destruction, as suggested in the more critical accounts of the impact of capitalism by environmental historians (Worster, 1979). Complaints about pollution, and concerns about unprofitable and inefficient waste, led mining, petroleum and paper companies, among others, to undertake significant innovations. Waste and pollution levels were in some cases significantly reduced, although the underlying negative environmental impact was not resolved (Gorman, 1999; LeCain, 2009; Söderholm and Bergquist, 2012).

Smoke controls, national parks, conservation movements and corporate innovation resulted in niche fixes for some of the more blatant unintended consequences from industrialization before 1914. However, for the following half-century, an era that included two world wars and the Great Depression, the environmental downsides of modernization and industrialization continued but attracted little attention (Jones, 2017: 55–7). Few new environmental organizations were founded in this period. Insofar as the environment attracted interest, fascist organizations expressed environmental concerns and introduced environmental policies during the interwar years (Conford, 2001; Brüggemeier et al, 2005). After 1945 the focus was on economic recovery and the Cold War. There were new industries such as computers and information technology. Huge increases in energy use occurred: one estimate was that the world has used more energy since 1900 than in all prior human history. The use of fossil fuels remained critical, but natural gas and nuclear energy also provided additional sources of energy (McNeil, 2000: 14–15). In Germany, the US and elsewhere, concerns about industrial pollution by manufacturing were brushed aside as the role of business was seen as essential to economic recovery. The German legal system formally prioritized economic performance over protection of pollution victims (Jones and Lubinski, 2014).

The lack of interest in the environment was not because environmental degradation had eased. As McNeil and Engelke argued in their aptly named book *The Great Acceleration*, the negative human impact on the natural environment was magnified after 1945, especially because of exponential growth in fossil fuel consumption and population growth (McNeil and Engelke, 2014).

Nor was the lack of interest caused because scientists stopped warning what was happening. In 1939 two British soil scientists, Graham Jacks and Robert Whyte, employed by the Imperial Bureau of Soil Science, a government agency, published the evocatively named book *The Rape of the Earth*. The book provided a global and historical survey of the problems of soil erosion, exploring the political and social consequences of environmental degradation, and discussing the trade-off between economic success and environmental cost. 'Movements of capital have been one of the mainsprings of progress, but capitalism has never seriously concerned itself with its repercussions on the humus content and structure of soils. Nevertheless, the repercussions have been shattering in their effect and can no longer be ignored' (Jacks and Whyte, 1939). Although the repercussions were evident, governments and industry pursued other priorities.

William Vogt's book *Road to Survival*, published in 1948, presented a compelling picture of rising populations and diminishing resources. The author had served as Associate Director of the Division of Science and Education of the Office of the Coordinator in Inter-American Affairs, a US federal agency, and the book included extensive discussions of environmental stresses in Latin America as well as Africa, Asia and the US. Vogt documented serious problems of soil erosion, declining fertility, water shortages and the depletion of non-renewable resources such as oil and minerals manifested by the 'waster's psychology', which he considered most visible in the US (Vogt, 1948: 67). He was particularly explicit about the trade-off between capitalism and the environment. 'Man assumes that what has been good for industry must necessarily be good for the land,' Vogt observed. 'This may prove to be one of the most expensive mistakes in history' (Vogt, 1948: 34–7). Few listened. As the environmental historian John McNeill later observed, before 1970 'environmental thinking appealed only to a very narrow slice of society' (McNeill, 2000: 337).

However, although there were serious warnings, the full scale of the environmental damage inflicted by business was also still not evident. There was almost no understanding of the impact of the burning of fossil fuels, as well as methane emissions, on the climate. In 1896 Svante Arrhenius, a Swedish scientist, observed the potential of carbon dioxide to raise the global temperature, but this was not central to his work, and he predicted that any impact would occur over the very long term. During the 1930s an American geologist, T.C. Chamberlin, raised the issue more forcefully after observing a warming of the North Atlantic region, but he was not taken seriously by the scientific community (Weart, 2008). It was not until 30 years later that even the possibility that human activity could impact the climate began to be more broadly discussed. In 1971, the first-ever conference to focus on the study of man's impact on climate was held in Stockholm. The concluding report, entitled *Inadvertent Climate Modification*, discussed in detail emissions of pollutants and greenhouse gases, although there was no consensus on what was happening, let alone on the solutions

(Wilson and Matthews, 1971; Weart, 2008: 71). Another lengthy period passed before the problem of climate change attracted extensive attention beyond the scientific community.

During the 1960s, however, environmental awareness as a whole began to increase again (Guha, 2000: 2–4, 68). There were several triggers. First, there were serious water pollution episodes. The synthetic detergents industry's use of non-biodegradable surfactants resulted in foam covering lakes and rivers across Europe and the US, provoking new regulations over the industry (Jones and Lubinski, 2014). In 1969 a disastrous Santa Barbara oil well blowout spilt 200,000 gallons of oil onto the Californian coastline for 11 days. This event led to the National Environmental Policy Act in 1969, a landmark piece of legislation that required US federal agencies to prepare environmental assessments and environmental impact statements (Hoffman, 2001: 53–6).

Second, a new generation of articulate writers reached a wider audience. Rachel Carson's *Silent Spring*, published in 1962, is sometimes credited for single-handedly starting a second wave of environmentalism by highlighting the impact of the pesticide DDT on poisoning wildlife, fish and birds (Guha, 2000). Subsequently, Jean Dorst and Paul Ehrlich extended the idea of environmental threats to include issues such as over-population (Dorst, 1965; Ehrlich, 1968). Meanwhile, the British economist Barbara Ward, who exercised considerable influence on policy makers both in Britain and the US, joined her long-term concerns for development and social justice with debates concerning environmental sustainability in *Spaceship Earth*, published in 1966 (Ward, 1966).

A third influence on the emergence of the second wave of environmentalism was the new social movements that fundamentally questioned existing social and political frameworks. During 1968 European capitals, Paris most famously, were swept up in radical student protests. Environmental concerns were only one small dimension of an emergent counterculture that embraced hippies and political dissent, but these wider social movements facilitated wider citizen participation in environmental protests. Charles Reich's *The Greening of America*, published in 1970, explicitly sought to integrate the need for environmental protection into a broader set of issues including feminism, gay rights, racial equality and an end to military conflict, excessive consumerism and corporate power (Reich, 1970).

Even the space race unwittingly contributed an iconic image that the nascent environmental movement adopted as a rallying point. On 24 December 1968 the Earth was photographed rising over the lunar horizon by the crew of Apollo 8, the first spaceship to orbit the moon. The stunning visual image of the small blue and white planet set against the darkness of space captured imaginations. Named 'Earthrise', the photograph was widely adopted by the environmental movement. As images of the Earth from space became pervasive, the environmental movement developed a new set of powerful non-governmental organizations (NGOs). Naturalist David Brower, a member of the Sierra Club, founded the Friends of the Earth in San Francisco in 1969 after the club refused to oppose the development of nuclear power in the US (Weber and Soderstrom, 2012; Jones, 2017: 88).

This second wave of environmentalism, as it was later termed by environmental historians, saw many countries introduce new environmentalism legislation. There was a new recognition that private and public interests were misaligned. New measures of environmental protection were introduced, including restrictions on the disposal of chemical waste, constraints on water and air pollution, and limits on the destruction of habitat (Bergquist et al, 2019). However, there was limited immediate response from business itself. Large corporations remained broadly resistant to what they perceived as the increased costs caused by new regulations.

Alternative green capitalisms

From the middle of the 19th century a small cohort of green entrepreneurs emerged, building for-profit businesses that had a more positive environmental impact. This impact was often inadvertent; but in other cases it arose from a specific identification of environmental problems and a belief that for-profit business was a way to solve them.

A first set of green entrepreneurs who emerged in the late 19th century were the pioneers of today's wind and solar industries. They faced a hugely successful incumbent industry based on fossil fuels. Coal power was a triumph of capitalist enterprise. In Britain, Europe's largest coal producer, landowners and increasingly specialist colliery companies pioneered the deep-shaft mining techniques that enabled massive amounts of coal to be mined. By the 1870s a huge industry had developed, employing half a million workers and exported four fifths of its output around the world. The American industry, favoured by laws that enabled corporations to keep all they mined on federally owned lands, featured both huge companies and thousands of small ventures with one or two employees. A second fossil fuel, petroleum, was initially much less important than coal. Nevertheless, by the 1920s large vertically integrated firms such as Standard Oil and Royal Dutch Shell had developed, spanning the production, refining and distribution of petroleum worldwide (Jones, 2017: 39). Fossil fuels enabled the generation of electricity that progressively lit up the world with light bulbs and streetlights, and allowed communication over distances with the new technologies of the telegraph, the telephone and cinema. As consumption grew, costs fell. The average price for electric energy fell 400 per cent in the US between 1902 and 1930 (Hausman et al, 2008).

As noted earlier, there was no understanding of the impact of fossil fuels on climate change, and the early endeavours in renewables were motivated by other, often practical, concerns.

The vast open spaces of the interior of the US prompted endeavours to develop businesses using wind technologies for mechanical water pumping using small systems with rotor diameters of one to several metres. Low-cost water-pumping windmills were sold to the transcontinental railways, which needed to draw water for their steam locomotives and faced high costs to transport coal for this purpose. During the 1920s wind generator electrical systems inspired by the design of airplane propellers and later monoplane wings found widespread use in the rural areas of the Great Plains, initially to provide lighting for farms and to charge batteries used to power crystal radio sets, and later to power refrigerators, freezers, washing machines and power tools. The Jacobs Wind Energy Company was among the most important wind energy businesses of this era (Jones, 2017: 41–2).

It was in Denmark, the second pioneer of the modern wind energy industry alongside the US, that wider social issues became integrated into the development of windmills. Denmark had a long tradition of using windmills to mill grain for flour, but Poul la Cour took the technology to a new level. In 1891 la Cour, who had become a teacher at a high school in the south of the country, began experimenting with how wind turbines could generate electricity. He was the first person in the world to carry out systematic experiments with artificial air currents in a wind tunnel. He was motivated by his dislike for what he regarded as the poor social conditions in towns as they industrialized, and sought a way to improve rural life so people would not leave for such towns. He considered access to electricity as the key, but as power plants were only built to serve the Danish cities, he wanted to find a way to generate electricity in rural areas. La Cour and one of his students launched a company called Lykkegaard to manufacture wind turbines. It was joined by a second venture organized by the cement group F.L. Smidth & Co, which, in cooperation with the aircraft company Kramme & Zeuthen, developed a new type of turbine with aerodynamic wings and a tower of concrete that had an output of 40–70 kW. Smidth became a leader in linking turbine manufacturing with the field of aerodynamics. However, the construction of national electricity grids supplied from coal-burning power stations during the interwar years blighted the wind energy industry in Denmark and elsewhere (Jones, 2017, pp 41–2).

There were parallels between developments in the wind and solar energy industries. Passive solar energy, or the use of the sun's energy for lighting and heating living spaces, had always been used, but no technology existed to store solar heat or even to capture it. There were new technical advances in the 19th century. The French mathematician Augustin Mouchot, motivated by a conviction that fossil fuels would eventually run out, created the first solar steam-powered plant using parabolic dish collectors. The production of steam using parabolic troughs remained the key technology for using solar power until after the Second World War, when the conversion of sunlight directly into electricity using photovoltaic panels was developed. Mouchot developed an experimental solar-powered steam engine, which received some government funding and won a prize, but was not developed. There were also experiments with the use of solar energy in the late 19th century to power water desalination plants in Chile's dry Atacama Desert (Jones, 2018: 59).

As with wind, entrepreneurs saw profitable opportunities where coal was costly and the sun shone. During the 1890s, several solar water heater companies were started in California, which had a lot of sun and no coal (Jones, 2018: 59–60). However, in time the growing availability of fossil fuels and the spread of grids made such businesses uneconomic. It was in the hot and sunny countries in the developing world where solar energy seemed to have better prospects. The most important example was in the British protectorate of Egypt, where the American entrepreneur Frank Shuman established a solar business.

Shuman was concerned about the finite supply of fossil fuels. In September 1911, he wrote in *Scientific American* that 'the future development of solar power has no limit … and in the far distant future, natural fuels having been exhausted, it will remain as the only means of existence of the human race' (Shuman, 1911: 291). He wrote at a moment when there was much public debate about imminent shortages of coal and petroleum, yet he still struggled to attract investor interest. He turned to the London capital market. In 1911 he and his partners floated a new company, Sun Power Company (Eastern Hemisphere), to launch a solar energy venture in Egypt. The British colonial government supported the project as a cost-effective way to upgrade Egypt's irrigation system and increase the country's lucrative cotton crop, but the outbreak of the First World War led to the closure of the pilot plant. Shuman died of a heart attack in 1918. After the war the momentum for further experimentation was lost, as the prices of fossil fuels fell sharply during the post-war recession (Jones, 2018: 60–2).

Cheap fossil fuels and electricity grids largely ended entrepreneurial experiments in renewable energy for the following half-century. When experiments resumed, they were often motivated by social concerns. During the 1950s and 1960s Farrington Daniels, a chemistry professor apparently consumed with guilt over his involvement with the Manhattan Project, promoted the use of solar energy as a cheap energy source for developing countries, and helped keep the nascent Solar Energy Society financially solvent. Purpose-driven entrepreneurs were also important in the new photovoltaic cell technology that emerged after the Second World War, which proved too costly and experimental for large corporations. During the

1970s, the most important figures included Elliot Berman, who developed a cheaper type of solar cell based on organic materials such as dyes, and Bill Yerkes, who achieved major costs reductions. Both were concerned to provide power for the rural poor in developing countries, and both eventually had to sell their businesses to large oil companies after failing to interest investors (Jones, 2018: 63–71). The development of wind energy was even more closely linked to social movements, especially in Denmark, where entrepreneurial wind energy ventures were closely linked with anti-nuclear activism and ecological concerns (Jones, 2017: 114–15).

A second area for green entrepreneurship from the 19th century onwards was food. In this industry the parallels with modern day environmental concerns were much clearer. As chemical fertilizers were applied to agriculture and chemical additives added to products, concerns rose about the impact on human health and the health of the soil.

The first such businesses often grew out of social and religious movements. In the US a social movement known as health reform provided a context and intellectual agenda for the first businesses. It emerged in early 19th-century Boston and was associated with Sylvester Graham. In 1829 this Presbyterian minister made the antecedent of what Americans know as the Graham cracker, made of whole-wheat and high-fibre flour, as an alternative to the increasingly popular white bread that employed chemical additives. His ideas became the basis for entrepreneurial start-ups, though not by him personally. These included 'Graham boarding houses' and small stores. Health reform was a central concern of the Seventh-Day Adventist sect established at Battle Creek, Michigan, in 1863. In 1876 Dr John Harvey Kellogg, a passionate vegetarian and consumer of Graham crackers, became medical director of a sanatorium on the site. Kellogg specialized in making healthy vegetable-based foods. This was the origins of the Kellogg Corn Flake breakfast cereal, though it was Kellogg's brother Will who commercialized the product by adding sugar and other non-healthy ingredients (Jones, 2017: 26–7).

The American health reformers were in frequent contact with counterparts in Britain, which also saw small businesses making health food products for sale in spas and sanatoriums. Among the first health food stores in the world opened in the industrial metropolis of Birmingham in 1898, when a group of vegetarian businesspersons established a vegetarian store, plus a restaurant and hotel. John Henry Cook, who coined the term 'health food store', managed it. Cook, a Seventh-Day Adventist and vegetarian, acquired the store in 1901, stocking it with fresh fruits and vegetables. By 1908 Cook had established a factory making health foods, and he became a supplier to other stores. Both in Britain and in the US the number of health food stores—most of which were small and family-owned and managed – grew in the interwar years. They catered to a niche market of people interested in healthier eating and lifestyles (Jones, 2017: 27–8).

In Germany, social movements concerning food and health also emerged. These social movements sometimes overlapped with Romantic, nature-worshipping ideologies. The Life Reform movement became the official name of a network of participating groups including naturopaths, nature healers, nudists and vegetarians, all of whom urged people to eat simple healthy food and take care of their bodies. Carl Braun, a naturopath, who noticed that it was hard to buy the wraps and towelling he recommended, opened the first such Reform House shop in Berlin in 1887. Within three years he had begun selling cocoa and chocolate, then seen as healthy foods, and later expanded more widely into food and health products. There were about eighty Reform Houses by 1914, distributed across Germany but sparsest in the south of the country. It was mostly, although not entirely, a matter of small-scale entrepreneurship, but a number of businesses grew larger. Although the First World War caused many difficulties, the Reform Houses survived and became an established feature (Jones, 2017: 28–9).

Although the Life Reform movement was primarily urban, some members began to work as farmers or gardeners, experimenting with composting, green manuring and mulching. In 1928 these farmers formed their own organization, the Arbeitsgemeinschaft Natürlicher Landbau und Siedlung (Working Group for Natural Agriculture and Settlement). It focused on fruit and vegetable production without artificial fertilizers (Vogt, 2000).

Among the Life Reform's agricultural suppliers was a venture called Eden. A group of vegetarians in Oranienburg, near Berlin, established this fruit-growing cooperative as part of a back-to-the-land settling movement in 1893. Eden's initial land quality was poor, with sandy soil, but the settlers engaged in building it up with mineral fertilizers alongside Berlin street sweepings and sewage sludge. Within a few years the use of natural fertilizers produced internally by the community was the norm. Although the original settlement did not envision producing Reform products for sale as opposed to communal use, they soon did so. The production of fruit, initially strawberries, as a for-profit business within the settlement began in 1898. Fruit and fruit juices were promoted as alternatives to alcohol and as free from chemical preservatives. Natural honey, vegetarian meat substitutes and margarine were added over the following two decades (Baumgartner, 1992: 125–33, 159–60, 179, 191–2).

The early 20th-century philosopher Rudolf Steiner laid the basis for a more radical alternative capitalism. Formally trained in science and philosophy, Steiner became involved in the movement known as Theosophy in the 1900s. In 1913 Steiner founded his own school of Anthroposophy, a 'science of the spirit', which sought to occupy the middle ground between science and religion. Steiner believed that humans had lost awareness of their ancient understanding that they had bodies, souls and spirits. He argued that humanity was engaged in an epic struggle against materialism, which had caused this loss of awareness. Steiner saw human beings as living both on earth and in the spiritual world, and asserted that they needed to operate competently in both. He developed an alternative view of human history as he described the evolution of consciousness. Humans were continuously reincarnated, changing genders and cultures as they evolved over time. Capacities acquired in one incarnation became new talents in the next, while misdeeds also came back. Reincarnation and karma meant, in Steiner's view, that everything in life had a meaning. There was a profound optimism in his work, arising from his belief that there was a spiritual dimension to human beings that was a source of hope for future possibilities. In this respect, it was a mental framing of the world well suited to equipping entrepreneurs with survival skills when facing the hardship of building a business (Lachman, 2007).

A distinctive feature of Steiner and his followers was a concern for practical applications of their world view. Before the First World War he worked with Ita Wegman on the healing power of ingredients derived from plants. After the war he moved to found a business after discussions with Emil Molt, a German entrepreneur who owned a cigarette company, the Waldorf-Astoria Cigarette Company, who was in the process of co-founding with Steiner a school in Stuttgart to serve the children of employees of the factory. The first school became the forerunner of the worldwide Waldorf educational system, which became characterized by a heavy emphasis on music, arts, movement and stories in the early stages of the programme, which were designed to inspire imagination and holistic understanding. Molt suggested that businesses could be established to provide the financial means for supporting the diffusion of Anthroposophy. Steiner proposed creating a 'bank-like institution' to support such businesses, which would promote Anthroposophical values by assisting other companies with financial and managerial support and building a new business culture. Although it was intended that the bank would be profitable, as that was the only way to make it sustainable, the profits were not seen as an end in themselves, but rather were to be used to repay loans, and to support educational and cultural institutions (Jones, 2017: 34–5).

Steiner's vision of a new business culture was part of an even broader vision for society. In the wake of the First World War and the turbulence of the post-war world he developed the concept of social threefolding, perceiving three domains of human society – economic, legal and cultural – that needed to remain autonomous, but needed to negotiate to achieve consensus. The holistic vison of threefolding was a key factor why his followers would, especially from the 1970s, become influential in the environmental movement.

It proved challenging to execute this vision of a new business system in the context of financially and economically unstable post-war Germany.

The proposed bank, whose German name translates to The Coming Day in English, launched in 1920 with Steiner as chair. A number of small companies and laboratories were also launched in Germany and Switzerland to make natural medicines. The ventures struggled to progress, which was hardly surprising in the conditions of post-war Germany. The earlier ventures were rolled up in 1924 into a joint-stock company, soon known as Weleda. Steiner, alarmed by the attempted coup by Adolf Hitler in Munich in the previous year, based the firm in Switzerland. The Anthroposophical Society and individual Anthroposophists were the shareholders. He saw the company as an 'economic-spiritual enterprise' (Jones, 2017: 35).

By then, Steiner had also developed ideas about a new agricultural system based on Anthroposophist principles. Working with a group of German farmers, Steiner gave a course of lectures on agriculture in 1924. He incorporated ideas already in circulation in Germany, including seeing farms as organisms and the avoidance of chemical fertilizers. However, he added new components, especially the value of mixed farming and the use of animals, the use of cosmic forces to enrich the soil and techniques to control pests and weeds without chemical pesticides. The health of the soil, plants and animals depended, he argued, on their connection with cosmic creative forces. Steiner saw his lectures as works in progress; they became the basic principles of what known as biodynamic agriculture, which would become one of the primary systems of organic agriculture. The principles featured the use of nine so-called 'preparations' designed for soil health and to stimulate plant growth alongside crop rotation, manuring and the integration of crops with livestock. The preparations were a mixture of mineral, plant and animal manure, which were fermented and applied to composts, soil and plants. The preparations were left in the soil for either six months or a year, two of them in cow horns and five of them in different animal parts, such as the bladder. Three were then sprayed on crops and six blended into compost. In addition, the method emphasized that plants come under astrological influences, and that planting and harvesting needed to coincide with movements of the moon and the planets (Norman, 2012: 214–18).

Steiner himself became ill, and during his last months before his death in 1925 he was cared for by Wegman as they wrote a book providing a theoretical basis to their new medicine. By the mid-1920s Weleda's product line included remedies against a wide variety of illnesses, as well as dietary supplements and digestive teas. Hair tonic and shaving soap were made from ingredients grown on biodynamic principles. The business was the founder of the modern natural beauty industry, although it would take half a century more for that industry to develop.

Anthroposophy survived the death of its founder in 1925, and experiments in the practical applications persisted. The movement remained tiny, but with a strong international focus and considerable impact over time. The most substantial legacy, for half a century, was the Waldorf school movement, which spread outside Germany elsewhere in Europe and beyond. After the Second World War the numbers of Waldorf schools grew, at first slowly and then rapidly from the 1970s. By the 1980s there were 600 Waldorf schools worldwide. D.N. Dunlop, an engineer in the British Electrical and Allied Manufacturers' Association who was inspired by Steiner's social threefolding model, organized a World Power Conference in 1924. He assembled electrical engineers, politicians and others to discuss collaboration worldwide on issues such as regulations and interconnectivity. This became a permanent annual event that has persisted until the present day, being renamed the World Energy Council in 1990 (Meyer, 1992).

The concept of business enthused with purpose by Anthroposophy also survived Steiner's death. However, the idea took a great deal longer to gain traction than the Waldorf education system. Weleda only issued its first dividend in 1929; it was not to issue another one until after the end of the Second World War. However, it remained in business, and continues so today, selling skin creams and other personal care products in over forty countries. It has continued to be closely held and controlled by the Anthroposophical movement.

Initially, the application of Steiner's ideas moved at a snail's pace. The principles of biodynamic agriculture were slowly but deliberately developed. The movement created institutions and established rules. An organization called Demeter, founded in 1927, advised farmers and engaged in the marketing of biodynamic products, once more operating internationally. The Demeter trademark was launched in 1928 to certify biodynamic products. Biodynamic farming survived the traumatic 1930s. There were multiple farms in operation in Germany, some with links to the Nazi Party, elements of which linked back to nature movements (Staudenmaier, 2014).

Meanwhile individuals who emigrated from Germany slowly diffused biodynamic ideas. During the late 1920s Ehrenfried Pfeiffer, a German chemist who had worked with Steiner, created a model biodynamic farm at Kimberton, Pennsylvania, in 1938, and this played an influential role in the embryonic organic food market after the end of the Second World War. His English language book *Bio-Dynamic Farming and Gardening* (1938) codified the agricultural practices that had become popular under Steiner, and coined the term 'biodynamic' (Paull, 2011; McKanan, 2018: 35–9).

However, as the second wave of environmentalism gained traction, Anthroposophy emerged as an inspiration for new businesses in industries as diverse as food and finance, particularly in Germany and surrounding countries. It effectively reinvented Anthroposophy as relevant to socially progressive, 'New Age'-type social movements, and this was accompanied by shifts within the movement itself towards a greater focus on developing practical applications of the philosophy (McKanan, 2018: 70–119).

Biodynamists became highly influential in promoting organic agriculture and in building organic food businesses. In 1984 Götz Rehn, who had been educated at a Waldorf school, launched an Anthroposophical food retailer in Germany called Alnatura. It began to develop a network of organic food supermarkets, and over time developed as a leading organic food retailer in Germany, with sales approaching $1 billion by 2020.

In 1974, half a century after Steiner had floated the idea of creating a financial institution; the first Anthroposophical bank was launched in Germany. Gemeinschaft für Leihen und Schenken was launched as a mutually owned cooperative bank that paid depositors no or little interest and screened lenders for values, lending especially to Demeter-certified farms and later to early wind power projects. More social banks followed in Europe. Triodos, started in the Netherlands in 1980, became the largest (Jones, 2018: 96–9).

While for-profit business drove environmental degradation, a small cohort of entrepreneurs believed it could also be a solution. By the 1920s a number of agricultural and retail businesses had been founded in Britain, Germany and the US to focus on natural foods, avoidance of chemical fertilizers and healthy lifestyles. The figures behind these endeavours were often motivated through connections with wider social movements, which also provided a customer base. The followers of Rudolf Steiner took a broader view. They saw the healing of the Earth and the healing of humanity as totally entwined. The healing of the planet was not a central goal but a component of a much wider and holistic world view.

Collectively these green entrepreneurs stood apart from the norms of their era. Most environmentalists saw capitalism as primarily a despoiler of the natural environment, which historically was largely true. Most businesses cared little for their environmental impact, because environmental externalities were irrelevant to their bottom lines. These alternative green entrepreneurs broke with multiple conventions, then. Not surprisingly, they were often treated by contemporaries as crazy. In all cases it was difficult to build a business against incumbents, especially the ones who were highly subsidized by governments, including the fossil fuel industry. And because these incumbents have not traditionally cared for the environment, they could keep their prices lower.

Corporate environmentalism

The sudden apparent mainstreaming of sustainability was remarkable when compared with the century before 1980. German chemical companies were among the first large Western corporations to embrace more proactive environmental strategies during the 1970s. This reflected the broader emergence of environmental issues in German society and government, but more specifically it was driven by the location of the head offices of leading firms Bayer and Henkel in the state of North Rhine-Westphalia near the Rhine. Senior management was directly exposed to criticism by local activists and regional politicians about polluted water and bad odours. This posed a threat to reputations developed over more than a century. Managements concluded that investing in technologies and products that were more eco-friendly could provide an opportunity to create value rather than simply impose costs on their firms, and that self-identifying as green had commercial as well as reputational benefits (Jones and Lubinski, 2014).

The more widespread 'greening' of big business from the 1980s, as manifested in a growing number issuing sustainability reports and gaining environmental certification, was driven by a number of interrelated factors. Probably the most important was the reinvention of environmental challenges as 'sustainability' by the Brundtland Commission in 1987. The commission's definition of sustainability as involving the three pillars of environmental protection, economic growth and social equality made it more compatible with large corporations, not least in apparently sanctioning practices that might not be environmentally positive but could, for example, be seen as helping society by providing employment. During the 1970s a series of books, including the Club of Rome's *Limits of Growth* (1972) and Schumacher's *Small is Beautiful* (1973), had argued that the environment was best helped by curbing growth. Schumacher was critical of large corporations and argued that half their equity should be socialized (Schumacher, 1971; Meadows et al, 1972). In contrast, the new ethos of sustainability saw growth as good. This legitimized large corporations as best equipped to deliver sustainability. Subsequently, the emergence of climate change as a global crisis raised sustainability to a commitment that was like a loyalty oath all were expected to uphold, including the chief executive officers of major corporations, which were ironically the primary drivers of climate change (Jones, 2017: 174, 360).

A number of other factors were also important in the growth of corporate environmentalism. As has been described by multiple recent authors, this period saw a sudden rise in the belief that business could solve all the world's problems. This belief was accompanied by the withdrawal of governments from many activities, low corporate tax rates and the virtual abandonment of anti-trust enforcement in the US (Andersen, 2020). An ecosystem of certifications and metrics was developed that enabled corporations to substantiate their claims to be sustainable. The concept of the triple bottom line, for example, resonated with the chief executives of leading global firms. The oil company Shell – a company that was almost by definition a force for environmental degradation – sought advice from its pioneer, John Elkington, and used the triple bottom line concept in its annual report for 1999 (Sluyterman, 2007: 358–9). The renewal of environmental awareness had also created a significant number of consumers who could be persuaded to purchase greener products. These green consumers wanted to buy organic food, install solar panels on their roofs, recycle their waste, buy homes marked green and stay in eco-resorts, although the premium they were willing to pay to do these things was not clear. As the green consumer came of age, large corporations perceived the possibilities of gaining value from green reputations – or at least deflecting unwanted criticisms of adverse environmental impacts (Markowitz and Rosner, 2002: 210–11).

Finally, governments and civil society provided a mixture of carrots and sticks that encouraged corporations to present themselves as forces for sustainability. Governments increasingly mandated more environmental policies, and also provided incentives in selected industries to invest in improving sustainability. Whether it was feed-in tariffs for wind and solar energy, tourism ministries' promotion of eco-tourism or government sponsorship of organic certification, public policies worked to reduce financial barriers of investing in sustainability and, sometimes, to make doing so very profitable. There was in some countries massive subsidization of renewable energy that attracted the attention of large conventional firms (Jones, 2017: 323–45). The role of public policy was also evident in smaller cases. By the 2010s Sweden had the world's highest consumption of organic wine. This came about because the country had a state-owned retail wine monopoly that promoted organic wine extensively in its shops. By 2018 Swedes drank $330 million of organic wine per year, over a fifth of total market. Sales of organic wine in the far larger American market were a mere $200 million (Jones, 2018: 155–6, 180). Meanwhile the growth in the number and impact of NGOs encouraged the greening of conventional capitalism, both through NGOs' ability to shame firms by publicly exposing poor environmental practices, but also by providing an institutional opportunity to enhance reputations through partnerships. By 2000 the United Nations estimated that there were about 35,000 large established NGOs, spanning a wide range of both social and environmental concerns (Lewis, 2010).

These pressures resulted in a mainstreaming of sustainability in large corporations. Wind energy, once the preserve of environmental activists, came into the hands of large multinationals such as GE and Siemens, alongside state-owned Chinese companies aiming to build capacity in an industry judged strategic. Organic food, once the preserve of radical idealists and biodynamicists, became progressively mainstreamed. In the US, by 2010 conventional retailers surpassed the specialty natural foods stores such as Whole Foods Market, the specialist and once radical organic retailer; they were responsible for 54 per cent of organic food sales, while natural retailers brought in 39 per cent of total organic food sales. Three years later the acquisition of Whole Foods Market by Amazon for $13.7 billion in

2017 took the entry of conventional business into organic food to a whole new level. One of the pioneers of organic food consumption in the US was reduced to being an affiliate of one of the least sustainable large corporations in the US (Jones, 2019: 374–5).

Overall, the extent of actual corporate commitment to sustainability was far from clear. There was a large element of greenwashing. The academic literature on this subject has focused on the selective disclosure of information about environmental impacts in annual reports and corporate sustainability reports. It has pointed to a wide spectrum of practices among large firms, but with little consensus on why firms differed in these practices. A body of theory in sociology suggested that an organization's visibility affected compliance with institutional pressures in environmental reporting. There was evidence that greater visibility made organizations more concerned with their legitimacy and anxious to avoid appearing to greenwash, although other research has suggested that the more powerful an organization was, the more it could afford to resist pressures from external stakeholders (Bansal and Roth, 2000; Okhmatovskiy and David, 2012).

In any case, the focus on selective disclosure captured only part of the greenwashing issue, which includes misleading claims about the eco-friendly nature of particular products or services, empty green claims, misleading labels and visual imagery, or indeed the reimagining of whole companies as green businesses. Large corporations were complex organizations that can make both sustainability improvements and greenwash at the same time. Unilever, for example, began developing environmental policies as early as the 1960s in response to consumer criticism and health scares about food additives, wasteful packaging and factory effluent. By the following decade these policies were increasingly proactive, if done in a very low profile way as befitted a decentralized corporation that generally preferred to be known for its hundreds of individual brands rather than as a single conglomerate (Jones, 2005b: 339–47). However, the firm followed the general trend in consumer products companies of inserting the word 'natural' into descriptions of consumer brands. During the 1970s it marketed, to give one of many examples, a successful shampoo brand called Timotei, which was packed in a white bottle with green text and cap and a small oval green and white flower and grass design, marketed as 'naturally mild' and advertised by models standing in fields (Jones, 2005b: 122).

Overall, the word 'natural' proliferated in both the personal care and food industries, helped by the fact that no regulatory agency defined what a natural product was. The meaningless term was an ideal vehicle for corporate greenwashing as it made no explicit claims. By the 2000s whole corporations were rebranded. The environmental strategy of the British-based oil company BP provides one much-discussed example. Rebranded as 'Beyond Petroleum' and lauded as a pioneer of emissions trading, the company was placed number one on Fortune and AccountAbility's annual rankings of the world's most responsible companies in 2007 (Vogel, 2005; Victor and House, 2006). Three years later an explosion on the Deepwater Horizon oilrig in the Gulf of Mexico that caused massive environmental pollution painfully exposed the gap between visionary rhetoric and reality. BP was revealed as a company that prioritized cost cutting over safety and environmental impact (Jones, 2017: 376–7). BP was far from alone in grandiose claims with little to show for them (Klein, 2014).

In fact, accusations of hypocrisy could be levelled at virtually any corporation claiming to be sustainable, as there were so many uncertainties about what sustainable really meant, as well as how it was interpreted over time. Greenwashing was a dynamic phenomenon that assumed new forms. There was some evidence that increased scrutiny, whether from social networking or other forces, might work against more blatant forms of greenwashing, but other forms were evident and probably increasing. The term 'symbolic corporate environmentalism' was used to describe situations in which managers did not explicitly pursue strategies to mislead, but in which greenwashing still occurred. For example, the commissioning of a Leadership in Energy and Environmental Design-certified head office might by association build the image of a company as green, even if the company avoided making explicit claims (Bowen, 2014).

Definitional difficulties made it impossible to quantify accurately the extent of greenwashing in the corporate world, but it was and is evidently a widespread and diffuse phenomenon. It has helped to undermine consumer confidence in the very idea of sustainability by encouraging widespread confusion and often cynicism. It has made efforts to create markets and to educate consumers and policy makers harder. Meanwhile, pioneering green entrepreneurs have faced the new and formidable challenge of having their cases heard in a world where every company claims to be sustainable.

The incentives for public corporations continued to encourage them to not take environmental protection seriously. The products and services of green businesses were always going to be more costly, and the gains were going to be more long-term than immediate. It was hard to reconcile heavy spending with maximizing profits for shareholders. The costs of environmental damage were still not incorporated in the calculations of profits and costs. Willingness to pay for more expensive green products still varied enormously between countries, and was very low in countries such as the US. In some respects that problem got worse because of the rise of e-commerce. This introduced a new price sensitivity with the ability for people to research and compare prices. It was observed that when people booked online vacations to eco-tourist locations, such as Costa Rica, decisions were primarily based on price rather than any specific green metric (Jones, 2018: 219). Meanwhile, willingness to pay was further eroded because corporate environmentalism resulted in enormous consumer confusion about what green and sustainable really meant.

Conclusion

Capitalism, at least in the form it assumed since the Industrial Revolution, drove the environmental decimation of the planet. The essential problem was that the environment – whether minerals or birds – was seen as a free good, while the consequences of dirty industrial and agricultural processes were seen as external the firm. By the early 20th century regulations had started to be put in place to control industrial pollution in industrialized countries, but they were not remotely comprehensive before the 1970s at the earliest. Even today only the most blatant environmental destruction is regulated, and in much of the world that regulation is nominal. Governments across systems and across time have manifested a preference for short-term economic growth, job creation and higher living standards over the natural environment.

This chapter has stressed that although capitalism as a system was highly problematic for the environment over the long term, the system was not monolithic. In the absence of public policies to protect the environment, niche for-profit entrepreneurs endured neglect and often ridicule to put in place the fundamentals of organic agriculture and renewable energy, while governments were largely focused on subsidizing ever greater use of chemical fertilizers and fossil fuels, and promoting nuclear energy. These firms were often purpose-driven, this being seen in its extreme form in the case of the Anthroposophical businesses. As such, they offered a radical alternative to conventional capitalism for which the generation of profit without regard for environmental costs remained at the core of strategies. They understood how for-profit business could assemble resources and innovate, contributing to sustainability at the micro-level in the hope it would eventually become the norm rather than the exception.

Over the last three decades green has become big business. Yesterday's marginal eccentrics are today's valuable brands. Yet the diffusion of certification programs, green brands and corporate sustainability reports has largely served to create confusion about what is really green rather than save the planet. Corporate sustainability has become one more product in corporate portfolios: the target markets are consumers looking for greener products and investors searching for respectability by claiming to invest in sustainable industries. The commodification of environmentalism by large corporations has confused consumers and turned sustainability into little more than a code for greenwashing. The pioneering green entrepreneurs embodied values in products, often philosophical or religious, and the empty rhetoric employed by large corporations has proved a poor substitute.

References

Andersen, K. (2020) *Evil Geniuses. The Unmasking of America: A Recent History*, New York: Random House.

Bansal, P. and Roth, K. (2000) 'Why companies go green: a model of ecological responsiveness', *Academy of Management Journal*, 43(4): 717–36.

Baumgartner, J. (1992) *Ernährungsreform: Antwort auf Industrialisierung und Ernährungswandel*, Frankfurt: Peter Lang.

Bergquist, A-K. (2019) 'Renewing business history in the era of the Anthropocene', *Business History Review*, 93(1): 3–24.

Bergquist, A.-K., Cole, S.A., Ehrenfeld, J., King, A.A. and Schendler, A. (2019) 'Understanding and overcoming roadblocks to environmental sustainability: past roads and future prospects', *Business History Review*, 93(1): 127–48.

Bowen, F. (2014) *After Greenwashing: Symbolic Corporate Environmentalism and Society*, Cambridge: Cambridge University Press.

Brüggemeier, F.-J., Cioc, M. and Zeller, T. (eds) (2005) *How Green Were the Nazis? Nature, Environment, and Nation in the Third Reich*, Athens: Ohio University Press.

Clapp, B.W. (1994) *An Environmental History of Britain since the Industrial Revolution*, London: Longman.

Conford, P. (2001) *The Origins of the Organic Movement*, Edinburgh: Floris Books.

Cushman, G.T. (2013) *Guano and the Opening of the Pacific World. A Global Ecological History*, Cambridge: Cambridge University Press.

Dorst, J. (1965) *Avant Que Nature Meure*, Neuchâtel: Delachaux et Niestlé.

Ehrlich, P. (1968) *The Population Bomb*, New York: Ballantine Books.

Fouquet, R. (2008) *Heat, Power and Light*, Cheltenham: Edward Elgar.

Gorman, H.S. (1999) 'Efficiency, environmental quality, and oil field brines: the success and failure of pollution control self-regulation', *Business History Review*, 73(4): 601–40.

Guha, R. (2000) *Environmentalism: A Global History*, New York: Longman.

Hardin, G. (1968) 'The tragedy of the commons', *Science*, 162(3859): 1243–8.

Hausman, W.J., Hertner, P. and Wilkins, M. (2008) *Global Electrification*, Cambridge: Cambridge University Press.

Hoffman, A.J. (2001) *From Heresy to Dogma: An Institutional History of Corporate Environmentalism*, Stanford, CA: Stanford Business Books.

Jacks, G.V. and Whyte, R.O. (1939) *The Rape of the Earth: A World Survey of Soil Erosion*, London: Faber and Faber.

Jones, G. (2005a) *Multinationals and Global Capitalism*, Oxford: Oxford University Press.

Jones, G. (2005b) *Renewing Unilever: Transformation and Tradition*, Oxford: Oxford University Press.

Jones, G. (2017) *Profits and Sustainability: A History of Green Entrepreneurship*, Oxford: Oxford University Press.

Jones, G. (2018) *Varieties of Green Business. Industries, Nations and Time*, Northampton, MA: Edward Elgar.

Jones, G. and Lubinski, C. (2014) 'Making "green giants": environment sustainability in the German chemical industry, 1950s–1980s', *Business History*, 56(4): 623–49.

Klein, N. (2014) *This Changes Everything, Capitalism vs the Climate*, New York: Simon & Schuster.

Lachman, G. (2007) *Rudolf Steiner. An Introduction to His Life and Work*, New York: Penguin.

LeCain, T. (2009) *Mass Destruction: The Men and Giant Mines that Wired America and Scarred the Planet*, New Brunswick, NJ: Rutgers University Press.

Lewis, D. (2010) 'Nongovernmental organizations, definition and history', in H.K. Anheier and S. Toepler (eds) *International Encyclopedia of Civil Society*, New York: Springer, pp 1056–62.

Matagne, P. (1998) 'The politics of conservation in France in the nineteenth century', *Environment and History*, 4: 359–67.

Markowitz, G. and Rosner, D. (2002) *Deceit and Denial: The Deadly Politics of Industrial Pollution*, Berkeley: University of California Press.

McKanan, D. (2018) *Eco-Alchemy. Anthroposophy and the History and Future of Environmentalism*, Oakland: University of California Press.

McKinsey Global Institute (2020) 'Climate risk and response: physical hazards and socioeconomic impacts'[online] January 2020 https://www.mckinsey.com/~/media/mckinsey/business%20functions/sustainability/our%20insights/climate%20risk%20and%20response%20physical%20hazards%20and%20socioeconomic%20impacts/mgi-climate-risk-and-response-full-report-vf.pdf [Accessed 4 August 2020].

McNeil, J.R. (2000) *Something New under the Sun: An Environmental History of the Twentieth-Century World*, New York: W.W. Norton.

McNeil, J.R. and Engelke, P. (2014) *The Great Acceleration: An Environmental History of the Anthropocene since 1945*, Cambridge, MA: Harvard University Press.

Meadows, D.H., Meadows, D.L., Randers, J. and Behrens III, W.W. (1972) *The Limits to Growth*, New York: Universe Books.

Meisner Rosen, C. (1995) 'Businessmen against pollution in late nineteenth-century Chicago', *Business History Review*, 69(3): 351–97.

Meisner Rosen, C. (2017) 'Business leadership in the movement to regulate industrial air pollution in late nineteenth- and early twentieth-century America', in H. Berghoff and A. Rome (eds) *Green Capitalism? Business and the Environment in the Twentieth Century*, Philadelphia: University of Pennsylvania Press, pp 53–76.

Meyer, T.H. (1992) *D.N. Dunlop. A Man of Our Time*, London: Temple Lodge.

Miller, S.W. (2007) *An Environmental History of Latin America*, Cambridge: Cambridge University Press.

Miller, S.W. (2012) 'Latin America in global environmental history', in J.R. McNeill and E.S. Mauldin (eds) *A Companion to Global Environmental History*, Chichester: John Wiley & Sons, pp 116–31.

Norman, A. (2012) 'Cosmic flavour, spiritual nutrition: the biodynamic agricultural method and the legacy of Rudolf Steiner's anthroposophy in viticulture', in C.M. Cusack and A. Norman (eds) *Handbook of New Religious and Cultural Production*, Leiden: Brill, pp 213–35.

Okhmatovskiy, I. and David, R.J. (2012) 'Setting your own standards: internal corporate governance codes as a response to institutional pressure', *Organization Science*, 23(1): 155–76.

Paull, J. (2011) 'Biodynamic agriculture: the journey from Koberwitz to the world, 1924–1938', *Journal of Organic Systems*, 6(1): 27–41.

Pontin, B. (2007) 'Integrated pollution control in Victorian Britain: rethinking progress within the history of environmental law', *Journal of Environmental Law*, 19(2): 173–99.

Reich, C. (1970) *The Greening of America*, New York: Random House.

Santiago, M. I. (2006) *The Ecology of Oil. Environment, Labor, and the Mexican Revolution, 1900–1938*, Cambridge: Cambridge University Press.

Schullery, P. and Whittlesey, L.H. (2003) *Myth and History in the Creation of Yellowstone National Park*, Lincoln: University of Nebraska Press.

Schumacher, E.F. (1971) *Small Is Beautiful: Economics as if People Mattered*, London: Blond and Biggs.

Shuman, F. (1911) 'Power from sunshine: a pioneer solar power plant', *Scientific American* (30 September): 219–2.

Sluyterman, K. (2007) *Keeping Competitive in Turbulent Markets, 1973–2007: A History of Royal Dutch Shell*, Oxford: Oxford University Press.

Söderholm, K. and Bergquist, A-K. (2012) 'Firm collaboration and environmental adaptation: the case of the Swedish pulp and paper industry 1900–1990', *Scandinavian Economic History Review*, 60(2): 183–211.

Staudenmaier, P. (2014) *Between Occultism and Nazism. Anthroposophy and the Politics of Race in the Fascist Era*, Leiden: Brill.

Uekötter, F. (2009) *The Age of Smoke: Environmental Policy in Germany and the United States, 1880–1970*, Pittsburgh, PA: University of Pittsburgh Press.

Victor, D.G. and House, J.C. (2006) 'BP's emissions trading system', *Energy Policy*, 34(15): 2100–12.

Vogel, D. (2005) *The Market for Virtue: The Potential and Limits of Corporate Social Responsibility*, Washington DC: Brookings Institution Press.

Vogt, W. (1948) *Road to Survival*, New York: William Sloane Associates.

Vogt, G. (2000) *Entstehung und Entwicklung des Ökologischen Landbaus im Deutschsprachigen Raum*, Bad Dürkheim: Stiftung Ökologie & Landbau.

Ward, B. (1966) *Spaceship Earth*, New York: Columbia University Press.

Weber, K. and Soderstrom, S.B. (2012) 'Social movements, business and the environment', in P. Bansl and A.J. Hoffman (eds) *The Oxford Handbook of Business and the Natural Environment*, Oxford: Oxford University Press, pp 248–65.

Weart, S.R. (2008) *The Discovery of Global Warming*, Cambridge, MA: Harvard University Press.

Wilson, C.L. and Matthews, W.H. (eds) (1971) *Inadvertent Climate Modification*, Cambridge, MA: MIT Press.

Worster, D. (1979) *Dust Bowl: The Southern Plains in the 1930s*, Oxford: Oxford University Press.

Worster, D. (2008) *A Passion for Nature: The Life of John Muir*, Oxford: Oxford University Press.

9

Capitalism and Income Inequality

Catherine Casson

Introduction

The extent to which capitalism has increased or decreased inequality has generated significant debate from the 18th century onwards. The capitalist system allows people to derive income and wealth from assets that they own. The most valuable assets are those that are scarce. For 18th- and early 19th-century classical economists such as Smith and Mill good quality agricultural land was the scarce asset and therefore the most important source of income and wealth (Smith, 1791; Mill, 1848). However, from the mid-19th century onwards, in the light of the Industrial Revolution, Marx and neoclassical economists emphasized the importance of capital with which to purchase machinery and factory buildings, and finance inventory (Marx, 1961). Gradually skills possessed by the individual moved to the fore. The second Industrial Revolution in the US emphasized the desirability of skill in organizing large businesses and trusts and in foretelling the future through speculation (Hayek, 1949; Kirzner, 1973). Scarcity factors have become more intangible over time. From the 1930s onwards 'knowledge' as possessed by professional managers and scientist became a value asset (Harper, 1995). Finally, from the 1970s onwards, entrepreneurship began to be recognized as a scarce factor.

The change in emphasis on scarce assets had the potential to remove the inequality that had existed whereby income and wealth were concentrated in the hands of large landowners. Land was passed on through inheritance, meaning that subsequent generations started in an advantageous position as they did not have to allocate time and money to acquire assets from scratch and the acquisition was not dependent on their personal performance (for example their skill as a cultivator). Skills-based assets, in contrast, were based to a greater extent on merit. This had implications for social mobility. The acquisition of land acquired significant amounts of capital and it was

212

hard for an outsider to break into the landowning elite. The acquisition of skills required less up-front capital. However, background could still provide a competitive advantage, as a good education enhanced the skills based. Opportunities for social mobility were more difficult for children, whose education was curtailed because they had to enter the workplace at a young age.

The change in emphasis to more personal attributes also impacted earning potential. Within each occupation, some people may be better than others and those people will possess a comparative advantage. There will also be someone who has the least ability and is therefore marginal. Everyone else in the occupation has some absolute advantage over that marginal person. The excess of each person's output over the output of the marginal person represents their economic rent to superior ability, and under competitive conditions this will be reflected in an earnings premium. Large differences in ability within an occupation have the potential to produce substantial inequalities in personal earnings.

While there have been important studies on income inequality in earlier periods using wage data and tax records (examples being Abel, 1980; Van Zanden and Soltow, 1998; Van Zanden, 2009), the majority of available data survives for 1850–2010. The benefit of studying this period is therefore that it allows us to draw on a wide range of data and to examine the impact of the Industrial Revolution of 1760–1850 and the second Industrial Revolution in the US of 1870–1914. The chapter examines inequality at national, regional and individual level, drawing primarily on information from the UK, US, Germany and France. It shows that a more meritocratic society emerged during the period. While inequalities between those with valuable land and those without it reduced, new inequalities emerged based on the possession of the new scarce factors. These had notable impacts at a regional level.

National

We begin by examining inequality at a national level. One way of doing this is to examine a country's wealth as a percentage of national income (Piketty, 2014: 50–2) National wealth is defined as 'the total market value of everything owned by the residents and government of a given country at a given point in time, provided that it can be traded on some market' (Piketty, 2014: 48). National income is 'the sum of all income available to the residents of a given country in a given year, regardless of the legal classification of that income' (Piketty, 2014: 43).

Figure 9.1 shows the ratio of net national wealth to net national income for the countries of France, Germany, the UK and US for the period 1850–2015, using data from the World Inequality Database. In 1850, for example, the UK's wealth/income ratio was 7 (which can also be expressed as 700 per

Figure 9.1: Ratio of net national wealth to net national income, 1850–2015

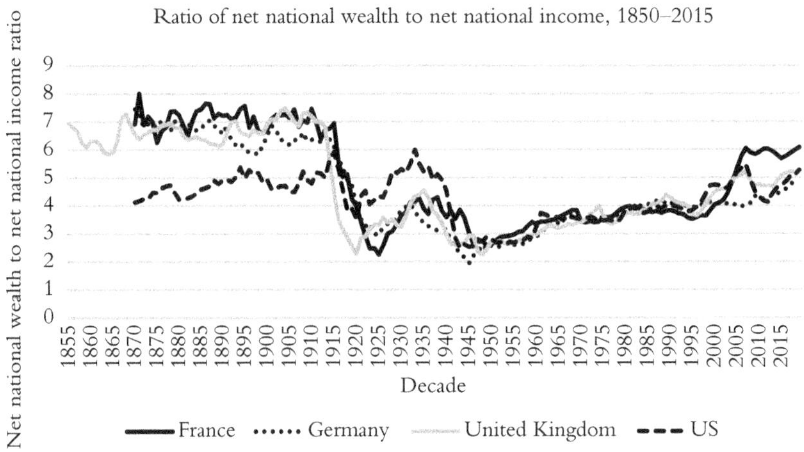

Source: World Inequality Database (2021)

cent), meaning that the UK's stock of wealth in that decade was equivalent to seven years of its national income.

Figure 9.1 shows that the stock of wealth in Germany, France and the UK was in the region of six to eight years of national income from 1850–1914. Data for the US begin in 1870, and relative importance of wealth was lower in the US in 1870–1914 compared with the other three countries. That the relative importance of wealth was lower in the US in this period is rather surprising, given that it corresponds with the second Industrial Revolution, in which US firms became the leaders in innovation in sectors including 'energy, materials and chemicals' (Mokyr, 1999: 219). However, it was also a period characterized by immigration into America. Immigrants usually arrived with limited capital, and often required support from, for example, local religious communities to raise the funds to start a business and thereby earn income (Godley, 1996). Possibly gains made in one area of the economy were offset by challenges in another.

The First World War emerged as a significant shock in all four countries, causing the stock of wealth to decrease. The US experienced the greatest recovery, with the relative importance of wealth in the American economy rising again in the 1920s and 1930s. During that period the US ratio was at a higher level – representing four to six years of national income – than that of the other three countries. Indeed, in the mid-1930s the importance of wealth in the national economy exceeded pre-First World War levels. In contrast, the stock of wealth in France, Germany and the UK never returned to its earlier levels after the First World War. This situation may have been brought about in the UK by British industry failing to remain internationally competitive after the war. Before 1914, the UK had been a major exporter. However, the First World War disrupted the UK's exports to its overseas customers. Instead, former customers such as Japan and the US began to invest in internal production, and started to export those products themselves. By the end of the war in 1918 the UK's international markets had declined significantly and competition in sectors such as textiles had intensified. Furthermore, the UK's coal sector began to face intense competition from the German Ruhr and Pas-de-Calais, France during the 1920s. The French and German coal industries mechanized coal cutting and underground haulage after the First World War, allowing the best quality coal to be extracted more easily from thin seams and increasing the volume and quality of output (Scott, 2006). In contrast, UK coal mines were slow to adopt mechanized cutting, and did not mechanize underground haulage (Scott, 2006).

In the UK the stock of wealth recovered more quickly than in France and Germany, with a peak in 1921 that corresponded with troughs in France and Germany. The UK possessed one advantage over France and Germany that aided its recovery. During the 1920s some American manufacturers, including Ford, opened plants in Britain in an attempt to avoid the high import duties charged on American goods (Dunning, 1958). These were often located in London as it was considered a more 'fun' location for American executives to live in and visit, although Ford opened a plant at Trafford Park, Manchester.

However, it was not long before the stock of wealth in France and Germany also began to increase again – and from 1947 to 2005 there was a convergence across the countries. The resilience of the European economies in the 1940s and 1950s may seem surprising given the disruption caused by the Second World War. In the case of Britain this corresponds with a further period of American investment in Britain (Dunning, 1958). US firms used the UK as a bridge to export goods and services to Europe as the country's infrastructure had remained relatively intact compared with Continental Europe. It was there that the new consumer products such as vacuum cleaners and fridges were manufactured and from where they were distributed (Scott, 2017). France and Germany also benefited from US support through the Marshall Plan, which aided their recovery (Vonyó, 2008).

While some differences between countries can therefore be observed, overall the figure shows that there was less variation than might have been expected.

National level: causes of inequalities

As discussed earlier, a number of writers have suggested that the key to inequality lies in one particular area, for example land, manufacturing or talent. If that were the case it would be expected that there would be significant differences in inequality between countries, owing to their different endowments. The fact that the countries exhibit similar patterns suggests that the root of inequality is more likely to be the result of capitalism's reward system, which is unlimited. How might this be addressed? Taxation, it has been proposed, is the main mechanism for resolving inequality because it makes people pay back a proportion of their gains to society. There are a number of factors that need to be considered in order for taxation to address inequality effectively. The first is whether they are applied to income or to wealth or to both. The second is how high they are and how progressive (Seligman, 1910). The level of taxation relates to what percentage of income is paid as taxes (for example 1 per cent or 5 per cent). The progressiveness relates to the proportion of income the tax is paid on. It may be the case that individuals are not required to pay tax on the first part of their income (for example the first £12,500) but that then the amount due goes up in instalments. Under the current UK income tax system, for example, 20 per cent is paid on £12,501–£50,000, 40 per cent on £50,000–£150,000 and so on. The third issue is the potential for taxes to act as a deterrent to entrepreneurship. If they are set too high then prospective entrepreneurs may perceive the risks of entrepreneurship to be greater than the potential rewards from profit. Finally, taxes are not effective as a means of reducing inequality if they can be avoided. Potential avoidance strategies include tax-deductible charitable giving and hiding money off shore.

Knight (1935) proposed that taxation would never truly address inequality of income and wealth. He questioned why inequalities remained despite the introduction of taxation. He proposed that it was because the rich were in a position where they could 'buy' influence, including political influence. They used that to lobby for policies that benefited themselves, including low tax rates. This opinion is echoed by Piketty, who suggests that the French Revolution of 1789 had little ultimate effect on reducing income inequality in France because the tax rate of 1–2 per cent introduced by the revolutionary assemblies was too low to make any significant impact on larger fortunes (Piketty, 2014: 365)

Regional

International comparisons and aggregate data can sometimes conceal variation in the distribution of income and wealth at the regional level. We therefore move on to this geographical level. A region can be defined as 'a geographical area at a subnational level' (Eurostat, 2018: 7). Regional inequality can be measured using gross domestic product (GDP) per capita, which is the 'total of goods and services produced in a given year' within the borders of a country of region, divided by its population (Piketty, 2014: 43).

We will undertake a comparison across regions in Europe before considering a case study of the UK, a country in which regional inequality is considered to be particularly pronounced (McCann, 2016).

Regional performance in Europe, 1900–2010

Rosés and Wolf (2018a, 2018b) examined the performance of 173 Nomenclature of Territorial Units for Statistics Level 2 regions in 14 EU countries and the UK and Norway (Eurostat, 2018: 7, 2021; Rosés and Wolf, 2018a: 3). They compared relative GDP per capita in 1900 with that in 2010, and evaluated the performance of each region relative to the EU average of 1 (Rosés and Wolf, 2018a: 16, 44).

The UK regions were fairly consistent in the 1900s and all were above the EU regional average. Scotland, Wales and all regions of England had GDP per capita of >1.2, and Northern Ireland was in the range of 1.0–1.2 (Rosés and Wolf, 2018a: 44). By 2010 regional variations were pronounced and a hierarchy had emerged (Rosés and Wolf, 2018a: 45). The South-East (including London) was the only region at >1.2, with the South-West at 1.0–1.2. All other areas of England were 0.8–1.0. Scotland's performance remained higher than some areas of England, but also dropped to 1.0–1.2. Wales and Northern Ireland both dropped below the EU average to 0.8–1.0 and 0.8–1.0 respectively.

In 1900 France's best performing regions with GDP head of >1.2 were the Ile-de-France region (home of the capital) and Haute-Normandie (a coal mining centre facing the English Channel) (Rosés and Wolf, 2018a: 44). Regions in the north-east and south also performed above the EU average. However the southern regions of Languedoc-Roussillon and Rhône-Alpes, and areas in the east, north and west performed below the EU average, with a GDP per person of 0.8–1.0. The weakest performance was in the far west, far east and south-west, which had GDP per person of <0.8. By 2020 regional distribution of GDP per head had changed significantly. Only the Ile-de-France region had GDP per head of >1.2. (Rosés and Wolf, 2018a: 45). The performance of the far west and some south-western regions remained stable, while GDP per person in all other regions declined (Díez Minguela and Sanchis Llopis, 2018; Rosés and Sanchis, 2018; Rosés and Wolf, 2018a: 29).

In Germany in 1900 Berlin (the capital) and Hamburg were the only regions with a high GDP per head of >1.2 (Rosés and Wolf, 2018a: 44). The west of Germany performed strongly, with a concentration of six regions with GDP per head at 1.0–1.2, including the main coal-mining areas in the Ruhr and in Saarland. However, the majority of north German regions had GDP per head below the EU average at 0.8–1.0, while many in the south had the lowest GDP per capita of <0.8. By 2010, however, the distribution of regional GDP per head had significantly shifted. GDP per person in Berlin had dropped below the EU average to 0.8–1.0. Regions in the west and east of Germany generally became poorer, while those in the south became more affluent (Rosés and Wolf, 2018a: 45). Rosés and Wolf attributed the lower growth rates in Berlin and East Germany to the consequences of partition in 1949–50 and to deindustrialization after reunification in 1990 (Rosés and Wolf, 2018a: 15, 29). In contrast, the south of Germany, notably Munich, reoriented its economy from agriculture to engineering, financial services and the high-tech sector (European Commission, 2021a).

All regions of Italy in 1900 had GDP per head below the EU average. The highest GDP per head, at 0.8–1.0, was in Lazio, where Rome is situated and Liguria, where the important port of Genoa is located – historically the busiest in Italy (Rosés and Wolf, 2018a: 44). The rest of Italy had a GDP per capita significantly below the EU regional average, at <0.8. By 2010 GDP per capita in Italy exhibited a strong north–south divide. Performance improved in northern regions to 1.0–1.2 and 0.8–1.0 GDP per head (Rosés and Wolf, 2018a: 45). Particularly notable was the strong performance of Lombardia, the location of Milan, which became the production hub for Italian clothing manufacturing and export after the Second World War (Merlo and Polese, 2006). Examining the cause of the north–south divergence, Felice (2018) proposes that the south may have been hindered by a relative lack of rapid rail and road connections to other European countries. However, she identifies human and social capital as the most significant factor, with the south having low levels of literacy and school enrolment, and limited social and political participation (Felice, 2018).

Comparison of the UK, France, Germany and Italy with Scandinavia reveals that some countries experienced significant improvements in regional GDP per head during the 20th century. GDP per head in Sweden in 1900 exhibited a strong north–south divide. Sweden's wealthiest region in 1900, with GDP per head of 1.0–1.2, was Stockholm, where the country's capital is located (Rosés and Wolf, 2018a: 44). The next wealthiest regions were the sparsely populated, heavily forested northern regions, with GDP per capita of 0.8–1.0, their wood being an important source of fuel for the extraction and production of iron (Enflo and Missiaia, 2017a: 15, 2017b; European Commission, 2021b, 2021c). The rest of Sweden's regions had a GDP per head of <0.8. By 2010 the situation had altered radically, with the performance of all Swedish regions exceeding the EU average at 1.0–1.2, and Stockholm and part of the north increasing to >1.2 (Rosés and Wolf, 2018a: 45).

Norway and Finland also experienced an increase in GDP per capita at regional level between 1900 and 2010. Most of Norway in 1900 had GDP per person significantly below the EU regional average, at <0.8. The exception was the Oslo og Akershus region, where Norway's capital is located, where it was 1.0–1.2 (Modalsli, 2018; Rosés and Wolf, 2018a: 44). By 2010 the GDP per person had increased in all areas except the far east, where there is little urbanization. Of particular note were increases in the two regions closest to the oil fields discovered in the 1960s, and a further strong performance in the Oslo og Akershus region, where GDP per head increased to >1.2 (Rosés and Wolf, 2018a: 45). Meanwhile in Finland in 1900 the Helsinki-Uusimaa region, where the capital is located, had the highest regional GDP in the country, at >1.2. All other Finnish regions had GDP per person <0.8 (Rosés and Wolf, 2018a: 44). In 2010 GDP per person in the Helsinki-Uusimaa region remained at >1.2 while levels rose across the rest of the regions to 0.8–1.0 (Enflo, 2014, 2018; Rosés and Wolf, 2018a: 45).

Regional performance in the UK

The UK has been identified as a country with 'large interregional inequalities' (McCann, 2016: 1). The work of Crafts (2005) and Geary and Stark (2002, 2015) has extended the examination of regional GDP per head in the UK back to 1861, allowing us to consider when these inequalities began to emerge. Crafts (2005) identified the emergence of inequality in the UK with the period 1871–1911. However, Geary and Stark (2015) have provided evidence have suggested that this earlier period was in fact one in which poorer regions were catching up with London and the South-East.

Geary and Stark (2016) have also examined on a decade-by-decade basis the transformation that occurred during 1900–2010 in the UK. Their work has shown that the 'convergence trend' was then disrupted by the First World War and volatile economic conditions of the 1920s (Geary and Stark, 2016). From 1918 to 1930 the gap between the South-East and the rest of the UK regions widened, with the South-East performing stronger. In 1931 the performance of the regions began to converge again, with the areas outside the South-East once again catching-up. The period 1931–71 was, they propose, 'the golden age of economic growth for the UK regions outside the South-East' (Geary and Stark, 2016: 223). Yet this was not to prove permanent. From 1971 onwards the regional inequalities re-emerged and the gap between the South-East and the other regions intensified (Geary and Stark, 2016: 223–4). Today three separate regional economies can be identified in the UK, as indicated in the Rosés and Wolf (2018a) data. The first is London and its hinterland (including the South-West), the second is the North and Midlands of England together with Wales and Northern Ireland, and the third is Scotland (McCann, 2016).

Regional level: causes of inequalities

In the late 19th and early 20th centuries regional growth appears to have been driven by the presence of coal and industries reliant on it, the presence of the country's major political city or the location of a key port. Regions with the highest GDP in each country had at least one of these characteristics. However, by 2010 we can see that the most successful region in each country was generally the one in which the capital city is located.

Deindustrialization and resulting migration effects may explain this transformation. When industrialization first occurred in the early to mid-19th century, there was a tendency from more enterprising members of the population to migrate from poorer agricultural areas to developing industrial ones in search of new employment (Enflo, 2014: 18; Hudson, 2014; Enflo and Rosés, 2015). However, the decline of traditional coal-based industries from the 1920s onwards reduced employment opportunities in industrial regions (Casson, 1983). A further wave of migration occurred, with the more enterprising members of the population relocating to seek employment elsewhere. The data suggest that cities proved an attractive destination. German regions encompassing the Ruhr, Düsseldorf and Cologne were able to retain GDP per head of 1.0–1.2 because the industrial area was in close proximity to three major cities that enterprising individuals could relocate to: Düsseldorf, Cologne and Bonn. In contrast, the former mining area of Saarland saw a decline in the level of GDP per head because enterprising individuals looking to relocate to a city would have had to leave the region entirely. In the UK, workers migrated from coal-mining areas of Wales and the North-East to the Midlands and the South (Scott, 2007). The Midlands offered opportunities in textiles and bicycle and car production in Coventry. In the Greater London area factories were seeking staff for craft and assembly production of furniture and radios, which were themselves items aimed at customers who were relocating from the inner city to the new suburbs (Scott, 2013). Migration from the North-West was less prevalent, as textile manufacturing still provided employment opportunities.

By the 1960s and 1970s many of those born in the post-Second World War baby boom were entering adulthood. Rather than seeking employment in the declining heavy industries, they looked to enter the growing professional and service sector. Cities were a hub for aspiring professionals, as they were home to many firms and therefore provided greater opportunities to progress upwards through new roles (Hall, 1966). The most attractive cities were those that combined political, trade, finance, professional function, luxury consumption opportunities and entertainment, a combination most likely to be found in a country capital (Gravier, 1947; Hall, 1966). A further wave of migration occurred, with young adults from traditional industrial areas relocating to regions that were hubs for professions and services, contributing to the higher GDP in the region of the capital city. In Britain, for example, the collapse of textile manufacturing in the North-West in the 1970s increased migration from the North-West to the South.

Individual

We conclude by focusing on income and wealth at individual level (Lindert; 2000; Lindert and Williamson, 2016). For income we examine income from labour and income from investment. For wealth we consider self-made success and inherited wealth.

Income from labour

Of particular concern to Marx, and of interest to subsequent writers on the Industrial Revolution, was the relationship between the three groups who were involved in the economy: 'the landed aristocracy, whose income derived primarily from rents, the bourgeoisie, whose income derived from profits, and the mass of the working population who were wage dependent' (Hudson, 2014: 203). As Hudson (2014) remarks, 'these three sources of income were potentially in conflict, because each could raise its share only at the expense of the other (Hudson, 2014: 203).

One way of investigating the situation of the 'mass' of wage dependent workers is to examine the relationship between their earnings and GDP. Figure 9.2 shows UK real GDP per capita and average real earnings, 1801–2010 (Clark, 2021a, 2021b; Thomas and Williamson, 2021). The best scenario for wage earners is for average real earnings to be above GDP. If average real earnings are below GDP than a worker's standard of living is likely to be negatively impacted, and they may need to work longer hours to maintain the same standard of living.

Figure 9.2 shows that average real earnings generally grew in a corresponding manner to GDP until 1864. During 1864–74 average earnings dropped below GDP per head, resulting in a situation where workers may have had to work longer hours in order to have maintained the same share as GDP. Wages fell below GDP again in 1915–18, corresponding with the First World War. Real earnings were significantly higher than GDP per head in 1920–39. With the onset of the Second World War this gap reduced in 1940, and in 1941–45 real earnings dropped below GDP per head. From 1946 onwards until 1977 real earnings and GDP per head were very closely aligned. From 1977 onwards, however, the increase in real earnings was slower than in GDP. This may indicate that the share of labour income in GDP was falling.

Figure 9.3 compares the long-term trends in US real GDP per head and an index of the average money wage of an unskilled labourer (1860 = 100). The money wage is an 'index of the average money wage of a "common" or unskilled labourer' which was converted from a weekly rate to an annual equivalent' (Margo, 2000: 6, 17; Johnston and Williamson, 2021). The range of values of these two variables are broadly comparable and they are therefore plotted using a common vertical scale.

Figure 9.2: UK Real GDP per capita and average real earnings, 1801–2010

Source: Thomas and Williamson (2021); Clark (2021a)

Figure 9.3: US Real GDP per capita and money wage of unskilled labour, 1800–2010

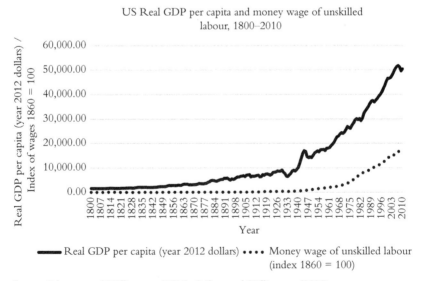

Source: Johnston and Williamson (2021); Officer and Williamson (2021)

The apparent static level of the initial years of the money wage index on the graph conceals some volatility in the data. The period 1801–47 saw the money wage index range between a low of 57 and a high of 111. From 1848 to 1869 there was an upward trend; there was then a downward trend from 1870 to 1879. Wages increased again after this, with the 1880s and 1890s seeing a period of stability. There was an increase in 1900–20. The 1920s and 1930s were rather volatile. However, from 1940 until 2010 the real wage climbed steadily. Unskilled workers in the US saw their wages rise in line with GDP for much of the period. It was therefore unlikely that they had much need to work longer hours in order to maintain their wages.

Figure 9.3 suggests that it would have been relatively easy for wage workers, including the unskilled, to maintain their standard of living during the period 1801–2010. It is notable, though, that for many wage earners in manufacturing the level of wages did not reflect the risks that they were exposed to, including injury by machinery.

Income from investment

Investment has been important historically in providing an income for women, thereby addressing some inequalities in access to employment and education. Female investors were both winners and losers from investment in the South Sea Company, founded in 1711. Richard Hoare, director of the original company, was also the founder of Hoare's Bank in London and introduced the scheme to his bank clients. Women comprised 10–12 per cent of the bank's customers, and surviving correspondence informs on why some of them purchased South Sea stock (Laurence, 2006, 2008: 567). The Earl of Huntingdon's five daughters and their friend Mrs Jane Bonnell were motivated by opportunity and necessity. As married women, Catherine and Margaret were probably less in need of supplementing their finances than their unmarried sisters. We know little of their investment activities, but Lady Margaret recorded some profit on her South Sea stock that she appears to have put into other investments. Lady Betty was the wealthiest of the unmarried sisters, with an income of £3,000 a year. This, however, was largely derived from income from family estates, which were difficult to liquidate; in contrast, shares could be bought and sold easily. Lady Betty also made a profit on her South Sea stock. Half-sister Lady Ann was significantly poorer, with a total wealth lower than Lady Betty's annual income. Despite investing to supplement her income, Lady Ann lost £800. Lady Frances derived an annual income from stock she held in the East India Company but also bought South Sea stock, although we don't know the details of its performance. Jane Bonnell invested out of necessity, after she was widowed and her nephew withheld an allowance. She borrowed money to invest, but unfortunately suffered such substantial losses that in later years she became reliant on financial support from her own sister.

In the first half of the 19th century women continued to embrace new investment opportunities as they arose in the UK, in both railways and joint-stock banks. However, shareholding was still dominated by male investors, who tended to have a consolidated portfolio focused on two or three companies and to take an active interest in their running (Green and Owens, 2003; Freeman et al, 2006; Maltby and Rutterford, 2006; Rutterford and Sotiropoulos, 2017).

The number of women owning shares, and the value of their holdings, expanded significantly in the UK in 1870–1935. This corresponded with a general broadening of the investment base among men too, with 'retailers, skilled workers and professionals' joining 'gentlemen, solicitors and peers of the realm' but also reflecting specific circumstances (Rutterford et al, 2011: 157). Demand-side influences for all groups were a rise in real incomes and the expansion of employment opportunities in the salaried and professional sectors (Rutterford et al, 2011: 158). For women, there were additional demand-side influences. The number of women in the population compared with men increased significantly during the period, from 600,600 more women than men in 1871 to 1,849,000 more women than men in 1931 (Rutterford et al, 2011: 171). This increased the proportion of single women who needed to support themselves financially. Secondly, while employment opportunities in the professions of teaching and clerical work expanded for women, not all women were eligible for such roles. Finally, the legal position of married women with regards to property ownership improved at the start of the period. Wives were granted full rights over any property that was 'brought into or acquired' during their marriage as a result of the Married Women's Property Act of 1870, its 1874 amendment and the 1882 Married Women's Property Act (Rutterford et al, 2011: 171).

Supply-side factors also encouraged share ownership by both genders. The introduction of limited liability in 1856, and its extension in 1862, reduced the risk to investors. If a limited liability company went bankrupt, a shareholder was only at risk of losing the value of their investment. Their remaining overall wealth was protected. Company securities were producing higher yields than government securities during this period, making them more attractive as an investment opportunity. Finally, overseas investment opportunities increased, particularly as a result of company foundations during mining booms in South America, India and Australia in the 1870s–90s (Rutterford et al, 2011: 160).

In the US the investment base for shares remained relatively narrow until the early 1900s, with industrialist and bankers being the dominant investors during the 1800s (Rutterford and Sotiropoulos, 2017). This was largely because of supply-side constraints. It was primarily after the 'merger boom' of 1897–1904 that large companies were founded, and prior to that there was little cause to issue common stock to fund their creation (Rutterford and Sotiropoulos, 2017: 491). Secondly, stock in the US was generally traded in batches of 100, with a surcharge applied if anyone wanted to purchases smaller amounts. This discouraged small-scale investors (Rutterford and Sotiropoulos, 2017: 491). Rutterford and Sotiropoulos (2017: 500) propose that prior to the First World War a greater proportion of the UK population (approximately 2.4 per cent) were shareholders compared with the proportion of the US population (approximately 0.9 per cent).

The First World War changed attitudes to the stock market in both the US and UK. The launch of war bonds in 1914 in the UK and Liberty Bonds in the US in 1917 and 1918 encouraged people to lend the government money, at a guaranteed rate of return, to help fund the war. Subscription to the bonds was emphasized as an investment (not a speculation) and they were heavily marketed to women, who were not engaged in front-line combat, as an alternative way to support the war effort.

More surprisingly, the number of shareholders in both the UK and the US continued to rise after the stock market crash of 1929, possibly because the investors thought that 'stocks were relatively cheap' (Rutterford and Sotiropoulos, 2017: 515). One 1937 estimate was that 6.2–7 per cent of the US population were shareholders (Rutterford and Sotiropoulos, 2017: 516). The recovery was not total, however, and there was decline in numbers from that point, with an estimated 4.2 per cent of the US population being shareholders in 1951 (Rutterford and Sotiropoulos, 2017: 524).

The decline concerned the New York Stock Exchange and led the institution to pay greater attention to attracting small investors. Women again turned out to be significant players. The New York Stock Exchange's 1951 survey found that 32 per cent of shareholders were housewives – although it suggested that they may have inherited shares from their husband or held them in their own name for tax purposes (Rutterford and Sotiropoulos, 2017: 524). Seeking to revive shareowner numbers, the New York Stock Exchange initiated the 'Own Your Own Share of American Business' from 1954 to 1969. This was targeted at individual investors and emphasized the consumer goods businesses that were considered to be particularly attractive to female investors (Rutterford and Sotiropoulos, 2017: 524). A significant success, the campaign resulted in an estimated 15 per cent of the US population being shareholders in the 1960s (Rutterford and Sotiropoulos, 2017: 528).

The UK was less impacted by the 1929 crash. However, the nationalization of the coal, electric, railway and iron and steel sectors by the Labour government in 1947–49 removed share ownership in those sectors and the London Stock Exchange did not take the initiative to promote share ownership in other areas. In 1949 the percentage of the population estimated to hold shares was 2.6 per cent, almost identical to the pre First World War level and significantly less than in the US (Rutterford and Sotiropoulos, 2017: 521). Women formed 40 per cent, men 47 per cent, joint holders 8 per cent and charities, nominees and corporate holders 5 per cent of shareholders (Rutterford and Sotiropoulos, 2017: 521). Yet there was a lack of diversity in the socio-economic profile of shareholders, with a dominance of retirees living in the South and South-West of England and in North Wales (a popular retirement location for those living in the North of England).

Share ownership could be a source of power in addition to a source of income. In the US from 1865 to 1900 bankers and industrialists wrestled for control of key railway routes by purchasing controlling shares of the companies concerned. In 1868, for example, Cornelius Vanderbilt attempted to gain control of the Erie Railroad, which connected New York, Buffalo and Chicago, by gradually buying a controlling share of the stock. A rival team of bankers and industrialists, led by Jay Gould, illegally issued 50,000 shares of Erie stock in an attempt to stop him (Klein, 1986).

On other occasions business magnates would cooperate in order to create efficiencies in their business or create a monopoly – depending on one's perspective. J.D. Rockefeller used his position as largest shareholder in Standard Oil, founded in 1863, to exercise control over the company's direction. During the 1870s he organized the acquisition of competing firms located across American states (Klein, 1986; Chernow, 1999). However, the growth of the company was exceeding state laws on company size. To consolidate the companies while circumventing that legislation, the Standard Oil Trust was created in 1882, and the stockholders in the individual companies transferred their shares to nine trustees (US National Archives, 2021). For every share transferred to the trust, the stockholder received 20 trust certificates. The profits of the combined companies were sent to the trustees and they determined the allocation of dividends and elected directors and officers for each of the companies. Thus a monopoly was created.

Yet power was disseminated as well as concentrated. Each ordinary or common share gave its owner the right to vote in the company's general meeting. UK shareholders initially had greater power than US ones, possessing the ability to dismiss company directors. UK companies made it easy for shareholders to attend annual meetings, and the relatively short distances facilitated attendance. In contrast, in the US directors could only be dismissed for misconduct and the large distances posed a barrier to attendance for many regional investors. Companies often deliberately introduced further barriers (such as small or inconvenient locations) to deter shareholder attendance at meetings (Rutterford, 2012).

The relationship between US companies and their shareholders changed in the aftermath of the stock market crash of 1929. Companies were required to be more transparent in their communications with shareholders, while shareholders began to hold them more accountable (Rutterford, 2012: 139). In the US, for example, shareholder Wilma Soss lobbied during the 1940s–80s for the introduction of female directors and for regional board meetings that would allow greater numbers of stockholders to attend (Rutterford, 2012). Rather than dismissing 'housewife' investors, companies began to actively court them. Inspired by the 'Own Your Own Share of American Business' campaign, US companies used general meetings to show off their new plants and products and sought to turn their investors into customers. Consumer goods firms led the way, finally recognizing that female stockholders had significant consumer purchasing power and influence on purchasing decisions made by their friends and relatives.

Wealth: self-made

Having looked at income from employment we now move on to consider wealth. We first examine self-made success and then examine the significance of inheritance as a source of wealth.

Andrew Carnegie's career exemplifies self-made success and the transformation from employee to firm owner and industrialist (Nasaw, 2006). Carnegie emigrated from Scotland to America as a child in 1848, after his parents became disillusioned by the failure of the Chartist movement, which had aimed to secure better political representative and working conditions for labourers. Aged 14, Carnegie worked as a telegraph runner, and then taught himself to be an operator. He used his new skill to obtain a job on the Pennsylvanian Railroad, eventually being promoted to superintendent at the age of 24. Colleagues and mentors signposted investment opportunities for him in transport related areas, and he took financial risks, such as mortgaging his house, to raise the necessary capital. In 1861 he invested some of the profits in an oil company, along with his business mentors. Carnegie's national profile was enhanced during the American Civil War of 1861–65 when he laid railway tracks and replaced wooden bridges with more durable iron ones to help Lincoln's side. This helped him to secure further government contracts. After the war Carnegie moved into the steel sector, which could be manufactured cheaply for the first time as a result of the Bessemer process that had been invented in 1856, and where the opportunity to make steel railway tracks could be exploited (Mokyr, 1999).

In 1901 Carnegie sold his steel company, becoming the richest man in the world in the process. He embarked on a major programme of philanthropy, with the goal of disposing of all his fortune before his death. Carnegie believed that 'there is no mode of disposing of surplus wealth creditable to thoughtful and earnest men into whose hands it flows save by using it year by year for the general good' (Carnegie, 1889: 14). Initiatives included the foundation of 2,509 libraries in America, Belgium, France, Ireland and the

UK (including in the industrial cities of Manchester and Birmingham). These were intended to provide workers, many of whom had received little formal schooling, with the opportunity to expand their knowledge and skills (Carnegie Corporation of New York, 2020).

Rubinstein found similar evidence of self-made success in his examination of the family backgrounds, secondary and higher education of the British elite of 1880–1970. He used a dataset of 312 top civil servants, 213 Church of England bishops, 211 vice chancellors of English and Welsh universities and 226 chairpeople of the largest British industrial companies (Rubinstein, 1986). Inheritance, he found, had little relevance to the social position of the individuals in his study. It was most significant in the case of the industrialists, some of whom had benefited from inheritance from their fathers, who had themselves been industrialists. However, even in that category there were many individuals who had risen up the ranks from middle management to become chairperson. Rubinstein suggested that the civil service and academia were particularly attractive professions for bright individuals from less affluent families, as the starting salaries were relatively high and the professions did not require the up-front capital needed to start a company or enter the legal profession.

Education was a more significant factor in explaining the social position of civil servants and bishops – over half of whom had attended public school. It was a less significant factor for industrialists, the majority of whom did not attend university during the period of study. Rubinstein proposed that, instead, those who were joining the family business were expected to do so straight from school.

Rubinstein (1977, 1986) also examined the main location of childhood residence. His findings were strikingly similar to that of McCann. London and the South-East were the dominant locations for all groups. Industrialists who were chairman in 1900–19 were more likely than the other three categories to have spent their childhood in the North-West of England, reflecting its industrial dominance at the time. However, from the 1920s onwards they increasingly also had their origins in the London area, reflecting the decline of industry in the North-West and the recruitment of Londoners as managers in the new American subsidiaries examined by Dunning (1958). Overall, Rubinstein found that entrance into these four 'elite' categories was largely based on merit. He suggested, however, that the same meritocracy might not have yet extended to 'large landowners, City of London merchant bankers and bankers and Conservative politicians and cabinet ministers' (Rubinstein, 1986: 192–3).

Wealth: inheritance

Inheritance involves the transfer of wealth from one individual to another, either as a gift during life or a bequest after death (Atkinson, 2007, 2018).

Benefactors of an inheritance have opportunities, for example to reduce or stop salaried work. However, they also have responsibilities. Receipt of an inheritance may require an investment of time, for example the assumption of a position of responsibility in a family business or the management of landed estates. Those with a source of independent wealth may also be expected to donate their time to, for example, charitable activities, as they are under less pressure to spend it engaged in salaried employment.

The lives of Samuel Jones Loyd, Baron Overstone (1796–1883) and his daughter Harriet Sarah Loyd- Lindsay, Lady Wantage (1837–1920) illustrate these issues. As a banker from a banking dynasty, and with a substantial inheritance, Overstone falls into one of the additional elites identified but not examined by Rubinstein (1986). Overstone was born in London to a former clergyman turned banker and the daughter of a banker. Educated at Eton and Cambridge, he joined the family bank as a partner two years before his graduation. Overstone benefited from three substantial inheritances, from two uncles (who died in 1819 and 1821 respectively) and from his father, who died in 1858. Overstone, however, continued to work for the bank after his first inheritances. Under his leadership the bank was successful and Overstone's annual income was supplemented by a share of the profits. In 1850 Overstone was awarded a peerage for services to the sector, a situation that required him to retire from active business and draw his income from capital (Reed, 2008).

Irrespective of the peerage, from his early 40s Overstone began to reorientate his income from a 'potentially larger but less stable income from the bank' to a 'steadier and more secure' one that would support his retirement (Michie, 1985: 61). From his father Overstone inherited an estate worth several million pounds, comprising land and securities. Overstone's father had been particularly successful with investments in railway shares, which he had purchased cheaply in the aftermath of the 1847 railway mania (Michie, 1985). Overstone continued to invest in railway stock during the 1860s when it remained relatively cheap, and thus benefited from its rapid rise in value in the 1870s. Overstone's main new investment was in the accumulation of agricultural land, which he saw as a secure source of rental income. He was almost unique, Michie (1985) proposes, in having both the wealth to buy estates and to make significant investments in improving them, for example through investments in drainage to improve agricultural productivity. In 1881 the composition of Overstone's income was estimated at 38 per cent from farm rents, 24 per cent from British government securities, 11 per cent from foreign government securities, 16 per cent from domestic railway stock and 11 per cent from 'his outstanding loans, his holdings of miscellaneous securities and money on deposit in the Bank of England and London and Westminster Bank (Michie, 1985: 61–2).

Overstone managed his income and capital carefully, saving 50–60 per cent of his annual income and using that to fund his land acquisitions. One third of his total expenditure in the period 1863–82 was spent on gifts to family members, friends, employees and charities. The remainder of his expenditure related to the running costs of his house and to unique events, such as his daughter's wedding in 1858, house building in 1861–66 and the funding of election campaigns in 1868 and 1879 (Michie, 1985: 63).

At his death in 1883 this careful stewardship meant that Overstone remained one of the wealthiest people in England. Michie suggests that Overstone's only misjudgement was that he continued to buy agricultural land for too long and did not exit the market when he would have received the greatest returns on his investment. Consequently, Overstone was hit by the decline in agricultural rents during the 1870s and 1880s.

Lady Wantage was Overstone's sole heir. Overstone had provided Wantage and her husband with a significant bequest on their marriage in 1858, and continued to provide substantial financial gifts during his life. As a married women of independent means there was little expectation that she would supplement her income by salaried work. She therefore focused on distributing the fortune, possibly motivated by the fact that she did not have descendants to bequeath it to. Both Wantage and her husband donated substantial time and money to supporting the British Red Cross, and other beneficiaries included the University of Reading, the Royal Berkshire Hospital and the National Art Collection fund (Corley, 2004). The family's ideas were not very socially progressive, however. Overstone had resigned from the senate of London University over the awarding of degrees to women, and his daughter campaigned against female suffrage in parliamentary elections.

Individual level: causes of inequalities

Income and wealth obtained by investment and inheritance is sometimes seen in a more negative light than that obtained by labour. The case studies here, however, suggest a more complex situation. Investment provided an important source of income for women, many of whom had limited employment opportunities available to them owing to social, legal and educational barriers. In an era before full female suffrage, shareholder meetings provided an opportunity to express opinions in a public forum, and afterwards they continued to be a platform to lobby for improved female representation in positions of responsibility in business. Inheritance was a responsibility as well as a gift, and it could be disposed of in ways that benefited society as a whole, and not just one person or family.

An income derived solely from labour carries risks, notably of unemployment. Those who are willing or able to be more mobile may be able to reduce those risks by moving to locations with better employment opportunities. Education can also improve prospects (Goldin and Katz, 2010). The connection between education and employment prospects was noted in Rubinstein's study, and Carnegie's belief in the power of education was demonstrated in his bequests to libraries.

Conclusion

Since capitalism allows people to market whatever they own (land and capital) they can also market themselves. There is no upper limit on what they can receive. The most able will receive a premium for the use of their resource. In the 19th century writers such as Ricardo and Mill thought that the premium was based on possession of a large amount of superior agricultural land. In the 20th century the quality of being the organizer of a large manufacturing business was perceived to be the most valuable talent. Now in the 21st century we perceive the resource in terms of qualities, such as entrepreneurial ability and successful speculation. We have a superstar culture in which people with those abilities receive spectacular rewards.

This new focus on the person as the resource has the potential to reduce the inequalities that derived from inheritance. However, it also has the potential to contribute to inequality based on earned income. Regional inequalities can result as well. Land as a resource was static, but a person is mobile. Those with valuable talents can therefore relocate with them. The threat of potential relocation to another business may cause their employer to award them an even higher salary, to retain their loyalty, thus further contributing to the existing income inequality. However, that incentive cannot be offered by a region that faces losing its talented residents to other areas that have greater opportunities.

References

Abel, W. (1980) *Agricultural Fluctuations in Europe from the Thirteenth to the Twentieth Centuries*, New York: St Martin's Press.

Atkinson, A. (2007) 'The distribution of top incomes in the United Kingdom 1908–2000', in A. Atkinson and T. Piketty (eds) *Top Incomes over the Twentieth Century. A Contrast Between Continental European and English-Speaking Countries*, Oxford: Oxford University Press, pp 82–140.

Atkinson, A.B. (2018) 'Wealth and inheritance in Britain from 1896 to the present', *Journal of Economic Inequality*, 16: 137–69.

Carnegie, A. (1889) *The Gospel of Wealth*, *Carnegie Corporation of New York*, [online]. Available from: https://www.carnegie.org/about/our-history/gospelofwealth/ [Accessed 20 December 2020].

Carnegie Corporation of New York (2020) 'Andrew Carnegie's story' [online]. Available from: https://www.carnegie.org/interactives/founde rsstory/#!/ [Accessed 20 December 2020].

Casson, M. (1983) *Economics of Unemployment: An Historical Perspective*, Oxford: Robertson.

Chernow, R. (1999) *Titan: The Life of John D. Rockefeller, Sr.*, New York: Vintage.

Clark, G. (2021a) 'What were the British earnings and prices then? (new series)', *Measuring Worth*, [online]. Available from: http://www.measuri ngworth.com/ukearncpi/ [Accessed 12 February 2021].

Clark, G. (2021b) 'What were British earnings and prices then? A question and answer guide', *Measuring Worth*, [online]. Available from: https://www. measuringworth.com/datasets/ukearncpi/earnguidenew.htm [Accessed 12 February 2021].

Corley, T.A.B. (2004) 'Lindsay, Harriet Sarah Loyd-, Lady Wantage (1837– 1920), benefactor', *Oxford Dictionary of National Biography*.

Crafts, N. (2005) 'Regional GDP in Britain, 1871–1911: Some estimates', *Scottish Journal of Political Economy*, 52(1): 54–64.

Díez Minguela, A. and Sanchis Llopis, M.T. (2018) 'Regional income inequality in France: what does history teach us?', *Carlos III University of Madrid. Figuerola Institute of Social Sciences History*, [online. Available from: http://portal.uc3m.es/portal/page/portal/instituto_figuerola/home/ publications/working_papers [Accessed 1 February 2021].

Dunning, J. (1958) *American Investment in British Manufacturing Industry*, London: Allen and Unwin.

Enflo, K. (2014) 'Finland's regional GDPs 1880–2010: estimates, sources and interpretations', *Lund Papers in Economic History: Department of Economic History, Lund University* [online]. Available from: https://ideas.repec.org/ p/hhs/luekhi/0135.html [Accessed 10 February 2021].

Enflo, K. (2018) 'Balancing east and west: evidence from Finland's regional GDPs, 1880–2010', in J.R. Rosés and N. Wolf (eds) *The Economic Development of Europe's Regions: A Quantitative History since 1900*, London and New York: Routledge, pp 103–28.

Enflo, K. and Rosés, J. (2015) 'Coping with regional inequality in Sweden: structural change, migrations and policy, 1860–2000', *Economic History Review*, 68(1): 191–217.

Enflo, K. and Missiaia, A. (2017a) 'Between Malthus and the industrial take-off: regional inequality in Sweden, 1571–1850', *Lund Papers in Economic History*: Department of Economic History, Lund University.

Enflo, K. and Missiaia, A. (2017b) 'Regional GDP estimates for Sweden, 1571–1850', *Lund Papers in Economic History*: Department of Economic History, Lund University.

European Commission (2021a) 'Internal market, industry, entrepreneurship and SMEs: regional innovation monitor plus: Bavaria', *European Commission* [online]. Available from: https://ec.europa.eu/growth/tools-databa ses/regional-innovation-monitor/base-profile/bavaria [Accessed 20 January 2021].

European Commission (2021b) 'Internal market, industry, entrepreneurship and SMEs: regional innovation monitor plus: Mellersta-Norrland', *European Commission* [online]. Available from: https://ec.europa.eu/growth/tools-databases/regional-innovation-monitor/base-profile/mellersta-norrland [Accessed 20 January 2021].

European Commission (2021c) 'Internal market, industry, entrepreneurship and SMEs: regional innovation monitor plus: Övre-Norrland', *European Commission* [online]. Available from: https://ec.europa.eu/growth/tools-databases/regional-innovation-monitor/base-profile/%C3%B6vre-norrl and [Accessed 20 January 2021].

Eurostat (2018) 'Methodological manual on territorial typologies 2018 edition', *Eurostat* [online]. Available from: https://ec.europa.eu/eurostat/ web/products-manuals-and-guidelines/-/KS-GQ-18-008 [Accessed 20 January 2021].

Eurostat (2021) 'NUTS and territorial typologies', *Eurostat* [online]. Available from: https://ec.europa.eu/eurostat/statistical-atlas/gis/vie wer/?config=typologies.json&ch=NUTSLEVL,NUTSLEVL2&mids= BKGCNT,NUTS2016LEVL2,CNTOVL&o=1,1,0.7&center= 60.89802,36.21534,4&lcis=NUTS2016LEVL2&nutsId=FI1B& [Accessed 20 January 2021].

Felice, E. (2018) 'Regional income inequality in Italy in the long run (1871–2010): patterns and determinants', in J.R. Rosés and N. Wolf (eds) *The Economic Development of Europe's Regions: A Quantitative History since 1900*, London and New York: Routledge, pp 177–203.

Freeman, M., Pearson, R. and Taylor, J. (2006) ' "A doe in the city": women shareholders in eighteenth- and early nineteenth-century Britain', *Accounting, Business and Financial History*, 16(2): 265–91.

Geary, F. and Stark, T. (2002) 'Examining Ireland's post-famine economic growth performance', *Economic Journal*, 112: 919–35.

Geary, F. and Stark, T. (2015) 'Regional GDP in the UK, 1861–1911: new estimates', *Economic History Review*, 68(1): 123–44.

Geary, F. and Stark, T. (2016) 'What happened to regional inequality in Britain in the twentieth century?', *Economic History Review*, 69(1): 215–28.

Godley, A. (1996) 'Jewish soft loan societies in New York and London and immigrant entrepreneurship, 1880–1914', *Business History*, 38(3): 101–16.

Goldin, C. and Katz, L.F. (2010) *The Race Between Education and Technology: The Evolution of U.S. Educational Wage Differentials, 1890–2005*, Cambridge, MA: Belknap Press.

Gravier, J-F. (1947) *Paris and the French Desert*, Paris: Portulan.

Green, D.R. and Owens, A. (2003) 'Gentlewomanly capitalism? Spinsters, widows, and wealth holding in England and Wales, c. 1800–1860', *Economic History Review*, 56(3): 510–36.

Hall, P. (1966) *The World Cities*, New York: McGraw-Hill Book Co.

Harper, D. (1995) *Entrepreneurship and the Market Process*, London: Routledge.

Hayek, F.A. (1949) *Individualism and Economic Order*, London: Routledge Arbitrage.

Hudson, P. (2014) *The Industrial Revolution*, London: Hodder Arnold.

Johnston, L. and Williamson, S.M. (2021) 'What was the US GDP then?', *MeasuringWorth*, [online]. Available from: https://www.measuringworth.com/datasets/usgdp/ / [Accessed 12 February 2021].

Kirzner, I.M. (1973) *Competition and Entrepreneurship*, Chicago: University of Chicago Press.

Klein, M. (1986) *The Life and Legend of Jay Gould*, Baltimore, MD: Johns Hopkins University Press.

Knight, F.H. (1935) *The Ethics of Competition and Other Essays*, London: G. Allen and Unwin Ltd.

Laurence, A. (2006) 'Women investors, "the nasty South Sea affair" and the rage to speculate in early eighteenth-century England', *Accounting, Business and Financial History*, 16: 245–64.

Laurence, A. (2008) 'The emergence of a private clientele for banks in the early eighteenth century: Hoare's Bank and some women customers', *Economic History Review*, 61: 565–86.

Lindert, P.H. (2000) 'Chapter 3: Three centuries of inequality in Britain and America', in A.B. Atkinson and F. Bourguignon (eds) *Handbook of Income Distribution Volume 1*. Amsterdam: Elsevier, pp 167–216.

Lindert, P.H. and Williamson, J.G. (2016) *Unequal Gains: American Growth and Inequality since 1700*, Princeton, NJ: Princeton University Press.

Maltby, J. and Rutterford, J. (2006) '"She possessed her own fortune": Women investors from the late nineteenth century to the early twentieth century', *Business History*, 48(2): 220–53.

Margo, Robert A. (2000) *Wages and Labor Markets in the United States, 1820–1860*, Chicago: University of Chicago Press.

Marx, K., (1961) *Capital Volume 1* (trans S. Moore and E. Aveling and ed F. Engels), Moscow: Foreign Languages Publishing House.

McCann, P. (2016) *The UK Regional–National Economic Problem: Geography, Globalisation and Governance*, Abingdon: Routledge

Merlo, E. and Polese, F. (2006) 'Turning fashion into business: the emergence of Milan as an international fashion hub', *Business History Review*, 80 (3): 415–47.

Michie, R.C. (1985) 'Income, expenditure and investment of a Victorian millionaire: Lord Overstone, 1823–83', *Historical Research: The Bulletin of the Institute of Historical Research*, 58(137): 59–77.

Mill, J.S. (1848) *Principles of Political Economy*, London: John W. Parker.

Modalsli, J. (2018) 'Regional income in Norway, 1900–2010', in J.R. Rosés and N. Wolf (eds) *The Economic Development of Europe's Regions: A Quantitative History since 1900*, London and New York: Routledge, pp 228–50.

Mokyr, J. (1999) 'The second industrial revolution, 1870–1914', in V. Castronovo (ed) *Storia dell' Economia Mondiale*, Rome: Laterza Publishing, pp 219–45.

Nasaw, D. (2006) *Andrew Carnegie*, New York: Penguin Press.

Officer, L.H. and Williamson, S.H. (2021) 'Annual wages in the United States, 1774–Present', *MeasuringWorth*, [online]. Available from: http://www.measuringworth.com/uswages/ [Accessed 12 February 2021].

Piketty, T. (2014) *Capital in the Twenty-First Century* (trans A. Goldhammer), Cambridge, MA and London: The Belknap Press of Harvard University.

Reed, M. (2008) 'Loyd, Samuel Jones, Baron Overstone (1796–1883), banker', *Oxford Dictionary of National Biography*.

Rosés, J.R. and Sanchis, T.M (2018) 'A long-run perspective on French regional income inequality, 1860–2010', in J.R. Rosés and N. Wolf (eds) *The Economic Development of Europe's Regions: A Quantitative History since 1900*, London and New York: Routledge, pp 129–48.

Rosés, J.R. and Wolf, N. (2018a) 'Regional economic development in Europe, 1900–2010: a description of the patterns', *CEPR Discussion Papers*, [online]. Available from: https://ideas.repec.org/p/ehl/wpaper/87242.html [Accessed 5 January 2021].

Rosés, J.R. and Wolf, N. (eds) (2018b) *The Economic Development of Europe's Regions: A Quantitative History since 1900*, London and New York: Routledge.

Rubinstein, W.D. (1977) 'The Victorian middle classes: wealth, occupation, and geography', *Economic History Review*, 30(4): 602–23.

Rubinstein, W.D. (1986) 'Education and the social origins of British élites 1880–1970', *Past and Present*, 112: 163–207.

Rutterford, J. (2012) 'The shareholder voice: British and American Accents, 1890–1965', *Enterprise and Society*, 13(1): 120–53.

Rutterford, J. and Sotiropoulos, D.P. (2017) 'The rise of the small investor in the US and the UK, 1895 to 1970', *Enterprise and Society*, 18(3): 85–535.

Rutterford, J., Green, D.R., Maltby, J. and Owens, A. (2011) 'Who comprised the nation of shareholders? Gender and investment in Great Britain, c. 1870–1935', *Economic History Review*, 64(11): 157–87.

Scott, P. (2006) 'Path dependence, fragmented property rights and the slow diffusion of high throughput technologies in inter-war British coal mining', *Business History*, 48(1): 20–42.

Scott, P. (2007) *Triumph of the South: A Regional Economic History of Early Twentieth Century Britain*, Aldershot: Ashgate.

Scott, P. (2013) *The Making of the British Home: The Suburban Semi and Family Life Between the Wars*, Oxford: Oxford University Press

Scott, P. (2017) *The Market Makers: Creating Mass Markets for Consumer Durables in Inter-War Britain*, Oxford: Oxford University Press.

Seligman, E.R.A. (1910) *The Shifting and Incidence of Taxation* (3rd ed.), New York: Columbia University Press.

Smith, A. (1791) *An Inquiry into the Nature and Causes of the Wealth of Nations* (4th edn), N.S.

Thomas, R. and Williamson, S.H. (2021)'What was the UK GDP then?', *MeasuringWorth* [online]. Available from: http://www.measuringworth. com/ukgdp/ [Accessed 12 February 2021].

US National Archives (2021) 'The Sherman anti-trust Act (1890)', *US National Archives* [online]. Available from: https://www.ourdocuments. gov/doc.php?flash=false&doc=51[Accessed 15 February 2021]

Van Zanden, J.L. (2009) *The Long Road to the Industrial Revolution: The European Economy in a Global Perspective, 1000–1800*, Leiden: Brill.

Van Zanden, J.L and Soltow, L. (1998) *Income and Wealth Inequality in the Netherlands 1500–1990*, Amsterdam: Het Spinhuis.

Vonyó, T. (2008) 'Post-war reconstruction and the Golden Age of economic growth', *European Review of Economic History*, 12(2): 221–41.

World Inequality Database (2021) [online]. Available from: https://wid. world/ [Accessed 6 January 2021].

10

Conclusion

Catherine Casson and Philipp Robinson Rössner

This volume has proposed that the evolution of capitalism was connected to the emergence of five distinct economic functions: entrepreneurship, finance, management, workers and political leaders. Some functions emerged as more dominant in particular locations and periods, and other functions in different locations and periods. Thus capitalism can be seen as a series of evolutions rather than a single one. This chapter will review the evidence in the book that informs on selected aspects of these functions. It will then highlight two key takeaways from the volume: geographical dimensions and values and beliefs. Finally, directions for future research will be proposed.

The book has reinforced the importance of situating capitalism in a wider historical context. Chapter 2 proposed that the modern market economy developed in 13th-century European towns and was stimulated by local and national regulation. Building on that analysis, Chapter 3 argued that during the 16th and 17th centuries elements of a shared philosophy pertaining to markets and their place in society can be identified in Continental Europe. Key themes were monetary regulation, customs and trade policies aimed at nurturing certain industries or branches of economy that were considered vital for the common good, and market regulation, in particular of urban product markets. These strategies and philosophies of market were invented, applied and modified centuries before modern capitalism, but were an importance influence on it.

While Chapters 2 and 3 emphasized the convergence of market regulation practices across locations, Chapters 4, 5 and 6 explored situations where countries developed different trajectories. Chapter 4 examined how the Scandinavian countries of Sweden and Norway developed ownership structures that differed both from the dominant US, UK and Continental models, but also from each other. Chapter 5 examined how merchants in Asia and Africa adopted cross-cultural and communal, rather than national or institutional, frameworks to underpin their global exchange with English and Portuguese merchants. This represented a different model to that employed in most instances of global trade, in which countries adopted a formal institutional framework for market regulation and aligned their practices with that of their trading partners. Chapter 6 demonstrated that a diversity of approaches also emerged in South America, Asia and Africa during the 19th and 20th centuries.

Chapters 7, 8 and 9 considered the impact of capitalism. The chapters showed that religious, social and political beliefs represented significant influences on entrepreneurial activity alongside the more commonly emphasized profit-seeking objective. Chapter 7 showed that religious and social beliefs had the potential to constrain some of the negative elements of capitalism, yet challenges remained in reconciling the two. Yet as the over-representation of certain religious denomination – such as the Quakers – in certain business areas shows, religion could also have manifestly positive impacts on capitalism, or predict a potentially positive attitude and performance for business. Chapter 8 demonstrated that attitudes to land as a unit of production have changed significantly from the 18th and 19th centuries. The exploitation of natural resources was a significant sector of entrepreneurship throughout evolutions of capitalism. Chapter 8 explored how and why entrepreneurs and business leaders began to see for-profit business as an opportunity for environmental sustainability rather than depletion. Chapter 9 considered the social consequences of capitalism with regards to income and wealth. It showed that capitalism has led to the uneven distribution of income and wealth, but that this distribution was arguably most noticeable at the regional level.

Entrepreneurship

A range of motivations for entrepreneurship have been identified in this volume. Necessity-driven entrepreneurship was a feature of the Nonconformists examined in Chapter 7. Legal restrictions prohibited their engagement in the law and politics, while their religious beliefs restricted involvement in other sectors. As pacifists, for example, Quakers did not wish to serve in the military, and they preferred to avoid involvement in the sale of alcohol or tobacco. Founding a business provided Nonconformists with a source of income and allowed them to operate in sectors that complemented their beliefs.

Opportunity-seeking remained, however, a key element of entrepreneurship. The chapters in this volume have placed particular emphasis on the exploitation of natural resources, investment in infrastructure and the identification of new markets. In the majority of locations entrepreneurship was aided by an institutional structure and by support from political leaders.

Chapter 2 has shown that England during the 13th century was a pioneer in this regard.

Entrepreneurship could have a positive impact, providing consumers with a greater choice of products and generating improvements in infrastructure. Mutually beneficial collaboration occurred within and between countries. Domestically, shareholders investing in joint-stock companies benefited by obtaining income, while the capital formed investment for large-scale infrastructure projects. Internationally, trade between countries provided consumers in both with an access to a wider range of goods, as Chapter 5 illustrated.

Entrepreneurship could also have a detrimental impact. The colonization of overseas territories was of little benefit to their local populations, who were frequently exploited. Urbanization during the Industrial Revolution impacted on workers' quality of life. There was a limited consideration of the long-term implications of intensive extraction of natural resources. Income and wealth became unevenly concentrated among certain groups or in specific regions. Chapter 8 showed that to start to address these problems, pioneers are needed in each sector who are willing to take the financial risk required to reorientate the business model. Even after a possible solution is validated, there are still significant challenges in ensuring that it is actively, and not passively, adopted.

Finance

Finance has emerged as significant with regard both to money invested in a business and to money generated from it. Considering first money invested, the volume has highlighted the importance of pooled capital and of foreign direct investment, characterized by the ownership of overseas investors in domestic assets. Most of the mechanisms that allowed entrepreneurs to extend their market, and thereby their production, were only possible by the pooling of capital from many different individuals. This practice commenced with the chartered companies of 1600 and the contractor state of 1640 and intensified with the joint-stock banks and railway companies authorized in England from 1825 onwards. The issuing of stocks to raise capital has been identified with the separation of ownership and management. However, it also enabled the engagement of a broader section of the population in the economy. Groups, notably women, who otherwise had little involvement in the economy as either entrepreneurs, managers or workers, became involved as investors. Women were able to give input into the running of those businesses before they were granted the ability to vote in parliamentary elections.

Foreign direct investment was initially practised by Western countries as they intensified their trading links with non-Western countries. It consisted of the establishment of outposts that used as depots for the collection of goods for exports and for the distribution of imports (Casson, 2020). This meant that when ships arrived they could be swiftly loaded up as the cargo was waiting. During the 17th century Western countries observed and emulated each other's foreign direct investment practices; for example the English emulated the Dutch and the Scottish emulated the English. Foreign direct investment was also associated with territorial expansion as Western countries expanded their activities into the interior and sought to achieve overall political control in order to secure their property rights.

Foreign direct investment retained its importance during the 20th century, although it was no longer closely associated with territorial expansion. In some situations there was little spill-over effect. There was significant Swedish investment in Norway during the 20th century, particularly by the Wallenberg family. However, Norway adopted a state ownership model that was distinctive from Sweden's predominant family ownership model. Spill-over effects were more significant with regards to US investment in the UK in the aftermath of the First and Second World War, and support for Italy in the Marshall Plan after the Second World War. The dissemination of US management practices aided the competitiveness of both economies and the regional performance of the locations in which US subsidiaries, or domestic firms those producing for the US market, were based.

Marx perceived money generated from business as a significant cause of inequality between entrepreneurs and workers. However Chapter 9 proposed a more complex situation, in which a wider range of groups received an income from the profits of business. Experiences also had the potential to vary between workers. The greatest benefits, in the form of higher wages and enhanced career progression, were obtained by workers who were mobile and who had a comparative advantage in their technical, leadership, managerial or organizational skills base.

Management

In most countries management emerged as a distinctive function from ownership as firms grew in size. It has been argued that the shift from entrepreneur owner-managers to a system of salaried managers and shareholders has negatively impacted on businesses' social responsibility by intensifying the focus on the maximizing of profits. Managers are often set profit targets that they have to achieve to receive a bonus and even retain their job. Shareholders, meanwhile, want to receive the maximum possible dividends (Mayer, 2018). Just as with political leaders, it is important that employees and shareholders have the opportunity to question and challenge management. We have seen that during the 19th and early 20th centuries trade unions provided a potential forum and a voting and meetings platform for shareholders. However, there were few overlapping priorities between the two groups. While labour remuneration was an element of shareholder activism, it was of limited priority, and direct appeals by workers to shareholders to lobby for improved working conditions met with little response (Rutterford, 2012: 139).

From the mid-20th century and into the 21st it is increasingly consumers who have the power to influence change in managerial strategies. Chapter 8 proposed that consumer pressure played a significant role in causing the managers of multinational companies to engage with environmental sustainability.

Workers

The value attached to the skills of workers in the manufacturing sector has varied substantially across periods and locations. Notable in these chapters is a distinction between attitudes in the UK and US on the one hand and Germany and Japan on the other. In the UK and US there was a significant deskilling of manufacturing workers during the 19th century, and the emerging field of management focused on the improvement of worker productivity. US and UK firms perceived the value of the product to be connected to the customer's opinion of it and their desired characteristics. The price was set according to the added value that the customer is considered to get from the exciting experience.

In contrast, Chapter 3 and Chapter 6 have suggested that in Germany and Japan the expertise of manufacturing workers was considered to be a source of competitive advantage with regards to product quality. Chapter 3 has shown that the importance of manufacturing was emphasized in German economic and political thought from the 16th century. The German model then provided an inspiration to Japan, as Chapter 6 demonstrated, as it sought to become more internationally competitive in the late 19th and 20th centuries. The Japanese state prioritized 'the technical, the scientific and the vocational' in their economic reforms, and remodelled their education system on that in Germany and France. Germany and Japanese companies perceived the value of the product as being in the high quality and functionality that are the result of the number of skilled hours that workers contribute to production (Fitzgerald, 2007; König, 2007). When Yamamura and Streeck (2001, 2003) examined why, from the 1970s, Germany and Japan's economic performance overtook that of the UK and US they emphasized political factors, particularly the non-liberal context, characterized by 'statist controls and authoritarian rule' (Yamamura and Streeck, 2001). However, it may be that the constant focus across many centuries on quality and industrial entrepreneurship also aided Germany's resilience and contributed to its success.

Political leaders

The relationship between political leaders and private enterprise has been described as a 'narrow corridor' that needs to be carefully trodden lest it becomes distorted and perverted on both ends leading to either neoliberal capitalist anarchy (no rules, or no one who can credibly enforce such rules) or coordinated economic regimes (where just one institution or actor centralizes decision making processes, such as Soviet-style planning) (Acemoglu and Robinson, 2019). However, rather than seeing capitalism and the state as potentially opposing forces in their need to be reconciled and carefully managed, chapters in this volume suggest that the relationship between capitalism and the state might better be described as symbiotic (List, 1841; Reinert, 2019).

Political leaders have engaged in the promotion of the economy by establishing systems of monetary and market regulation. Investment in the underpinnings of trade and the institutional framework contributed to 'first-mover' advantage. Chapter 2 showed that England's economic success in the period 1200–1400 was closely connected to the introduction of market regulation. Chapter 3 examined the intersections between state, capitalism and economic growth. Economists have emphasized the proactive role of entrepreneurial states and mission-driven industrial policy (Mazzucato, 2013, 2021; Kattel and Mazzucato, 2018) without usually acknowledging their deep historical ramifications: most medieval and early modern European states applied mission-driven proactive manufacturing policies (Reinert, 2019; Rössner, 2021). Chapter 3 demonstrated that industrialization in 16th-century Europe was driven by proactive state policy based on a political economy or economic doctrine – cameralism – that emphasized industry and manufacturing, not agriculture, as the principal sources of the nations' wealth (Reinert, 2019; Rössner, 2020).

Investment in the institutional framework was also a significant factor in enabling 'catching up countries' to become more economically competitive. Armenian traders in the 17th century were able to maintain a successful trading network with merchants from Western countries without introducing a corresponding institutional framework. However, the lack of transition from informal to more formal practices may have contributed to the decline of their trade during the 18th century. Japan in the mid-19th century, alongside the educational reforms mentioned earlier, also redesigned its government along German lines and its banking system on US ones. In Norway, meanwhile, the transformation from an agrarian to industrial economy was aided by state ownership of Norwegian firms.

Political leaders have the potential to use their power to promote or to address inequalities. The volume has shown situations where some individuals received preferential treatment over others. In the contractor state of 1640s

England, the Crown was criticized for rewarding business opportunities as a form of patronage or in exchange for money rather than according to merit. In his discussion in this book of the situation in South America in the late 19th century and in the mid- and late 20th century, Lewis has examined how 'the state granted privileges to specific groups of national and/or foreign capitalists'. In contrast, Chapter 9 identified taxation as an important way in which politicians can seek to address inequalities in income and wealth resulting from capitalism.

Schumpeter had an optimistic assessment of how capitalism might result in improvements to the established democratic system. However, for the majority of the period covered in this volume, the majority of workers and a substantial proportion of investors were denied any direct political voice on the grounds of income or gender. Urban working men in England and Wales fulfilling a property qualification did not receive the vote until 1867; full political representation for all women and men over the age of 21 was not achieved until 1928. For women in particular, the political system took decades to catch up with the leverage they were exercising as shareholders.

Geographical dimensions

The first key takeaway from the case studies presented in this volume is that the locations in which functions emerged earliest did not necessarily continue to replicate that speed of progress. The function of entrepreneurship emerged in England at an early date, in 1200, aided by the strong institutional framework. Financial reforms that enabled the pooling of capital and the reduction of risk allowed the UK economy to maintain a strong performance up until about 1860. However, the UK was not proactive in responding to the increased competition from the US, Japan and Germany from 1870 onwards. Despite pioneering railway construction, it failed to recognize the opportunity to apply management lessons from the railways to the manufacturing sector. Instead, the US became a first mover in the field of management. The UK failed to modernize its coal sector after the First World War, leaving France and Germany to forge ahead. In the financial sector, the UK firms failed to use their pre-existing positive relationship with shareholders to transform them into customers and informal salespeople, instead allowing US firms to adapt and extend UK best practice in the sector.

During the period 1200–1350 Italy innovated new financial instruments, which benefited entrepreneurship. Venice served as an important hub of international trade, which was the most prevalent form of entrepreneurship during the period. However, unlike the UK, Italy seems to have struggled to build on those earlier advantages. Its lack of significant natural mineral resources meant that it was not in a position to industrialize to the extent of Germany and the UK. What is perhaps more surprising is that it did not use its combined seafaring and financial expertise to initiate a programme of overseas expansion. Chapter 9 showed that the Italian economy exhibited intense regional inequality from the 19th century, which may have had even earlier origins. The vitality of northern Italy was enhanced by the dissemination of American management practices to Italian firms.

The Spanish and Portuguese were engaged in long-distance seaborne trade at an earlier period than the English and Dutch, but retained their existing institutions without adopting chartered companies. Instead, activities were coordinated by the state. The Spanish coordinated their trade with America through the Casa de Contratación (House of Trade), established by the Crown in Seville in 1503 (Fisher, 2008a, 2008b). The Portuguese organized their trade with Africa and India through the state-run Casa da Guiné (founded 1443) and Casa da Índia (founded 1500) (Diffie and Winius, 1977; Scammell, 1982). The state granted monopolies to individual merchants to trade with the overseas colonies and to individual settlers to produce the items to trade (Roper and Van Ruymbeke, 2007; Fisher, 2008b).

Both Spain and Portugal developed permanent outposts in the overseas locations. Portugal focused on India, the East Indies and Brazil and Spain on the West Indies and central and South America. The Portuguese and Spanish strategies focused on the extraction of natural resources, in the form of minerals and spices. However, the lack of proactive entrepreneurship in other areas eventually caused problems for both the countries and for their colonies. In Portugal's case, the Portuguese imports to India, the East Indies and Brazil were worth less than the cost of the exports, and not perceived as very desirable by the local population. The difference in price had to be made up by money, and merchants trading with the Portuguese preferred to retain the money rather than spend it on the imported Portuguese goods. As a result, in the mid-16th century the maintenance of the trading posts began to be financially unsustainable and the Crown began a process of withdrawal. In Spain the reverse situation occurred when an influx of silver from America raised domestic prices. Consequently, products imported from other European countries became more desirable because they were more competitively priced. Colonization, therefore, had few spill-over effects in terms of creating a branch of dynamic domestic manufacturing or industrial entrepreneurship.

The function of entrepreneurship emerged in Germany at a relatively early date, during the 16th century. Germany benefited from having its own natural coal and mineral resources, and these rapidly emerged as large industrial enterprises. Including the (in)famous Saiger huts – large smelting plants erected in central and southern Germany since the 1460s where the argentiferous copper mined in the central European mining regions weas separated into its basic components of pure copper and silver, using imported lead – these enterprises were also at the forefront of the attacks levied on the Imperial Diets and during the religious, political and socio-economic conflicts from the Peasant War (1524–25) to the Reformation. The financing of those processes was arguably less sophisticated, relying on wealthy family companies – led by Augsburg late medieval super-companies of Fugger and Welser – and not on pooled capital (Häberlein, 2012). Likewise there was an absence of a comprehensive system of market regulation, partly because Germany was made up of a series of independent states during the period. Regulation focused on the quality of the currency, which political leaders were interested in from the perspective of owners of mineral mines as well as collectors of tax. Yet Germany benefited from a consistent focus on manufacturing. In the 17th century cameralism emphasized the value added through industry, knowledge and creativity as key factors in triggering economic development, and this attitude continued to influence Germany in subsequent decades, as evidenced in the modernization of German industry after the 1820s (Reinert, 2007, 2019).

The Scandinavian countries of Norway, Sweden and Finland were slower to industrialize than many other locations. In contrast to the UK and US, where the pooling of capital aided industrialization and where joint-stock companies led to a separation of ownership and management, in Sweden and Norway ownership was more concentrated. Family ownership was the dominant form in Sweden, while state ownership was significant in Norway. Unlike family firms in 19th-century UK and Italy, where managerial positions were usually given to family members regardless of their talent, in Sweden family companies sourced their managers externally. The activities of managers were, however, closely supervised to ensure that the problems in excessive managerial autonomy identified by Berle and Means (1932) did not emerge. In Norway state ownership played a significant role in coordinating the large-scale exploitation of the country's natural resources. Rather than only seeking the income from the sale of rights, as occurred in the contractor state of the 1640s, the Norwegian state participated actively in resource exploitation. It took a long-term perspective, which reflected an understanding of potential resource depletion in the future. Income from the oil was saved, rather than spent, so that the accumulated wealth could be used for economic downturns or to support the needs of an ageing population.

The US emerges as a clear example of a country that caught up and overtook (Allen, 2014). From the first colonies the US was proactive in learning from others' best practice. The 13 colonies established by England proactively used the degree of political self-autonomy they had been granted by the Crown to introduce their own policies. After the American Wars of Independence of 1776–83 immigration and industrial espionage emerged as significant factors in the development of US entrepreneurship. Two causes of this were the failure of UK factories to fully appreciate the capabilities of their workers and the failure of UK political leaders to introduce full suffrage. Workers emigrated in the hope of greater wages, bonuses for knowledge of trade secrets and a more representative political system. By the 20th century the relationship between the two countries had reversed dramatically, and it was now the UK that was reliant on the expertise of US companies.

We can also consider the experience of the countries that were subject to Western political or cultural influences, particularly through colonization. It might be expected that colonization would produce a knowledge spill-over that allowed newly independent former colonies to rapidly accelerate their economic performance. However, Chapter 8 showed that South American countries that had formerly been Spanish and Portuguese colonies struggled to engage with the competitive international economy when they gained their independence. The reasons were complex, but included the absence of a positive legacy from the colonists (such as a strong institutional framework) and limited initiative from new political leaders to fill the gaps. Instead of a long-term plan focused on investing in the local population, including their education and training, political elites tended to favour short-term measures such as generating income by awarding contracts to entrepreneurs from overseas or using contracts as a form of domestic political patronage. Ultimately it was Japanese imperialism that was more significant in disseminating capitalism.

Values and beliefs

A second key takeaway from the volume is that systems of power should not be able to perpetuate themselves; they should always be challenged. Capitalism has been perceived as having two very different potential impacts on society. Marx (1961 [1867]) perceived capitalism to be an oppressive force in which industrial wealth promoted inequality. Conversely, Schumpeter (1992 [1942]) saw the opportunity for capitalism to liberate people from oppression through democracy. Knight (1935) noted that capitalism provided the rich with the opportunity to gain influence and use it to their own advantage. However Carnegie (1889), in *The Gospel of Wealth*, proposed a situation in which income and wealth generated by capitalism were employed for the benefit of society.

Challenges to systems of power have been examined in this volume. The American Revolution of 1775–83 stemmed from anger among the colonists that the English government was increasing the burden of taxation without providing the colonies with political representation in the English Parliament. It sought to prevent further national inequality between the UK and US. The French Revolution of 1789, meanwhile, was intended to reduce economic inequalities within the population. Both challenges were successful, but their success was dependent on substantial violence and military conflict.

Improving the condition of those who undertook the labour in the capitalist system was a focus of challenges to established systems in the 19th century. Chapter 7 outlined how religious and political beliefs motivated the campaign for the abolition of slavery, which was eventually achieved in the British Empire in 1833 and in the US in 1865. However, many politicians and avowed Christians were complicit in the trade in enslaved people and resisted the abolition of slavery, despite the efforts made by others to end it. They extracted significant amounts of compensation from the government in the aftermath of the abolition of slavery in the British Empire in 1833. Meanwhile, the UK trade union movement of the 1830s challenged the power of firm owners and sought to improve the working conditions of UK workers in industry and agriculture. When formal deterrents proved unsuccessful, the UK government switched to informal ones, such as sentencing six agricultural workers from Tolpuddle, Dorset, tried in 1834 on charges of taking an illegal oath after forming a union, to deportation to Australia. Workers launched challenges to the established political system too, calling for greater political representation. The Chartists demanded universal male suffrage, secret ballots, equal sized constituencies, annual general elections and salaries for Members of Parliament as well as the abolition of their property qualification (to increase the pool of eligible candidates). Petitions presented by the Chartists to the UK parliament in 1838, 1839 and 1842 failed, but pressure generated by the movement is now considered to have been a significant step in the subsequent parliamentary reforms and extension of the franchise (UK Parliament, 2021).

By the 20th century the main challenge was environmental pollution and resource depletion, and the solutions were driven by the social values of entrepreneurs. Barriers in that instance were institutional, financial and political. In the organic food sector, companies failed to be proactive in developing an institutional framework among themselves, or in partnership with government, to fully define the concept to customers and to allow international standardization. In green energy there were significant costs entailed in research and development (R&D), which made the sector heavily dependent on government subsidies, an insecure situation when government policy on the topic fluctuated significantly between administrations and according to the price of oil.

Perhaps the reason why capitalism has been perceived as having two very different potential impacts on society is because it has had two very different impacts. Motives for reform have varied, entrepreneurs have both caused problems and sought solutions. As indicated in the next section, future research is needed on this area to fully understand motivations for, and barriers to, reforms.

Future research

China and Russia, rather than the US, are now dominating the world economy. China in particular possesses the important combination of the exploitation of natural resources, investment in R&D and a focus on the education of the workforce – a combination that was never fully met in UK or US industrialization, where the skills of employees were generally undervalued. We have only touched briefly on these locations in this volume, but the importance of better understanding the operation of firms under communism has been demonstrated in the recent work of Scranton and is a significant area for future research (Scranton, 2018, 2019).

Compassionate capitalism may provide a solution to addressing the inequalities that still exist today in the capitalist system. This requires actions from political leaders, entrepreneurs, managers and consumers. More research needs to be done to consider how political leaders can better monitor the distribution of income and wealth and ensure that firms and entrepreneurs recognize that progressive taxation reflects the benefits they derive from the infrastructure and institutions provided and maintained by government. Social norms and values may also be able to significantly alter the behaviour of entrepreneurs and informally encourage them to redistribute their wealth according to Carnegie's model. Ongoing research into entrepreneurial philanthropy may start to unlock answers to this (Harvey et al, 2011, 2019, 2020). Consumers and investors also need to consider their responsibility. Consumers need to hold brands more accountable for passive engagement (such as greenwashing), but they also need to consider a wider spectrum of a company's activities. In the fashion sector, for example, consumer awareness of the environmental impact of textile production and disposal has increased significantly, thanks partly to a growing body of academic research on the topic. Expectations surrounding the low price of clothes also need to change in order for wage levels and living standards of textile workers to improve, and research is needed to address how that can be achieved. Shareholders need to consider if they are happy with how profits are obtained.

A revival of the shareholder as lobbyist is under way, largely spearheaded by the Church Commissioners of England, managers of the Church of England's investment fund. Their solution to challenge environmental exploitation and social inequalities has been to retain, rather than sell, shares in companies where they felt that reforms were required. While selling might have had a short-term impact, retention is a long-term strategy that utilizes the authority and access to the companies provided to shareholders (Church of England, 2021; *The Guardian*, 2021).

References

Acemoglu, D. and Robinson, J. (2019) *The Narrow Corridor: How Nations Struggle for Liberty*, London: Penguin.

Allen, R.C. (2014) 'American exceptionalism as a problem in global history', *The Journal of Economic History*, 74(2): 309–50.

Berle, A. and Means, G. (1932) *The Modern Corporation and Private Property*, New York: Macmillan.

Carnegie, A. (1889) *The Gospel of Wealth, Carnegie Corporation of New York*, [online]. Available from: https://www.carnegie.org/about/our-history/gospelofwealth/ [Accessed 20 December 2020].

Casson, M. (2020) 'International rivalry and global business leadership: an historical perspective', *Multinational Business Review*, 28(4): 429–46.

Church of England (2021) 'Responsible investment', *Church of England* [online]. Available from: https://www.churchofengland.org/about/leaders hip-and-governance/church-commissioners-england/how-we-invest/resp onsible-investment-1 [Accessed 4 March 2021].

Diffie, B., and Winius, G. (1977) *Foundations of the Portuguese Empire, 1415–1580*, Minneapolis: University of Minnesota Press.

Fitzgerald, R. (2007) 'Marketing and distribution', in G. Jones and J. Zeitlin (eds) *The Oxford Handbook of Business History*, Oxford: Oxford University Press: 396–419.

Fisher, J.R. (2008a) 'Casa de Contratación', in J. Kinsbruner and E.D. Langer (eds) *Encyclopedia of Latin American History and Culture: Volume 2* (2nd edn), Detroit, MI: Charles Scribner's Sons, pp 168–9.

Fisher, J.R. (2008b) 'Colonial Spanish America', in J. Kinsbruner and E.D. Langer (eds) *Encyclopedia of Latin American History and Culture: Volume 2* (2nd edn), Detroit, MI: Charles Scribner's Sons, pp 543–8.

Guardian, The (2021) 'Church of England to step up pressure on firms to improve diversity', *The Guardian*, [online] 17 January. Available from https://www.theguardian.com/business/2021/jan/17/church-of-engl and-to-step-up-pressure-on-firms-to-improve-diversity [Accessed 4 March 2021].

Häberlein, M. (2012) *The Fuggers of Augsburg: Pursuing Wealth and Honor in Renaissance Germany*, Charlottesville: University of Virginia Press.

Harvey, C., Maclean, M., Gordon, J. and Shaw, E. (2011) 'Andrew Carnegie and the foundations of contemporary entrepreneurial philanthropy', *Business History*, 53(3): 425–50.

Harvey, C., Maclean, M. and Suddaby, R. (2019) 'Historical perspectives on entrepreneurship and philanthropy', *Business History Review*, 93(3): 443–71.

Harvey, C., Gordon, J. and Maclean, M. (2020) 'The ethics of entrepreneurial philanthropy', *Journal of Business Ethics* [online pre-issue] Available from: https://doi.org/10.1007/s10551-020-04468-7 [Accessed 4 March 2021].

Kattel, R. and Mazzucato, M. (2018) 'Mission-oriented innovation policy and dynamic capabilities in the public sector', *Industrial and Corporate Change*, 27(5): 787–801.

Knight, F.H. (1935) *The Ethics of Competition and Other Essays*, London: G. Allen and Unwin Ltd.

König, W. (2007) 'Design and engineering', in G. Jones and J. Zeitlin (eds) *The Oxford Handbook of Business History*, Oxford: Oxford University Press: 374–95.

List, F. (1841) *Das Nationale System der Politischen Ökonomie*, Stuttgart/ Tübingen: Cotta.

Mazzucato, M. (2021) *Mission Economy: A Moonshot Guide to Changing Capitalism*, London: Allen Lane.

Mazzucato, M. (2013) *The Entrepreneurial State: Debunking Public vs. Private Sector Myths*, London: Anthem Press.

Marx, K. (1961 [1867]) *Capital Volume 1* (trans S. Moore and E. Aveling and ed F. Engels), Moscow: Foreign Languages Publishing House.

Mayer, C. (2018) *Prosperity: Better Business Makes the Greater Good*, Oxford: Oxford University Press.

Reinert, E.S. (2007) *How Rich Countries Got Rich ... And Why Poor Countries Stay Poor*, London: Constable.

Reinert, E.S. (2019) *The Visionary Realism of German Economics from the Thirty Years' War to the Cold War*, London and New York: Anthem.

Roper, L.H. and Van Ruymbeke, B. (eds) (2007) *Constructing Early Modern Empires: Proprietary Ventures in the Atlantic World, 1500–1750*, Boston: Brill.

Rössner, P.R. (2021) *Managing the Wealth of Nations: Political Economies of Change in Preindustrial Europe*, Bristol: Bristol University Press.

Rössner, P.R. (2020) *Freedom and Capitalism in Early Modern Europe. Mercantilism and the Making of the Modern Economic Mind*, Cham: Palgrave Macmillan.

Rutterford, J. (2012) 'The shareholder voice: British and American accents, 1890–1965', *Enterprise and Society*, 13(1): 120–53.

Schumpeter, J.A. (1992 [1942]) *Capitalism, Socialism and Democracy*, London: Routledge.

Scranton, P. (2018) 'Managing communist enterprises: Poland, Hungary, and Czechoslovakia, 1945–1970', *Enterprise and Society*, 19(3): 492–537.

Scranton, P. (2019) *Enterprise, Organization, and Technology in China: A Socialist Experiment, 1950–1971*, London: Palgrave Macmillan.

Scammell, G.V. (1982) 'England, Portugal and the Estado Da India c. 1500– 1635', *Modern Asian Studies*, 16(2): 177–92.

UK Parliament (2021) 'Chartists', *UK Parliament* [online]. Available from: https://www.parliament.uk/about/living-heritage/transforming society/electionsvoting/chartists/overview/chartistmovement/ [Accessed 4 March 2021].

Yamamura, K. and Streeck, W. (eds) (2001) *The Origins of Nonliberal Capitalism: Germany and Japan in Comparison*, Ithaca, NY, and London: Cornell University Press.

Yamamura, K. and Streeck, W. (eds) (2003) *The End of Diversity?: Prospects for German and Japanese Capitalism*, Ithaca, NY, and London: Cornell University Press.

Index

Note: References to figures appear in *italic* type;
those in **bold** type refer to tables.

'The 15 families' 78–9

A
Abbasid caliphs 158
abolition of slavery 175–6, 178, 181, 247
active financial ownership 89
active ownership 86–7, 91
Act of Union 12
*Address to the Christian Nobility of the German
    Nation* (Luther) 60, 61
advertisers 40
advertising 41, 42–3
Africa 108, 119, 131, **132**, 133, 192
African slave labour 175
agency costs 86, 87, 89
agency, human 53
agency theory 91
Age of (European) Discoveries and
    Exploration 127
agricultural goods 106
agricultural land 229, 230, 231
agricultural revolution 9
agricultural specialization 44
agriculture 3, 188, 200, 201, 202,
    207
Ahmadabad 108
air pollution 194
Akan 101–2, 114–19
Akbar 111
Albuquerque, Afonso de 117
Aldworth, Thomas 108
Aleppo 111
algeravias 117
algeravias tenezes 118
alienability 33
alienation 6
Alnatura 202
Alteuropäische Ökonomik 54
America 131, **132**, 133, 142–4, 146–8,
    188–9
    and the environment 192

and slavery 175
    South 145, 243, 244, 246
    see also US
American Revolution 18, 246
Amsden, A.H. 139, 140, 146
Amsterdam 111
animals 188, 189, 190, 200
Anstey, Roger 178
Anthropocene Age 188
Anthroposophical businesses 207
Anthroposophical Society 200
Anthroposophy 198–9, 200–2
anti-scientific outlook 158
anti-Trinitarianism 171
Apollo 8 193
Aquinas, Thomas 57, 163
Arabs 105–6
Arbeitsgemeinschaft Natürlicher Landbau
    und Siedlung 198
arbitrage 39–40, 47, 54
Årdal 81
Argentina/the Argentine 146, 189
Arians 171
aristocracy 190, 221
Arkwright, Richard 16
Armenian merchants/traders 109–14,
    242
Arrhenius, Svante 192
artisan production 34
asbestos 180
asbestosis 161
ascending price 39
ASEA 80, 86
ASEA 87
Ashton, T.S. 164, 174
Asia 109, 113–14, 131, **132**, 133,
    138–41, 148
    and the environment 192
    South 108, 110
Aslanian, Sebouh David 109–10, 112
Assas, King of 117

Assembly of Merchants 112
asymmetrical bargain 62
Atacama Desert 196
atomistic competition 40
auctions 39
Aufwexl 65
Authentic Narrative (Newton) 179
autonomy 150, 245
average real earnings 221, *222*
avoidance strategies, tax 216

B
backwardness 134–5, 137, 139, 150
Baigan, Ishida 159
Bailey, Mark 16
balance of payments crises 143, 148
banana plantations 188–9
bank account 11
Banking Co-Partnership Act 13
Bank of England 11–12, 20
bankruptcy 170, 173, 174
banks 13, 199, 200
  Anthroposophical 202
  German 62
  Italian 11, 18, 48
  medieval 11
  Norwegian 83
  state 137
  Swedish 78, 87
Baptists 164, 175
Barnevik, Percy 88
barter 30, 34, 55, 108
Bateson, M. 48
Bayer 203
Bayly, C. 102
Beckert, S. 156
Bellah, R.N. 159
benchmark 38
Benezet, Anthony 179
Bergens Tidende 83
Berle, A. 5, 245
Berlin 217–18
Berman, Elliot 197
biases 40
bicycle production 220
bidding 39
bill of exchange 10–11, 55
bio-based economy 188
biodynamic agriculture 200, 201
Bio-Dynamic Farming and Gardening
  (Pfeiffer) 201
biodynamists 202
birds 190, 193
bishops 228
Bitu 100–2, 114–15, 119
Black Death 15
black smoke 190
boarding schools 170
Bolivia 189

Bonn 220
Bonnell, Jane 223–4
bonum commune 56, 57
boroughs 47
Botero, Giovanni 55, 67
bourgeois capitalism 162, 164, 180
bourgeoisie 79, 221
BP 205–6
brands 38, 248
Braudel, F. 1, 10, 48
Braun, Carl 198
Brazil 175, 244
Bretton Woods institutions 129
bridges 44
Bridgewater, Duke 9
Bridgewater Canal 9
Britain 144–5, 146–7, 215
British and Foreign Unitarian
  Association 172
British West Indies 175–6, **177**, 180,
  181
Britnell, R.H. 1
Bronze Age 29
Brower, David 194
Brown Boveri 86
Brundtland Commission 203
Bubble Act 13
budget deficits 143
budget price retailers 41
buffalo 190
burgesses 36, 47
Busbecq, Ogier Ghiselin de 159
business founder 5
business morality 163
business organization 8, 136
Buxton, Thomas Fowell 180
buyers 30, 38, 39, 47, 110
  and sellers 30, 31, 35, 48

C
Cadbury chocolate manufacturer 171
Cadiz 111
Cain, P.J. 145, 146
caldeirões 117
Calvin, John 163–4
Calvinists 163
cameralism 54, 57, 59, 242, 245
canals 9
Canon Law 11
capital
  accumulation of 134, 135, 136
  concentration and centralization of 133
  pooled 239
Capital (Marx) 14
capital city 220
capital-intensive industries 34
capitalism
  bourgeois 162, 164, 180
  crony 142–4

gentlemanly 145
industrial 129, 130, 139–41, 145, 169
managerial 81, 87, 135, 136
national 138
service 145
state 138, 141, 148
Capitalism, Socialism and Democracy
(Schumpeter) 3–4
Capitalisms: Towards a Global History (Yazdani
and Menon) 102
capitalist modernization 149–50
carbon dioxide 192
Caribbean 175
Carl Zeiss Stiftung 160
Carnegie, Andrew 227–8, 231, 246
cars 37, 220
Carson, Rachel 193
cartels 36, 54, 137, 138
Casa da Guiné 244
Casa da Índia 244
Casa de Contratación 244
cashless payment system 55
Casson, C. 9
Casson, M. 9
'catching up countries' 128, 134, 135,
159, 242
Catholics 169
cattle 188
CEIFs (closed end investment funds) 78, 87
Central America 189, 244
cepalismo 144
ceramics 105, 106
ceremony 29, 30
Chaebols 138
Chamberlin, T.C. 192
Chandler, Alfred D. 5, 14, 136
Chaney, E. 158
chartered companies 8, 20, 239
Chartists 247
chemical companies 202–3
chemical factories 190
chemical fertilizers 197, 207
chemical waste 194
Chibber, V. 142
Chicago 191
child labour 16–17
Chile 189, 196
China 103–8, 133, 140–1, 157, 204, 247–8
chinchilla pelts 189
choice, and human economy 53
Christian ethic 161
Christian Frontier Council (CFC) 160
Christianity 158, 159
Christianity and Social Order (Temple) 159
the Church 7, 55
Church Board of Finance 162
Church Commissioners of England 248
Church Congress, Hull 159–60
Church of England 162, 164

Cipolla, C.M. 159
Cistercian monastic order 6
cities
capital 220
hub for aspiring professionals 220
City of London 145
city-states 163
civic elite 47
civil servants 228
Clapham Sect 179–80
Clarkson, Thomas 179
climate change 193, 195, 203
Club of Rome 203
coal 134, 188, 194, 219, 220, 244
mechanized cutting 215
pollution problem 190
coin debasement 62, 63, 65
coins 10, 34–5, 63–4
Cold War 84, 136, 191
Collin, Sven-Olof 76
Cologne 220
colonialism 129, 149, 150
colonization 147, 148, 239, 244, 246
On Commerce and Usury (Luther) 54, 58,
60, 61
commercialization 1, 59, 197
commercial mediation 43
Commercial Revolution 55
Commission of Public Acts 11–12
commons, enclosure of 6
communication 5, 10, 30, 117, 134,
194, 226
company securities 224
comparative advantage 33, 34, 85,
213
comparison, and the market 35
compassionate capitalism 248
competition 36, 38, 40–1, 54, 57
competitive advantage 139, 158
competitive bidding 39
competitive capitalism 130
compulsory purchase of land 10
concentrated ownership 76, 86, 89
Conference on Christian Politics,
Economics and Citizenship
(COPEC) 161
Confucianism 157
conglomerates 130, 133, 138, 140, 141,
148, 205
J. & J.W. Pease 171
Norsk Hydro 87
Congregationalists 164, 165, 175
Congregational Union 173
conscience 163, 175, 176, 180
conservation 89, 190, 191
Constantinople 111
consumer brand 38
consumer capitalism 189
consumer cooperative 17

consumer goods firms 227
consumer products 215
consumers 6, 37, **42**, 102, 146, 160, 248
  and branded products 38
  and Courtauld 160
  and entrepreneurship 239
  female stockholders 227
  and greener products 203–4, 205,
    206, 207
  and pressure 241
  and shopping 40
contract curve 34
contractor state 8–9, 20, 239, 242–3
control, and ownership 20
Cook, John Henry 197
cooperation 40, 77, 79, 84, 85, 89
cooperatives 17, 198, 202
copper 7, 63, 244
corporate environmentalism 202–7
corporate governance 74, 75, 84, 88, 89,
  90, 91
corporate innovation 191
corporate social responsibility (CSR)
  159–60
Correia, Fernão Lopes 117–18
Costa da Mina 114, 116
cotton masters **166**
cotton spinners 173
cotton spinning industry 164
Courtauld, George 173
Courtauld, Samuel 160, 173
Cowper, William 179
craft guilds 36
Crafts, N. 219
craft skills 34
creative destruction 37–8, 134
credit 6, 10, 30
Crompton's spinning mule 16
crony capitalism 142–4
crops 188
the Crown 8, 9, 243
culture 43–4
Cunningham, Rev William 159–60
currency 7, 63–4, 65–6, 245
Czarist Russia 137

D
Daaku, K.Y. 101
Dahmén, Erik 85
Daniels, Farrington 196
Darien Scheme 12
debt 13, 39, 65
debt recovery 10
decolonization 131
Deepwater Horizon oilrig 206
defence 43, 138
deflation crisis 78
deindustrialization 147, 150,
  218, 220

demand-side influences 224
Demeter 201
democracy, and capitalism 6
Democratic People's Republic of
  Korea 138, 140–1
Deng, Gang 105, 106, 107
Denmark 195, 197
Den Svenska Handelsbanken 78
dependency 130, 147, 148–9
dependistas 130, 147, 148
deregulation 88
development 148, 149, 193
development-promoting 139
diffused ownership 75
directors 160, 226, 227
dispossession 6
Dissenters 164–71
divergence 131, **132**, 133
domestic growth 149
domestic manufacturing 67, 244
domestic market liberalization
  141
domestic ownership 141
Dorst, Jean 193
Drescher, Seymour 178
Dreschler, W. 157
dual-class shares 78, 86, 88
Du Halde, Jean-Baptiste 104
Dunlop, D.N. 201
Dunning, J. 228
Düsseldorf 220
Dutch East India Company 8
Dutch traders 106
dynastic leader 32

E
earls 32, 33
earnings 213, 221, *222*
the Earth 193–4
'Earthrise' 194
East Asia 133, 141
East Germany 218
East India Company 108, 113
East Indies 244
e-commerce 206–7
economic backwardness 139, 150
Economic Commission of Latin
  America 143
economic growth 134, 203
Economic Miracle, Japanese 138
economy, and the state 20
ecotourism 204, 206–7
Eden 198
Eden, R. 108
Edgeworth, F.Y. 34
Edison, Thomas 10
education 33, 139, 228, 231, 248
Education Act, 1880 (UK) 17
Edwards, Bryan 176

Edwards, William 108
egrets 189
Eguafo 116
Egypt 105, 196
Ehrlich, Paul 193
elected leader 32
electrical industry 139
electricity 194, 195
electricity grids 196
Electrolux 87
electro-technical companies 87
electro-technical industry 79–80
elites 36, 47, 145
Elkington, John 203
emissions trading 206
empire, scramble for 134
employers 5, 16, 17
energy 191, 247
  see also coal; electricity
Engelke, P. 191
Engels, Friedrich 5
England
  and chartered companies 20
  dissolution of monasteries 7
  Norman period 32–3
  regions 217
English East India Company 8, 113
English Industrial Revolution 149
English merchants 113
engrosser 46–7
Enskilda Bank 78, 85
enslaved people 8
  see also slavery
entrepreneurs 16, 20, 37, 247, 248
  green 194, 196–8, 202, 207–8
  and Knight 5
entrepreneurship 4, 6–10, **19**, 134, 238–9
  in Germany 244
  in Italy 243
  as scarcity factor 212
  and taxes 216
  in the US 245
environment 187–208
environmentalism legislation 194
environmental protection 194, 203, 206
episcopacy 164
Equiano, Olaudah 179
Ericsson 78, 80, 87, 88
Erie Railroad 226
ethical norms 35
ethics, religion-based 161, 181
Etruria pottery factory 9, 16
Eurasia 112, 129, 133, 150
Europe
  regional performance 217–19
  share of global GDP **132**
European Economic Area (EEA) 86
European Union (EU) 85, 86
exchange depreciation 143

exploitation 5, 54, 66, 131, 161
  of natural resources 8, 80, 81, 82, 147, 238,
    245, 248
export-led growth 141
export-led industrialization 140
export-orientated industrialization 141
Eyde, Sam 79

F
factories 14, 16, 17
Factory Acts, 1833, 1879 (UK) 17
factory production 188
familias empresarias 142
family companies 60, 75–6, 78, 84, 130, 138,
  240, 245
family financial–commercial–industrial
  businesses 143
family-owned conglomerates 140
farmers 7, 15, 20
Fear, J.R. 79
feathers 190
feedback mechanism 3
feed-in tariffs 204
Felice, E. 218
female investors 223–4, 225, 226, 227, 243
Ferns, H.S. 146, 147
Ferrier, R. 113
fertility, declining 192
fertilizers 197, 207
Fetu 116
feudalism 15, 20
finance 1, 3, 4, 10–13, **19**, 20, 145, 239–40
finance capital/capitalism 129–30, 145
Finland 218, 219, 245
first-mover advantage 138, 242
First World 150
First World War 214–15, 219, 221, 225
fiscal-military state 145
fish 193
F.L. Smidth & Co 195
food 33, 197–8, 202, 204–5, 247
Ford 215
foreign borrowing and investment 147
foreign direct investment 79, 138, 239–40
foreign ownership 80, 88
forestaller 46
Fossen, E. 82
fossil fuels 188, 191, 192, 194, 195,
  196, 207
Fox, George 169, 170, 171
France 11, 214, 215, 217
Frank, A.G. 148
fraud 7, 32, 49
freedom 54
  of entry 32
  from regulation 32
freeholders 47
freeman 47
free-riding 88

free trade imperialism 144–8
French Revolution 3, 18, 216, 246
Friends of the Earth 194
Fry chocolate manufacturer 171
Fugger family 7, 245
funding, religious organizations 161–2
fur clothing 189
Futo, King of 117

G

Gallagher, J. 144–5, 146
GDP (gross domestic product) 74, 75, **132**,
    133, 220
  and average real earnings 221
  per capita 216–19, *222*
Geary, F. 219
Gemeinschaft für Leihen und Schenken
    202
*The General Theory of Employment, Interest and
    Money* (Keynes) 4
gentlemanly capitalism 145
geo-based economy 188
Germany 7, 80, 81, 191, 202–3
  banking houses 62
  and coal 215
  and entrepreneurship 198, 244–5
  and manufacturing 241
  Peasant War 59, 63, 66, 245
  regions 217–18, 220
  wealth/income ratio 214
Gerritsen, A. 107
Gerschenkron, A. 134, 135, 137, 139, 150
al-Ghassani, Wazir 100
gift-giving 117
Gladstone, John 175–8
Glete, J. 86–7
global GDP (gross domestic product) **132**
globalization 150, 188
global temperature 188, 192
global trade 108–14
Glorious Revolution 18
goats 117
Golconda 111
gold 7, 67, 115
Gold Coast 114
The Gospel of Wealth (Carnegie) 246
Gould, Jay 226
governments, and environmental policies 204
government securities 224
Goyder, George 160
Graham, Sylvester 197
Graham crackers 197
Grassby, R. 163
The Great Acceleration (McNeil and
    Engelke) 191
Great Britain, and ownership 73
Great Divergence 131, **132**, 133
The Great Divergence (Pomeranz) 103
Great German Peasant War 59, 63, 66, 245

Great Power rivalry 134, 144
green consumers 204
Greene, Benjamin 175
green energy 247
green entrepreneurs 194, 196–8, 202,
    207–8
greenhouse gases 192
The Greening of America (Reich) 193
green products 207
greenwashing 205, 206, 207
Greg, Thomas 175
grupo familiar 142
grupos económicos 142
guano industry 189
guilds 6, 7, 15, 36, 47
Gujarat 108

H

habitat, destruction of 194
Hamburg 217
Hamilton, Alexander 76, 135
Handelsbanken 78
happiness 57, 129
Hardin, Garrett 190
hats 190
Hausbanken 74, 87
Hausväter 54
health food products 197
health reform 197
heavy industry 130, 137, 138, 139, 220
Helsinki-Uusimaa 219
Henkel 203
Henrekson, M. 74
Hibbert, George 176, 180
Hibbert family 175
higher education 139
high-price shop 43
Hirschman, Albert 144
Hirschmeier, J. 159
Ho, E. 113
Hoare, Richard 223
home-workers 7
honesty 35, 163
Hopkins, A.G. 145, 146
horizontal specialization 6
Hörnigk, Philipp Wilhelm von 67
Howe, A. 164, 166
Hudson, P. 221
human agency 53
human capital 141
human choices 53
hunting 190
Huntingdon, Lady Ann 223
Huntingdon, Lady Betty 223
Huntingdon, Lady Frances 223
Huntingdon, Lady Margaret 223
Hussain, R. 112
Hydro model 81, 82–3, 85, 89, 90
hydro power 79–80

I

Ibn al-Mukhtar 100
Ibn Khaldun 109, 113
Ideals and Industry (Courtauld) 160
Ile-de-France region 217
immigration 214
imperialism 127, 128–9, 130, 133,
     144–9
  and first Industrial Revolution 150
  and Japan 138, 140, 246
import substitution 141, 143, 148
incentives 33–4, 46, 86, 113, 162, 206,
     231
  in China 141
  for peasants 15
  and sustainability 204
income equality 141
income inequality 213–31, 239
incomes, per capita 149
incorporation 149–50
Independents 164, 169, 173
India 112, 244
individualism 163–4, 180
indulgences 55, 62
industrial capitalism 129, 130, 136, 139–41,
     145, 169
industrial centres 44
industrial-financial conglomerates 138
industrialism 135, 136, 139, 149, 150
industrialists 3, 13, 143, 228
  and Nonconformists 164
  in the US 224, 226
  and Wesleyans 173
industrialization 5, 128, 131, 133, 148, 150,
     220, 242
  late 137, 138, 139–41
  and natural environment 189–90
  transnational 147
industrial modernization 138, 148
industrial ownership 86, 89
industrial policy 66–9
industrial pollution 190–1, 207
Industrial Revolution 14, 149, 188,
     239
  first 2, 134, 148, 150, 164
  second 10, 133, 135, 136, 212
  third 141
industrial rivalry 134
industry 3, 5, 20, 139, 148, 242
Industry and Property (COPEC) 161
inequality 212–31, 239, 240, 242–3,
     246, 248
inflation 143, 148
infrastructure 9, 44, 49, 239
inheritance 228–30
innovation 37–8, 49, 85, 140, 191
institutional ownership 86, 88, 89, 91
instrumentum ex causa cambii 55
intellectual property rights 49

*The Interesting Narrative of the Life of Olaudah
     Equiano* (Equiano) 179
intermediation 36–7
international agreements 85, 189
international finance 145
international maritime trade 106
international trade 8, 11, 101, 129,
     131, 134
  Bitu 101
  China 105, 106
  Latin America 147
  and Ricardo 33
  Venice 243
international trading networks 105,
     106–7
interventionism 57, 62
invention 9, 140, 166, **168–9**
inventors 166, **167–9**
investment income 223–7
investor 88
Ireland, Northern 217, 219
iron 134, 188
Islam 157–9
Italy 55, 240, 243–4
  banking 11, 18, 48
  city-states 163
  GDP per capita 218
Izmir 111

J

J. & J.W. Pease 171
Jacobs Wind Energy Company 195
Jakobsson, U. 74
James II 18
Japan 106, 138–9, 140–1, 159, 241, 242,
     246
Japanese Economic Miracle 138
jasper ware 173, 179
Jeremy, D.J. 172, 174
Jevons, W.S. 34
Jews 169
Jiangdezhen 107
job creation 143
joint-stock banks 13, 239
joint-stock companies 5, 8, 10, 14, 20,
     239, 245
joomiat 112
Judaism 163
Justi, Johann Heinrich Gottlob von 59, 68
just-in-time delivery 141

K

Kadane, M. 172
Kapital (Marx) 68
karma 199
Katzenstein, P.J. 77
Kellogg, Dr John Harvey 197
Kellogg Corn Flake breakfast cereal 197
Kershaw, Nellie 161
Keynes, John Maynard 4

Kindersley, Lord 162
Kirzner, I.M. 4
Klein, H.S. 178
Knibb, William 180
Knight, F.H. 4–5, 216, 246
knights 32–3
knowledge, as value asset 212
knowledge-based learning 140
knowledge centres 44–5
Kongsberg 83
Korea 138, 140–1
Kramme & Zeuthen 195
Kreuger, Ivar 78
Kreuger Crash 78
Kuomintang refugees 141
Kuran, T. 158

L
labour
  income from 221
  and Marx 5
  vertical division of 16
labour hours 5
labour-intensive industries 34
labour management 171
la Cour, Poul 195
laissez-faire 54, 56, 58, 134, 144–8, 147
lambeis 117, 118
land 10, 32, 212–13, 231
landed aristocracy 221
Landes, D.S. 157–8
Lange, E. 80
Langholm, O.I. 56
La Porta et al 75, 76
late industrialization 137, 138, 139–41
Latin America 131, **132**, 133, 142–4, 146–8, 188–9, 192
Latourette, K.S. 157
Laurence of Ludlow 36
leaders 32
Leipzig Monetary Ordinance 63–4, 65–6
leisure 43–4
Lever, William 161
Levi-Faur, David 76
liberalism 54
liberalization 86, 88, 129, 141
Liberty Bonds 225
libraries 227–8
Lie, E. 80, 81
Life Reform movement 198
limited liability 10, 224
Limits of Growth 203
Lingwai Daida (Qufei) 106
List, Friedrich 76, 77, 135
Liverpool and Manchester Railway 9
loans 7, 11, 12, 13, 78, 199, 229
local elites 144, 145, 146
Lockyer, Charles 111
Lombardia 218

London 219, 220, 228
London Committee for the Abolition of the Slave Trade 179
London Stock Exchange 225
Long, Edward 176
long-term loans 13
Lopez, Fernão 116
lot 47
low-price shop 43
Loyd, Samuel Jones, Baron Overstone 229–30
Loyd-Lindsay, Harriet Sarah, Lady Wantage 229, 230
Luther, Martin 54, 58, 59, 60, 62, 163
Lykkegaard 195

M
Madras 113
madrasas 158
Malian empire 100
Malthus, T. 3
management 4–5, 13–15, **19**, 20, 240–1
managerial autonomy 245
managerial capitalism 81, 87, 135, 136
managers 5, 20, 136, 140
Manchus 157
Manila 106, 111
manufactories 68
manufacturing 14, 33, 67, 143, 148, 241, 242, 245
maritime trade 105, 106
market information 37
marketing 14, 136, 201
marketplaces 46
market regulation 57, 242
markets
  alienability 32–3
  co-location of transactions 35
  comparison 35
  definition 31
  economic theory of 38–43
  evolution 29–31
  incentives 33–4
  and innovation 37–8
  intermediation 36–7
  money 34–5
  policy intervention 46–8
  private property 32
  regulations 46–8
  towns 44–5
  trust 35–6
market towns 35, 41, 43–6
married women 224
Married Women's Property Act 224
Marshall, Alfred 39
Marshall Plan 215, 240
Marx, K. 1, 2, 5, 6, 14, 212, 221
  and feudalism 15, 20
  on industry 3

on inequality 240, 246
on manufactories 68
Marxists 66, 145, 147, 148, 149
Mason, Hugh 173
McCabe, Baghdiantz 112
McCann, P. 219, 228
McNeil, J.R. 191
McNeill, John 192
Means, G. 5, 245
mechanization 2, 16
mechanized production 134
mediators 43
Medici bank 11
medieval banks 11
medieval markets 35–6, 46
Meiji Restoration 138, 140
memory 30
Menlo Park, US 10
Menon, D. 102, 104
mercantile capitalism 129, 130
mercantilism 54
mercantilist imperialism 144
merchant guilds 36
mergers and acquisitions 86, 136
metals 166, 188
methane emissions 192
Methodism 160–1, 173–4
Methodist Church 162
Methodists 164, 179
metropoleis 60
Mexico 189
Michie, R.C. 229, 230
Middle Ages 20, 56, 57–8, 69
middle axioms 159–60
Midlands of England 219, 220
mid-range retailers 41
mid-technology sectors 139, 140
migration 220
military-industrial complex 138
military modernization 139
millionaires 165, 171
minerals 7, 244
Mines Act 17
Ming dynasty 157
Ming Shi-lu 106
Ming state 106
mining 61, 189
Missionary Christianity 159
Model T 37
modernization 138, 146–7, 148
Mokyr, J. 10
Molt, Emil 199
monasteries, dissolution of 7, 15
monetary ordinances 62
monetary regulation 62–6, 242
money 34–5, 137–8
money wage 221, *222*, 223
monitoring 87–8
monopoly 38, 40, 49

monopoly capitalism/monopoly finance
 capitalism 130, 133–4
monopoly rents 143
Moosvi, Shireen 110
Morck, Randal 75–7, 90
motor-mechanical industry 139
Mouchot, Augustin 195–6
Mughal India 112
Muir, John 190
multinational companies 138, 188–9,
 204, 241
multipliers 43
Munro, J. 11

N
national capitalism 138
national debt 13
National Environmental Policy Act (US)
 193
national income 213–15
national industrial capitalism 141
national industrialization 131
nationalism 76, 77, 90, 91
national ownership 76, 77, 85, 86, 90, 91
national wealth 213–15
natural beauty industry 200
natural foods 202
Natural Law 57
natural product 205
natural resources 8, 82, 147, 238, 239,
 244, 248
 Norway 80, 81, 82, 85, 245
Nazi Germany 80
negotiation 30, 31
neoclassical economic theory 31
neo-colonialism 149
neo-Marxists 130, 149
'New Age'-type social movements 201
Newalls 161
New Economic Policy (NEP) 137–8
New Julfa 109–11, 112
New Lanark Mills 14
Newton, John 179
New York Stock Exchange 225
NGOs (non-governmental
 organizations) 194, 204
night-watchman states 66
non-biodegradable surfactants 193
Nonconformists 164–71, 180, 238
non-profit intermediation 43
Nordic Welfare model 84
Norman England 32–3
Norsk Hydro 75, 80, 81, 82, 83, 87
North, D.C. 6
North-East England 220
Northern Ireland 217, 219
North of England 219
North-West England 220, 228

Norvik, Harald 89
Norway 75, 76, 77, 218–19
  banks 83
  state ownership 73–4, 75, 77, 79–86, 87–9,
    90, 91, 240, 242, 245
  stock market 90
nuclear energy 207

O
obligation 30, 32, 47, 159, 163
O'Brien, P.K. 133, 149
*Observations on … the Manufactures of Great
  Britain which Have Been for the Most Part
  Established and Supported by Protestant
  Dissenters* (Worsley) 164
Ohlin, B. 34
oil 82
oil well blowout 193
Oldham, Joseph H. 160
oligarchic state 142–3, 144
open auction 39
opportunity-seeking 238
ordoliberalism 54
Ordonnances 62
organic agriculture 200, 202, 207
organic certification 204
organic food 202, 204–5, 247
organic wine 204
Orkla 79
Oslo og Akershus 218, 219
Oslo Stock Exchange (OSE) 73, **83**
Ottoman Empire 111
Overend, Gurney & Co 171
overindulgence 163
overpopulation 3, 193
overseas investment 12, 224, 239
overseas trade 147
  see also international trade
Overstone, Baron, Samuel Jones
  Loyd 229–30
Owen, Robert 14
ownership 20, 76, 77–9, 88, 89–90, 91,
  141
  private 73, 138
  state 73–4, 75, 77, 79–86, 90, 240,
    242, 245
'Own Your Own Share of American
  Business' campaign 225, 227
Oxford Dictionary of National Biography
  (*ODNB*) 166

P
Panama 12
Paris 193
partnerships 20, 112, 135, 204, 247
passive industrial ownership 89
Paterson, William 12
path dependency 159
patronage 20, 243
peasants 15

Peasant War 59, 63, 66, 245
per capita incomes 149
Pereira, Duarte Pacheco 117
Persia 110, 111, 112
Peru 189
pesticides 193
petroleum 189, 194
Pfeiffer, Ehrenfried 201
philanthropy 227–8, 248
Philpotts, Rev Henry 175
photovoltaic cell technology 196
piece rates 7
'pie-powder' courts 36
Piketty, T. 18, 216
pilgrimages 43, 62
pin factory 16
plague, 1348–9 7
Platt, D.C.M. 146, 147
political leaders 5–6, 18, 20, 242–3, 248
political leadership **19**, 20
political representation 227, 243, 246, 247
politics, and entrepreneurship 20
pollutants 192
pollution 190–1, 193, 194, 206, 207, 247
Pomeranz, K. 103
pooled capital 239, 245
populism 143
porcelain 105, 107
Porter, M.E. 5
Port Sunlight 161
the Portuguese 106, 115–19, 175, 244
Portuguese Indian Ocean trading empire 62
power, concentration of 91
Prebisch, Raúl 144
precedence, for office-holders 48
precious metal 34–5
Presbyterians 164, 171–2, 175
price comparison websites 40
price deflation 60–1
price fixing 54
price inflation 57, 61
Price Revolution 60–1
principle-agent problem 109
printing press 158, 163
private ownership 73, 138
private property 32, 138
productivity 14, 16
professional sector 220
profiteering 54
profits 30
property ownership 224
protectionism, selective 77
Protestantism 2
Protestant Nonconformists 164–71
Protestant Reformation 162–4
protests, environmental 193
public ownership 49
  see also state ownership
Purgatory 55

Puritans 164
putting-out system 7
pyramid ownership 74

Q

Qing dynasty 106, 108, 157
Quakers 164, 165, 166, 169–71, 179, 238
quality control 7, 48, 171
Queen's ware 173
Quesnay, François 104
Qufei, Zhou 106

R

Ragion di Stato (Botero) 55
railway companies 14, 239
railways 5, 9–10, 14, 18, 188
Rank, J. Arthur 162
Rank, Joseph 162
Rank family 162
The Rape of the Earth (Jacks and
    Whyte) 191–2
real earnings 221, *222*
reciprocity 30
redistributionist policies 143
Reformation 2, 7, 60, 61, 162–4
Reform Houses 198
regions, income inequality 216–20, 231
regrator 46
regulations, market 46–8
Rehn, Götz 202
Reich, Charles 193
reincarnation 199
Reinert, S. 10
religion 156–81
religion-based ethics 161, 181
religious belief 35–6
Religious Census, 1851 165
relocation 15–16, 17, 195–6, 197, 220, 231
renewable energy 196, 204, 207
rentier capitalism 145
rent-seeking 54, 139, 142
reputation 36, 41, 48, 163, 170, 203, 204
research and development (R&D) 247, 248
resource depletion 245, 247
resource exploitation 80, 81, 82, 188, 189,
    238, 245
resource rent 85
The Responsible Company (Goyder) 160
retailers 36–7, 41
retailing 40–3
reunification, Germany 218
revaluations 62–3
Revolution of 1525 63
Ricardo, D. 3, 33
Rise of the Rest (and the Remainder) 131
Road to Survival (Vogt) 192
Robinson, J. 77
Robinson, R. 144–5, 146
Rochdale 17
Rockefeller, J.D. 226

Roe, Mark 75, 76, 89–91
Roman Empire 158
Roman towns 45
Rosés, J.R. 217, 218, 219
Rössner, P.R. 58
Rostow, Walt Whitman 135–6
Rousseau, J.J. 178
Rowntree chocolate manufacturer 171
Royal African Company 8
royal patronage 8
Rubin, Jared 158, 159, 163
Rubinstein, W.D. 165, 228, 231
Ruhr 220
Rukuo, Zhao 105–6
rules, political leaders 6
Russia 137–8, 247
Rutterford, J. 225
Ryder, Joseph 172
Rylands, John 173

S

Saarland 220
Safavid Persia 110, 111, 112
Saiger huts 244
Salt, Titus 173
Sandvik, P.T. 79
Santa Barbara 193
São Jorge da Mina 116, 117, 118–19
Saxony 63–4, 65–6
scale 135, 136
Scandinavia 76, 77, 218–19, 245
    see also Norway; Sweden
scarcity factors 212
Schnyder, G. 78–9
scholasticism 54, 55–6
schools 170–1, 201
Schumacher, E.F. 203
Schumpeter, J.A. 3–4, 5–6, 48, 243, 246
Scientific American 196
scientific management 14
Scotland 12, 217, 219
Scots 166
Scottish Missionary Society 175
Scranton, P. 248
Second World War 53, 80, 84, 221
securities 78, 224, 229
security 29, 101, 158
Sejersted, F. 77, 79
selective disclosure 205
selective protectionism 77
self-denial 163
self-interest 46, 163, 190
self-made wealth 227–8
sellers 32, 38, 39, 46
    and buyers 30, 31, 35, 48
Sequeira, Diogo Lopes de 116–17
serfdom 137
service capitalism 145
services 145, 220

Seventh-Day Adventist sect 197
shareholders 225–7, 239, 240, 241, 243, 248
share ownership 224
shares 78, 86, 88
Sharp, Granville 179
sheep 188
Shell 203
Shingaku movement 159
ships 8, 105, 188
shopkeeping 34
shopping 40
shops 40, 41–3
short-term loans 13
Shuman, Frank 196
Sierra Club 190
Silent Spring (Carson) 193
silk 106, 111, 113
silver 7, 63, 67, 244
Sino-Japanese War 140–1
Sjögren, H. 77
Skandinaviska Banken 78
skills-based assets 212, 213
slave owners 175–6
slavery 174–80, 181, 247
small- and medium-sized
    enterprises 134, 140
Small Is Beautiful (Schumacher) 203
small shops 40
Smith, Adam 16, 30, 33, 68, 178
smoke 190–1
social audit 160
social banks 202
social control, instrument of 160–1
social democracy 75, 76, 91
Social Democrats 84–5, 86, 90
social equality 203
socialism 4, 137
'Socialism and Private Industry: a New
    Approach' (Goyder) 160
social justice 193
social mobility 212, 213, 230–1
social movements 193, 197, 198, 201, 202
social network 41–3
social norms 35, 248
social skills 34
social status 36
social threefolding 199
Society of Friends 164, 169–70
Socinians 171
soil erosion 192
solar energy 195–6, 204
Solar Energy Society 196
solar water heaters 196
Sombart, Werner 1, 56, 68, 163
Song dynasty 104–5, 107
Songhai Empire 100
Soss, Wilma 227
Sotiropoulos, D.P. 225
Soto, Domingo de 58

South America 145, 243, 244, 246
South Asia 108, 110
South East Asia 109
South-East England 217, 219, 228
South of England 220
South Sea Bubble 49
South Sea Company 12, 13, 223
South-West England 217
Soviet Russia 137–8
space race 193
Spaceship Earth (Ward) 193
Spain 67, 159, 175, 244
Spanish Manila 111
specialization 33, 34, 59
spinning jenny 16
spinning mule 26
stage-model of industrialization 135–6
stages of growth hypothesis 136
Stamp, Sir Josiah 162
Standard Oil 226
Stark, R. 163
Stark, T. 219
the state
    and the economy 20
    and markets 30–1
state action 131, 134, 140
state-assisted industrial capitalism 140
state-assisted industrial growth/
    development 149–50
state autonomy 142
state banks 137
state-building 142
state capacity 63, 66, 142
state capitalism 138, 141, 148
state capture 142
state companies 82, 83, 138
    see also state ownership
state-directed industrial capitalism 140
state-owned Chinese companies 204
state-owned factories 137
state ownership, Norway 73–4, 75, 77,
    79–86, 87–9, 240, 242, 245
    Hydro model 90
    and institutional ownership 91
Statoil 82, 83, 84, 89
Statute of Labourers 16
steam power 134, 188
steel 133, 188
Steier, L. 75–6
Steiner, Rudolf 198–201
Stephen, James 179
sterling 129, 145
Steuart, James 58–9
Stirling, William 175
Stockholm 218
Stockholm Stock Exchange 78–9, 86
Stockholms Enskilda Bank 78
stocks 78, 225, 239
Stockton and Darlington Railway 9

Stone Age 29
Stothert, William 175
Sträng, Gunnar 85
Streeck, W. 241
structuralism 144, 147, 148
student protests 193
sub-infeudation 33
sub-Saharan Africa 108
subsistence rights 48
sugar 174–5
Sung dynasty 157
Sunni Revival 158
Sun Power Company 196
supervision, of merchants 48
supply chains 141
supply-side factors 224
surplus value 5, 30
sustainability 203, 204, 205, 206, 207, 241
Sweden 74–5, 76, 79, 204
  GDP per capita 218
  ownership 77–9, 84–7, 88, 89–90, 91,
    240, 245
symbolic corporate environmentalism 206

T
Tagliacozzo, Eric 109
Taiwan 140, 141
tariff protection 68, 77, 135, 137, 143
Ta'shï 105
Tawney, R.H. 163
taxation 3, 216, 243, 248
Taylor, Frederick Wilson 14
technology 85, 135, 136, 138, 139, 171, 173
technology-based manufactured exports 141
Teixeira, P. 111
Telenor 83, 84, 89
temperature, global 188, 192
Temple, Archbishop William 159, 160
tenezes 118
textile factories 17
textile manufacturers 166
textiles 7, 16, 44, 139, 220, 248
thaler 63, 64
Theosophy 198
Third World 147, 149, 150
Thompson, E.P. 160–1
Thornton, Henry 179
Thoughts upon Slavery (Wesley) 179
threefolding 199, 201
Timbuktu 100
Timotei 205
Tokugawa era 159
Toleration Act 169, 171
towns
  and competition 36, 41
  location 43–6
trade 33–4, 105–7, 133, 134, 147, 239
  global 108–14
  and markets 29–30

trade guilds 36
trade routes 105
trade unions 5, 17, 240–1, 247
trading networks 101, 105, 106, 107, 242
'The Tragedy of the Commons' (Hardin) 190
transactions
  co-location of 35
  costs 31, 62
transnational corporations 149
transnational industrialization 147
transport 2, 9, 16, 44
  see also railways; ships
trans-shipment 44
Trent and Mersey Canal 9
Trevor-Roper, Hugh 163
Trinitarian Calvinism 173
Triodos 202
triple bottom line 203
Troeltsch, Ernst 162
trust 35–6
Turner, Robert 161
Turner & Newall (T&N) 161
Turner family 161

U
UK
  failed to modernize 243
  government 18
  income tax system 216
  and investment income 223–4
  and manufacturing 241
  real GDP per capita and average real
    earnings 221, *222*
  regions 217, 219
  and shareholders 225–6
  and US 240, 245–6
  wealth/income ratio 213–15
  and worker migration 220
underdevelopment 147, 150
ungleiche hendel 62
uniform equilibrium price 39
Unilever 205
unions 17, 85
Unitarians 164, 165, 169, 171, 172–3,
  175, 179
Unitarian Toleration Act 171
United Methodist Church (UMC) 161
United Nations 204
United Secession Church 175
Upper German banking houses 62
urbanization 1, 61, 63, 104, 143, 219, 239
urban marketplace 45–6
urban markets 56
US
  and banana plantations in Central
    America 189
  and entrepreneurship 245–6
  and the environment 192
  government 18

and health reform 197
industry 5
investment income 224–5
and investment in the UK 215, 240
manufacturing 14, 241
National Environmental Policy Act 193
and organic food 204–5
and ownership 73
and political leaders, entrepreneurs and
   private investors 20
real GDP per head and money wage of
   unskilled labour 221, *222*, 223
revolutionary war 18
and second Industrial Revolution 212
and shareholders 226–7
and smoke pollution 190–1
wealth/income ratio 214
and wind technologies 195
Yellowstone National Park 190
'The Use of Money' (Wesley) 173
user–producer relations 85
usury laws 158
utilities 38, 49, 79

V
value added 68
Vanderbilt, Cornelius 226
Van Opstal, W. 17
Vaz, Gonçalo 118
Venezuela 189
Venice 111, 243
Venn, John 180
vertical division of labour 16
Vieira, João 117
Vogt, William 192
Von Kauffshandlung vnd Wucher/On commerce
   and usury (Luther) 54, 58, 60, 61
vote differentiation 74, 78, 88
voting, right to 226, 239, 243

W
wages 143, 221, 223
wage workers 15–16
Wakelin, M. 162
Waldorf educational system 199, 201
Wales 217, 219, 220
Walker, Rev George 173
Wallenberg, Marcus 79, 85
Wallenberg Bank 78
Wallenberg companies 85
Wallenbergs 74, 76, 78–80, 85, 86, 88,
   240
   and electro-technical companies 87
   and Norsk Hydro 75
Walpole, Robert 67
Walvin, J. 170
Wansey, George 172
Wantage, Lady, Harriet Sarah Loyd-
   Lindsay 229, 230
waqf 158

war bonds 225
War Communism 137, 138
Ward, Barbara 193
Warren, B. 128, 148–9
Washbrook, David 109
Washington Consensus 129, 146
watchfulness 172
water desalination plants 196
water frame 16
water pollution 193, 194
water-pumping windmills 195
water shortages 192
Watts, M.R. 164, 165, 166, 170, 171,
   172, 174
wealth 2, 3, 163, 213–15, 227–30, 239, 248
Wealth of Nations (Smith) 68
weavers 17
Weber, Max 2, 162–3
Weberian modernization theory 136
Wedgwood, Josiah 9, 16, 173, 179
Wedgwood's factories 105
Wegman, Ita 199, 200
Weleda 200, 201
Welser 245
Wesley, John 173–4, 179
Wesleyan Methodists 161–2, 164, 169, 173–4
Wesleyan Methodists' Centenary Fund 166
West Africa 119
Western Europe **132**
Western Railway 14
West Indies 175–6, **177**, 180, 181, 244
Whitehorne, James 175
Whole Foods Market 204–5
wholesalers 36–7, 47–8
Whyte, Robert 192
Wilberforce, William 179, 180
wildlife 190, 193
Wilks, I. 100, 101
William III, William of Orange 11, 18
Williams, Eric 102, 178
Williamson, J.G. 133
Willoch, K. 82, 83
Winchcombe, John 7
wind energy 197, 204
wind generator electrical systems 195
windmills 195
wind technologies 195
wind turbines 195
wine 204
Wolf, N. 217, 218, 219
women, and investment 223–4, 225, 226,
   227, 243
wool 7, 67
worker directors 160
workers 5, 7, 15–17, **19**, 20, 220, 241
work ethic 163
World Energy Council 201
worldly affairs 2
World Power Conference 201

World Trade Organization 85
Worsley, Israel 164

X
Xarife 117

Y
Yamamura, K. 241
Yara 83

Yazdani, K. 102, 104
Yellowstone National Park 190
yeoman farmers 7, 20
Yerkes, Bill 197
Yui, T. 159

Z
the Zaibatsu 138
Zhu Fan Zhi (Rukuo) 105